POLITICS *in* UNIFORM

PITT LATIN AMERICAN SERIES

Catherine M. Conaghan, Editor

POLITICS *in* UNIFORM

Military Officers and Dictatorship in Brazil, 1960–80

MAUD CHIRIO

University of Pittsburgh Press

Published by the University of Pittsburgh Press, Pittsburgh, Pa., 15260
Copyright © 2018, University of Pittsburgh Press
All rights reserved
Manufactured in the United States of America
Printed on acid-free paper
10 9 8 7 6 5 4 3 2 1

Cataloging-in-Publication data is available from the Library of Congress

ISBN 13: 978-0-8229-6537-4

Cover art: Army soldiers in front of the National Congress on April 2, 1964. O Globo Archive.
Cover design: Joel W. Coggins

To Anouck, Ulysse, and Paul

CONTENTS

Acknowledgments *ix*
Abbreviations *xi*

Introduction   The Unusual Face of the Brazilian Dictatorship *1*
Chapter One   Conspiracies: 1961–1964 *15*
Chapter Two   Continuing the Revolution: 1964–1965 *54*
Chapter Three   Consolidation and Divergences: 1966–1968 *97*
Chapter Four   Shaking the Ground: 1969 *138*
Chapter Five   At the Heart of the System: 1970–1977 *168*
Chapter Six   The Final Campaign: 1977–1978 *208*

Conclusion 233

Notes *241*
Bibliography *257*
Index of Names *271*

ACKNOWLEDGMENTS

This book is based on my doctoral thesis, defended in 2009 at the University of Paris I. It is the fruit of a long journey: five years of reflection, of archives and of distance covered, which took me far from my country, my familiar surroundings, and my political, social, and cultural milieu. It tells the story of individuals as far from my own identity and story as one can get: men, in uniform, locked in a radically conservative political battle, whose worldview I have tried to make my own so as to understand their careers and the course of their lives.

Among all the guides and companions I have had along this journey, it is to my doctoral supervisor, Annick Lempérière, that I owe thanks first and most. She gave me her time, she had faith in me, and she always pushed me to think in more depth and to look further. I owe too much to Celso Castro to mention here—his availability, his fertile ideas, his support at crucial moments, and his encouragement right up to the very last lines of this work. I extend my gratitude also to Renato Lemos and João Roberto Martins Filho, for their help and their dicas, and to Armelle Enders, Carlos Fico and Marcelo Ridenti, who opened the door of research into Brazil for me, and who gave me the taste for it.

An enormous thank you is also due to my "milicólogos" friends Rodrigo Nabuco de Araujo and Angela Moreira; to Eugénia Paliéraki, Marianne Gonzalez Alemán, and Marina Franco, invaluable colleagues and friends; and to the members of my Carioca family, who made Brazil a second home to me.

This book could never have existed without the support of the Thomas Skidmore Prize, which helps finance translations of works on contemporary Brazilian history into English. Winning the prize in 2013 also allowed me to meet James N. Green, whose excellence and luminous enthusiasm are a treasure of the academic world, on both sides of the Atlantic.

The fine translation and revision of this work were done by Melanie Moore and Nadine Wilstead. Publication also benefited from funding by the ACP Laboratory (Université Paris-Est Marne-la-Vallée) and by the Center for Research on Colonial and Contemporary Brazil (Centre de Recherches sur le Brésil Colonial et Contemporain, at France's main social sciences university, l'École des Hautes Études en Sciences Sociales, in Paris).

ABBREVIATIONS

AAB	*Aliança Anticomunista Brasileira.* Brazilian Anticommunist Alliance
ABI	*Associação Brasileira de Imprensa.* Brazilian Press Association
ACE	*Alto Comando do Exército.* Army High Command
ACFA	*Alto Comando das Forças Armadas.* Armed Forces High Command
AI	*Ato Institucional.* Institutional Act
AMAN	*Academia Militar das Agulhas Negras.* Agulhas Negras Military Academy
ARENA	*Aliança Renovadora Nacional.* National Renewal Alliance
CAMDE	*Campanha da Mulher pela Democracia.* Women's Campaign for Democracy
CCC	*Comando de Caça aos Comunistas.* Communist Hunting Commando
CENIMAR	*Centro de Informações da Marinha.* Navy Intelligence Center
CEPAL	*Comisión Económica para América Latina y el Caribe.* United Nations Economic Commission for Latin America and the Caribbean
CGI	*Comissão Geral de Investigações.* General Investigations Commission
CIE	*Centro de Informações do Exército.* Army Intelligence Center
CISA	*Centro de Informações da Aeronáutica.* Air Force Intelligence Center
CODI	*Centro de Operações e Defesa Interna.* Operational Commands for Internal Defense
CSN	*Conselho de Segurança Nacional.* National Security Council
DOI	*Destacamento de Operações de Informações.* Intelligence Operations Detachments
DOPS	*Departamento de Ordem Político e Social.* Departments of Political and Social Order
DSN	*Doutrina de Segurança Nacional.* National Security Doctrine
ECEME	*Escola de Comando e Estado Maior do Exército.* Army Command and General Staff School
EME	*Estado Maior do Exército.* Army General Staff
EMFA	*Estado Maior das Forças Armadas.* Armed Forces Staff

EsAO	*Escola de Aperfeiçoamento de Oficiais.* Officer Improvement School
ESG	*Escola Superior de Guerra.* Superior War School
EsNI	*Escola Nacional de Informações.* National Intelligence School
FAB	*Força Aeronáutica Brasileira.* Brazilian Air Force
FEB	*Força Expedicionária Brasileira.* Brazilian Expeditionary Force (BEF)
GAP	*Grupo de Ação Patriótica.* Patriotic Action Group
GR	*Guerra Revolucionária.* Revolutionary War
IBAD	*Instituto Brasileiro de Ação Democrática.* Brazilian Institute for Democratic Action
IPES	*Instituto de Pesquisas e Estudos Sociais.* Institute of Research and Social Studies
IPM	*Inquérito Policial Militar.* Military Police Inquiry
ISEB	*Instituto Superior de Estudos Brasileiros.* Higher Institute of Brazilian Studies
LIDER	*Liga Democrática Radical.* Radical Democratic League
MAC	*Movimento Anticomunista.* Anticommunist Movement
MDB	*Movimento Democrático Brasileiro.* Brazilian Democratic Movement
OAB	*Ordem dos Advogados do Brasil.* Order of Attorneys of Brazil
OBAN	*Operação Bandeirante.* Bandeirante Operation
PARASAR	Parachute Search and Rescue.
PCB	*Partido Comunista Brasileiro.* Communist Party of Brazil
PSD	*Partido Social Democrático.* Social Democratic Party
PTB	*Partido Trabalhista Brasileiro.* Brazilian Labor Party
SNI	*Serviço Nacional de Informações.* National Intelligence Service
STF	*Supremo Tribunal Federal.* Federal Supreme Court
STM	*Superior Tribunal Militar.* Superior Military Court
SUDENE	*Superintendência do Desenvolvimento do Nordeste.* Superintendency for the Development of the Northeast
TFP	*Sociedade Brasileira de Defesa da Tradição, Família e Propriedade.* Brazilian Society for the Defense of Tradition, Family and Property
UDN	*União Democrática Nacional.* National Democratic Union

POLITICS *in* UNIFORM

INTRODUCTION

The Unusual Face of the Brazilian Dictatorship

AN EASY VICTORY

In the early morning hours of March 31, 1964, the army barracks in the city of Juiz de Fora, in the south of the state of Minas Gerais, were abuzz with unusual excitement. Under orders from General Olímpio Mourão Filho of the Fourth Infantry Division, thousands of soldiers had gathered at headquarters where they were issued instructions to march on Rio de Janeiro, about 180 kilometers away, and there to depose the Labor Party president, João Goulart, who had been the country's leader for two and a half years. They were told that it was a matter of defending order, the constitution, and democracy against the communist revolution, in which Goulart had become complicit. At the crack of dawn, rows of tanks began their descent toward the *cidade maravilhosa*, which had lost its status as capital in 1961, but which the president was currently visiting. The operation, baptized "Popeye" after the pipe the general continually smoked, was launched in secret. With a few rare exceptions, conspirators and other malcontents were kept in the dark, despite being plentiful among the political classes, the business community, and the armed forces. The unorthodox, aging, and somewhat megalomaniacal Mourão Filho, who had brimmed with anticommunist zeal since his formative years, took the initiative single-handedly.[1] It should be noted that he was an old hand at this: his previous claim to fame, nearly three decades earlier, had been writing and distributing "the Cohen Plan," a document falsely attributed to the international communist movement that laid out plans for an alleged Brazilian insurrection.

The release of this spurious text in September 1937 had helped justify the coup d'état that instigated the Estado Novo dictatorship (1937–45) a month and a half later. For the second time in the course of his career, Mourão Filho hastened the march of history, helping to suspend democratic guarantees and establish an authoritarian regime in Brazil.

But the old general's decision to go it alone belied a broader movement. Seeing this handful of battalions march on the former capital was enough to galvanize all the country's troops. Most of the army's major units rallied in just a few hours: the "military apparatus" set up by the Labor government did not defend the rule of law, and officers loyal to Goulart refused to engage their troops. The streets remained deserted: neither the unions, nor leftist parties, nor progovernment civilian organizations would take up arms to defend it. The majority of state governors, however, cheered on the insurgents. The defeat was resounding. On April 1, Goulart, forsaken by almost everyone, left Rio for Brasilia, where he would soon make tracks for the south, and then for Uruguay where he would weather a fourteen-year exile. The president of the Senate, the conservative Auro de Moura Andrade, hastily nominated a new president for the leaderless Republic. As stipulated in the 1946 Constitution, his counterpart at the Chamber of Deputies, Ranieri Mazzili, would hold the office until a successor could be elected. But most of the power was already concentrated elsewhere. By April 2, in Rio, a self-proclaimed "Supreme Command of the Revolution" made up of generals of the three armed forces, had already announced the beginning of the "Revolution," intended to rid the nation of its many scourges, the foremost of which was communism. One week later, the Command would announce an Institutional Act legitimizing the suspension of the rule of law and declaring open season for the first wave of political persecutions. Numerous deputies would lose their mandates as well as their political rights. The congress that elected army chief of staff General Humberto de Alencar Castelo Branco to the presidency had been purged of all opposition.

Supporters were so numerous that it makes sense to speak of a civilian and military coup rather than an armed putsch. The overwhelming majority of leading press outlets could not find words enthusiastic enough to welcome the "Revolution," which was already being described as "glorious," "redemptive," and of course "democratic." And this exuberance was shared by the political class, with the exception of the Labor Party's closest allies, the business class, the clergy, and numerous civilian organizations that had been openly at war with the government for several months. The urban middle class, too, breathed an audible sigh of relief. In Rio a "Victory March" (initially planned as a reprisal of the March 20 "March of the Family with God for Freedom" in São Paulo) drew more than a million people on April 2. For everyone else, the coup d'état, and especially the Left's inability to deal with it, was a "political cold shower," as expressed by historian and former militant José Murilo de Carvalho:

> We thought the country was on the eve of a great social transformation which, as the agents of history, we were to have been active participants in. Socialism was within our reach.
>
> And suddenly, the shock. The military movement, with the support of politicians and religious and anticommunist demonstrations by the middle classes, toppled the government by merely moving its troops. The government, the openly progovernment *generais do povo*, the unions, the parties, and leftist movements—all of them disappeared, evaporated into thin air, put up no resistance. After the first surprise came a second: the military did not hand over power to their political allies as was customary. They came, they saw, they triumphed, and they stayed.[2]

Why was a moderate, legalist, and democratically elected government so easily swept away by this wave of conservatism? Why did its foundations topple like a house of cards? Whose arms did such large swaths of the Brazilian population think they were jumping into?

THE POWDER KEG

The April 1964 putsch was no bolt from the blue: for several weeks, political tensions had been running high. The whole conservative political class, along with the most affluent sectors of the population, had convinced themselves that Goulart was about to open the door to a communist revolution once and for all. João Goulart, nicknamed "Jango," was actually no communist. His party, the Brazilian Labor Party (Partido Trabalhista Brasileiro, PTB), had rolled out a program of reforms aiming to increase social entitlements for the lower classes, reduce the country's most glaring inequalities, and regulate the economy. He embraced the legacy of Getúlio Vargas (1882–1954), particularly when it came to social issues and his closeness to urban workers. Vargas, despite being dead for ten years, continued to be a central and deeply divisive figure in Brazilian politics. Twice elected president of the Republic, first after a coup d'état dubbed a "Revolution" (1930–45), and then after democratically held elections (1951-54), Vargas had been the leader of what came to be called Brazilian "populism."[3] Exercising strong, and even blatantly dictatorial power between 1937 and 1945, he also revolutionized the Brazilian state through policies of centralization, social intervention, economic action, and management of the masses. Both he and his memory were as lionized by the urban working classes as they were deplored by the economically liberal Right, which was concentrated in the right-wing National Democratic Union (União Democrática Nacional, UDN) party.

It was thus Goulart's position as Vargas's heir apparent that the Right held against him. Since the death of the great populist leader, Jango had become the principal face of the Labor Party, serving as vice president of the Republic twice: first under Juscelino Kubitschek (1955-60), with whom he had been allied, and then—since the president and vice president are not on a single ticket in Brazil—under the right-wing Jânio Quadros (January to September 1961). Indeed, in January 1961, the conservative Right got its wish: after the *getulista* (from "Getúlio") camp's almost uninterrupted thirty-year reign, a strong and moralist Right finally returned to power in the figure of Jânio Quadros. While the latter raised a few eyebrows with his personal eccentricities and some of his political positions—such as not being sufficiently in step with the United States on foreign policy—his sudden resignation in late August 1961 plunged the UDN, and all of the Right's anticommunists and *antigetulistas*, into utter disarray. Under the 1946 Constitution, it was none other than his vice president, João Goulart, who was mandated to finish the term that had scarcely begun. This was unthinkable for the ministers of the three armed forces, who attempted a coup to prevent him from taking office. It was a failure, but it did not bode well for the remainder of Goulart's term.

In addition to the rejection of Vargas's heir, a growing panic had taken hold of the upper classes as to the intentions of what was seen as a populist, even socialist, government. This was late 1961, when conservatives across the Americas were on tenterhooks. Several months earlier, in Cuba, Fidel Castro had acknowledged the Marxist-Leninist inspiration of his revolution, placed until then under the banner of the nation, anti-imperialism, public freedoms, the restoration of the constitution, and greater social justice. The announcement of his alignment with the Eastern bloc came as no surprise of course, but it nonetheless aggravated the political climate across South America. To parody Ernesto "Che" Guevara's 1967 address to the Tricontinental Conference after the event: there were "two, three, many *Cubas*" (not Vietnams) that the

Right already feared would blossom on Latin American soil. The conservative forces prepared for battle by setting up financing networks, organizing propaganda and armament campaigns, and manipulating as many civil society sectors as possible behind the scenes. The United States provided them with logistical, financial, and diplomatic support in these tasks. Each country was a powder keg waiting to explode.

Brazil was the first. João Goulart had begun his term in a spirit of reconciliation, albeit under duress. To come to power, he was forced to bring an end to the presidential system and grant wider powers to the conservative Congress he had inherited from the outgoing president. But against the backdrop of a radicalized political climate, his term evolved into a test of strength. Congress blocked his plans for reform, which were seen as having a socialist bent, and this led to a resurgence of popular support for the government. Red flags were brandished as symbols of defiance at mass demonstrations, strikes and union meetings drew hundreds of thousands, and a few acts of disobedience by rank-and-file soldiers set Brazil's political life aflame. For the demonstrators, the struggle was that of a people fighting for its rights against moneyed interests, U.S. intervention, and brutish military "gorillas"; for the Right, the communist revolution was knocking at the country's door, perhaps even already inside. The two camps mirrored each other's rhetoric and criticism: both claimed to be defending democracy, the nation, and the constitution against their adversaries' putschism, their submission to Washington's or Moscow's imperialism, their disregard of the people's will. It was by accusing João Goulart of plotting an imminent coup d'état, that the military General Staff seized power in early April 1964.

THE UNUSUAL FACE OF THE BRAZILIAN DICTATORSHIP.

Few observers at the time could have fathomed that the military regime was destined to endure twenty-one years, only coming to an end with the inauguration of a civilian president in March 1985. The coup was interpreted by its detractors and many of its supporters as a temporary interruption in the rule of law involving the armed forces, which had been a relatively frequent phenomenon in Brazil since the beginning of the Republic. In reality, South America's first "National Security" dictatorship had just been established, and it was to be followed by its cousins in Uruguay (1973–85), Chile (1973–90), and Argentina (1976–82). These were regimes that would all last more than a decade, except for the Argentinean dictatorship, which fell prematurely after losing the Falklands War to the British. These regimes had more in common than just their authoritarian nature, or even their high level of militarization—for Latin America had grown accustomed to heavy-handed governance, military or otherwise, since the early twentieth century. What truly distinguished them was their chief justification: that they stood in the way of a communist offensive. Even though anticommunist paranoia had taken root in Latin American armies since as early as the 1930s, the onset of the Cold War, and especially the Cuban Revolution changed its standing. Now the anticommunist struggle was both a political emergency and a military duty. Under the influence of both American and French doctrine, the latter shaped during recent wars of decolonization, the armies of Latin America convinced themselves of the legitimacy of suspending the rule of law and seizing power. Though some regimes may have had a strong personality leading them, they were still military institutions, governed by the chain of command principle, which took over governments and occupied state apparatuses, rather than caudillos acting in their own names.

These military coups, often supported by large swaths of civil society, paved the way for strongly militarized, anticommunist, and repressive authoritarian regimes. However, the Brazilian dictatorship differed from its neighbors on several levels. First, while the Brazilian coup d'état had enjoyed the overwhelming support of a business class wedded to the virtues of economic liberalism, the military period was not accompanied by a neoliberal revolution, as it was elsewhere. It was still too early, in 1964, to draw inspiration from the Chicago boys and the theories of Milton Friedman, and the ideal of a strong, interventionist state enjoyed wide support among civilian and military putschists. Though the generals would pursue industrialist policies that were favorable to employers and deeply hostile to the workers' movement, exacerbating social inequalities in the process, this was done without widespread privatization of the economy.

The Brazilian dictatorship's other distinguishing feature was that it respected much of the legal and democratic process, which simultaneously curbed and concealed the violence of its political persecutions. Hence the rule of law was continuously upheld by a series of constitutions: that of 1946 was initially maintained as the guarantee of a "non-radicalization of the revolutionary process," as the authors of the First Institutional Act were eager to point out in their preamble. Two new constitutional texts followed, in 1967 and 1969, which were markedly more authoritarian than the first. Seventeen institutional acts, which trickled out piecemeal from 1964 to 1969, suspended or modified their powers. These documents constructed an increasingly authoritarian order, and although they did not preclude the use of arbitrary powers, they always posited the latter within a legal framework.[4] In this way, the appearance of democracy was maintained. Congress continued to meet, except during an intensified period of authoritarianism from December 1968 to November 1969. In its chambers, the opposition party, which had been pushed into the minority, debated against the pro-military party with its hands tied. As outlined in the successive constitutions, this Congress elected five president-generals who governed the country from 1964 to 1985. Elections were held regularly at all levels of government, though they were regulated by restrictive and biased legislation, and excluded large parts of the Left. Last, a relatively independent judiciary remained in place, though it was militarized and obviously very much geared toward purging the opposition.

These unusual characteristics help to explain why the Brazilian dictatorship was less deadly than many others, its last and perhaps most distinctive feature. In December 2014, the National Truth Commission established a list of 434 politically motivated deaths and disappearances. Even though the report's authors rightly point out that the list is probably incomplete, the figure remains a far cry from the 30,000 likely victims of the Argentinean dictatorship, or the 3,000 Chilean disappeared, especially given the population of the country and the longevity of the regime. The number of dead is obviously not the only indicator of a regime's level of authoritarianism, or even its repressiveness. The systematic, widespread, and professional use of torture in Brazilian prisons, the thousands of political detentions, the hurdles placed in the paths of undesirable government employees, the reactionary propaganda, and the weight of censorship, clearly designate the military regime as fundamentally distinct from a democracy and the rule of law. But this relatively low murder rate speaks to the military regime's choices, to the balance of power between the forces present, to a tradition of conciliation, and to a lower level of political conflict than that found in neighboring countries.

Brazil's less murderous brand of state repression also stems from the context in which it was imposed and the opposition it subsequently met. The level of polarization of Brazilian society in 1964, though high for the country, cannot rightly be compared to the state of latent civil war reached in the Chile of the Popular Unity alliance (1970–73), or the Argentina of Isabelita Perón (1974–76); and in Brazil no one had yet taken up arms. In the Brazil of 1964, while the leftmost fringe of the Labor Party supported using strong-arm tactics to push through reforms, and certain popular movements (in particular the Peasant Leagues that struggled against the great landholders of northeastern Brazil) were ready to take up arms, these strategies only enjoyed the support of a small minority and there is no guarantee they would have been carried out. The Brazilian Communist Party (Partido Comunista Brasileiro, PCB), which supported Goulart's Labor government, adhered to a legalist policy. The Brazilian military thus came to power battling windmills in the form of revolutionary movements that did not exist yet. Except for very isolated initiatives, it was only several years after the coup that part of the Brazilian Left chose armed struggle, and then it was to fight a regime made considerably tougher by the mobilizations of 1968. Indeed, all through that year, mass demonstrations, student protests, workers' strikes, and the rebirth of Congressional opposition, put the generals on the defensive. In December, the regime enacted a Fifth Institutional Act, which would make history. The decree dramatically increased the regime's despotism, set off a new wave of political persecutions that would quickly come to rely on a far-reaching repressive apparatus, and clearly militarized power. Only then did thousands of young people choose the path of clandestine and violent action. And so began the Years of Lead (1969–74), which would only come to an end with the suppression of the armed movements. Ernesto Geisel, the president-general appointed in March 1974, announced a process of "détente," a long and hesitant thaw, which finally gave way to the return of civilians to government in March 1985.

Hence, in the regional context of "National Security" dictatorships, the Brazilian military regime was a horse of a different color. This was due to the country's specific context, to traditions and characteristics already present when it fell under twenty-one years of military rule. But they also resulted from political choices that emerged out of negotiations, debates, and conflicts. These occurred between the military and civilians, of course, but the voices of the latter were increasingly silenced as the regime militarized. It was above all within the armed forces themselves that the narrative of this dictatorship was negotiated, debated, and written about. It is this story we are setting out to tell: of political life inside an institution especially resistant to internal disputes, the army under a dictatorial regime.

THE DILEMMA OF THE POLITICAL

Anyone who is interested in political life inside the Brazilian Army in the second half of the twentieth century comes up against several obstacles. First, the smokescreen of a ubiquitous institutional discourse, at the time of the dictatorship and even to this day: "the military stays out of politics." The assertion is almost as old as the intercession of military men in the life of the body politic. Indeed, since the beginning of the century, the Brazilian military found itself torn between two ethical and professional orientations: on the one hand, the temptation to get involved in state business, for which they considered themselves more technically competent, better organized, and morally superior to the civilian elites; and on the other hand, a growing concern for the internal strife such behavior could potentially engender. Politics implied debate and conflict, and their deleterious effects on the institution's efficiency and chain of command were feared.

This dilemma was not resolved by adopting a stance of "political muteness," as was the case with most of the European armies. Since the beginning of the Republic in 1889, the Brazilian military was, on the contrary, omnipresent in the political arena. But its regular forays into politics were increasingly the doing of its generals, while restrictions on demonstrations and political action weighed more heavily on the rest of the institution. In the early days of the Republic, agitators were most often junior officers. The main architects of its founding were the student officers of the Praia Vermelha School, who put forth the idea of the "citizen soldier," in other words, each officer's individual responsibility to society.[5] Generals quickly co-opted the podium, but some military youth continued to be important political agitators in the coming decades. In the 1910s, a group of lieutenants and captains known as the "Young Turks" formed a pressure group around the review *A Defesa Nacional*, which tried to reform the military into an institution better adapted to modern times. Though they rejected insubordination and frowned on individual participation in politics—their ideal, after all, was European professionalism—they did nevertheless defend increased military intervention in the public sphere, even from their low ranks. A dozen years later, in July 1922, another group of junior officers had fewer qualms about bucking discipline and the hierarchy. This handful of lieutenants rebelled at Fort Copacabana in Rio de Janeiro in the name of democracy, political integrity, the nation, and modernity. Despite the repression it suffered, the "Lieutenant's movement" (*tenentismo*) rallied hundreds of supporters in the following years, becoming a "destabilizing force" for the established regime.[6] The political and military force of the *tenentes* contributed decisively to the Revolution of 1930 and Getúlio Vargas's rise to power.

The Brazilian Army paid the price for tenentismo when, in the 1930s, it experienced one of the most severe disciplinary crises in its history. The first objective of the military hierarchy became to reestablish the chain of command, to prevent the involvement of the military in politics, and to limit civilian interference on army bases. The great pioneer of this new direction was Pedro Aurélio de Góis Monteiro, an eleventh-hour revolutionary in 1930, war minister from 1934 to 1935, and army chief of staff from 1937 to 1943, the most authoritarian period of the Vargas era. It was then that the sanctification of discipline and the chain of command, and the rejection of political debate took root in the discourse and imagination of the armed forces. These demands remained the leitmotif of the Brazilian military and civilian elites into the second half of the century, even as the rules and regulations themselves evolved. Disciplinary sanctions for officers who engaged in political activism grew harsher under the dictatorship of the Estado Novo. On March 4, 1938, a new addition to the disciplinary code forbade officers from partaking in any political discussion, demonstration, or act of propaganda in public or on military bases.[7]

According to this reading of twentieth-century Brazilian military history and, in particular, the political consequences of the professionalization process, the individual blended into the organization as its internal cohesion grew. According to José Murilo de Carvalho, the concept of the "citizen soldier," dominant at the time of the Republic's founding, but representing a risk for the institution, would disappear in favor of the "professional soldier," and then the "institutional soldier."[8] Contrary to the prediction of the U.S. political scientist Samuel Huntington at the end of the 1950s, this professionalization did not translate into a distancing from the political sphere.[9] On the contrary, professionalization paved the way for the political interventionism of Latin America's armies because it isolated the military institution, strengthened its internal cohesion and structure, and allowed for the organized dissemination of new doctrines.[10] However, instead of a "military interventionism," founded on the politicization of officers of all ranks, an "interventionism of the Generals" would emerge.[11]

The April 1964 coup d'état, as an initiative increasingly reserved for high-ranking officers, seems to fit this historical dynamic. After the coup, power quickly realigned according to the chain of command, and the supreme post, the presidency of the Republic, would be filled by a succession of five generals: Humberto de Alencar Castelo Branco (1964–67), Artur da Costa e Silva (1967–69), Emílio Garrastazu Médici (1969–74), Ernesto Geisel (1974–79), and João Batista Figueiredo (1979–85). Even though men in uniform exercised direct and lasting political power, with the support of the army and in its name, that did not preclude a paradoxical insistence on apoliticism—but one that could only therefore apply to the bottom of the military hierarchy. This contradiction was handily summarized by General Orlando Geisel, army minister of the Third Military Government, during a meeting of the Army High Command:

> Whether we like it or not, we are involved in politics. Generals are often forced to pretend they are not involved, that they only deal with the professional side of things, but generals must necessarily get involved in politics, if only behind the scenes. . . . Captains, majors, colonels, and even brigadier generals must stay out of politics; politics must only happen in the highest spheres. The Chief of the Army engages in politics, but less than a minister like me does; and I am less involved than the President. We must project the image that we do not think about politics.[12]

The reality of a progressive depoliticization of subordinate and middle-ranking officers and of the troops, coupled with the institutional discourse demanding their strict apoliticism, has thrown social science researchers off their scent. In a play whose major actors were the generals, the military regime relegated rank-and-file soldiers and the bulk of officers to nonspeaking roles, or even pieces of historical scenery. The behavior of junior and senior officers was generally considered apolitical. The overwhelming majority of them, it was said, were stationed on bases where they were confined to apolitical "professional tasks," far away from decision-making circles. Meanwhile, a small minority, having participated in state repression, were more often portrayed as a group of criminals whose "fanatical" behavior did not deserve political analysis. When we talk about junior officers, we thus either associate them with absolute passivity, or radicalism, emotionalism, and collective effervescence. Only the generals were credited with a philosophy, a doctrine, a strategy, in short, a political rationalism. Only the generals were granted the status of political players.

THE PERSISTENCE OF POLITICAL AND "REVOLUTIONARY" FOMENT

Even so, the reining-in of the armed forces and the assertion of the military elite as sole political actor does not represent the whole picture. These were rules and ideals that came to be enforced over time, but they did not prevent the continuing mobilization of soldiers, sergeants, and junior officers in the second half of the century.

Let us now turn back to the two decades leading up to the coup d'état. The fall of the Estado Novo, in 1945, resulted first and foremost from Vargas's abandonment by the military General Staff that had advised and supported him. The presidential elections immediately afterward, which inaugurated the democratic postwar period, were disputed between two general officers: the air chief general and former tenente Eduardo Gomes, representing the economically liberal Right, and the candidate from the getulista camp, General Eurico Gaspar Dutra, who would win the election. All subsequent elections between 1950 and 1964 were won by civilians, despite the fact that their opponents were always general officers: thus Getúlio Vargas won the 1950 election against Air Chief General Gomes; Juscelino Kubitschek won in 1955 against General Juarez Távora, also a former revolutionary lieutenant in the 1920s; and Jânio Quadros won the presidency in 1960 against General Henrique Teixeira Lott. Hence, in the upper echelons of the state, political clashes directly involved the military top brass.

However, during this same period, the entire armed forces came to mirror the mobilization and growing polarization of Brazilian urban society. For proof of this, one need only observe the mood of excitement that permeated the Military Club, a political and cultural association for army officers. Here, they hotly debated the big issues animating the national political scene, and the "getulista" nationalist faction clashed with the economically liberal and anticommunist Right, sometimes violently. Under Vargas's second government (1951–54), infighting between factions turned into a full-blown war involving officers of all ranks. But the club was far from an isolated hotbed of politicization in an otherwise disciplined army. While the majority of activism was concentrated in Rio de Janeiro, where the Military Club's headquarters were located, an atmosphere of debate and even conflict spread to bases all over the country: turnout for the club's elections was massive and manifestos signed by hundreds of officers were frequently publicized. This state of political turmoil was diametrically opposed to the hierarchical precepts that, it seems, sought to construct a new "military identity" hostile to sectarian embroilment and other acts of indiscipline.

Astonishingly, the highly mobilized military Right continued to insist on a depoliticized and strictly professional institution, while the nationalist camp was decried as the troublemaker, an enemy of the hierarchy, the Trojan horse of civilian interests. And yet, this faction, which was very close to the UDN, was just as involved in partisan issues as its opponent. It had its own heroes in the political class: Jânio Quadros, until his sudden resignation put him in the category of dashed hopes; and especially Carlos Lacerda, a radical UDN politician, a virulent anticommunist orator, and governor of the State of Guanabara (where Rio is located) as of 1960. To defend them, or challenge their opponents, groups of officers increasingly engaged in acts of rebelliousness and disobedience throughout the 1950s. In August 1954, following an attempted assassination of Carlos Lacerda, in which Vargas's inner circle was implicated, an internal air force investigation began to look like an insurrection. The military top brass put increasing pressure on the President's Office, contributing to Getúlio Vargas's suicide several days later. From then on, there was no way to calm hearts and minds. Juscelino Kubitschek's election was met with an attempt at armed resistance from aboard the cruiser *Tamandaré* in November 1955, and his inauguration touched off an uprising deep in the Amazon by what then appeared a handful of wing nuts. In fact, their rebellion would come to be seen as a founding act for important architects of the 1964 coup d'état (Jacareacanga Rebellion, January 1956). When the candidacy of Jânio Quadros began to take shape, the same officers would try once again to influence the course of events with a final rebellion (the Aragarças Rebellion, December 1959) before effectively seizing power less than five years later. And yet this right-wing military faction recruited far beyond the generals: its ranks included few of the young sergeants, lieutenants, and captains who tended to favor nationalist theses and social reform projects, but majors, lieutenant-colonels, and colonels were legion.

Hence, well before the Goulart government came to power, part of the army lived in a state of permanent intrigue and uprising.[13] This situation lent the rebellious a sense of impunity (for they were granted amnesty on several occasions), solidified antiestablishment practices, helped form peer networks, and reinforced an idea within the military that was totally at odds with professionalism and apoliticism: the mystique of an anticommunist and authoritarian "revolution" that was hostile to the majority of the political class.

Nor did this activism stop in 1964. Despite the influence exerted by the hierarchical ideal and the victory of their own camp, numerous young officers saw the coup as their "revolution," their chance, their moment. They felt responsible for the new regime and were fully intent on influencing its path. Their protests were thus at the origin of a genuine political life, but whose actors were armed forces officers, under a military dictatorship. Their career paths and their networks, their modes of organization and action, their convictions and strategies were more than just a footnote to a larger history: they allow us to grasp the regime's evolution, its progressive militarization, its hardening by fits and starts, and its repressive confinement. Moreover, the activism of these officers, because it was considered legitimate by a great number of the putschists, sheds light on the nature of the military regime itself and, in particular, its symbolic ambiguities. Was this the collective work of a military Right galvanized by the word "revolution" or a hijacking of state power by generals imbued with the dream of a perfect hierarchy? An authoritarian perversion of the Republic or a "revolutionary" state of emergency? Somewhere between these models, the putschists would, through negotiation and conflict, collectively improvise their own regime.

CHAPTER ONE

Conspiracies
1961–1964

> If we don't educate our children and grandchildren, then the communists will. They are our great enemy. Nothing important happens in this country without action by the communists. There is red dust in the eyes of the people and a large proportion of the leaders of Brazil.
> —GENERAL MILTON TAVARES DE SOUZA

The coup d'état of April 1964 has long seemed an oddity in the history of the Republic of Brazil. First, because the image of the Brazilian Army in Latin America at the time was one of legalism and respect for the authorities. Unlike its counterparts in Argentina, Brazil's neighbor and historical rival, the Brazilian military had not exercised power directly on behalf of its own institution since the 1890s. To be sure, the country had experienced numerous armed uprisings, and no break with the rule of law had ever occurred without the backing of the Military High Command or significant sections of the armed forces. To be sure too, since the Revolution of 1930 at least, generals had operated behind the scenes at the highest levels and in the ministries of the republic, but neither the central authorities nor the machinery of state had been subordinated to the military for any length of time. Just a few years prior to the coup, senior officers still reveled in that reputation. In Brazil there would be no caudillo or dictator heading a "totalitarian dictatorship" of the kind seen in "poxy little South American republics," General Castelo Branco declared at the Superior War School in September 1955. He would go on to be the first president of the actual dictatorship. He also said that a "professional armed forces mentality" prevailed over a "militia mentality" sustained by the "volatility of a political mindset that wavers constantly between taking power and preserving it." "If we adopt this regime, what comes in by force, will be kept in place by force and removed only by force. What a backward and reac-

João Goulart (foreground, sitting) being greeted by general Ladário Teles. August 1, 1962.
O Globo Archives.

tionary objective! And then there will be no escape."[1] Castelo Branco was speaking in a particular context: that of the presidential election campaign in the run-up to the November 1955 vote that brought Juscelino Kubitschek, heir to Getúlio Vargas, who had died a year earlier, to power. Part of the Brazilian Right, both civilian and military, was already organizing to prevent his becoming president but this putschist state of mind was far from that of the majority, and respect for the ballot box prevailed among General Staffs and the officer corps as it did among the general population. To everyone's surprise, even the putschists themselves, less than ten years later almost nothing was left of this legalist tradition and identity.

Indeed, the second surprise of 1964 was the ease with which the rebels seized power. Not only did the army break with its tradition of republican legalism but, to begin with, its initiative met only extremely limited resistance. João Goulart appeared to fall like a ripe fruit: neither the lower ranks of the armed forces, despite having given assurances of their support on numerous occasions, nor the trade unions, nor people on the Left, took to the streets or took up arms to try to prevent it. Opponents of the coup went to ground then opted for silence or exile. At the same time, the urban middle classes, half the political elite, and the business community were noisily exultant, giving the coup d'état all the hallmarks of a concerted and consensual initiative by conservatives, whether civilian or military.

When the republic collapsed like a house of cards, it evidently provoked soul-searching and even an identity crisis within the Brazilian Left. It has subsequently inspired a large number of studies focused on a simple but often crucial question in recent-history research: "How was it possible?"[2] What changes in military and civilian thinking and behavior, what structural alterations to Brazilian society permitted such a break with legality that the army took power? These questions and, arguably, this anxiety are the motives behind the present study of the 1964 coup d'état and the political and party restructurings that followed. We will not revisit all the debates over the origins and causes of the putsch here but will confine our research to a specific and key issue: how the military came to subscribe en masse to the prospect of a coup d'état.

BUILDING THE CONSENSUS

Many factors enabled the putschists to achieve easy and speedy victory. It is our hypothesis that the lack of any real military resistance and, indeed, the confidence and enthusiasm with which the overwhelming majority of officers regarded the overthrow of João Goulart played a major role. We believe also that the building of this consensus, which conflicted with the constitutional requirements of the military institution, was of fairly recent date, that is, later than 1961. The liberties taken with democratic principles by some of the military Right were nothing new. Since the end of the Second World War, the nomination of any candidate connected to the legacy of Getúlio Vargas had resulted in sporadic military revolts and challenges from sections of the conservative National Democratic Union or UDN. We might, for example, recall the remark by Carlos Lacerda, an eminent member of the UDN and darling of the military Right, regarding the possibility of Vargas returning to power in 1951: "As a senator, he must not run for president. As a candidate, he must not be elected. If elected, he must not take office. If he is in office, we must resort to revolution to prevent him from governing."[3] Nor was virulent anti-communism new in Brazil, particularly in the armed forces. Last, João Goulart had been despised for at least a decade when his move to the Ministry of Labor during the second Vargas government (1953–54) entrenched accusations that he was in cahoots with the unions and promoting the "communization" of Brazil. He had been accused ever since then by the UDN, the conservative press, and the military Right of workerism, demagoguery, and sympathy for the Peronist "syndicalist republic" in neighboring Argentina.

Nevertheless, this self-confident military Right was unable to prevent Vice President Goulart from coming to power in August–September 1961 after the unforeseeable resignation of the extravagant Jânio Quadros—albeit not for want of trying. Quadros left office on August 25. On August 30, the three armed forces ministers (General Odílio Denys for the army, Admiral Sílvio Heck for the navy, and Brigadier Gabriel Grün Moss for the air force) put out a manifesto accusing Goulart of being compromised by his involvement with the unions, of betraying the authentic interests of the working classes, and of being complicit with "international communism," particularly by promoting the infiltration of its agents into the machinery of state. In the ministers' words, "[the] support, protection, and encouragement" Goulart would give to the "agents of disorder, disunity, and anarchy" in Brazil would inevitably lead to "chaos, anarchy, [and] civil war," with the armed forces—the main bulwarks against such a state of affairs—unable to resist since they would already have been "infiltrated and tamed" and then "transform[ed] into simple communist militias as has happened in other countries."[4] The ministers were, however, unable to garner sufficient support within their own forces to achieve their goals: the legalist resistance of the military, particularly the Third Army in Rio Grande do Sul, together with that of the Labor Party and within it of Leonel Brizola, governor of Rio Grande do Sul, forced the rebels to back down. Yet by March 1964, when the Left had been in power for two and a half years and Goulart believed he had set up a "military apparatus" meant to allow only loyal generals to hold senior troop commands, he appears to have been abandoned by the entire institution.

A shortage of suitable sources means the scale, mechanisms, and key causes of this abandonment are difficult to access as subjects of research. Military unit archives for the post-1945 period are not open to researchers and hold the internal reports that are the only means of providing an accurate description of who in each unit supported, resisted, or abandoned the coup. Also out of reach is the opinion of the military, which had no public space for expression and was surveyed by the General Staffs only rarely or in partisan fashion. The main available source is in fact the statements of the military personnel themselves, both at the time and today, in the form of published testimonies or those taken down by researchers and journalists: since the mid-1970s publishers and the media have given considerable space to officers' memoirs.[5] It should be noted that until the 1990s studies did not focus on the discourse and practices of the protagonists, particularly the military putschists. The recollections and even discourse of the military were (and, for certain audiences, remain) suspect and disparaged: collecting them and, especially, making them part of the interpretation of events is often seen as a kind of political betrayal, a betrayal of memory, if not the "moral pollution" of the researcher.[6] These memoirs only really entered the academic space when, thirty years after the coup, researchers at the Contemporary Brazilian History Research and Documentation Center (CPDOC-FGV/Rio de Janeiro) published officers' testimonies using a systematic interviewing approach.[7] The novelty of the undertaking lay not so much in the fact that putschist officers were given the chance to "speak out" as from the fact that the army no longer had a monopoly on the production of its memory: beginning to create a scientific corpus of oral sources that offered the "military take" on the coup d'état and the dictatorship has allowed it to be included in the construction of a historical narrative.

These military witness statements must, of course, be used with a degree of caution. They give information only about the military personnel who make them, leading players perhaps, but not the only ones in the conspiracy against and overthrow of the civilian president;[8] most come from senior officers under the military regime; last like any testimonies, they are reconstructions and distortions, particularly in the context of the "memory war" under way since the end of the dictatorship.[9] Even so, they are a vital resource for research into the precise methods of constructing unanimity in the military or at least a broad consensus within the officer corps.

Did this consensus really exist, however? The first factor adding grist to the mill was the small number of sanctions meted out immediately after the coup. While the "cleanup operation" that ensued primarily concerned the military institution—it was far and away the main body of public servants affected—the 1,013 troops disciplined by the regime's first "institutional act" were merely a drop in the ocean of the institution as a whole. In the army, 252 sergeants and subofficers were expelled from their force, discharged, or retired, out of the nearly 59,656 who held these ranks (i.e., 0.4 percent).[10] Proportionately, eight times as many army officers were disciplined but this was still only 264 (3.3 percent) of the nearly 7,929 the institution included at the time, according to figures from the *Boletim do Exército*. Only army generals were significantly affected, with a quarter being disciplined. Navy and air force personnel were proportionately more affected, particularly the rank and file and subofficers, although the figures do not suggest mass involvement in politics or resistance to the putsch.

The small scale of this intra-institutional crackdown may be interpreted in various ways. First, it is possible that sergeants and subofficers openly resisted the coup d'état but the new authorities opted for a moderate response. There are several reasons that this hypothesis is unlikely, the first being that, while traces of skirmishes can be found in a few sources, there is nothing to suggest the existence of any large-scale armed resistance.[11] Furthermore, had the latter existed, it is highly likely that it would have been emphasized in the victors' memoirs as evidence of the communist convictions of the armed forces' lower ranks. Last, several authors have called attention to the high level of tension and animosity between the Left and the military Right at the time, expressed in instances of violence since the 1950s, suggesting that the penalties would have been harsh.

The second hypothesis is that the majority of military personnel accepted or supported the coup d'état. What cannot be known, however, is whether this consent was the result of a need to obey the chain of command, a group mentality or a more enthusiastic commitment. The sources have little to say about this: written documents are, in fact, extremely rare and later testimonies (published memoirs, interviews with journalists or researchers) generally come from service personnel who are clearly identified with one camp or another and are justifying their choice rather than recounting their memories, which, in any case, are reconstructions. Barely any are moderate, nonpartisan, or even guarded. On the basis of a limited number of interviews, Lausimar Zimmermann concludes that sergeants essentially accepted the putsch rather than actively supporting or resisting it, so as to comply with the orders of officers of intermediate or senior rank, the majority of whom were, for their part, in favor.[12] The vast majority of officers' testimonies depicts a reckless and impatient youth, the core of the discontent, which drew an apathetic and negligent military elite along in its wake. For General Cordeiro de

Farias, "With very few exceptions, the generals kept their heads down. They were all hostile to the government but they did not have the courage to express their positions. [By contrast] there was a far higher number of senior officers—lieutenant-colonels and colonels. The great bulk, however, was made up of young officers—lieutenants, captains and majors. The difference in behavior was obvious. While the generals and senior officers held back, the young soldiers were impetuous, intense, and determined to throw themselves into the fight."[13] It must be noted, however, that the overwhelming majority of testimonies available are from officers who either supported or agreed with the coup at the time. There is nothing straightforward about how this political aspect should be interpreted: are the sources biased because researchers and journalists were less interested in the losers than the winners who, in addition, had more networks, resources, and space for self-expression within the armed forces? Or is it in fact the sign of mass support for the putsch? It is hard to say. At most, we can state that, in the testimonies, the barracks' "enthusiasm" and "fervor" are linked to their proximity to urban centers, which may have facilitated internal military communications and access to the civilian media's anticommunist propaganda. It is true, however, that there is a dearth of information about the peripheral regions. Rio has a special place since the Military Club, on the one hand, and the military schools (Officer Improvement School [Escola de Aperfeiçoamento de Oficiais, EsAO] and Army Command and General Staff School [Escola de Comando e Estado Maior do Exército, ECEME]), on the other, were spaces in which political expression by young officers was tolerated.[14]

What happened to the Brazilian armed forces between September 1961, when João Goulart came to power relatively easily despite the surprise, and despite a right-wing Congress and the openly hostile military ministers (although he did have to broker a deal whereby his inauguration only went ahead in exchange for a restored parliamentary system that drastically truncated his powers); and March 1964, when the arrival of a column of troops from the plateaus of Minas Gerais forced him to flee into exile? Awareness of the international context in the years after the Cuban Revolution and, even more, the revelation of its Marxist-Leninist nature, the North American cultural and military offensive and the extremely polarized political climates of Latin America tend to make this U-turn appear natural. And yet, in the spring of 1961, the Brazilian Army's fate and ideological course was not yet set in stone: its political development was and would continue to be the result of doctrinal innovations, contacts with political and economic circles, and outside influences, which constructed a politically oriented reading of the national and global situation and the legitimate ways of confronting it.

Initially, observers and researchers identified a single guilty party, which had invented and disseminated a new military doctrine, with which the South American Right had been injected and brainwashed since the beginning of the Cold War. The guilty party was, of course, the United States, with its National Security Doctrine (NSD), a major offensive weapon in the "psychological warfare" being waged in Latin America. From the end of the 1970s, the NSD was considered the official ideology of Southern Cone dictatorships to the extent that they were known as "National Security Dictatorships."[15] The NSD was based on the notion of imminent war against an omnipresent enemy (primarily communist), an external and, above all, internal armed conflict of a psychological and all-encompassing nature since it affected not just the armed forces but also entire societies and machineries of state. The certainty of war meant that all political systems, economies, education, the mass media, and social policies, in short, all public institutions and policies, had to be reassessed in terms of the impending conflict. This program for restructuring states and societies entered the Southern Cone armed forces from the higher military schools which had been modeled on the U.S. National War College in the early hours of the Cold War. In Brazil, it was from the Superior War School (Escola Superior de Guerra, ESG), founded in 1949, that army officers Cordeiro de Farias, the first head of the school, Castelo Branco, future president of the dictatorship, and Golbery do Couto e Silva, geopolitical expert and post-1964 éminence grise, theorized and disseminated their version of the NSD.[16]

South American historiography from the 1990s to 2010 subsequently queried the dogma of a single, unique, and omnipresent NSD, imported from the United States. This was first the result of a closer analysis of individual national cases, which revealed fragmentary, partial, and differentiated appropriations of the National Security Doctrine depending on the country and understood as the result of its history. In Brazil, while the War School's theoretical output often resorted to a highly specific "national security" jargon—"Permanent National Objectives" had to be met by a "National Strategy" combating "Antagonisms," which were not to be confused with "Adverse Factors"—its ideological content was neither systematically new nor always present in the "ready-made thinking" provided by the Americans. In fact, the essence of the

NSD, the internal enemy, had been a pillar of the Brazilian Army's strategic thinking since the 1930s. Unlike their European and even North American peers, when the Cold War broke out it had already been a long time since the Southern Cone military had regarded external, border warfare as the main military threat to their countries. The internal enemy revolution had, in fact, already taken place: the NSD added "only" total warfare, psychological especially, and a particular conceptualization. Moreover, the political program that was meant to respond to the threat and thus to ensure "national security" stood at the crossroads of several schools of thought.[17] It spoke of the planned authoritarian demobilization of society, abolition of class conflict, propaganda, and increased police pressure that can be seen in the various versions of the NSD. At the same time, a centralizing and authoritarian developmentalism can also be seen, inspired by Alberto Torres and Oliveira Viana, two very conservative thinkers of the 1920s and 1930s, and the ideologues of the Estado Novo. This inspired the forced-march industrialization, infrastructure construction, and territorial organization proposed and planned by the ESG (especially, it must be said, after the coup).

What in Brazil is called the "National Security Doctrine" of the 1950s to 1970s was then the result of an innate syncretism and cannot, moreover, be considered the sole "ideology of the regime." Last, it was not a theory immediately intended to indoctrinate the troops. The officers most rapidly acculturated to the NSD were in fact the elite who attended the Superior War School, in other words, the cream of the colonels and generals, along with handpicked civilians. Other than in very few ways and only very belatedly, the version of the policy devised was not included in the curriculum of the schools open to the youngest officers or to sergeants. As for manuals and handbooks bearing the hallmarks of NSD jargon, these also made a belated appearance, from 1967 onward. In other words, if the ESG, as a civilian and military think tank, was of real significance in the growing political ambitions of some of the Military High Command and in the contacts they established with the conservative civilian elites, its influence on the ideological education of the vast bulk of officers is more debatable.[18]

BETWEEN THE UNITED STATES AND FRANCE: AT COUNTER-INSURGENCY SCHOOL

South America and especially Brazil were certainly the target of a North American ideological offensive at this time but until the mid-1960s it came only very partially in the form of a new military doctrine. The story began in the Second World War, which launched the rapid Americanization of cultural and consumer goods in Brazil. From 1942 onward, the country was effectively in the allied camp and even secured a role in the "liberation" of Europe, hoping thereby to gain access to benefits and privileged partnership with the United States. As a result, 25,000 Brazilian soldiers went off to Italy at the end of 1943 as members of the Brazilian Expeditionary Force (BEF) (Força Expedicionária Brasileira, FEB). Brazil was the only South American country to have troops on the ground.[19] The wartime alliance and the experience of combat contributed to an upsurge in U.S. influence over the Brazilian Army and civilian elites and beyond them to the whole of society. At the same time and in parallel, the influence of France, by then in ruins and lacking diplomatic autonomy and economic power, collapsed after hegemony of more than twenty years.[20] The military was affected in two ways. On the one hand, in 1945 the United States became Brazil's main arms supplier and military financial partner, as subsequently confirmed by an agreement signed in 1952.[21] Personal links were established during the war, such as those between future General-President Castelo and Vernon Walters, the U.S. liaison officer for the BEF and Fifth Army Command and future military attaché to Brazil between 1962 and 1967. On the other hand, the Brazilian military, like the whole of the country's middle class, found themselves immersed in a "cultural Cold War" in which promotion of the American Way of Life and the denigration of communism and socialism pervaded the mass media.[22]

The Cuban Revolution (January 1959) and especially the revelation of its Marxist-Leninist nature (April 1961) inaugurated a radically new phase on both these fronts. As described by Phyllis Parker since the 1970s and by Carlos Fico on the basis of more recently declassified U.S. documents, the Goulart years were marked by an explosion of U.S. investments in propaganda campaigns, most often under cover of the Alliance for Progress, set up by Kennedy, and designed to shore up the "progressive, democratic center" (i.e., the Right opposed to the labor president) and to "reveal the true face of communism."[23] First to be affected by the offensive were the big media, the business world, intellectuals, academics, and the conservative political class whose campaigns and even local administrations were given support and massive financial backing. In addition to the conquest of "hearts and minds" designed to keep the masses from the temptation of the "red peril," a real campaign was mounted to undermine João Goulart's presidency, especially from the middle of 1962 and the start of debates over whether or not to restore the presidential system. These operations, which ran to several tens of millions of dollars, were orchestrated by the United States Information Service (USIS) and increasingly encouraged by Ambassador Lincoln Gordon (1961–68), convinced that Goulart would inevitably slide into populism and communism. It was Gordon who, at the end of 1963, urged the U.S. secret services and armed forces to consider logistical and military assistance for a coup d'état. This was Operation Brother Sam, the provision of light weapons and the deployment of a fleet off the Brazilian coast, which was ultimately surplus to the putschists' requirements.

There is no doubt that the rise in aggressive anticommunist propaganda, together with an operation to destabilize and discredit the Goulart government, helped push officers into open opposition to the incumbent authorities, primarily because, coming from the urban middle classes as they did, they were the core target of this conservative discourse. Moreover, several dozen officers belonged to political organizations inspired and sometimes funded by their U.S. counterparts. As of 1961 these fueled what Rodrigo Patto Sá Motta calls the "second great anticommunist surge" of 1961–64 (the first being in 1935–37).[24] They included the Patriotic Action Group (Grupo de Ação Patriótica, GAP) and Anticommunist Movement (Movimento Anticomunista, MAC) to name only the most important. It was not unusual to find these officers' wives in groups aimed at the female public, such as the Women's Anticommunist League (Liga Feminina Anticomunista) or the Women's Campaign for Democracy (Campanha da Mulher pela Democracia, CAMDE).[25] Last, the military were the target of specific anticommunist and moralist campaigns, particularly through films shown in barracks and schools or on ships. In 1963, for example, more than 1,700 films were distributed by the USIS, reaching an audience of around 180,000 officers, subofficers, and soldiers.[26] Several book translations were also funded although it is not possible to assess their reach.

And yet when they are asked about the foreign influences and doctrinal changes of those years, most Brazilian officers say nothing about the United States or the NSD—the contents of which very few would be able to give any idea about—or even the counterinsurgency theories that were just starting to be drawn up by the U.S. General Staffs. Instead, they all talk about the "theory of revolutionary war," which was a conception of the communist enemy rather than of the exercise of power, and imported from France rather than the

United States.[27] Here is what Otávio Costa, serving at the ECEME, recalled three decades later:

> Right then we were confused about what direction to take . . . what should we do? Which way should we go? What war were we supposed to be preparing for? . . . So we started looking into new experiences: the civil war in Greece, France's wars in Indochina and Algeria, even the internal problem in France itself, with the violent reactions to De Gaulle. On this occasion, we were gripped by French military literature . . . [and], despite America's influence, we started contemplating its colonial and domestic experience, conceiving of a new kind of war. It was an infinitely small war—insurrectional war, revolutionary war.[28]

The fact that the officers' testimonies insist on the predominant influence of French rather than U.S. doctrine in the years leading up to the coup is not the result of a desire to conceal American input into the "democratic revolution" of which they are so proud. Of course, the putschists' recollections generally tend to play down, if not deny outright, any U.S. involvement in the conspiracy and the coup d'état, sometimes despite the evidence. In this particular case, however, from the point of view of doctrine, there was indeed a "French presence where the United States had been thought to dominate," as Rodrigo Nabuco says.[29] He explains that at the outset of the Cuban Revolution, U.S. strategists were comparatively short on doctrine: without any real on-the-ground experience—for massive engagement in Vietnam would only begin in 1964—their knowledge of anti-guerrilla techniques is still only theoretical, acquired from their French Army counterparts returning from Indochina and Algeria. Moreover, the French General Staffs had turned their "military know-how into an export product that could create a community of interest with the target countries." In other words they could deliver a sufficiently adaptable and universal theory to be used in "law enforcement" everywhere, to increase French military influence and to sell arms.[30] Last, despite the drastic decline in its diplomatic and military influence since the Second World War, France could still draw on older networks: a good many Brazilian Army generals had passed through the French Military Mission, based in Brazil from 1919 to 1939, and had retained an intellectual and emotional attachment to France.

The theory of revolutionary war was imported into Brazil between 1957 and 1961. Between 1961 and 1964, it was systematically disseminated to army officers and, to a lesser extent, to sergeants and subofficers. Nothing of the kind existed for U.S. counterinsurgency theories and techniques at the time. These appeared in the Brazilian military press after the coup d'état and only really replaced French references at the end of the 1960s.[31] Nor did counterinsurgency training come from attending the famous School of the Americas in the Panama Canal region since it only began to accept Brazilian armed forces personnel from the end of 1964, much later than service personnel from other nations of the subcontinent (furthermore, Spanish became the teaching language in 1962). Prior to the 1964 coup, it was attended only by the Military Police for general training, and by a small number of officers and subofficers for specific weapons training (90 mm cannon). Only eight officers received intelligence or command training there between 1960 and 1962. Between 1964 and 1966, the first generation of Brazilians was trained in "jungle warfare," which had been perfected in light of the initial U.S. engagements on the ground in Vietnam, and thus anticipating the importance of this type of warfare even before the conflict there had mutated into full-blown war. Only in 1966 did the military curriculum for Brazilian officers and sergeants in Panama really come to include intelligence, counterinformation, and "psychological operations."[32]

The theory of revolutionary war in Brazil can be traced back to the autumn of 1957 in the form of French military journal articles published in translation in Brazilian military journals. This was also when the innovative doctrine reached Argentina, its point of entry into the subcontinent.[33] Faced with failure in Indochina and Algeria, the French Army had been developing its analysis of an ideal-type enemy, separatist, insurgent, terrorist, or communist, since the middle of the 1950s. The theory quickly became seen as an export product. Unlike the National Security Doctrine drafted in the muffled corridors of the War School, which sought to build a political program for the elites, the theory of revolutionary war was designed from the start as a mass-market product intended for troop training. It needed no tweaking—or not much. It was intended to be disseminated. Within a few months, its words, concepts, and practices had invaded Brazil's military reviews, military school courses and the schedules of barrack conferences. Leading the field was the *Mensário de Cultura Militar*, published by the Army General Staff (Estado Maior do Exército, EME), with an article titled "A guerra revolucionária" in autumn 1957. This was a translation by Lieutenant Colonel Moacyr Barcellos Potyguara of a document that had appeared a little earlier in the *Revue Militaire d'Informations*, linked to the French Defense Ministry.[34] Presented as setting out the "bases" of revolutionary war, the document included the main theoretical features that would subsequently be used in articles, at conferences, and in courses aimed at Brazilian officers: the objective of revolutionaries was the "physical and moral conquest" of the population in order to overthrow the authorities. To achieve this, they used "destructive techniques," on the one hand, including strikes, "terrorism," "manipulation of the masses (huge meetings and demonstrations)," and guerrilla warfare; and "constructive" techniques on the other—propaganda, activist training, control of the masses through the creation of "parallel hierarchies," construction of a clandestine government apparatus. Last, there were several clearly identified phases to any revolutionary conquest: four in this article—although it would be the five-phase division of another French author, Colonel Jacques Hogard, that would come to dominate.

Colonels and lieutenant colonels, some of them instructors at the ECEME, were the first to set about translating such documents and demanding that officer training included classes on revolutionary war. In 1958, a Modern Warfare Workshop Report (*Relatório do Seminário de Guerra Moderna*) published recommendations from the ECEME Instructors' Study Groups that "subjects to do with insurrectional war" should feature on the curriculum. Potyguara was far and away the trailblazer. During Goulart's presidency, he was also a very active conspirator, especially as cadet corps commander at the Agulhas Negras Military Academy (Academia Militar das Agulhas Negras, AMAN), the army cadet training school. As of 1960, he was joined in his translation venture by a handful of General Staff officers, most frequently colonels.[35] We will keep in mind the names of those born around 1920—Moacyr Potyguara (1919), Ferdinando de Carvalho (1918), Adyr Fiúza de Castro (1920), and Amerino Raposo (1922). After the coup, they would gain a reputation for demanding participation in the political process and the toughening up of the process itself.

Born in the 1910s and 1920s, these men were from middle- and upper-class families and the number of officers' sons among them was above average for their rank.[36] While they themselves were unambiguously opposed to Kubitschek's so-called getulista presidency (1956–61), their concerns were not those of a single faction. In the Brazilian Army of the day, anticommunism was an official and largely shared discourse. So, in 1958, Army Chief of Staff General Zeno Estillac Leal, a leading light of getulista nationalism, gave an interview to the press in which he portrayed "modern warfare" as potentially "subversive," "insurrectional," and "social-revolutionary."[37]

Initially, the revolutionary war scenario was not adapted to fit the Brazilian context (French articles were translated without commentaries or introductions). It appeared as an aspect of professional competence and separately from splits and internal political debates. And yet the original texts were laden with political implications. A particular vision of the social order, the "masses," the political class, and the role of the military seeped through the strategy reports. An article by Colonel Hogard, then an intelligence officer in Algeria, translated in the July 1959 *Mensário*, for example, highlighted the need for wholesale reform of society and the establishment of a "new order" to combat "the Revolution"—particularly because a "corrupt society" would be fragile in the face of the enemy. From this, the author deduced the need to reorganize society around "men beyond question, whom we must select and, on occasion, train. Many of them will have to be 'new men,' often from the people, because it is far easier for the Revolution to discredit and isolate the old persons of distinction."[38] Linked to this stated desire for social and political reorganization was a contempt for the working classes and an appreciation for the new elites, among whom the military stood out. "When the salvation of the Motherland is at stake and when it seems that they alone hold the truths that could save it. Twentieth-century warfare is too serious a thing for the military to keep silent about what they have learnt, to accept it not being taken into consideration."[39]

In this way, the export of French doctrines of war in the 1960s and 1970s helped justify the entry into the public arena of the Latin American military who read them. On numerous issues—suspicion of the civilian political class, considered out of date or corrupt; an organicist concept of social issues; paternalism and contempt for the masses; belief in the military's political mission within a modern warfare framework, extending as far as social and political "reorganization," and so forth—the thinking of the French writers echoed topics that had historically been very much present within the Brazilian military Right. The documents were, however, identified with military training and aspects of professional competence, inspired, moreover, by a European army—and all these features legitimized them in the eyes of their readers and depoliticized them.

Before 1961, the spread of revolutionary war theory in Brazil was confined to certain military journals, and to the ESG and ECEME. From 1961 onward, which corresponds to the brief term in office of the conservative Jânio Quadros, the Army General Staff embarked on indoctrination on a far greater scale, in particular by issuing a directive governing revolutionary war training in the military schools and troop units.[40] Officer school courses and curricula were changed. At the EsAO, which primarily trained captains, several documents and handbooks, endorsed by the school's education department in 1961, were used to train units in the years that followed.[41]

If the presidency of Jânio Quadros corresponded to a broader and more systematic dissemination of the theory of revolutionary war, his resignation in August 1961 seemed paradoxically to enhance the military focus on troop and officer indoctrination. The Left's return to power led to a wave of lectures on the subject being held at the military schools in order to complete the disrupted campaign to instill the fight against communist revolution.[42] At the same time, the journals gave greater space to the issue. As for October 1961, the Army General Staff's *Boletim de Informações*, previously focused on barely politicized economic, social and diplomatic studies, drastically altered its structure and ideological content, with a vast number of anticommunist and revolutionary war texts. In March 1962, the *Mensário de Cultura Militar*, a trendsetter in the field (its first special edition on revolutionary war having appeared in November 1960), changed the guidelines for its distribution from "restricted circulation" to "as wide as possible." The key weapon, however, was intensive officer training courses outside the usual curriculum, with the course content subsequently published internally. Several dozen officers from the three branches of the military, from General Staffs and directorates-general, as well as military school trainers, took part. The first was held in April 1962 and included AMAN instructors. The second was in September–October 1962 and that month's issue of the *Mensário* consisted of training material. The third and last in December 1963 ended with a lecture by Army Chief of Staff Castelo Branco, attesting to the institutional importance given to the courses.[43]

João Goulart's coming to power in September 1961 did not then put a stop to revolutionary war indoctrination within the armed forces. It delayed the introduction of courses and moderated indoctrination in the military schools but boosted the activity of the journals and the number of conferences. Most important, it intensified military anticommunism and encouraged the application of the new theories to the Brazilian situation. As of 1961, the *Mensário de Cultura Militar* explicitly depicted Brazil as an operational area for the communist revolution. The fragility of democracy, the culpable disarming of the civilian elites, the credulity of the masses and enemy operations were topics now applied to the domestic situation. In February 1962 it was possible to read that "the communists, almost entirely unrestrained, are endeavoring to take power." The armed forces must prepare for this threat by learning to know the enemy and "his dialectic in order to remain beyond the reach of its insidious and treacherous effects; his methods of action in order to neutralize or suppress him, including by violence if necessary."[44] In addition, as of 1962, reports of revolutionary war scenarios were accompanied by a collective debate as to how it could be taken on board by Brazilian officers: from then on, propaganda became considered, organized, and coordinated despite the executive's misgivings.

The military Right's freedom to indoctrinate the troops during the Goulart presidency can be partly explained in terms of the political position of the officers who headed the teaching departments, commanded the schools, or served at the EME. The new authorities did not immediately overturn the military's organizational structure and, subsequently, envisaged administrative and teaching work as an effective means of distancing opponents from troop commands. For Colonel Otávio Costa, who was in favor of the coup, Goulart's mistake was precisely "to exile the officers he didn't trust to the schools, assuming that the schools didn't stand for very much. By his own action, therefore, the schools were full to bursting with the best military assets, more so than ever before. This mistake made it easier for his opponents to mobilize because it concentrated the military at the ESG and in the three General Staff schools."[45]

While it has been proved that the theory of revolutionary war spread to the EsAO and ECEME, AMAN's piecemeal archives do not allow a similar development to be ascertained when it comes to the cadets. Moreover, the academy was a far less central venue for political agitation than the schools for older officers. Nevertheless, the presence of Moacyr Barcellos Potyguara as head of the cadet corps in charge of overall training in 1963 and 1964 and of Emílio Médici, an active conspirator and future general-president during the dictatorship, as academy commander, certainly encouraged the inclusion of considerations of revolutionary war in its tuition. Colonel Francisco Ruas Santos, author of the leading course on revolutionary war (used systematically after the coup d'état at AMAN but also at EsAO and ECEME), taught history at the academy.[46] The presence of a course on revolutionary war in cadet training is confirmed only in the 1964 program, which was drawn up in 1963, and the number of hours explicitly given over to revolutionary war teaching remained low (at 5 hours in the second year and 20 in the third out of a training timetable of around 150 hours). Nevertheless, it seems instructors had great freedom to bring these topics into their lessons.[47]

In the country's barracks, outside the "youth in the schools," acculturation to the theory of revolutionary war was more varied and closely linked to the beliefs and activism of senior and general officers of influence in a given region. Under Goulart's government, there was an increase in informal "conferences" bringing revolutionary war to the attention of officers, sergeants and troops, which were systematically an opportunity for more or less veiled attacks on the incumbent authorities. The archives of General Antônio Carlos Murici reveal, for example, the efforts he made as commander between 1961 and 1964 of the Seventh Military Region (based in Recife in northeastern Brazil) to "train" his unit: a kind of homemade training manual, a compilation of journal articles and notes of military school lessons, was even put together in 1962.[48] In May 1963, he held a conference for officers of the Natal Garrison, which was later repeated for the town dignitaries, to great fanfare. It led to Murici being dubbed a "gorilla" by Leonel Brizola, governor of Rio Grande do Sul, a left-wing member of the Brazilian Labor Party (Partido Trabalhista Brasileiro, PTB) and Goulart's brother-in-law.[49] The conference demonstrated how the theory of revolutionary war was used as "scientific" validation of criticism of the incumbent authorities, naming the specific phases of the revolutionary process (as used by France's Hogard), which Brazil had already allegedly entered. We should note that General Castelo Branco, commander of the Fourth Army, to which the Seventh Military Region was subordinate, did not approve of such a conference being held for a civilian audience although he had no objections at all to it taking place at a barracks. In the one case, it was military training. In the other, it was politics and under no circumstances could the army get involved in politics, he said.[50] Nevertheless, he sanctioned Murici only with a minor reprimand.

Support for the theory of revolutionary war did not translate into identical involvement in the conspiracy. Castelo Branco, for instance, steered clear of the conspirators' networks for a long time. While he fully concurred with the theory of revolutionary war, he did not initially look on it as a political weapon or an extra-military propaganda tool. By contrast, the opposition of a great proportion of officers to the Goulart government grew without it being possible to attribute the rising discontent solely to the spread of the new doctrine of war within the military. Indeed, many officers, serving away from the schools and the missionaries of revolutionary war, only became properly acquainted with it after the coup d'état or through civilians. General Agnaldo del Nero, for example, a lieutenant promoted to captain at the end of 1963 and an instructor at the Sergeants' School (Escola de Sargentos das Armas), only came across the revolutionary war theory through a speech made by UDN president Bilac Pinto to the Chamber of Deputies on January 23, 1964, which was subsequently transcribed in the press. And yet Nero had evinced clear distrust of Goulart and fierce hostility toward Brizola well before that date.[51] At that point, part of the UDN and of conservative public opinion was indeed familiar with the vocabulary of revolutionary war, an acculturation evident in political speeches, parliamentary debates, and increasingly heated media polemics. The doctrine therefore spilled across the symbolic boundary between civilians and the military.

The transmission of the revolutionary war theory from a center (the General Staffs and military schools) to a periphery (the officer corps and the affluent sectors of civil society) cannot then be explained solely by growing opposition to the powers that be. The image of "imminent revolution" was developed within the officer corps by more complex and multifaceted propaganda, in which internal indoctrination and, more particularly, the teaching of revolutionary war, were only one piece. A diversity of vehicles helped mobilize the themes and images traditional to anticommunism in the Brazilian military. The objective was to present the coup as a counterrevolution.

TO "INFORM" AND PERSUADE: THE PROPAGANDA WAR

More often than the notion of a doctrine to be communicated to their military colleagues, it is the notion of informing, revealing, and urgently emphasizing the abyss into which Brazil was about to plummet that recurs in officers' testimonies. To begin with, the conspiracy was in fact an immense propaganda operation that sought to deny the government the legitimacy to exercise power. The campaign was not covert. On the contrary, the growing polarization of the political scene and a media backlash against Goulart made violent attacks and, in the later months, calls for a coup d'état routine topics in the public space.

It was from 1962 onward in particular, as tempers flared after Cuba's move to the East, that the high level of social mobilization in Brazil, the government's "basic reforms" plan (a set of structural measures affecting land, education, taxation, and industry) and its pursuit of an independent foreign policy spread the use of the terms anarchy, disorder, and political and social subversion by the Right and the conservative press. The Right retained a slim parliamentary majority in the legislative elections of mid-October 1962, confirming the growing political polarization that was sealed by the January 1963 plebiscite, which restored the presidential system suspended in 1961. From that day on, suspicious tolerance of the president disappeared to be replaced by accusations, no longer merely of weakness regarding radical groups set on outstripping him on the Left, but also of personal putschist ambitions.

Society was very highly mobilized at this time, both for and against the government. There was an upsurge in the number of strikes, rallies, and mass demonstrations, and public debate had never been so heated. The mobilization of the military reflected and echoed this. Most officers acted no differently from the urban middle classes, with which many of them identified, moreover, even if it was good form for those in uniform to appear to be outside classes, groups, and vested interests. Affected by galloping inflation, they feared becoming downwardly mobile, particularly when the status of subofficers (corporals and sergeants) was by contrast being economically and symbolically enhanced: highly mobilized, they had particularly good access to Goulart, for whom they were a vital support. The rejection of an impoverishment of the officer corps that would bring it closer to the rank and file, together with the fears of the urban middle classes about their own proletarianization, cannot be detached from the specter of "subverting the existing order" that was brandished by the putschists as evidence of the communist advance.

Assiduously reading the daily press played a decisive role in the political situation being interpreted as unstable and then insurrectional. While the media still wore the colors of a degree of political diversity when João Goulart took office, the main newspapers in Brazil's major cities came together in radical opposition during 1962 and 1963. In this way, each with its own methods and in its own time, most newspapers thus declared open war on the government against a backdrop of anticommunism. Moreover, critics of the authorities were much exercised by the fact that the mainstream media did not extend to the whole country. They saw it as a key instrument in "systematic anticommunist indoctrination," as General José Pinheiro de Ulhoa Cintra wrote in a letter to a São Paulo dignitary on January 1, 1964. In it, the general set out plans for a weekly newspaper that would pull together the most "important" articles in the national press, with a preference for the very conservative *O Estado de São Paulo*, and seek to "expand, defend, and consolidate the democratic spirit of the armed forces." He was particularly anxious about the south of the country where "the military usually read just one newspaper (if they read one at all). They wake before dawn and are then completely taken up with the absorbing and exhausting tasks of the barracks." "And so they live virtually in a world apart, with no clear perception of the facts, vulnerable to political distortions as shown by the events of August–September 1961." "So then, what is to be done? Indoctrinate, enlighten. In the form of speeches on the radio, newspapers, and journals, convey healthy ideas, adapted to fit the discernment and intellectual ability of officers and sergeants. In short, the opposite work to that of Brizola who, let's say in passing, although lowbrow, manages to 'spew forth' his own language, accessible to the simpleminded, and creating illusions, hopes, and ambitions."[52] It should be noted that among the general officers, Ulhoa Cintra was one of the most involved in active collaboration with USIS to the extent that he was briefed on the details of Operation Brother Sam.[53]

Behind the media, in the background, there were businessmen, press barons (including Júlio de Mesquita Filho, owner of *O Estado de São Paulo*), politicians, intellectuals, and military personnel engaged in a vast fund-raising, propaganda, and political destabilization operation. They would encounter one another at two organizations: the Institute of Research and Social Studies (Instituto de Pesquisas e Estudos Sociais, IPES) and the Brazilian Institute for Democratic Action (Instituto Brasileiro de Ação Democrática, IBAD), with which the Superior War School was closely associated.[54] The prevailing media discourse followed that of these anticommunist institutions and organizations, which were proliferating in the country, with or without U.S. encouragement. The press also acted as a mouthpiece for the civilian Right and intelligentsia, linked or not to the conservative party, the UDN, of which an extremist fringe had shown scant respect for legality in regard to its political adversaries since the mid-1950s. The UDN had a lot in common with the military Right, in fact: a political vision tinged with hostility toward parties, a hatred of popular mobilizations, a degree of moralism, and an aggressive anticommunism.

The contempt many officers showed for civic politics, which was systematically associated with embezzlement, the protection of vested interests and weakness of character, paradoxically existed alongside admiration for certain individuals who were set apart with the title "leader" (*líder*) rather than politician. Two people in particular stood out as the great hopes of conservative officers: Jânio Quadros (briefly president in 1961) and Carlos Lacerda (a UDN politician, peerless orator, and governor of the State of Guanabara, which at the time corresponded to the city of Rio de Janeiro, from 1960 to 1965). They represented a real political alternative for a part of the military Right that proclaimed its disdain for the party political system. For Colonel Tarcísio Nunes Ferreira—who when he was a captain took part in the Aragarças Rebellion, the uprising of air force and army officers that, in December 1959, attempted to undermine the Kubitschek government and pressure Jânio Quadros into remaining a candidate for the presidency of the republic—"Jânio Quadros wanted to achieve revolution at the ballot box." In fact, this officer made belief in revolution the rationale of his life, as can be seen in the letter he is believed to have written to his wife at the time of the 1959 rebellion. He was already expecting revolution.

> The last hopes are extinguished. No one believed more than I did in a bloodless revolution, through the ballot box. And no one wanted it more than I did.
>
> All I can do now is to join forces with some comrades I've encountered who, on the other side of shame, have the courage to go for broke. I have thought a lot about you and [our son]; I have not abandoned you, I have been trying hard to find a motherland for you, of which you would not be ashamed. If we fail, I will have left you the very greatest legacy: an honorable name.
>
> We leave, convinced that we will be able to stir this "sleeping giant" through this act we do not want; so that men, especially those in uniform, rise up with new zeal and regain their lost virility, abandoning creature comforts and vested interests and, united, seek Brazil's best interests.[55]

Even Tarcísio did not believe completely in Jânio Quadros's revolution, however, since to his mind the new executive would not be able to oppose the "deputies representing the ruling class" once they had allied themselves to the judiciary. "With Jânio, we were deluded ourselves," he suggested nearly fifty years later. "The whole movement more or less petered out, putting its hopes in Jânio Quadros."[56] The latter's resignation was a huge disappointment for this part of the military Right.

Carlos Lacerda was the other person who aroused enthusiasm, not just because he was a champion of moralistic diatribes and soaring anticommunist tirades—all the more virulent since he had been a Communist Party member in his youth—but also because these military groups saw him as an honest, authoritative, and dynamic leader able to ensure the development and greatness of Brazil if he became its president.[57] Lacerda cultivated this aura. He was happy to present himself as the favorite target of the enemy camp, as corroborated by two assassination attempts. The first, in August 1954 by the bodyguards of Getúlio Vargas, was the key moment in politicizing many young officers who would go on to support the coup. Lacerda was only slightly injured but his bodyguard, Air Force Major Rubens Vaz, was killed, becoming a martyr in the eyes of a whole generation. The second attempt (never confirmed) is said to have been in October 1963, incited this time by members of the parachute brigade of Vila Militar, a huge garrison on the outskirts of Rio de Janeiro. It was another failure. The crime was prevented by opposition mounted by the commander of the Airborne Division Howitzer Corps, Lieutenant Colonel Francisco Boaventura Cavalcanti Júnior, according to claims he made himself. Boaventura, who a few months later would attract a lot of attention in the ranks of the putschists, made a great deal of the affair at the time. Transferred to another regiment, he wrote to Goulart's war minister, Jair Dantas Ribeiro. The letter was a public event. It was read out in the Senate by UDN Deputy Daniel Krieger on November 23, 1963. Boaventura believed he had been punished for "failing to support the attack and the violence, for refusing to encourage his subordinates to commit a criminal act, for opposing a stain on the army's dignity." "It is a bizarre identification that the war minister establishes in a ruling obsessed with party politics, between loyalty to the Constitution and disrespect for it; between obedience to the existing laws and their violation; between continuing to exercise the mandate of state governor and the treachery of those who, through the irregular use of an army unit, sought to deal the democratic regime a mortal blow."[58] In this way, Lacerda, who had so little respect for republican legality, was built into a symbol of the putschism of the authorities, presented as disrespectful toward the Constitution and democracy. By way of a mirror image, the conspirators were presented as paragons of republican legality and legitimacy.

At the beginning of 1963, as the economic and social crisis deepened and political tensions grew, the discourse about the ongoing "revolution" changed. The authorities were directly accused of fomenting a coup d'état, said to be set for May 1, 1963. A movement of civilians and the military formed around this phantom menace in April 1963, taking the name "constitutionalist revolution" in a reference to the liberal revolt of that name that in 1932 opposed the exceptional regime installed by Getúlio Vargas two years previously. The movement's slogan was "the constitution is untouchable," and its raison d'être to resist a communist coup d'état.[59] No longer therefore was the "communist revolution" a military theory, a political threat, or even a diffuse and underground process: it was a concrete and identifiable plan for a coup d'état of which the actors and the date were known. In this catastrophic scenario, the features bestowed on the men in power had particular significance in that they did so much to support the argument that a putsch was imminent.

The "red" enemy was distinguished primarily by his moral degradation: treacherous, duplicitous, mendacious to the point that the name "cryptocommunist" was a better fit, self-seeking and power-hungry. He was also described as cruel and bloodthirsty, in keeping with the international canons of traditional anticommunism. This dual image was projected onto the incumbent government as represented by João Goulart (a demagogue, weak and opportunistic) and Leonel Brizola, governor of the State of Rio Grande do Sul between 1959 and 1963 (rabid). The military Right's hatred of Brizola, which had also developed during the second Vargas government (1951–54), was now honed by his resistance to the coup d'état of September 1961. The loathing of Brizola increased in the years that followed as his involvement with the unions and left-wing organizations grew. The final straw was his use of the words "gorilla" and "putschist" to describe General Murici in his speech in Recife on May 5, 1963.[60] The insult was such a scandal that it produced outpourings of solidarity with the general from civilians and officers of all ranks. Antônio Carlos Murici kept 420 of these letters and telegrams—271 were from military personnel.[61]

The verbal spat between Brizola and Murici met such a response in the army that some anticommunist officers reclaimed the name "gorilla" in an eponymous statement issued in June 1963. In it, gorilla was considered "an honorable distinction" for whoever "fights for freedom, desires greater well-being for the people, without actually turning the people into a slave." "We, the GORILLAS, are the majority. We will march shoulder to shoulder when the time comes to carry out the reforms that PEACE requires, to do good to the people, to defend DISCIPLINE AND THE HIERARCHY, to maintain the dignity of households in order to eliminate the corrupt and the corrupters, in order finally to be able in the best traditions of our soldiers' plumes to give account to GOD and our COMPATRIOTS with the real and solemn cry of TRUE PATRIOTS [capital letters as printed]."[62] Right-wing propaganda in the barracks, the mainstream media and the discourse of a part of the political class thus gave credit to the notion of an imminent coup d'état, supported or even organized by the powers that be. The idea of the military hierarchy being "subverted" or "inverted" was a key argument of this propaganda. That army sergeants, sailors, and marines during Goulart's presidency were highly mobilized acted as evidence that the destruction of the established order was under way. It was not, however, one aspect among many in the argument intended for the armed forces, as strikes, mass demonstrations, or the taking up of arms by occasional protest groups might be but a structural element in a military worldview that looked to the long term and was linked to a particular representation of the action and political system regarded as acceptable.

DEFENDING THE HIERARCHY AND DISCIPLINE

The words of the military who favored the coup are extraordinarily stereotypical when it comes to what encouraged them to overthrow the civilian authorities. They all highlight in particular two main "perils," against which the coup was to be the sole and final bulwark: that of a communist revolution often with greater or lesser emphasis specifically on the "phase" the country had already reached, using a clearly identified "revolutionary war" vocabulary; and that of a "breakdown in the hierarchy" of the armed forces by lower-ranking troops and incited by "subversive agents" who had infiltrated their ranks; two dangers allegedly tolerated if not actually whipped up by President Goulart. These arguments did not appear in 1963 or 1964, however. They had been part of the military Right's discourse well before Goulart took office but had been linked specifically to him for nearly a decade. They were the arguments used by the three armed forces ministers who sought to use force in September 1961 to prevent the labor leader from taking presidential office. The bulk of the argument in favor of the overthrow of João Goulart, therefore, which the conspiracy developed and spread among the officer corps—widespread disorder, the slide toward communism, the destruction of the armed forces—existed even before his term of office began. While the political and military events of 1961–64 were decisive in mobilizing the putschists, their interpretation belonged to preestablished scenarios.

Of course, the armed forces did not discover anticommunism with the Cold War or the Cuban Revolution, nor when a group of officers convinced themselves a "revolutionary war" was being waged on national soil. It was a hatred cultivated over several decades, buttressed by the references, images, and words employed by the most active conspirators in the political circumstances of the 1950s and 1960s. In this way, the new threats of the Cold War, the discourses to describe them, and the weapons with which to face them often seemed like a simple reordering of elements that had long existed in Brazil's anticommunist repertoire: the internal threat, and linked to it the image of treachery; condemnation of the social movement (strikes, demonstrations) as a "disorder" that "would break apart" the institutions, the values, and the unity of society; subversive propaganda as a weapon, and the need for counterpropaganda. These were, moreover, features of a conservative anticommunism extending well beyond the frontiers of Brazil.

One topic had a special place: the fear of mass infiltration of the army by communist agents and the betrayal of comrades in arms. It had its own origin myth: a 1935 revolt by communists in the military, disparagingly known as the *Intentona* (the Attempt), its heroic "martyrs" and suppression commemorated with devotion ever since.[63] The event was one more proof of the long-standing red peril in the beating heart of Brazil. It established a simplistic, unnuanced "national narrative" in which Brazil and its army were defined in opposition to the constant threat of their being fragmented by the army itself. The comparison with the climate of the 1930s was a particular obsession of the 1960s, and also of how they are remembered. To many, a new Intentona was about to be hatched in 1964. The frame of reference was thus a national one in Brazil: with Castro's revolution at the forefront of everyone's mind, and its advent causing the Latin American Right to redefine all the subcontinent's progressive and labor movements as potential communist insurgencies, it was to 1935 and to the peculiarities of Brazil's history that the military made constant reference, rather than to events in Cuba. General Sérgio de Avelar Coutinho said forty years later that the political mobilization of junior soldiers in 1963–64 forcefully revived recollections of 1935: "There was the memory of '35. . . . The sergeants' revolt in Brasília and the navy revolt in Rio left no one in any doubt: there was a communist conspiracy in the country."[64] There was only one, eternal bulwark against this communist threat with its changing strategies and faces: the army. Revolutionary war appeared, therefore, as a modernized form of international communism's age-old strategy of seizing power, of which the Intentona was considered the first attempt on Brazilian territory.

The parallel had been ubiquitous in military utterances since 1960. On November 27 that year, the twenty-fifth anniversary of the revolt, War Minister Odílio Denys revealed an agenda in which he described a communist movement with immutable objectives but changing methods, forever presenting "a new appearance and insidious phrases to seduce new generations." "The watchword from abroad has also changed: force and violence must be kept for the final stage. . . . The preliminary actions now take shape in the psychological domain and its main concern is to conquer the human mind."[65] The official memory of 1935 therefore identified the main enemy as doubly internal—within the country and within the army. He was the opposite of oneself: that is, the opposite of the ideal soldier. This black-and-white approach took on a particular intensity in the army itself and went some way toward explaining the violence of intramilitary conflicts between 1961 and 1964, as well as the extent of the internal purge of the armed forces after the coup d'état.

What the putschist military were fighting had a name that they repeated incessantly: "subversion of the hierarchy," where the word "subversion" had a double meaning: overturning the internal order of the military institution and destabilizing or destroying the political and social order. The ambiguity reflected the overlap between hierarchical military thinking that demanded that subordinates were obedient and not politically mobilized, and a fear of working class and necessarily "subversive" mobilization that gripped society as a whole.

The 1950s had already seen heightened political tensions within the officer corps. In the Military Club, campaigns were bitterly and aggressively debated and when meetings came to an end the various factions often continued the discussions with their fists.[66] João Goulart's coming to power marked the entrance of new players into this highly factious political space: subofficers and soldiers. These were not the first political demonstrations by military of these ranks. They had occurred since the establishment of the republic and peppered the first third of the twentieth century. In 1910, for example, naval crewmen, the majority of them black, mutinied against the humiliations and harsh treatment they endured on a daily basis. This was the "Revolt of the Whip" (*Revolta da Chibata*).[67] In the 1920s and 1930s, sergeants took an active part in the tenentismo movement.[68] After the Estado Novo (1937–45) cracked down on intramilitary politics, the sergeants returned only timidly to center stage, initially to support getulista officer movements and then more independently. The crisis of September 1961 launched a veritable "political movement" of the sergeants who, distancing themselves from strictly professional demands, now called for greater rights and took a stance on national politics. The key battle was for the right to be elected to local and national assemblies under the banner "The Sergeant is also the people!" (*Sargento também é povo!*). It was fought primarily in the "trade union associations" (the Armed and Auxiliary Forces Sub-Officers, Sub-Lieutenants and Sergeants Club, of which the naval counterpart was the Sailors and Marines Association of Brazil), which were authorized in Brazil unlike in most of the neighboring countries.[69]

There was an upsurge in these mobilizations in 1963. In a context of political radicalization after the January plebiscite, the "ineligibility" of sergeants who were victorious in the October 1962 legislative elections came to a head. The 1946 Constitution was unclear about their right to take office, resulting in arguments that suggested the sergeants were attempting to subvert the military hierarchy. War Minister General Amaury Kruel issued a "Recommendation on Political Demonstrations," in which he drew the army's attention to three prohibitions: on attending legislative assemblies in uniform, on talking "party" politics in the barracks, and on taking part in political meetings where "they might be implicated and exploited to the advantage of more experienced and more invested third parties."[70] Kruel, regarded as a legalist by the authorities, was also a great critic of the sergeants' cause, which he interpreted as an unacceptable attack on the army's Disciplinary Rules. Nor did he hesitate to subject activists to disciplinary sanctions. As a result, a Military Police Inquiry (*Inquérito Policial Militar* or IPM: a police inquiry carried out by armed forces personnel because of its target) went ahead at the end of May and found that "day after day, agitators' activities increase in intensity through meetings, rallies, gatherings, pamphlets, and the broadcast and print media," helping "to bring down discipline and order, the fundamental principles of our institution."[71] The IPM looked into a ceremony held by sergeants and sublieutenants on May 11, 1963, in nonmilitary premises to honor General Osvino Ferreira Alves, commander of the First Army. In fact, even more than the subofficers' political activism, it was the closeness to, even fraternization with, a general that amounted to sacrilege since it disrupted the chain of command. The officers who compromised themselves by such promiscuity, the "people's generals" (generais do povo) as they called themselves, were committing a crime. Often very strongly left-wing, they found themselves on the blacklist of the military Right.

The executive, and João Goulart most of all, was also suspected of encouraging this "inversion of the hierarchy." The attention Goulart paid the sergeants' and subofficers' associations, as well as their demands, was seen by a

Sailors' rebellion. Rio de Janeiro, March 1964. Geraldo Tonel / O Globo Archives.

number of officers as an unearned privilege, a show of clientelism, the insertion of party political loyalties into the armed forces but also as an improvement in the social and symbolic status of the military's lower ranks, the immediate subordinates of the junior officers, whose own position was thus downgraded. The chain of command "subverted" was then disciplinary, political, economic, and symbolic in the eyes of the discontented officers.

A tribute to General Osvino from the sergeants of Rio, just after the start of the "gorilla" spat between Brizola and General Murici, was the final straw, particularly in the historic capital, which saw regular clashes between military factions and demonstrations between May and July 1963—at which point the Military Club recovered its former fervor. On December 12, sergeants, corporals, and subofficers staged a revolt in Brasília when the Federal Supreme Court confirmed that they could not run in the legislative elections. This had a profound influence on officers' thinking and was subsequently presented as the opening event in a series of acts of indiscipline and inversions of the chain of command, which reached a peak in March 1964. On March 13, Goulart held a massive rally outside Rio's central railway station to introduce and defend his "basic reforms" program. It was attended by workers, militants, and hundreds of soldiers in uniform. This "reform rally" petrified the conservative camp. Ten days later on March 25 came what the Right dubbed the "Kronstadt *tupiniquim*": a sailors' uprising in Rio to oppose the forced closure of their professional association which had been ruled illegal.[72] On March 30, sergeants and sublieutenants held a meeting at the Automobile Club of Rio de Janeiro. President Goulart, who had been invited, put in an appearance.

Testimonies from conservatives in the military present an almost "official" sequence of events that led to the coup d'état: the sergeants' activism pushed as far as mutiny, the military leadership of the "people's generals," and the authorities' benevolent tolerance no doubt helped rally many officers to the theory that the existing order was being subverted. Moreover, some in the Military High Command, who had so far kept their distance from the government's critics, demonstrated their hostility to what seemed to them to be a dangerous internal disorder. They included the above-mentioned General Kruel, who had cracked down on the mobilizations of junior ranks from the ministry, until June 1963; but also General Peri Bevilacqua who, despite being identified with legalist nationalism (and having supported Goulart's inauguration in 1961), reacted to the Brasília sergeants' uprising with a harsh instruction that was very widely distributed in the barracks.[73] Anxiety about the breakdown of order transcended military factions, convinced many legalists that a line had been crossed, and constructed a new unanimity against the government.

The association between disorder within the armed forces and communist infiltration became a fixture after the sergeants' revolt of September 1963, significantly dubbed the "Brasília Intentona" by General Bevilacqua. Appointed army chief of staff the following day, General Castelo Branco delivered an inaugural address on the topic of turning the military institution into a "people's army." A few weeks later, he sent a note to the war minister, offering a tortuous analysis of "military indiscipline"—the result of a strategy taken on by subversive forces more or less affiliated to international communism, it was also said to be fueled by the self-serving conduct of "politicos" and "collusion by civilians" that divided the army. The note clearly pointed out the overlap between what Castelo Branco regarded as two pernicious phenomena: communist infiltration of the army, and its politicization, for which he blamed civilians. This twofold condemnation became the leitmotif of speeches by the future general-president intended for the youngest officers. In the early months of 1964, Castelo Branco increased the number of statements in military schools and units centered on a single topic: the politicization of the institution. "The officer must remain above party political conflicts and, especially, their injunctions and compromises,"[74] he told EsAO officer cadets in January 1964. "We are not obliged to take sides, in either the government camp or that of the opposition." Legality must be maintained and the battle against the communist enemy fought, Castelo Branco said, not through party political engagement but through participation in ideological combat, information, and clear awareness that "the communists want an end to the cohesion of the Armed Forces and want to overthrow the military organization of the country." It was a curious, legalist speech that used the same political repertoire as did the militant putschists by condemning "left-wing" destabilization of the military hierarchy.

For Castelo Branco, civilian, party political, or communist penetration splitting the military corpus had an innate negative value, separate from anticommunism. For many officers indeed, the threat to the institution, to which the coup would put a stop, was its invasion by communist agents and also by "party politics." The same process was at work in the Argentinean Army in the 1960s: the fact that officers who were regarded as "legalist" supported the 1966 coup d'état was the result of their rejection—paradoxical though it seems—of "politicization" of the officer corps, for which civilians (not necessarily communists) were blamed.

In fact, the military Left in the 1960s (and especially its lower ranks) was seemingly more accepting of military personnel being involved in political issues and of collaboration with civilian groups with the goal of a collective struggle against "reaction." This discourse could be backed up by the notion that the military elite was at the service of the bourgeoisie and endeavoring to silence soldiers and sergeants who put forward their demands as the dominated. By contrast, for advocates of the "hierarchical pyramid," social classes had been invented either for subversive ends—to separate society and the army—or by professional politicians to conceal their vested interests. The political participation and mobilization of the military were not merely alternative ways of operating therefore but an outside disruption caused by alien and minority elements within a professional corps that was by definition solid and united.

These two concepts of the hierarchy and the military's involvement in politics were not, however, explicitly owned by the conflicting factions: first, because strict compliance with the military regulations and the chain of command was presented as a duty by the overwhelming majority of actors, despite occasionally contradictory practices. The two camps accused one another of being rebels and conspirators, each regarding attacks on legality and military professionalism as their adversary's preserve. Moreover, not all conservative officers made the same virtue out of the requirements to be apolitical and disciplined. They all considered them absolutes for sergeants and the "people's generals" but when it came to themselves and their peers, officers' comments vary more widely, although personal insubordination is rarely acknowledged or appreciated.

It is difficult to assess the respective role of the largely interwoven fears of communist revolution and the collapse of their own institution in officers' support for the conspiracy and then the coup d'état. The common factor in using these two themes in intramilitary propaganda was to target officers' conservative feelings, not just against the policies of the labor government and the demands of Brazil's working classes (civilian and military), but also in defense of values such as the hierarchy and discipline, together with ensuring that the border between the military and civilians could not be crossed. This discourse built up collective support for a conservative revolution that would restore Brazil to its essential state as a "democratic" country (exempt, that is, from any social mobilization inspired by "totalitarian" communism), Christian, untouched by "exotic" ideologies such as Marxism, ordered, and subject to a strong and enlightened government. This was the basis for the line of argument that legitimized the coup, although it did not represent it in its entirety. The conspirators' final media offensive also highlighted the idea that the putsch had legality and constitutionality, an argument that was evidently false from a judicial point of view but that makes it possible to understand why almost all officers ultimately came on board, despite belonging to a body historically regarded as "legalist."

THE LEGALITY ARGUMENT

The hammering home of stereotypes and anticommunist fear and hatred, the drip-fed idea that history would repeat itself and that the military hierarchy was on the verge of collapse, the inclusion in the broad array of "military skills" of a doctrine urging that social movements be seen as signs of insurrection: archives and testimonies converge to identify these features as generating a radical rejection of the incumbent government. Still unanswered is the question as to how action came to be taken and, especially, how there came to be collective acceptance of this breach of legality. The specific reasons for the rejection of legalism by the Brazilian armed forces and, within the Southern Cone, by military institutions historically subject to the civilian authorities, initially took researchers by surprise, particularly in the United States, which, given that country's strong encouragement of coups, is not without irony. This conduct went against the theory developed a few years earlier by Samuel Huntington, for whom professionalizing the armed forces would serve as protection against political intervention (*The Soldier and the State*, 1957). Studies after 1964 and, especially, those into the coups in Chile and Uruguay (countries with armies generally respectful of the powers established since independence), continued to put "professionalization" at the center of research but reversed its effects. Professionalization was said to have isolated the military institutions from civil society in the 1950s–1960s, strengthening the former's sense of superiority and contempt for the democratic resolution of political and social conflicts.[75] A "new professionalism" was thought to have emerged, producing not caudillos set on taking advantage of their uniform and the troops they controlled to build up personal power but corporations collectively persuaded of their ability to stand in for the civilian elites in situations of political crisis and of the legitimacy of so doing. The Cold War heightening of tension was thought to have stimulated the move to action, positing the military not as mere shadowy powers or one-off players in the political game but as potentially taking and then exercising power directly and lastingly.

In the weeks leading up to the coup d'état, however, documents circulating inside the military institution bore no trace of this new identity. If the most involved conspirators sought to run the country in the long term, and this was not true of all of them, then no one was saying so. Nor was it what the bulk of officers were being told. On the contrary, the imminence of the coup led to the emergence of a new kind of argument aimed at officers who were still undecided: legal language on the use of force. The goal was to build on the "legalist" convictions of military youth, by proving that respect for the Constitution, for order and the republic, required support for the coup. Illegality, putschism, and "revolutionary" ambitions belonged solely to the opposing camp. Any legalist was duty bound to turn against Goulart.

The aim was to justify the planned coup without abandoning the earlier discourse about protecting the legal order and the constitution. Castelo Branco, army chief of staff since June 1963, was an expert at these arguments. In March 1964, an obsession with constitutional analysis permeated his discourse, giving ever-less-implicit support for military intervention. The best known was the "reserved circular" sent by Castelo Branco to all general officers in command of troops on March 20, 1964, which was regarded as the signal that he had joined the rebel camp. His reasoning was based on the need for a "countercoup" to block the government convening a Constituent Assembly (for which there was no evidence), which he held to be an illegitimate and illegal "revolutionary objective." To Castelo Branco, the armed forces "are committed to guaranteeing constitutional powers" and should remain "within the limits of the law."[76]

A pamphlet was making the rounds at the same time, titled "Loyalty to the Army" (*Lealdade ao Exército*), or LEEX, which was probably written at least in part by General Ulhoa Cintra.[77] Not only did it champion the constitutionality of armed intervention since "the text of the Constitution itself includes the measures to be employed in such circumstances,"[78] it also stated that "our goal is not to plot the overthrow of the present government nor to replace it with an extraconstitutional regime." The objective was for "the current leaders to see out their mandates without besmirching the regime of representative democracy. . . . We are fighting as is our Duty for the respect of the free exercise of the Constitutional Powers, which are the very structure of the regime, without breaking away from the functions, duties and prerogatives that are inherent to it"—a passage that, in hindsight, seems bitterly ironic.[79]

The same day that Castelo Branco put out the secret note in which he informed his peers of his acquiescence in a coup d'état that, until then, he had only helped plan indirectly, General Augusto César Moniz de Aragão launched a series of columns in the Rio de Janeiro newspaper *O Globo*, titled "Message to Young Soldiers." Seven of them appeared until May 1964. Moniz de Aragão was the popular commander of the prestigious Parachute Brigade in Vila Militar (Rio). He also wanted the presidency of the Military Club, up for renewal at the end of May. The legal justification for the coup was the subject of a column published ten days after the coup itself: "Violation of the law, disruption of social harmony, and arbitrary rule cancel out the duty to obey. The Armed Forces draw the sources of their legitimacy from tradition and the Constitution. As a result, they owe no subordination to the agents of state power whose initiatives are harmful to the interests of the Motherland and who flout the law, encourage disorder and seek subversion. It is not just disobedience that is incumbent upon the Armed Forces but also an explicit *pronunciamento* or a coup d'état."[80] Not content with making "legality" the motive for a coup d'état, General Aragão also insisted that the military uprising honor the hierarchy. In documents from March 20 and 26, he insisted on the need to allow the highest ranks to take the initiative in the putsch so that it did not do any damage to the institution itself. Moniz de Aragão and Castelo Branco thus achieved the extraordinary rhetorical and intellectual feat of using the pillars of the army's identity ("professional and apolitical") to justify the installation of a military regime. Most astonishing perhaps is that this was no passing utilitarian discourse. It continued after 1964 and fed into the policy toward the army of the first military government, in which friends of Castelo Branco held positions of power. Unsurprisingly, the topic of "constitutional intervention" permeated putschist propaganda just when those generals whom the authorities deemed loyal rallied to the coup. Furthermore, this supreme discursive strategy also made possible the hope of winning over an officer corps universally assumed to be basically "legalist" and therefore susceptible to this reasoning.

A HIERARCHICAL AND "ARCHIPELAGO" CONSPIRACY

The extent of support for the coup varied hugely, from the officer exposed to the prevailing catastrophizing discourse, but little involved in politics, who went over to the putschist camp at the last minute, more or less sincerely persuaded he was defending "the Constitution and order"; to the active conspirator who, together with his peers, had been involved in the campaign for several years, working to establishing civilian connections and international backing. It was a broad spectrum and the lines between the groups are hard to determine. The most active core of conspirators has since been presented by historiography and by observers in two contrasting ways. Initially, the conspiracy was said to be two-pronged. One faction consisted of intellectual officers, in contact with civilian political circles and united around General Castelo Branco. This "castelista" hub, also called the military "Sorbonne," was thought to be opposed by a barracks-based conspiracy of young radicals who admired General Artur da Costa e Silva. In actual fact, the rivalry between the two men arose only at the last minute. Once the putsch was under way, both wanted to be president. Castelo Branco, born in 1897, had a number of advantages. He was army chief of staff, in other words, held the highest army office apart from government posts. Then there were his intellectual qualities, his contacts with U.S. military and diplomatic circles, his prestige as a theoretician at the Superior War School, and his reputation for moderation among the civilian elites. His rival, Artur da Costa e Silva, born in 1899, was head of the Department of Production and Works (Departamento de Produção e Obras, DPO), a major logistics role. His long-standing involvement in the conspiracy against Goulart and his great popularity with the officer corps also worked in his favor. The balance of power between the two generals in early April showed the importance of the hierarchy. While Castelo Branco's supporters constantly stressed his role as chief of the Army General Staff (EME), Costa e Silva justified his claim to leadership in two ways. First, more than forty years before, he had graduated from military school with better grades than Castelo Branco. Second, in Rio de Janeiro, he had served in the Army High Command (Alto Comando do Exército, or ACE: the council of four-star generals, the highest army rank, in a command or leadership position) longer than any other general. There was no document or even any tradition that deduced hierarchical preeminence from these qualities in the event of a breakdown of legality. Costa e Silva, as many of his comrades would do over the next twenty years, had to improvise. On April 2, he proclaimed himself "Supreme Commander of the Revolution" and, until Castelo Branco was elected president on April 11, it was he who ran the country. Costa e Silva became war minister and throughout that first "revolutionary" term of office, he would offer a silent challenge to his rival.

If the aftermath of the putsch and the first military government were marked by the opposition between these two men, the conspiracy itself was not built around two clearly identified factions. Rather—and this is what many military testimonies teach us—there was an "archipelago" of clandestine mobilization, the islands being "revolutionary" generals, with little to connect them. Air Force Lieutenant Colonel João Paulo Moreira Burnier's testimony has been available since 1965: "There was no general command. Until the end. There were no joint meetings to resolve this or that to do with overthrowing the government. Anyone who says there was is lying. There were no unions of the three services to approve this or that. At most, there were bilateral meetings: army people meeting air force people, individuals from the air force meeting others from the navy. Or on other occasions from the army. Right to the end."[81]

In the nest of conspirators, senior officers (lieutenant colonels and colonels) had a special place. If lower-ranking officers were restless, some of their seniors became organized: a National Renewal Movement (Movimento Ren-

Carlos Lacerda (center, with glasses), governor of the State of Guanabara. Rio de Janeiro, April 1, 1964. O Globo Archives.

ovador Nacional), which was probably relatively informal since it is mentioned only by one witness, was even set up by members of this intermediate generation.[82] The colonels, as regimental commanders, had a degree of freedom to organize and train troops at the local level for a potential coup. Nevertheless, taking action and installing a new government were not envisaged without the endorsement and even command of a decorated and prestigious general. Here is General Leonidas Pires Gonçalves, a lieutenant colonel in 1964: "The Revolution of '64 was fomented for a very long time by lieutenant colonels and colonels, including myself. But we—although this is a personal opinion—were looking for a leader. Because the Army has reservations about tenentismo, which subverts the hierarchy. Discipline and hierarchy are the cornerstones of our institution. Why didn't Castelo come on board until the end? Why did we wait for a Castelo Branco to run things? Because if we broke the hierarchy, we were sure the revolution would not be structured or institutionalized and there would be one less ideal to justify it."[83] Despite the right-wing radicalization of Brazil's military youth at the beginning of the 1960s, the "revolution" of 1964 was not another tenentismo, something neither the lieutenants and captains nor their immediate superiors and commanders wanted to see happen. Indeed, paradoxically the coup was both organized in accordance with the principle of hierarchy *and* driven by a fervent and impatient military youth. As they plotted, the young officers said they endeavored to respect certain hierarchy rules. Cyro Guedes Etchegoyen, a young major training at ECEME in March 1964, explained:

> INTERVIEWER. Were you in contact with people of your own rank or only those of higher ranks?
>
> ETCHEGOYEN. At our level, captain, we did accomplish a lot of missions. "Do this, listen to so-and-so, talk to so-and-so, take that to someone else." Normally, though, when you're in a conspiracy, you work at your own level. Despite the concerns, even in a conspiracy, the hierarchy is respected in the Army. I am not going to "bag" a major or a colonel when I'm a captain. The most I can do is sound him out. But I'm not going to come along and indoctrinate the guy, "bag" the guy to come over to us. We worked from captain down.[84]

The opposition to João Goulart, driven to extremes when he was overthrown, was therefore a transgenerational phenomenon in the Brazilian officer corps. Although there were generals at the top, a wide variety of actors regarded themselves as partly responsible for the "civilian and military movement" of March 31. And they were equipped with widely differing political projects. As stressed by General Adyr Fiúza de Castro, a lieutenant colonel in 1964, who was subsequently much involved in repression by the dictatorship, beyond the "counterrevolution" which had everyone's support, was a very inexplicit "revolution" that everyone invested with meaning. And why "revolution," incidentally? Didn't the campaign for a putsch imply a movement "against"— against communist subversion, against inversion of the hierarchy?[85] To be sure, some word was required and this one had been part of the political vocabulary, designating and legitimizing the overthrow of legal authorities since the beginning of the century. The preamble to the First Institutional Act (Ato Institucional) of April 9, 1964. goes further:

> [The] civilian and military movement . . . has been and will continue to be, not

only in the spirit and behavior of the armed forces but also in national public opinion, an authentic revolution.

Revolution is distinguished from other armed movements by the fact that it expresses not merely the interest and will of a group but the interest and will of the Nation.

Victorious revolution is vested with Constituent Power. This is achieved through election by the people or by the revolution.

This is the most expressive and most radical form of Constituent Power. Thus, victorious revolution, as Constituent Power, is its own legitimacy. . . . It contains within it the normative force inherent in Constituent Power. It enacts legal standards within, in so doing being confined by those that predated its victory. The leaders of the victorious revolution, thanks to the action of the Armed Forces and the unequivocal support of the Nation, represent the People in whose name they exercise Constituent Power, which belongs to the People alone.

The Institutional Act confirms the similarities between the "31 March Revolution" and the *pronunciamientos* of Spanish America's nineteenth century. According to their authors, they restored the original sovereignty of the people, they had the same legitimacy as elections, and could occur when a government showed itself to be clearly unjust or harmful to the common good. It was not therefore in any way a question of starting again from scratch, of a radical break with the old order, or of a new man, but simply of waving the banner of the people's sovereignty. And yet the word "revolution" is riddled with other significations, the legacy of the Russian and Mexican revolutions, of tenentismo and Vargas, that were borne in very different ways by the putschists. Last, the First Institutional Act has little to say when it comes to assigning the title "leaders of the victorious revolution." What past, what situation was needed to claim it? A hierarchical position, political and intellectual standing, "revolutionary" credibility? So many factors in a precarious balance leaving the field largely open to political players, civilians, and military, able to claim power—which, incidentally, they set about doing without further ado.

CHAPTER TWO

Continuing the Revolution
1964–1965

> Revolution is a very serious matter. It is a break in the chain of command system. Once the revolution is over, the break does not end when someone takes office. Because all those who have taken an active part in the revolution think they have rights. They think they have the right to approve, to direct, to be heard. This is where the conflict between the leader of the revolution and the revolutionary groups begins.
> —GENERAL CARLOS DE MEIRA MATTOS

Despite General Costa e Silva's attempt to impose himself by force in the early hours of the coup d'état, the very beginning of Castelo Branco's term of office encountered an apparent media, political, and military consensus. Castelo cut a strange figure in the army. A small, stocky man, calm and reserved, he was always (in the putschists' eyes) on the right side of history, while rarely getting his hands dirty. He had sympathized with the tenentes movement, without taking part, although he had not supported the Revolution of 1930. Back from Europe in 1945, where he had fought as part of the Brazilian Expeditionary Force, he was in favor of removing Getúlio Vargas, but once again had no direct role. In the 1950s and at the beginning of the 1960s, he presented two faces: that of a man of influence, very much involved in the operation to disseminate the theory of revolutionary war, plus a public face of moderation and legalism. A former student at the French Military Mission with links to North American military circles, he was also a polyglot, open to foreign influences and regarded as respectful of liberal democracy. He immediately showcased that attachment, moreover, by insisting on being formally elected by the National Congress a few days after the coup. This was achieved with an overwhelming majority on April 11, 1964, by the conservative assembly and already purged by the First Institutional Act (AI-1, April 9, 1964).

Generals Castelo Branco (left, in suit and glasses) and Costa e Silva (using binoculars), during the coup. March 31, 1964. Domício Pinheiro / Estadão Conteudo Archives.

THE REVOLUTIONARY "HARD LINE"

The consensus had its limits and its behind-the-scenes activity. First, the repression that followed the putsch was harsh. Thousands of opponents were hunted down, arrested, publicly humiliated, and tortured, often without due process despite the opening of hundreds of military inquiries (IPMs). Second, within the armed forces, the dismissal of hundreds of officers created a race for command posts and ministerial duties. When troops occupied buildings in early April, it sometimes led to senior officers assuming de facto duties within the machinery of state. Prominent among these colonels and lieutenant colonels were men with the past and the aura of active conspirators or "revolutionaries," as they themselves put it. They included Parachutist Colonel Francisco Boaventura Cavalcanti Júnior, who had saved Lacerda from attempted assassination in 1963. Uninvited, he and a few associates pushed their way onto the president's Military Cabinet. Castelo Branco spent several weeks ridding himself of this unwelcome guest, who was closer to his rival and new war minister, Artur da Costa e Silva.[1]

The general disorder was short-lived but a degree of agitation continued in the military schools and barracks in the weeks that followed. The heightened politicization of previous years, the responsibilities assumed during the conspiracy and the coup, the break in the chain of command, the purge, and the start of repression all contributed to the emergence of military indiscipline and, even more so, of political demands. The Presidential Palace and its military base had to confront the agitation of various scattered "revolutionary groups," both inside and outside of the state apparatus. An expression began to be used to describe these turbulent officers in the media and then in their own statements: they were the revolutionary "hard line," versus hesitant, moderate authorities inclined toward caution and compromise.

Initially, for the officers who claimed the title, the "hard line" did not mean a group or faction but a vaguely defined political approach, a "state of mind," an ethic almost, together with a particular interpretation of the "revolution" of March 31, 1964. You could be "hard-line" the way you could be right or left, reformist or revolutionary, rather than belonging to a particular party. It was journalists and political analysts who, in August 1964, transformed what until then had been an expression of identification into a genuine group, with leaders, representatives, and, therefore, a degree of internal cohesion.[2] The officers only made the category their own later on. It was the incumbent authorities that first gave the name to one of its political adversaries. In September 1964, a report from the National Intelligence Service (Serviço Nacional de Informações, or SNI, the domestic intelligence service set up in the wake of the putsch) referred to one of the three groups of the government's "revolutionary opponents" as the "so-called hard line."[3] The protesting officers themselves then took up the title in a manifesto distributed in parliament in April 1965, which said "the hard line, guardian of the Revolution, [hereby] communicates to all its civilian and military members the instruction that is to guide joint action toward safeguarding the revolutionary ideals."[4]

Originally, therefore, the "hard line" was only a means of expressing a degree of opposition to the Castelo Branco government. It was a political leaning rather than a party. Its transformation into a faction in the vocabulary of those involved was a political weapon. For the authorities, it delimited an enemy. For the protesters, it created the image of an organized force, of which each officer could claim a monopoly or the leadership. All the military personnel who marched under this banner now shared a common discourse: anchored to the Right and more or less reformist. They did not champion a particular program but had one or two demands. The first was for a radical purge regardless of the methods employed or their conformity with the law. Immediately after the putsch, the hard-line officers were advocates of state violence and political repression. The second was a set of economically nationalist measures that had, until 1964, been the preserve of the Left. For want of any concrete proposals, the turbulent officers now brandished words of symbolic power as weapons against a government they deemed to be ultra-liberal and to have sold out abroad. A degree of anti-Americanism was sometimes associated with this, to the tune of "neither Washington nor Moscow." This dual position (repressive radicalism and economic nationalism) was of course a contrast to the liberal prudishness of the *castelista* government and the policy of openness to foreign capital conducted by its planning minister, Roberto de Oliveira Campos, and Finance Minister Octávio Gouvêa de Bulhões. These disagreements between the government and the "hard-liners," however, were not only evidence of political differences. They also stemmed from a strategy of opposition on the part of the protesting officers and an assertion of their political role within the new regime. They played a part, therefore, in developing the officers' line of argument and invective regarding a specific image of the government as "civilian," lukewarm, internationalist, and horse-trading—and regarding the idea of usurping power.

Historiographically, the period studied in this chapter—from the coup d'état (in April 1964) to the passing of the Second Institutional Act (AI-2, October 1965)—has generally been presented as the incubation stage of a clearly identified hard-line faction with a coherent ideology, a faction that would remain unchanged for the duration of the regime, challenging the central authorities, pushing for its authoritarian and repressive radicalization and then seizing control. This was indeed one impression afforded by hindsight in the months that followed the coup. Certainly, this period saw a group impose its vision of power and build a regime rather than merely stage an intervention into the existing civilian democracy. That vision was then enshrined in AI-2. It saw that group broaden and deepen the political purge and define the new authorities as *military* and *revolutionary*. To understand what happened next, however, it is necessary to go far beyond this one reading of 1964-65, focusing, on the one hand, on the construction of the two military parties and identities that appear to have confronted one another during that time.[5] On the other hand, it must be also be observed that "hard-line" demands were closely linked to providing a rationale for the politicization of lower-ranking officers in the new regime. The latter was said to be *military* because, for the officers making themselves heard, the army itself was in power—not just a "citizen from its ranks" or an "ex-soldier," as General-President Castelo Branco liked to repeat, but the organization as a whole.[6] As Colonel Etchegoyen, a captain at the time of the putsch, said: "Middle-ranking officers . . . felt responsible for Brazil. A historic event had taken place. The army had never been in power. It was the first time the army had been in power. When they conspired, every time they took action and were given power, they messed up. 'We've got to take power once and for all to see if we can do it.' That was the theory."[7] It was thus primarily as military men that the protesting officers believed they could legitimately exercise power. They were encouraged in this by the relative autonomy they were granted by their superiors during this post-coup period. Their mobilizations were generally met only with verbal condemnations and they themselves were not looking for a higher-ranking leader as had been the case during the conspiracy and would be again in decades to come. It must be said that the political climate was still not determined by the presidential elections, which would later tend to rally officers of all ranks around potential candidates, all of them generals.[8]

The latitude given to the protesting military was essentially due to the fact that, with their past as conspirators to support them, they called themselves *revolutionaries.* The title included them symbolically in a government that defined itself the same way. Some writers have stressed that, encouraged by its first president, the military regime remained a prisoner of its initial "democratic" rhetoric and that this subsequently obliged successive governments to maintain a democratic facade.[9] We might add that President Castelo Branco was himself a prisoner of the word "revolution," as used to describe the coup. Not only did the name allow the political orientations adopted to be challenged on the pretext that they were moving away from the "ideals of 31 March"—which everyone claimed to be the sole person to know and defend—it also allowed all "revolutionaries" to be granted a portion of sovereignty.

THE OLD AND YOUNG REVOLUTIONARY GUARDS

The first government of the military regime seems to have been at the center of a paradox. Its political base within the military per se, a group of intellectual generals nicknamed the "Sorbonne," was described as both the brains behind the coup—they were the theoreticians of Brazil's version of the National Security Doctrine and sincere believers in the theory of revolutionary war—and as a hub of semilegalism within the Brazilian military Right, the unwitting creators of dictatorship and the victims of successive "coups d'état within the coup d'état," allegedly preventing them from seeing through their plan for a one-off intervention, circumscribed by the rules of law.[10] The U.S. political scientist Alfred Stepan was the first to sketch this ambiguous portrait at the beginning of the 1970s. He showed that the castelista generals stood out among their generation because of their brilliant careers—they had often been top of the class at the military schools—their participation in the Brazilian Expeditionary Force during the Second World War, their permanent status at the ESG, and their foreign education (which for many had been in the United States). These experiences were thought to have strengthened their feeling of belonging to the Western democracies, as well as their trust in the capitalist system and the alliance with the United States. They were also believed to have created their hostility to "excessive nationalism" and their "deep distrust of emotional appeals."[11] As observed by Stepan once again, the policies implemented in the years after the coup were in keeping with these officers' profiles: diplomatic and economic openness to things foreign, a semi–free-enterprise system and trust in democracy despite the choice to make it tutelary for the time being.[12]

Stepan's description of the castelista military faction had a profound influence on historiography and on its representation by observers, whether civilian or military. It painted a picture of the military regime as an experiment gone wrong after slipping through the fingers of its most reasonable founders. In fact, the other members of the military, who lacked the specific experiences and intellectual capacities that apparently made the handful of castelistas "dictators in spite of themselves," were condemned to support an authoritarianism and often a nationalism that were taken as the natural order of things and in need of no particular explanation. These more boorish, less educated officers, supposedly less familiar with Western military cultures, were said to have gradually transformed what was intended to be a quick operation to maintain order and clean up the political system into a real dictatorship. However, the non-castelista generals, much less the other generations of politically active officers, have never been subject to a specific study of the reach of Stepan's research into the "Sorbonne."[13] Their professional profile, political options, and conduct are almost always considered as automatically ascribed to crude stereotypes and described as the mirror opposite of those of the group in power. The officers who described themselves as "hard-liners" immediately after the coup (especially the senior officers, lieutenant colonels, and colonels in the protest network) have thus been virtually eclipsed by historiography and remain very little known—even though some of them, who spoke out in the media or signed widely circulated manifestos, were public figures. It is possible nevertheless, with some limitations, to establish their profile, origins, and careers.

The first ones to make a public stand were officers in the reserve, whose positions were no longer restricted by the army's disciplinary rules after the enactment of Decree no. 54.062 on July 28, 1964, at Castelo Branco's instigation. As the protest spread, they were joined by serving officers who had no troop commands but were running the political inquiries, opened in their hundreds after the coup. Ultimately, military opposition to the government reached its peak when the barracks themselves protested through their officers in Rio de Janeiro at the end of 1965.

Who were all these men? We do not have an exact list, first, because the "hard line" was a fluctuating group identification that went beyond public protesters. Each witness drew up a list of names, depending on the reconstructions of their own memories, their positions within the institution, and any potential settlings of scores. The lists were never placed in a historical context, since memory tends to prefer permanent states to fluctuations. Second, the officers who considered themselves "hard-liners" tended to describe a small group, their own, whereas soldiers outside the movement often favored a radical "profile" that applied to a greater number. Our own corpus of actors, focused on the most visible protesters, is the result of combining official archives and sometimes conflicting memoirs.[14]

We start with the old reserve officers who launched the protest. Some had been regularly involved in public manifestos for a long time. They were professional conspirators, present on the political stage, who had attacked the authorities constantly over several decades. These "historical revolutionaries" rapidly deemed themselves "marginalized" by the authorities, according to an interpretation offered by one SNI report in July 1965.[15] A reserve admiral, the troublesome Sílvio de Azevedo Heck, was a pioneer of this early protest as well as something of a loose cannon. In July 1964, Heck leaked a manifesto denouncing "the infiltration of the Castelo Branco government by enemies of the Revolution" to the Brazilian Press Association (*Associação Brasileira de Imprensa*, ABI) in Rio de Janeiro. He depicted himself as an "authentic revolutionary" representing "a broad range of civil and military sectors concerned at the direction taken by the revolutionary process" and a "repository of the hopes of the Armed Forces' youth, the rural and urban workers, the middle class and the forces of production which need to flourish."[16] Born in 1905 and so barely younger than the tenentes brought into the circles of power after the

1930 Revolution,[17] he only entered the political arena much later so that for a long time it was his father (Vice Admiral Conrado Heck, navy minister from December 1930 to June 1931) who bore the title of the family revolutionary. After a textbook career, devoid of any clear political involvement, he entered history in November 1955 when, as commander of the *Tamandaré* cruiser, he took part in the start of a movement linking leading politicians, including acting president Carlos Luz, with military conservatives set on preventing the inauguration of Juscelino Kubitschek.[18] The endeavor failed and Heck found himself reduced to the position of a bitter critic of the Kubitschek government, indirectly involved in unsuccessful revolts, like the one in Aragarças (1959). His political statements set back his career and earned him numerous punishments.

His conspiratorial leanings blossomed during João Goulart's presidency, after he had attempted, as navy minister from January to September 1961, to prevent Goulart's inauguration. Along with General Odílio Denys and Brigadier Gabriel Grün Moss, he wrote a manifesto calling for a coup d'état on August 30, 1961, and he retained a special relationship with the first of these, who described him as "Revolutionary No. 1."[19] Denys, far more discreet than his naval colleague, was, moreover, regarded by the president's services as one of the historical conspirators most likely to inflame the malcontents.[20] Between 1961 and 1964, Heck conspired on all fronts. According to the French military attaché, he "took part in all the plots and, through his inopportune statements castigating the president's policy, drew the authorities' wrath (arrested 9 times from the end of 1961, he spent a total of 85 days in jail)."[21] He was in contact with business circles in Rio and São Paulo, with the conservative pressure group and think tank IPES (Institute for Research and Social Studies), with civilian anticommunist organizations and networks of conspiring officers—particularly through Odílio Denys—and his great work was the Civil-Military Patriotic Front (Frente Patriotica Civil-Militar). Set up in January 1963, this was a network of paramilitary groups, consisting essentially of rural militias created by big landowners and navy personnel. Again according to the French military attaché, the front had as many as 4,000 men, mostly in Minas Gerais and the State of São Paulo. He went on to say: "During the revolution, Heck did not consider the role of the Civil–Military Patriotic Front to be at an end. On the contrary, he intended to raise its numbers to a total of 8,000, of whom around 1,200 would be tasked with visible anticommunist action and provocation, the remainder being tasked with the infiltration and elimination of cells." In fact, after the putsch, the protesters partially maintained the structure of the front. One of its leaders, Reserve General José Alberto Bittencourt, was also the first leader of the Radical Democratic League (Liga Democrática Radical, LIDER), which, beginning in September 1964 and initially under the aegis of Heck, sought to organize a radical opposition to the presidency.

Already retired or at the end of their careers, officers like Heck no longer had recourse to troop commands on which to base their political influence, and they nursed a rancor against the government from which they were excluded that was all the greater because they belonged to the same generation as almost all its ministers. Moreover, they were often the scions of important families of officers or elected officials, which were powerful, at least within their home state. They regarded themselves as natural and legitimate members of the conservative elite that had been utterly opposed to the getulista authorities for nearly fifteen years and had come to power with the coup d'état. In 1965, a journalist with the very conservative *O Estado de São Paulo*, José Stacchini Júnior, published a book titled *Marco 64: Mobilização da Audácia*, which gives a snapshot of this frustration on the part of the old revolutionary guard. In it, General Olímpio Mourão Filho, the initiator of the putsch whose move to the reserve in September 1964 had seen him rapidly pushed aside, even developed the topic of "revolutionary deviance." Stacchini agreed wholeheartedly, pointing out that the "Mourão-Denys rebellion" (the coup d'état) had led to the "victory of sympathizers" with revolution (the military Sorbonne).[22]

Olímpio Mourão Filho, whose troops' move from the Juiz de Fora garrison triggered the coup, was another early dissident. He too, in quite a different way, was a very individual figure in the putschist camp. Dogged by his reputation as eccentric if not disturbed, he was a more marginal figure than Heck in terms of networks and support. Nevertheless, his happy initiative of March 31, 1964, made him an obligatory member of the revolutionary pantheon. Showered in praise in the regime's early days, he was even given a personal promotion to the rank of army general by a parliamentary vote on April 30. He too belonged to the generation of 1900, the year he was born, but did not take part in politics either during the tenentismo movement or the 1930 Revolution. It was anticommunism and "integralism," a peculiarly Brazilian form of fascism that had launched a mass movement in the 1930s, which had drawn him in. Crowned with the prestige of a war veteran—he commanded the First Infantry Division in the Second World War—he alternated between troop commands and ministries throughout the 1950s. During Goulart's presidency, he became almost overtly involved in conspiracy in Minas, where he commanded the Fourth Military Region. Highly satisfied with the repressive measures taken immediately after the putsch, he was soon disappointed in Castelo Branco. In August 1964, he began by following in the footsteps of Sílvio Heck, presenting himself as "very hard-line" when he became head of the Fourth Army (Northeast).[23] He invited Admiral Heck to the event amid great fanfare. The tone of his utterances rapidly made him an embarrassment to the authorities who, a month later, transferred him to the reserve and gave him the title and role of magistrate of the Superior Military Court (Superior Tribunal Militar, STM). This relegation—he had lost an important troop command—nevertheless gave him greater freedom of expression and made his spectacular U-turn visible: an advocate of unbridled repression, hostile to the application of habeas corpus and a champion of ultraconservative political reforms, he joined the newly created opposition party, the Brazilian Democratic Movement (Movimento Democrático Brasileiro, MDB), with much ado in January 1966. Together with General Peri Bevilacqua, another STM magistrate who had championed the rule of law and condemned the slide toward authoritarianism for a longer time, he declared in *Manchete* magazine that he was in favor of the political amnesty and the restoration of direct elections for all offices.[24] We will come back to the reasons for, and context of, this change of heart later on.

Heck, Mourão, Bittencourt, and others made public appearances because, as long-standing militants, they were used to making statements and political provocations but they also had a sense of frustration and injustice, experiencing being kept at a distance from government as a betrayal after a "life" of conspiracy. Within the serving forces, the heralds of authoritarian radicalization were legion, but disciplinary pressure to be discreet made them less easy to identify. The public was well aware, for example, of the admiralty's immense conservatism but this was kept out of the public arena. Five admirals, nicknamed the Dionnes after the much-publicized Canadian quintuplets born in the 1930s, stood out: Ernesto de Mello Batista (navy minister until January 1965), Augusto Hamann Rademaker Grünewald, Levi Pena Aarão Reis, Mario Cavalcanti de Albuquerque, and Saldanha da Gama. There is less consensus over whether there was a radical elite serving in the army. The testimony of Moraes Rego, a colonel close to Carlos Lacerda, talks about eleven "hard-line" general officers, two of whom were to have a particular role in the early days of the military regime: João Dutra de Castilho, commander of a Vila Militar parachute unit and, especially, Afonso de Albuquerque Lima, who became chief of staff of the First Army on October 1, 1965.[25] Colonels at the time of the coup, they were both promoted to brigadier general in July 1964 and in many ways served as a bridge between the generation of the 1900 revolutionaries and that of the "hard-line colonels."

These hard-liners have gone down in history as "IPM colonels," named after the political inquiries some of them chaired. They were the most visible opposition of their generation and the first to voice their dissatisfaction before unit commanders joined the dissenters during the 1965 crisis. Of the twenty-eight hard-line colonels quoted by Moraes Rego, two "groups" affiliated to more publicly exposed figures are of particular interest.[26]

The first was associated with Lieutenant Colonel Francisco Boaventura Cavalcanti Júnior, whom we have already met. An artillery officer and parachutist, he returned to active service in May 1964 when he was ousted from the president's Military Cabinet. His profile belied the image often given of the hard line as the exact opposite of the "castelista generals," as much "of the troops"—firmly rooted in the barracks and locked into narrow-minded nationalism—as the castelistas were said to be intellectuals, "top of the class" at the military schools, and acquainted with foreign armies. Born in 1919 in an old military family from Ceará (northeast Brazil), he graduated top of his class from the Military Academy in 1943 and joined the Brazilian Expeditionary Force (BEF) as a lieutenant. Within a few years, he had gained a Marshal Hermes medal—the army's highest academic distinction—with three laurel wreaths, in other words, had the title "thrice crowned," having also graduated top of the class from EsAO and ECEME. He became involved in the stormy debates that split the Brazilian Army at the beginning of the 1950s, initially in the nationalist camp, before breaking away in July 1950 after an article appeared in the *Revista do Clube Militar* criticizing U.S. intervention in Korea. Festooned with medals (the Order of Military Merit, plus the Campaign, Military, War, Peacemaker, and Caxias medals), he spent several periods of time abroad and at the end of the 1950s was a UN special adviser on Latin America. Back in Brazil, he attended the ESG staff and command course even as he actively conspired against the Goulart government. Overall, the career profile of Boaventura, who was twenty years younger than the men in power, was very close to the ideal-type castelista general, as described by Alfred Stepan.

Idolized as he was by some of his generation and regarded as a brilliant mind, Boaventura was no marginal figure among the young hard-liners. There were numerous BEF veterans among his closest comrades: Amerino Raposo Filho, an artillery officer born in 1922 to a middle class Carioca family (his parents were teachers), also enrolled as a second lieutenant and was even more heavily bedecked in medals for his combat prowess. An instructor at ECEME for several years, he published numerous articles on military strategy in the *Mensário de Cultura Militar* and, in 1960, a book titled *A manobra na guerra: síntese filosófica* (Maneuvers in war: a philosophical overview). Relegated to a remote garrison in Rio Grande do Sul during the Goulart presidency, he reentered the higher spheres of power at the time of the coup. Under the orders of General Golbery do Couto e Silva, head of Castelo Branco's Civil Cabinet and *éminence grise* of the Presidential Palace, he took part in setting up the National Intelligence Service, the SNI. He was trained at the Inter-American Defense College (Washington, DC) in 1968 and took the ESG warfare course in 1973.

Another "hard-line" colonel with an equally brilliant career worked in the president's Civil Cabinet, the slightly older Hélio Duarte Pereira de Lemos (born in 1914), a Second World War veteran who had gone to the ESG somewhat later. Last there was Colonel Dickson Melges Grael, who only appeared on the intramilitary political scene at the end of the 1960s. Another artillery officer born around 1920 and a parachutist like Boaventura, he was not a Second World War veteran, graduating from the Military Academy only at the end of 1944. He was, however, much decorated and trained in "intelligence techniques for foreign superior officers" in the United States.

This section of the "first hard line" (as it will now be called to distinguish it from a second network to be discussed shortly) of colonels linked to Boaventura was a close-knit generation. Its members had shared experiences, which were highly valued in professional terms (the war) and in politics (conspiring together, in many cases while still ECEME students). For the military institution, they remained outstanding officers and were barely involved in acts of insurgency until 1961, even though their politics were well known. They became acquainted with one another before the coup, valued their peers, and generally acknowledged Colonel Boaventura's moral authority.

A few younger officers had been linked with this group of colonels since conspiracy days. There was Tarcísio Célio Carvalho Nunes Ferreira, who was ten years younger. Born in 1930 to a middle-class intellectual family—his father was a secondary school philosophy teacher, his mother a painter—he was a parachutist whose renown as a participant in the Aragarças Rebellion brought him into the protestors' circle:

> COLONEL TARCÍSIO NUNES FERREIRA. Colleagues of my generation and I, we used to exchange ideas. Now we're all colonels, plus a few generals. Hélio Lemos, Hélio Mendes, Boaventura, Grael, I can give you a whole heap of names.
>
> MAUD CHIRIO. Are they all of your generation?
>
> FERREIRA. A bit older. Hélio Lemos is a bit older. But since I was a revolutionary very early on, I skipped a generation. I became part of the one before mine without really abandoning my own, but I was very much involved with the generation just before.... I was plotting with those guys back in '63. When I returned from exile [after the Aragarças Rebellion] ... once Jânio resigned, we started planning the '64 revolution.[27]

Last, the parachutist Kurt Pessek deserves mention. Born in 1934, he was even younger than Captain Tarcísio, and of humbler origins (his father was a recent Austrian immigrant, his mother a primary school teacher). Dickson Grael, who had been his superior officer and was also a parachutist, introduced Pessek to the group when he was a captain.

Within the group, Grael and Tarcísio Nunes Ferreira stood out as bearers of the political heritage of various attempts at sedition since the 1950s. For the former, who had been on the cruiser *Tamandaré*, it was the 1955 attempted coup to prevent Kubitschek taking office (the so-called *Novembrada*); for the latter, it was Aragarças, where he rubbed shoulders with army and, especially, air force officers who went on to become famous for their radicalism and their recourse to political violence. Membership of the "elite" parachutist troop, frequently involved in political disturbances in Brazil as in other parts of the world, also created specific networks and loyalties. This made General Moniz de Aragão, who commanded Brazil's one parachute unit (the Nucleus of the Vila Militar Airborne Division) after the coup, a central figure in these officers' accounts—despite his being a friend of President Castelo Branco.

In addition to the military and militant prestige that surrounded them, these officers shared common origins in middle-class, very occasionally upper-class, intellectual and civilian families. Nearly all had parents who were teachers. Only their leader, Francisco Boaventura, stood out as the descendent of a long line of officers from the Northeast. These shared origins, which probably aided their academic success in the military schools, also increased their sense that they had the political legitimacy to take part in the ongoing "revolution" and the ability to do so.

Conspiracy and putschist experience was an even greater feature of another hard-line group that was less generationally and professionally coherent and revolved around another colonel, Osnelli Martinelli. An officer in the reserve and a geography teacher at the Rio de Janeiro Military High School, he had none of Boaventura's aura, authority, or prestige. Of the same generation (he was born in 1922) and the son of a naval officer, he initially went into the navy before entering the Realengo Military Academy and the army. He joined the BEF as a lieutenant and spent ten months fighting in Italy. He then served for five years in the Infantry Regiment School in the Vila Militar, eventually took the improvement course, and, with the rank of captain in 1955, gave up troop commands to devote himself to teaching. He taught at the Rio Military High School until 1973. An unconditional supporter of Carlos Lacerda and a passionate anticommunist, in 1966 he became leader of the Anticommunist Movement, the MAC, set up when Goulart restored diplomatic relations with the Soviet Union and specializing in political acts of violence and attacks. In his own words, he was a professional conspirator even though he had not taken part in the main protests of the 1950s. He "almost [went] to Aragarças," he said. "I didn't go because no one asked me at the time. Because I was always mixed up in that kind of thing."[28]

Martinelli insisted he had a huge variety of contacts in the armed forces and in conspiracy circles, which he claimed were due to his early career—"I went to Navy School. After 1941 I was in the army. In '41, the Air Force Ministry was set up. And lots of guys from my navy intake and plenty from the same year's army intake went into the air force. So, I knew lots of people in all the service branches"—or, he said, due to the fact that "since I was always someone whose position was clearly defined, no one ever needed to ask me whose side I was on. It was always known. That meant I was also involved in these things. Everyone trusted me. And I was in contact with colonels, lieutenants, sergeants, generals, I had dealings with everyone."[29] He said that before the coup d'état he had headed a group of around sixty people (civilians and military personnel, serving and in the reserve), initially organized from the Rio Military High School. In his testimony forty years on, Martinelli alluded in particular to his group's importance in "the defense of Guanabara Palace," the seat of state government and where Carlos Lacerda was at the time of the putsch.

The same idea occurred to a group of radical air force officers led by João Paulo Moreira Burnier (born in 1919), Márcio César Leal Coqueiro de Jesus, and Júlio Valente. Burnier was to be a key figure in the history of the Brazilian military dictatorship, as an activist but above all for authorizing particularly harsh repression during the Years of Lead. Like Martinelli, he was the son of a navy officer. He went into politics only in the 1950s when he led the Aragarças Rebellion (1959). Coqueiro (1917), another Aragarças veteran, enjoyed the classic career of an air force staff officer before and after the revolt, including several months at the Inter-American Defense College at the end of 1964. Also to be added to the list are Roberto Brandini (1922), a BEF veteran who joined the reserve prematurely to work in the Guanabara state administration after Lacerda's election and chaired an IPM in 1964; Carlos Affonso Dellamora (1920); and Roberto Hipólito da Costa (1918), an army officer's son, who graduated with Burnier and was his close friend. He was also the nephew of General Castelo Branco with whom he continued to be on good terms. Last, at the Guanabara Palace on the morning of April 1, there was a group associated with Air Force Reserve Colonel Gustavo Eugênio de Oliveira Borges (1922), son of a navy officer, Guanabara State security secretary during Lacerda's time as state governor (1960–65), most faithful among the faithful, and another Aragarças veteran. Indeed, in 1964, this network of radicals was essentially united by these revolts and their commitment to the famous governor, even though he betrayed them in 1959 by informing the authorities of an undertaking he did not believe in.

The last person to keep in mind is Colonel Ferdinando de Carvalho. His professional profile (apart from not being a parachutist and being of far humbler origins) was very similar to that of Boaventura. Born in 1918, an artillery officer and a much-decorated veteran, he had a brilliant and rapid academic career that led him to a command and staff course in the United States (1953) and then to the ESG at the same time as Boaventura (1962). He was one of the busiest translators of French articles on "revolutionary war" at the beginning of the 1960s. His anticommunist obsession, established once and for all when he headed up the IPM into the Brazilian Communist Party in September 1964, was expressed in abundant writings published throughout the 1970s.[30]

The careers of most hard-line colonels, although twenty years shorter, was fairly similar to those of the "military Sorbonne" members who were in government. The first group, linked to Colonel Boaventura, was more intellectual, as stressed by their civilian descent from teachers and scientists (although this did not apply to Boaventura himself). The second group, for its part, was made up of activists, permanent conspirators since at least the 1950s, almost all of them the sons of officers (frequently naval officers). Whether it was a past as "professional revolutionaries," their professional excellence, or the ordeal of the Second World War, the radical nexus of 1964–65 was made of up officers with a degree of prestige within the military institution, which fostered a sense of political legitimacy. Given their professional and revolutionary credentials, the generational monolith of a government in which almost all ministers had been born between 1900 and 1910, seemed unfair to this small group of officers, frustrated about their exclusion from the state apparatus.

Their personal prestige explained their sense of injustice and their demand for a greater role. By contrast, the profiles do not explain their political orientations, particularly, their repressive radicalism, their scant attachment to democratic norms and their exaggerated economic nationalism. There is an unexpected element in the testimonies of some officers born around 1920 that should be noted: an ambiguity in their recollection of Getúlio Vargas and the Estado Novo. They appear to associate the Vargas era with dictatorship pure and simple and to contrast it with their own allegedly "democratic and antitotalitarian" convictions. The second Vargas government from 1951 to 1954 is disparaged as a grotesque episode of widespread corruption—a "sea of mud" as the title of a book by Gustavo Borges has it—and poor governance. For many, it was the beginning of their political engagement. Tarcísio Nunes Ferreira remembers:

> [In 1952] I went to serve in the First Infantry [Hunters] Battalion in Petrópolis [in the hills overlooking Rio], which was the presidential battalion because the president spent a quarter of the year in Petrópolis, during the summer. And I was able to be there, as a lieutenant, I guarded the Rio Negro Palace and I got to know the Republic up close, intimately, at the top. . . . I was disappointed by what I witnessed in the intimacy of power. It pushed me in the opposite direction. I mean I started to react to the government's, the state's, lack of ethics.[31]

For other members of that generation, however, condemnation of the Vargas "dictatorship" went hand in hand with nostalgia for the greatness of the nation, for the order and authority that supposedly prevailed during their adolescence. This generation had been particularly steeped in the teaching establishments' indoctrination and in state propaganda between 1930 and 1945. This is recalled by Colonel José Eduardo de Castro Portela Soares, born in 1921 and with connections to protest networks: "In Getúlio's day, there was one thing that doesn't exist nowadays. There was a particular propaganda and that propaganda encouraged young people's patriotism and enthusiasm. Ah, and another thing. I went to the military high school. It had discipline and I liked it. I thought it was a good thing. When he was dismissed, I discovered things weren't the same."[32] In this way, for these generations too young to have taken part in the regime, 1930 continued to be a revolutionary reference point and the Vargas era an example of authoritarian nationalism, albeit not fully assumed.

BONES OF CONTENTION

Recurring issues brought these men together between April 1964 and November 1965. There were the conditions for holding the political inquiries (the IPMs), instituted for the most part in the weeks immediately after the coup. These followed from Article 8 of AI-1, which stated that crimes against "the State or its property or the political and social order" and "acts of revolutionary war" could now be investigated by these means. The supreme courts (the civilian Federal Supreme Court and the Superior Military Court), however, regularly granted habeas corpus to prisoners held longer than the legal limit on preventive detentions, allowing them to go underground or into exile. At the time, in fact, these courts took a relatively autonomous line vis-à-vis the executive and often ensured compliance with a certain number of prescriptions of the rule of law in spite of the police and orders to "clean up."[33] A good many IPMs came up against the defense of this basic right, leading to considerable frustration for the officers who were conducting the inquiries and who had been robbed of participation in the "revolution" that they considered essential.

AI-1 also gave the executive the authority to impose temporary exclusion from public office on its opponents, to suspend their political rights and to withdraw the mandates of popularly elected officials (the so-called *cassação*). An immediate challenge was to decide which politicians should be deprived of their rights in this fashion and then how to conduct punitive operations with the legislative tools at hand. In fact, AI-1 included a certain number of restrictions: civil servant exclusions and retirements had to take place within six months and withdrawals of electoral office within sixty days. Added to these purely repressive issues was the matter of extending Castelo Branco's term. The president did not want an extension, unlike the radicals who initially saw it as a means of postponing the elections they dreaded. Several months later, however, having pushed for its adoption, they changed their minds and condemned the planned extension as evidence of the authorities' "continuism." The U-turn is intriguing. It demonstrates the ambiguous position of the hardline officers, wanting to deepen and perpetuate the "state of emergency" and the purge while being totally opposed to the head of state responsible for them.

These subjects were constantly discussed in the military debate that gradually expanded from June 1964 onward. At that point, the government resolved to deprive Juscelino Kubitschek of his political rights under pressure from the General Investigations Commission (Comissão Geral de Investigações, CGI), the IPM regulatory authority, even though ex-president Kubitschek had grudgingly consented to the coup d'état. A few weeks later and also under duress, Castelo Branco ruled to extend his mandate until March 1967.[34] Protest remained muted and patchy until November 1964—manifestos were produced by isolated individuals—and of little concern to the authorities. In September, an SNI report believed that: "The hard-line group, even if it does cause difficulties for the government in its administrative task and stated projects to normalize the life of the nation, does not have the resources—nor indeed any plan at present—to block the government and can, at most, apply pressure in favor of certain substitutes, primarily within the military. Furthermore, there is a sense that a weakening of these pressures and a weariness are permeating the hard-line circles."[35] The author of this report was not particularly perceptive. This was in fact just when the radical officers became really organized. They revealed their political and media strength during the "Goiás crisis" of November 1964. Since May 1964, Reserve Colonel Mauro Borges Teixeira, governor of this state in the high central plateaus (which is home to Brasília), had been harassed by local "revolutionaries." Although he had backed the coup, he had long been identified with the nationalist camp and had committed the unpardonable crime of traveling to communist countries in recent years. An IPM was set up to investigate the man and his administration, although he continued to enjoy support in both the army and the Presidential Palace. After a few months, the situation deteriorated and took on national importance, sparked by the Federal Supreme Court (Supremo Tribunal Federal, STF) granting Borges preemptive habeas corpus, sufficient, no doubt, to antagonize the IPM colonels who saw it as a defeat for their cause and the sign of the "revolution's" inability to impose itself on the existing institutions. The outcry on the Right forced Castelo Branco to repudiate the court in a "note to the nation" and to opt for a federal intervention led by General Meira Mattos, which deposed Borges at the end of November.

Granting habeas corpus was the perfect way to antagonize the protestors. Not only did it inhibit the radicalism of repression, it also came to symbolize the resistance of the institutions and the old order to the momentum of revolution. It was no surprise, therefore, that another STF habeas corpus in April 1965 lit the powder keg and launched the second phase of military protest. The armed forces had had their fingers burned by the "aircraft carrier crisis," which had rendered the navy and air force uncontrollable since December.[36] Moreover, the authorities had been weakened by the revival of an opposition in Congress that, until then, had been entirely at their mercy but had been encouraged toward greater independence by the suspension of punishments and the first dissent by civilian "revolutionaries." The reaction of the military far Right was all the stronger since the beneficiary of habeas corpus was one of its most reviled figures, former Pernambuco governor Miguel Arraes. Held for a year in the island prison of Fernando de Noronha, off the coast of Natal, his release was forcibly prevented by First Army Commander General Otacílio Ururahy and Colonel Ferdinando de Carvalho, chairman of the IPM into the Brazilian Communist Party. Castelo Branco had to intervene personally once again, this time in the opposite direction. He demanded the release of Arraes, to whom he was distantly related. The ex-governor immediately sought asylum at the Algerian embassy before going into exile. The general-president's gesture was seen as a serious betrayal.

After this event, the protest camp enjoyed an unprecedented phase of expansion. June–December 1965 was especially tense. In September, Colonel Jayme Portella talked of a "climate of elation" in the barracks.[37] In October, state elections provided the pretext for the worst political and military crisis of Castelo Branco's term of office. Two factors were involved in the standoff between the government and the colonels' radical nexus: the threat from the barracks, particularly that of the Vila Militar, which concentrated 20,000 armed men in the northern suburbs of Rio, and War Minister Costa e Silva who was skillfully ensuring the continuity of the government while opening up a highway to the presidency for himself.

INQUIRIES AND A FACTIOUS LEAGUE: THE TOOLS OF INTERNAL PRESSURE

In the months after the coup d'état, the protestors continued to rally to the same banners. It was their ways of organizing and their practices that developed to the point of threatening to bring down the government. Hard-line officers used two main tools to apply political pressure: their role in the machinery of repression, through the IPMs, and the creation of a far-right civilian and military movement, LIDER.

The 763 IPMs set up in the weeks after the putsch acted as a space for, and powerful driver of, political protests. During a year of inquiries, 50,000 members of the opposition—10,000 accused and 40,000 witnesses—are thought to have been affected by this witch hunt, which involved more than 3,000 officers.[38] They were general officers, serving or in the reserve, and a good many other less senior officers (colonels, lieutenant colonels, and even majors)— even on the most important IPMs—the purge having pruned the upper echelons of the hierarchy. For these men, the IPMs were symbolic (and financial) retribution for "services to the revolution," giving them visibility, prestige, and power, to which they attached the utmost importance. Their rejection of any impediment to IPM proceedings, such as the granting of habeas corpus, did not stem solely from their political beliefs. It was also a matter of preserving and extending a specific space of power, a source of substantial social value within the institution.

Many of the colonels in charge of IPMs were staff officers who had been through the ECEME, where they were assumed to have received thorough training in "revolutionary war," although this had not equipped them for their new legal and policing roles. They were largely left to their own devices, despite the oversight provided by the CGI, which was headed until mid-July 1964 by the highly conservative Marshal Taurino de Rezende.[39] The lack of training and the number of officers involved were such that the *Noticiário do Exército*, the War Ministry's official mouthpiece, published a manual in May 1964 aimed at the heads of the IPMs, in order to communicate the principles and rules to as many people as possible.[40] Ignorance of the rules of law encouraged these thousands of officers, removed from chain of command structures and their usual professional environments, to conduct their inquiries like crusaders, often very much prone to violence.

The use of violence, contempt for and ignorance of the legal rules and regulations, and the officers' ideological radicalism were in fact all interlinked. On the scale of "revolutionary" values, the mass elimination of opponents and the exposure of the allegedly widespread communist infiltration of Brazilian society took precedence over respect for justice, the limitations on preventive detention, and human rights. There was a purifying dimension to the use of violence: it guaranteed the existence of an ongoing revolutionary process and the unique value of those who led it. Ultimately, the deviations, excesses, and acts of disobedience were so many signals to the authorities from the "IPM colonels," demonstrating their de facto autonomy and desire for confrontation.

Between August 1964 and January 1965, indiscipline on the part of officers entrusted with police tasks proliferated: noncompliance with writs of habeas corpus, such as those of the governor of Sergipe, Seixas Dorias, in August 1964 or in November, those of the elderly and ailing author, Astrojildo Pereira, founder of the Brazilian Communist Party; threats to resign en masse; systematic challenges to legal decisions that forced Castelo Branco on several occasions to make certain that "the inquiries will take their normal course before the court."[41] These were local matters until November, when the case of the governor of Goiás, Mauro Borges, took on a nationwide dimension. Until then, acts of opposition were generally collective and anonymous if in the press, without widespread slogans or violent challenges to the government. They related to the ongoing inquiries because of a shared feeling that the authorities had created the artificial tool of the IPMs without really wanting them to succeed. Tempers were calmed when the president backed down in the Goiás affair, but only temporarily.

The "IPM colonels" returned to the intramilitary political stage in April 1965 when a second Federal Supreme Court habeas corpus was challenged (granted to the Pernambuco governor, Miguel Arraes), but only a handful remained and both the context and their organization were very different. Of the 763 IPMs opened in the months after the coup d'état, only nine were still ongoing owing to the reluctance of those in charge to bring the "revolutionary" purge to an end. Still left were, in particular, Colonel Ferdinando de Carvalho, heading the IPM into the Brazilian Communist Party; Colonel Osnelli Martinelli of the IPM into the Group of Eleven, a popular militia organization set up by Leonel Brizola in 1963 to resist putschist forces; Colonel Gérson de Pina, Martinelli's colleague at the Rio Military High School, who headed the IPM into the Higher Institute of Brazilian Studies (Instituto Superior de Estudos Brasileiros, ISEB), a progressive and developmentalist think tank, founded ten years before; and Major Cléber Bonecker, chairing the IPM into the communist press. Protests by these officers, dubbed the "crisis of the IPM colonels" by the press, lasted from April to June 1965. This was no longer "corporate radicalism," collective, anonymous, scattered, and localist as it had been at the end of 1964. The "IPM colonels" were now the figureheads of an organized military opposition to President Castelo Branco, which for several months had been presenting a "revolutionary" alternative.

In the background was the LIDER, set up in September 1964, which rapidly came to embody another force of military and public opposition to the castelista government. It took up the earlier demands of the IPM heads—freedom of investigation, restricted judicial powers, the extension of the Institutional Act's purge articles—while promoting even from its very first manifestos a much broader political platform of "revolutionary policies," especially when it came to the economy. In part, the LIDER adopted the political rhetoric of Admiral Silvio Heck: economic nationalism and the "authenticity" of a radical revolution. Its first appearances in the press and intelligence services archives (at home and abroad) date from September to October 1964. What SNI analysts thought of it at the time is a puzzle: they denied it had any "capacity for appreciable mobilization although it must be remembered that it is able to promote agitation at any moment, and as of now."[42]

A note in the French Army Archives is more explicit: "The Radical Democratic League was set up in Rio de Janeiro the night of 23 September 1964 by civilian and military elements, with a greater number of the latter. They all belong to various bodies connected by a single ideal: the uncompromising defense of the spirit that drove the 31 March revolution. . . . The league does not unite *all* 'hard-line' forces; it is one of the extremist wings, unhappy with the current state of affairs, which is organizing."[43] Several military traditions and factions were represented in the LIDER. Behind Admiral Heck were the conservative networks of the states of São Paulo and Minas Gerais, as well as the anticommunist Patriotic Action Group (GAP). Founded in Minas, the GAP would be a paramilitary organization bringing together civilians and reserve military personnel.[44] Heck and his associate, reserve general José Alberto Bittencourt, former leader of the Civil–Military Patriotic Front, were LIDER's first strongmen before being succeeded at the beginning of 1965 by a triumvirate made up of Colonel Osnelli Martinelli, lawyer Luis Mendes de Moraes Neto, and Colonel Joaquim Pessoa Igrejas Lopes. Martinelli and Gérson de Pina, teachers at the Rio Military High School and the heads of IPMs, epitomized Carioca anticommunist activism, linked to the small MAC terrorist group and subordinate to the state governor Carlos Lacerda. Luis Mendes de Moraes was an Aragarças veteran—one of the only civilians to take part in the revolt—for which he wrote the official manifesto.[45] Many of his contemporaries from that revolt and the one in Jacareacanga were in LIDER. Captain Tarcísio Nunes Ferreira, Major Alberto Fortunato, Brigadier João Paulo Moreira Burnier, and Charles Herba, a civilian, who had all taken part in one of the revolts, were active members.

There is great continuity in the profiles of the league's leaders. They were anticommunist activists inclined to violent action, involved in the revolts and conspiracies of the previous decade, and linked to civilian extremist circles. A changeover occurred in 1965, however, when the old generals' generation passed the baton on to the colonels' generation while the movement's center of gravity switched from Minas Gerais to Rio, where the bulk of the troops and the most highly mobilized military youth were concentrated. LIDER had its headquarters in Rio. It was run by a fifty-member "Leaders Council," twenty-five of whom were elected for life by a general assembly. These then appointed the other half, which was regularly replaced. The word "leader" (*líder* in Portuguese), for both the organization and those who ran it, was key. Recurrent and highly valued in the military lexicon, it was associated with charisma, natural authority, and aggressive political voluntarism. The activist officers used it to denigrate their rivals, to place themselves symbolically in a group or to describe their own actions without using the discredited term "politics." Osnelli Martinelli, for example, believes Carlos Lacerda "wasn't a politician to us, he was a leader. And at one time, there were lots of leaders, including in the navy and the air force . . . they don't exist nowadays. Today, unfortunately, there isn't any leadership anymore."[46] He relates with remarkable pride that General Costa e Silva introduced them, along with General Gérson de Pina, with the words: "They are our leaders," a description somewhat contemptuously denied him by Colonel Amerino Raposo Filho, a "hard-liner" close to Boaventura and not a member of the league. For him, Martinelli "had the hallmarks of leadership" but "somewhat overstated their exercise."[47] Between these two groups from the first hard line (LIDER and Boaventura's), despite clear political collusion, there was a gulf that widened over time. The former accused the latter of inconsistency and in return was often described as sectarian. This mutual contempt and future differences of political opinion can be explained by the disparity in their profiles. The league was a disparate union of far-right activists, civilian and military, who ran political investigations. The network run by Boaventura and Amerino Raposo was made up of serving officers with outstanding professional careers and troop commands.

It is difficult to calculate the number of LIDER members with any certainty. When it was set up, the league claimed to have 2,000 officers. In January 1965, the press mentioned 3,700 officers while a few days later Silvio Heck put the number who had rallied to him at 5,000 (serving or in the reserve). The authorities by contrast spoke of a few dozen individuals. In June 1965, the military hierarchy's punitive offensive against the league was preceded by statements about its "ultra-minority" status in the armed forces with 40 members, too few even to constitute the "Leaders Council." Other documents talk about 200-300 officers attending meetings in Rio, which gives no indication about support in other states or the number of vigorous activists.

LIDER expressed itself through manifestos distributed in the barracks and then passed on to the press. Between September 1964 and November 1965 when Justice Minister Juracy Magalhães banned the league, three documents were sent out: in February, June, and November 1965. They expressed the different tendencies within the organization, which focused on repressive radicalism and economic nationalism. There was a degree of internal specialization based around "sections" ("Diffusion and Propaganda," "Women's Sector," "Professional Sector," "Special Affairs," etc.) and members' own leanings. Martinelli, for example, admitted he had little interest in the economic issues that were the particular concern of Admiral Heck and Colonel Igrejas Lopes.[48]

Despite the small activist groups represented in it, LIDER did not engage in acts of violence and was not known for its role in street demonstrations. Its only action of this kind took place at the end of March 1965 at Largo de São Francisco outside one of the Federal University of Rio de Janeiro buildings. Activists from the league and the Women's Campaign for Democracy (CAMDE), along with political police officers (Departamento de Ordem Político e Social, DOPS) who belonged to LIDER, confronted the signatories of an "Intellectuals' Manifesto" gathered in the square, who were ultimately arrested by the police. The event caused a great stir and disturbed certain ministers of the Superior Military Court, such as General Peri Bevilacqua, who was becoming increasingly critical of the regime's excessive repression. Bevilacqua clashed with General Mourão Filho over this within the court itself. A few months later, they would be allies in the liberal opposition to the government.[49] The altercation also showed that LIDER was now part of a civil and military network of small right-wing groups. Links with CAMDE were particularly strong owing to political and personal affinities. In October 1965, two hundred dissidents, encouraged by Elizabeth Martinelli (Osnelli's wife), left CAMDE to join the league.[50] Last, the league had representatives in Congress, where some deputies acted as harbingers of repressive radicalism, notably Reserve Colonel José Costa Cavalcanti, brother to Francisco Boaventura and Nina Ribeiro who, in May 1965, took the Miguel Arraes habeas corpus case to the Guanabara Legislative Assembly, accompanied and applauded by two hundred hard-line officers.

As of December 1964, LIDER occupied the majority of the political space held by the military opposition to Castelo Branco. Its spokesmen were often reserve military personnel less liable to disciplinary sanctions than their serving colleagues. The "IPM colonels" crisis from April to June 1965 must be understood in this context of the league at its height. Utterances from the heads of the inquiries were, of course, still focused on the purge and on repression and never on the economy, but they now had a political project to pit against that of Castelo Branco. So, on May 13, 1965, the nine IPM chiefs issued the government with an ultimatum. They threatened to resign unless the STF was reformed and the time-limited punitive provisions of the Institutional Act reinstated. Both demands were effectively met by the passing of the Second Institutional Act on October 27, 1965. With their requests not yet satisfied, however, at the end of June Osnelli Martinelli, Gérson de Pina, Cléber Bonecker, and Ferdinando de Carvalho resigned one by one from their IPMs. The first two were jailed for antigovernment declarations, as were Lieutenant Colonel Júlio Valente, an Aragarças veteran, and Admiral Rademaker, who expressed solidarity with the IPM colonels and visited them in prison. The tradition of "visits to detainees" as a sign of protest became established.

Having seen the part played by LIDER and the "IPM colonels"—the leading lights of the military protest—we must look next at the role of the officers at barracks and in schools.

They were considerably more low-key because they were subject to stricter disciplinary rules. Even so, the real political risk to the authorities lay with the bulk of officers and the serving military elite. The hard-line colonels were also looking in their direction because the "opinion of the barracks" and the voice of their chiefs were vital sources of legitimacy and political strength.

Indeed, these colonels were imbued with a dual mindset of hierarchy and leadership. The first, effectively, ruled out promoting an individual from their own ranks as a potential political rival to the ruling generals. It defined them as subordinates, whose opinions needed to go up through the military ranks to be heard at the top. Leadership had a different connotation since it valued the political charisma and authority of a "strongman" amid his peers and subordinates. The opposition colonels were therefore awkwardly balanced between seeking support among the rank and file and the necessary patronage of a general. As a result, they looked upward even as they drew their legitimacy from the bulk of officers, for whom they claimed to speak—a numbers-based reasoning the putschists had claimed in 1964 to want to eradicate from their institution.

THE BARRACKS AND THEIR MINISTER

The backdrop to these political protests was a certain notion of and, particularly, a debate about the reality of the "revolution" and the regime that was being built. Was it a military government? Had the nation's sovereignty been entrusted to the armed forces as an institution? If so, why retain a congress, elections, or parties? If not, why did the executive with its disproportionately enhanced powers consist almost entirely of military men? President Castelo Branco's answer to these questions was to retain the appearances of civil and democratic normality as far as possible and to attempt to depoliticize and demobilize the serving army. He stressed the continuity of the legislature and judiciary as well as unequivocal popular support for the "revolution." He was rarely seen in uniform.

This initial representation of the dictatorial regime is the one that, after the transition to democracy, was highlighted in military recollections from whatever faction or political persuasion: the coup d'état was said to have been a "civil–military revolution," the government to be staffed by technocrats, the civilian political class fully involved in the regime's approaches, and the population universally delighted by its successes in repression as much as in the economy. Furthermore, it should be noted that, for partly identical reasons, this representation and the name "civil–military dictatorship" are winning the battle of words in recollection and historiography. Since the mid-2000s, the desire of a certain number of activists and historians to talk up collaboration and support for the dictatorial government within civil society has encouraged an end to the use of the single adjective "military."[51] First, however, this new name conceals changes in the composition, organization, and methods of legitimizing the authorities and the state apparatus as of 1964. The Brazilian state became profoundly military at every level. Second, it encourages people to forget the debates that took place among the putschists themselves about the nature and future of the regime. From 1964–65 onward, the "hard-line" officers based their political action on a disagreement. In the eyes of the castelista camp, a proportion of the military elite had worked its way into the existing system to save the motherland and adapt Brazilian democracy somewhat to the challenges of the Cold War. To the protesting colonels, the "revolution" was a military one and the government therefore answerable to the armed forces.

The confrontation between the government and its radical opposition went hand in hand therefore with a disagreement over the authorities' political base and political legitimacy. The practical application of these two contradictory discourses was full of ambiguities. The protesting officers drew their political legitimacy from the fact that, as they saw it, they represented the mass of the military rank and file, but continued to look for a leader who would act as a political outlet; while the government, on the pretext of depoliticizing the armed forces, planned to establish a long-term generals' regime.

The protest camp had a considerable resource in its opposition to the authorities: the growing anxiety and discontent of more numerous and younger officers, who were harder to restrain. "Turmoil in the barracks" is always difficult to assess. To begin with, it was probably limited. SNI documents, which offer a regular overview of the general situation in the country from August 1964 to July 1965, present a picture of isolated activist networks within the officer corps.[52] "The anxiety of the Armed Forces" regarding "the Government's economic and financial policy and the decisions of the STM [which allowed numerous instances of habeas corpus]" is mentioned at the beginning of that period.[53] Bulletins soon identified the protesters more clearly, while playing down their influence among the officers. In November 1964, at the height of the conflict over the Mauro Borges case, the military was considered to be calm, "the clean-up task . . . giv[ing] rise only to fleeting and minor criticism" and "the meanderings of the so-called hard line seemingly peter[ing] out."[54] In April 1965, when the crisis of the "IPM colonels" over habeas corpus for Miguel Arraes broke out, the SNI agent believed that "The Armed Forces . . . are also troubled by these disruptive agents, albeit to a lesser extent given their concern for the armor of discipline and their sense of military duty.

Not all will remain unscathed, however. And, already, the threat is at the door."[55] Last, in July 1965, after the sensational resignations of some IPM chiefs, and with LIDER seemingly at its height, a final document felt that their "attempts at agitation do not appear to impress the military world."[56]

The available sources make it possible to presume that certain centers of military agitation did exist at this time, contained within the Vila Militar on the outskirts of Rio de Janeiro. The first was the Officer Improvement School (EsAO), a hotbed of conspiracy during the Goulart government. After the coup, there were indirect signs of dissatisfaction among the captains who lived and studied there. It was there that the head of state and the war minister made their main speeches calling for calm and the restoration of discipline. When courses closed in July 1964, Castelo Branco spoke there, giving an unusually frank overview of the dissatisfaction of the young officers he urged to respect their "military duty." The reasons given for their discontent (a purge that had not gone far enough and the authorities' shilly-shallying negotiations) were entirely consistent with future utterances by the "hard line."[57] A year later, during the same ceremony, it was War Minister Costa e Silva's turn to issue a reminder of the need for discipline. He had the colonels in his sights: "Now, more than ever, the youth, the army's heart and marrow, must have its face, thoughts, and aspirations turned toward its chiefs. Trusting them . . . Just as a captain does not allow himself to be overtaken by a lieutenant, nor a lieutenant by a sergeant nor a sergeant by a corporal, so the generals of today will not let themselves be overtaken by their subordinates whatever their posts or ranks."[58] As well as a sign of tempers flaring at the school, the speech is also evidence of the war minister's complex strategy regarding military dissatisfaction. Costa e Silva was from the same generation as Castelo Branco. He was from the south (a *gaucho*), of less aristocratic origins than Castelo (his father was a Portuguese shopkeeper whereas the president's was an officer) but he was equally outstanding at school and in his career. Athletic and outgoing, he was in many ways the antithesis of the president. From the days immediately after the coup until the height of the military crisis of October 1965, Costa e Silva used his ministry to call consistently for respect for discipline and the hierarchy. "The time has come for the troops to return to the barracks and to maintain discipline," he said in the wake of the putsch.[59] There were ambiguities in his public statements, however. He presented himself as the legitimate repository of military dissatisfaction. While his position as war minister made it natural that he should receive the officers complaints and expressions of concern, he would often become a de facto spokesman, as the subjects dear to the protestors occupied more and more space in what he had to say. During the IPM colonels' crisis in April 1965, he blew openly hot and cold: one day, he would be championing "ten years of revolutionary government . . . with or without . . . Castelo Branco," the next he would be lauding the head of state to the skies.[60] This shift from being a purely hierarchical leader to, in effect, a political one as the voice of the protesting officers is what made him a threat to the government's authority.

Moreover, Costa e Silva's constant calls for discipline and calm at the barracks made him the guarantor of these as far as the powers that be were concerned, since he was a "strongman" with undoubted influence over the officer corps. It was exactly this firefighter–arsonist position that the war minister took up in October 1965 when the state governor elections turned hard-line protests into a direct threat to the authorities. Holding elections as Castelo Branco wanted was in itself unpalatable to the military Right. The final straw came when the opposition won two of the federation's main states—Francisco Negrão de Lima in Guanabara, replacing Lacerda, and Israel Pinheiro in Minas Gerais, both for the center-right getulista Social Democratic Party (Partido Social Democrático, PSD). To the radicals, this seemed like the official end of the "cleanup" process the hard-liners wanted to perpetuate.

Costa e Silva then made a still-famous speech to the First Infantry Regiment of the Vila Militar, in which he made several radical catchphrases his own even as he defused the revolt:

> I want to tell you, and I do so with pride, that the revolutionary spirit prevails more than ever today. We have a sui generis Revolution, a Revolution of which, a year after being established, the only problems are containing those who are too revolutionary. (*Applause*) We are not afraid of counter-revolutions. (*Applause*) . . . On the contrary, we are concerned about the enthusiasm and zeal of the youth who want more revolution. But I guarantee you, my friends, I guarantee you, young men under my command, that we know where we are going. The current leaders, as I said yesterday and as I say again today, are as revolutionary as the young revolutionaries. (*Applause*) I guarantee you that those who have been set aside will not come back. (*Standing ovation*) . . . They will never take possession of this country.[61]

The threat to the authorities at the time came from the Vila Militar officers' widespread discontent with the election results and, more profoundly, from the respect inside the country as a whole for certain rules of democracy. The core of the Vila Militar, the parachute brigade, had been another proven center of activism since the end of 1964. Known as the "Nucleus of the Airborne Division," the battalion was of very recent date (1953), small (fewer than one hundred troops), and regarded by the military as elite. General Ulhoa Cintra, who worked closely with Castelo Branco, gave evidence of its agitation in a letter sent to General Otacilio Terra Ururahy, commander of the First Army, in July 1965, talking about "an unease that always exists in the parachute force," the result of a "pernicious mentality of supermen, which leads them to underestimate comrades in other units" and to take on "inappropriate attitudes."[62]

Moreover, some parachute officers and particularly the brigade's chief of staff, the infamous Lieutenant Colonel Francisco Boaventura Cavalcanti, were involved in a conspiracy to topple the president, which was hatched by First Army Chief of Staff Afonso de Albuquerque Lima and Admiral Silvio Heck. The available information is piecemeal. At the end of November, the press spoke of a "Junta de Humaitá," named after the district of Rio in which the conspirators were based, and implicated Heck and two other hard-line colonels, Heitor Caracas Linhares and Plínio Pitaluga. The rebellion, which was extremely amateurish, did not take place however. Colonel Kurt Pessek recalls a handful of officers gathering in Rio de Janeiro's 15 November Square. Seeing the complete lack of coordination and preparation, Boaventura persuaded them not to march on the palace.[63] Ernesto Geisel, who was head of the president's Military Cabinet at the time, regarded the rebellion as mere bluff.[64]

In October 1965, therefore, Minister Costa e Silva won his place as leader of the military protest. He was granted it by the troops whereas the activism to be seen (in the archives and, to some extent, by the authorities) had since the coup been primarily concentrated in a "hard-line" nucleus kept away from the barracks by their police inquiries or their move to the reserve. He also won his place in opposition to the protesters' historic leader, Carlos Lacerda, governor of Guanabara until October 1965. Since July 1964, Lacerda had been dancing around the government, aiming to establish himself as the inevitable successor to Castelo Branco, while retaining his political base among the radical officers. This was no easy task, since his plan to run in the next presidential elections (scheduled for October 1966) entailed positions that often ran counter to those championed by the hard-liners. For example, he opposed extending Castelo Branco's mandate, abandoned his vehement putschist stance for a moderate position more likely to win the support of the civilian political class, and objected to postponing the governor elections in October 1965.[65] His ambitions required that an electoral routine and a degree of autonomy for the civilian elites be maintained. The latter would have no further role if a military and authoritarian regime was established. It was, however, his military support that offered him the best chance of influencing the balance of power within the palace and the barracks. No stranger to contradiction, in July 1965 he declared his solidarity with the hard-line colonels fighting for a more thorough-going purge. He went to see Martinelli in jail, following in the footsteps of the "blue and white group" that had "defended" Guanabara Palace during the coup. He was similarly opportunistic during the October 1965 crisis when, after wanting gubernatorial elections to be held in Guanabara and Minas Gerais, he then blamed the government for the defeat, claimed he would no longer be running for the presidency, and declared the revolution at an end. While the intervention of the war minister appeared to have temporarily shelved the likelihood of a Vila Militar uprising, the *lacerdistas*' networks remained in a ferment. On October 15, a demonstration outside the Military Club rallied a great many LIDER and CAMDE members to calls of "the doors of the Military Club are shut, those of Guanabara Palace are open," "Lacerda, Lacerda," "these are the revolutionaries of 1 April not 31 March."[66]

Lacerda's fate was sealed in a few weeks. On October 3, he ceded the post of governor of Guanabara to the opposition and on October 27, the provisions of a brand new, Second Institutional Act included the abolition of existing political parties, particularly the UDN, which, one year earlier, had endorsed him as a presidential candidate. Among other provisions, AI-2 introduced a two-party system. The former governor's hopes were extinguished all the more definitively since the acclamations greeting Costa e Silva at the Vila Militar made him a far more likely successor to Castelo Branco. This had been clear in any case inasmuch as the act established a genuinely military regime for the long term.

The interventions of the war minister and the promulgation of AI-2 did not entirely calm the turmoil among the officers. Some of those who had organized the abortive uprising at the beginning of the month were back at center stage throughout November and December, seeking to prevent the new governor of Guanabara, Negrão de Lima, from taking office. Colonel Ferdinando de Carvalho called for his political rights to be suspended while Parachute Brigade Chief of Staff Francisco Boaventura had the same aim when he issued the first political manifesto by a serving colonel since the coup d'état. Punished and jailed, he was visited by Martinelli. Colonel Hélio Lemos, who had declared his solidarity with Martinelli, also found himself behind bars. The radical core had never been as cohesive as it was over trying to prevent the governor from taking office. It should be noted that, despite its great diversity, it had a shared commitment to Lacerda (there was talk of *lacerdismo*) and a shared lack of trust in Costa e Silva. This is stressed by Jayme Portella de Mello, a friend of the war minister, in his memoirs: "The group of officers linked to M. Carlos Lacerda tried to play its last card."[67] Moreover, it was Costa e Silva, as their supervisory minister, who punished them with transfers out of the city of Rio. Boaventura was sent to Campo Grande in Mato Grosso, Hélio Lemos to Bagé in the far south of the country, and Martinelli to the Salvador Military High School. Negrão de Lima and Israel Pinheiro took office on December 5, 1965.

The disparate "first hard line," a visible part of the process of military politicization, only indirectly supported the war minister for the presidency. While some of the youngest officers mixed with the people close to Costa e Silva before 1964, he did not himself belong as Lacerda did to the networks of these indefatigable conspirators. However, Costa e Silva's position as "commander"—the only person able to avoid widespread insubordination—and his hierarchical legitimacy were enhanced by cleverly shifting of his discourse to the right and, more particularly, by the discontent of serving officers, especially in Rio. He overtly laid claim to the role in his first speech after the promulgation of AI-2, addressing officers of the Second Army meeting in Itapeva (São Paulo). He launched a head-on attack on the chairman of the STF, talking of a "judicial dictatorship" maintained by "civilian mysticism." He went on to conclude with a highly ambiguous question: "Some say the President of the Republic is politically weak. What's the problem in being politically weak if he is militarily strong?"[68] In addition, the speech was extemporized in the presence of Castelo Branco, after the president had spoken, violating the order of precedence.

Costa e Silva's candidacy said a great deal about the nature of the regime. It pointed out that the legitimacy of the authorities came directly from the barracks, where uproar demanded a political leader (identified as "strong-willed" and steeped in "the revolutionary idea") who was also a military commander. According to the hard-line officers, the barracks were, therefore, sovereign. More precisely, the "revolutionary armed forces" constituted the "permanent assembly" to which the government was accountable.[69] This had been indicated several months earlier in LIDER's second manifesto, published in the press on June 23, 1965: "The Head of Government is nothing more than a Delegate of the Supreme Command of the Revolution and, therefore, may not, under any circumstance, act against the ideals of the revolution, which take precedence over the Constitution itself."[70] The sovereignty of the "revolutionaries" was a problem, however, since the group lacked definition after a multipolar conspiracy and a coup d'état that everyone claimed to have initiated.

The position of the castelista government was quite different. Imbued with the imperatives of a professional army, it defended and enforced measures to depoliticize and subjugate the military institution, sovereignty remaining in theory with the people, purged of its nonnational elements, who were "subversive and corrupt."

Calls to respect the military hierarchy and military discipline were in no way the preserve of any one faction but Castelo Branco added a further requirement: the barracks must keep out of political debate and submit to the constituted authorities without endorsing or criticizing their decisions. Addressing EsAO captains in July 1964, he made the following statement:

> It seems I have to talk to you and even to ask you what your position is. Is it one of solidarity with the government? No. Because the army is not a political party to be in solidarity with the government or with anyone at all. Whoever is entitled to be in solidarity is also entitled to offer condemnation. Does the government hope for your support? No. The National Army is not an organization which should demonstrate its support for one element or another here and there because then it would be entitled to condemn it as well. I think your position has to be the one that is found in doing your military duty.[71]

Keeping politics out of the barracks had sustained a degree of legalism before the coup, but had also been part of the putschists' arguments. To them, the sergeants' protests, the positions adopted by the people's generals and, more generally, military support for the Goulart government all posed a threat to the integrity of the institution. Castelo Branco seized on these marks of constitutional legalism as well as on highly conservative objections to "the introduction of party politics" and any degree of internal democracy in the army to combat the activism of the protesting troops. Added to this was the stigma repeatedly attached to civilians as responsible for politicizing the military. These "over-excited serving wenches [*vivandeiras*] [who since 1930 had been] coming into the camps to torment the grenadiers and to rouse the Military Power to excesses" were, in his mind, the civilian leaders of the revolution,[72] Lacerda of course, but also the Minas Gerais governor, Magalhães Pinto.

This demand for political reserve sanctified some spaces (the barracks itself where officers and soldiers rubbed shoulders in combat training exercises) and ranks (from junior officers to colonels) still further. The new authorities did not confine themselves to mere words: new legislation was introduced aimed at distinguishing between the political involvement of individual service personnel who must not be on active service and the pursuit of a professional career. In July 1964, a decree gave permission for reserve troops to engage in politics since "in a democratic regime," "there is no inherent justification for restrictions on the military as regards the free expression of their thinking and party political activities . . . other than the specific requirements of being and acting as a member of the military on active service. . . . There is no reason for these restrictions when the serviceman is no longer active." At which point he "fully regains his rights as a citizen" and was no longer subject to army disciplinary regulations.[73] This document, astonishing precisely at a time when antigovernment rumblings were climbing up through the ranks of reserve and retired officers, satisfied the desire to prevent all-powerful serving military leaders from appearing on the political stage and creating factions. The main plank in this plan was a law passed in December 1965, restricting the length of time spent in the rank of army general (at that time, the highest rank in the army's active service), or the air force or navy equivalent, to four years with a move to the reserve after two mandatory years out of active service in the event of holding elected office.[74]

Nevertheless, the authorities only belatedly adopted a punitive policy toward activist officers. As a result, although under threat since January 1965, LIDER was only shut down in November as a "subversive entity" after publishing its third manifesto. The first disciplinary incarcerations, limited to thirty days with no subsequent loss of office, date back to the "IPM colonels" crisis of June 1965. The systematic breakup of the hard line was not undertaken until December. Castelo Branco thereby demonstrated the fragility of his military support. Unable to crack down sufficiently quickly and harshly on the troublesome "revolutionary" colonels, of whom, moreover, his powerful war minister was making good use, he allowed a concept of the regime to develop that was not his own. This was not so much because he was too liberal, too moderate, or too humanistic to adapt himself to the political system brought into being by AI-2. On the contrary, he would accommodate himself to it very well, ultimately delighted about this "institutionalization of the revolution," even if he was somewhat coerced into doing so. The political process got away from him on another level as it became a common understanding that the army was the country's electoral college and military chiefs the country's legitimate leaders.

MONOPOLY ON REVOLUTION

Political dynamics in the early years of the military regime centered on what seemed to be binary opposites. At the level of sovereign principles, there was "revolution" versus "constitutional legality." At the level of legitimate participants in the political process, there was the government versus the "revolutionaries." In reality, the division was simplistic since all players defined themselves as revolutionaries and many of them as legalists forced to support the coup because of the desperate nature of the situation. Nevertheless, defining the "revolutionary idea" was a leitmotif of military protest.

The first documents disseminated by activist officers depict the putsch as the pursuit and accomplishment of a century-long task: "the" Brazilian Revolution. Even so, while many members of the 1964 government were veterans of the 1922 revolt and the Revolution of 1930, the new authorities did not formulate an official discourse about the legacy of these movements unlike, for example, the recurrent parallel made with the victory over the 1935 communist Intentona. The fact that the General Staffs and government included former tenentes and officers who had helped put down their uprising—although many had backed the regime produced by the Revolution of 1930—made it difficult to establish an official line on the past. Nor indeed is there a single collective memory or consensus on how to remember this period in history.

On the contrary, fitting the coup into a "revolutionary tradition" was a frequent rhetorical recourse of protesting officers, particularly members of LIDER. It served to justify the elimination of the "old civilian political class," certain economic choices, and their own political engagement. Admiral Heck was a great fan of referring to "revolutionary" tradition, of which he declared himself a representative, even though he did not become a political agitator himself until the 1950s.[75] His associate Odílio Denys, who was far more involved in the uprisings of the twentieth century and who publicly declared his opposition to the Castelo Branco government during the October 1965 crisis, gave an interpretation that stuck closely to this revolutionary tradition: 1922 was the start of "the great struggle [for] democracy," which ended in 1964. In Heck's first manifesto, disseminated on July 21, 1964, he defined it as the rejection of "collusion with forces compromised by corruption and playing at politics" followed by the building of a "New Republic, Christian and democratic." "This has always been the hard line of the Brazilian revolution," he concluded.[76] Sílvio Heck focused his attacks on two main targets, each "antinational" in its own way: those who defended vested interests, as in the case of horse-trading and corrupt politicians who lacked ideals; and those in service to the foreigner, to communist internationalism or U.S. imperialism. These two groups did not have the same status. The first were impediments to revolution, a "corrupt civil power. . . which has debased all revolutions since that of 1922, through that of 1930, to the present day," as the first LIDER manifesto stressed in January 1965,[77] while the second were its enemies. In the manifestos of the "first hard line," references to these past events were largely for effect. They gave historical legitimacy to a political vocabulary (the oligarchies, politicking, the denationalization of Brazil) recycled in order to condemn a government they believed had betrayed a collective, national project. In February 1965, the second LIDER manifesto made the coup d'état the heir to the tenentismo struggles, which Castelo Branco was said to have betrayed, again, by promoting the "PSD-ization [bringing into line with the getulista party, the PSD] and denationalization" of Brazil.[78]

In an overly simplistic representation of the political situation, there was only one, multifaceted enemy of the revolution: the corruption of the political class, which favored subversion, while its tendency to sell itself to the foreigner, driven by shameful personal interests, kept Brazil from greatness and weakened it vis-à-vis both Washington and Moscow:

> [The revolutionaries cannot accept] that international cupidity, organized into monopolistic systems that bleed the national economy, should influence the fate of Brazil. The people are subjected to an inhuman, excessive, brutal and unbearable burden which is taking them to the brink of exhaustion. . . .
>
> I wish to condemn the silence of patriots at a time when the reactionary forces of corruption, opening the gates for subversion to return, abuse, attack and do moral harm to the brave officers who, obeying orders, engage in the most grueling missions, the only ones perhaps to have so far subjected the revolution to the judgment of the Brazilian people.[79]

This symbolic construct, common to the personal manifestos of Silvio Heck and the communications of the Radical Democratic League, went hand in hand with an inflated economic nationalism. The Castelo Branco government's economic policy was accused of being too open to foreign capital, particularly from North America, but also of excessive state interventionist ambitions that ran counter to the dogma of private initiative and tended therefore toward socialism. The most virulent opposition to this economic policy came first from the governor of Minas Gerais, Magalhães Pinto, and especially from the governor of Guanabara, Carlos Lacerda—although he had been the voice of economic antinationalism for many years. His economic choices since the Second World War had in fact been profoundly opportunistic. He had systematically opposed the choices of the incumbent authorities, whichever they happened to be.[80] This attitude was confirmed after 1964 when, in order to maintain his most precious political bases—the urban middle classes and the radical junior officers—he was thus encouraged to stress the cost of living as a major issue and to condemn the symbols of penetration by foreign capital. As was his wont, Lacerda did this with a great deal of sound and fury. His principal target was economy minister Roberto Campos (nicknamed Bob Fields by his detractors, the English translation of his name, in order to depict him as the henchman of U.S. imperialism), against whom he had long nursed animosity. His attacks, which began on July 1964, intensified in November 1964, when the government granted a mining concession to the Hanna Mining Company at the expense of the state-owned Companhia Vale do Rio Doce and Companhia Siderúrgica da Guanabara. He sent President Castelo Branco a series of letters, accusing the government technocrats of orchestrating a "denationalization of industry and the big estates," and thereby denaturing the revolution.[81] Lacerda's U-turn from antinationalist, agrarian, and anti-industrialist positions to a pro-industry nationalism that was much more popular among the "first hard line" was an attempt to tap into military dissatisfaction. The timetable of his offensives (July 1964, November 1964, and April–July 1965) attests to this eloquently, timed as they were to coincide with the moments of greatest military protest.

Most certainly influenced by Sílvio Heck, until February 1965 these nationalist theses were central in LIDER's declarations before gradually disappearing once Martinelli's group joined its leadership, given their obsession with resuming the purge. In regular dispatches in the *Jornal do Brasil* in January and February 1965, anonymous LIDER members defined their group as "clearly nationalist, especially when it comes to the defense of the economic riches vital to the development and strategic security of the Country."[82] The genealogy of this military nationalism, which was very strong in the activist colonels' generation, was not self-evident. Despite the ambiguous nostalgia some evinced for the "greatness" of the Vargas period, the majority were actively involved in the "antinationalist" camp in the 1950s and at the start of the 1960s. Moreover, there were very few who showed radical hostility to the United States, where they had often been proud to receive military training. Last, while Lacerda made himself the main harbinger of economic nationalism after the coup, the lacerdismo of these officers was driven by anticorruption moralism, virulent anticommunism, and what they identified as Lacerda's great capacity for leadership rather than his economic nationalism, which was only recently acquired. We will return to the content and origins of these nationalist tenets when, in a few years' time, they become one of this radical Right's pillars of identity and a bridge between opposing groups.

Between April 1964 and November 1965, a particular representation of the authorities came into being that was a direct product of the overly simplistic revolutionary views of the protesting officers. Since the eternal enemies of the revolution were the old oligarchic politics, foreign interests, and left-wing subversion, the government, the immediate adversary of the "radical nexus," had to acquire their features. To begin with, this was said to be through the infiltration of these elements into the governing team: the planning and finance ministers were designated emblems of foreign imperialism while the president was allegedly surrounded by harmful professional politicians. This bad company pushed him into governing in too "civilian" a fashion, which implied a lack of moral rectitude and a propensity for compromise and the defense of private interests. As of July 1964, when, as already mentioned, he addressed an audience of captains at the Officer Improvement School, Castelo Branco challenged these constant insinuations head-on: "No. The government is not running away from this mission. It is not giving itself over to lunches, barbecues, parties, and sensationalism. In an ordered fashion and with unity of thought and action, it is accomplishing the tough mission of fine tuning the life of Brazil. . . . The government is said to be giving itself over to bargaining and collusion. This is not an injustice, it is a serious accusation."[83] Castelo was playing the card of the "ex-soldier," entrusted with a mission and characterized by asceticism and moral rectitude. It was the head of the president's Civil Cabinet, Reserve General Golbery do Couto e Silva, who was portrayed as virtually the caricature of a civilian politician by the radicals. Only Heck, some of whose manifestos employed an unusually violent turn of phrase, accused the president too of being guilty, a "new political magician, drunk on power, who does not raise the wages of the needy but has his own monetarily adjusted because he is a revolutionary only when his own interests coincide with the exercise of power. . . . By relying on the enduring oligarchies responsible for so much disorder, he has marginalized most of the protest's authentic leaders, he has painfully slowed the revolutionary dynamic, [he has abandoned] real punishment of tie-wearing crooks, including by ceasing to confiscate illegally acquired assets."[84]

According to its radical critics, the castelista government was intrinsically not revolutionary. Its composition and even the character of some of its members were considered unfit to achieve the "ideals of 31 March." Two elements were linked to this representation of the authorities. First, the terms "usurpation" and the "revolution betrayed" began to appear systematically in the military protest. As part of the endless discussions of who took the first step toward the coup, the protesters saw the castelista clan as a "fellow traveler" of the revolution who came on board at the last moment. Second, if the contents of the revolution championed by the "hard-liners" were not very precise, they did have a very clear vision of themselves as "authentic revolutionaries." Not surprisingly, they had all the features denied the "tie-wearing crooks," the "wily old foxes" of politics, or the technocrats, who had colonized or contaminated the incumbent authorities. They were fighters, idealists, men of practical experience. Here is how Osnelli Martinelli told the commander of the First Army (General Otacílio Ururahy, who was sympathetic to the colonels' cause) that he was standing down from the "Group of 11" IPM:

> We are accused of acting in line with political interests whereas our action is typically revolutionary, indifferent to names and parties. . . . From a political weapon we did not know how to use, the inquiries have turned before our eyes into new weapons of the revolution, sure as we are that the next [revolution] will be carried out by those who were spared by this one, and will shed blood—unlike that of 1 April. That is when the true democratic and revolutionary leaders will be revealed, forged in street fights or battles on the ground with no refuge in the apartments, cabinets and corridors of politics.[85]

The revolution had to "make a clean break" with the scourge of "petty politics."

CHANGING THE OLD TRADITION

Support for the coup d'état was largely generated by the notion of an imminent communist revolution although no left-wing force with national appeal had opted for armed action at that time. Demonstrations, strikes, the reforming ambitions of the labor government, and even avant-garde art and philosophy were interpreted as portents of revolution, if not its first phases. After 1964, this interpretation of what was happening in society allowed for great disparities in defining the enemy who had to be fought. The hard-line officers unsurprisingly opted for a very wide definition of the red peril, as permitted by AI-1, which was vague about the individuals liable to "revolutionary punishment." In this way, broad swathes of civil society and the political class were identified as subversive, although they had sometimes supported the coup in its early days.

This initial "Operation Cleanup" (Operação Limpeza) was regarded by these officers, who themselves often belonged to police squads, as the enabling condition and cornerstone of the "revolution." As a result, part of formulating their political thinking was guided by a single concern: to mete out punishment unimpeded, in other words, without constitutional guarantees for the accused. To this end, the colonels envisaged existing legislation as subordinate to the Institutional Act and, moreover, turned that subordination into a sign that the old order had been rejected and that a genuine revolutionary process therefore existed. From a May 1965 manifesto:

> The Constitution of 1946 is subordinate to the AI and not the other way around as suggested by the latest rulings from the STF. . . .
> The IPM investigators therefore continue to be vested with the authority bestowed upon them by AI Article 8 [which set up the inquiries] to promote all types of measures which seem indispensable to the pursuit of the inquiries, including imprisoning the accused, to whom constitutional guarantees do not apply.
> [As a result], by granting habeas corpus within the framework of the IPMs, the STF places itself outside the law and this distortion of the duly institutionalized revolutionary order should be urgently corrected.[86]

The comment was in part ad hoc, intended simply to pursue the purge process. Gradually, however, these legal arguments took on the form of a political alternative. "Extreme revolutionism" eclipsed the separation of powers since only the executive was the result of 31 March. The judiciary had no legitimacy and nor did the legislature, which suffered additionally from the officers' negative image of its members. The call to purge the political class did not relate solely to the UDN's historical adversaries (the Brazilian Labor Party and the Social Democratic Party): the profound contempt in which these officers held the political class as a whole led to the systematic denigration of elected officials and fueled the demand to close Congress, abolish political parties, and control elections.

The prospect of elections in eleven states of the federation in October 1965 and a presidential election a year later were obvious rallying calls for the radicals. Their main concerns were the "ineligibility" of undesirables, the postponement of the 1965 elections and indirect suffrage at all levels of the state. LIDER raised the issue in January 1965 when, according to its members, the government was allegedly so unpopular that it was impossible to hold elections that would favor "the return of ousted elements."[87] It recurred repeatedly until, in April 1965, the "hard line told its adherents what steps to take in the October elections" in a manifesto distributed in Congress by Deputy Costa Cavalcanti. The lack of time justified their position: "Voting in the state elections is approaching" and "the clever and persistent enemy is seeking to deceive the voter's good faith in order to restore the prerevolutionary status quo." The hard line only issued one instruction, in fact: to prevent "communist candidates, subversives of all kinds, the corrupt and their agents" being registered as election candidates. "Timely and robust action by the hard-line military, according to this instruction, is necessary since any compromise could jeopardize the revolutionary enterprise."[88]

All in all, the regime the hard-line officers wanted was a model authoritarian regime: an all-powerful executive with no Congress and no independent courts, police repression with no legal constraints regarding the rights of individuals, the abolition of political parties, and only a bare minimum of election procedures. The most uninhibited version of this wish list came once again from Colonel Martinelli, in a statement for the press, dated October 20, 1965:

> We do not accept what is. We are for closing Congress, a measure that should have been taken on the first day of the Revolution. We do not want to do away with it, of course, but the intention is, first of all, to clean up the space and only then to hold elections and all the rest. We are acting as the real revolutionaries we are. . . .
>
> As long as this state of affairs continues, we will oppose it. We repeat that it is

necessary, first of all, to clean up what is here. We will be against any antirevolutionary, from whatever party. We even think we should put an end to all the existing political parties, alter the election law and create new ones with other acronyms so that there is no trace of the current ones. After that, then yes, we will accept any candidate for any post.[89]

The main provisions of AI-2 match these manifesto demands word for word. It abolished existing parties, instituted indirect presidential elections, made civilian suspects of crimes "against national security or the military institutions" answerable to military justice, resumed the process of repealing mandates and withdrawing political rights, increased the opportunity for federal intervention in the individual states, and boosted the number of Federal Supreme Court justices (from eleven to sixteen) in order to take control of the court. The act was therefore the direct outcome of mobilization by the "hard line," the visible face of military protest. Furthermore, it was a meticulous and systematic assent to all hard-line demands drawn up since August 1964 at the political but not the economic level.

October 1965 was a tipping point. AI-2, adopted under pressure from the radical sectors under the auspices of the war minister, committed the government that resulted from the putsch to building a new regime. It was to be an authoritarian regime but not just any authoritarian regime. Framed by a succession of decrees that maintained part of the existing system and also made it tougher, it bore the clear hallmark of the "hard line's" repressive radicalism as well as that of the castelista authorities, keen to keep control of the "revolution" and to give it an institutional framework. It was to be a military regime but not just any military regime. However involved and enthusiastic the mass of officers, however broad their appeal in the barracks, or "revolutionary" their credentials, there was no political future for anyone outside the generals' circle.

This draft model was not the project of the so-called hard-line military, who were far-right activists, anticommunists, antigetulistas and often fanatical lacerdistas. They would have preferred a dictatorship in which they could play a central role and yet they made a massive contribution to bringing this profoundly hierarchical military and authoritarian regime into being and so to their own continuing political subordination. The position in the state apparatus, which they were granted by the "revolution," often at the forefront of the "cleanup operation" they regarded as unfinished, generated specific demands, of which AI-2 was the direct result. It is indisputable that the "first hard line" brought about this decisive authoritarian watershed in the history of the regime by voicing, indeed hammering home their plan in the public arena from mid-1964 onward. AI-2, however, launched the process of excluding the civilian political class from power and thereby increased the influence of the military, in which these "young officers" were far from the largest political force. The hierarchical structure and mindset, which the Castelo Branco government was set on enhancing and maintaining, tended to reduce the political stage to the generals' circle. Moreover and more important, the military protest had fanned the radicalism of the barracks and made them more of a threat, leading to the seesaw effect that produced the ambiguous figure of Costa e Silva, both a bulwark against "subversion of the hierarchy" and the protesting officers' candidate.

The protesting officers, whose political mourning for Lacerda was both lengthy and difficult, were unaware of all this at the end of 1965. They believed they could benefit from newly opened opportunities to increase their political space. If Costa e Silva could be a new leader, why could they themselves not be his entourage? For every right-wing activist, the militarization of the political game also enhanced each man's status as a high-flying officer, as well as his personal pride. They all had a very lofty notion of themselves at this level—with medals and claims to fame to prove it—and to them their political legitimacy in a "military regime" seemed obvious. The "first hard line's" failure to take power—which only became obvious a few years later—therefore has as its key moment this Pyrrhic victory of October 1965, which turned its "revolution against the political class" into the precursor of a "regime of the generals."

CHAPTER THREE

Consolidation and Divergences
1966–1968

> And each time it's required, like today, we will make new revolutions within the revolution!
> —GENERAL ARTUR DA COSTA E SILVA, PRESIDENT OF THE REPUBLIC

The promulgation of the Second Institutional Act (AI-2) on October 27, 1965, challenged the hypothesis of a quick, "surgical" revolution. The additional powers the act conferred on the executive took the regime ever-farther away from representative democracy but did not allow Castelo Branco to slow the irresistible ascent to the presidency of his war minister, General Costa e Silva. The latter was elected by Congress in October 1966 and sworn in on March 15, 1967. On December 13, 1968, three years after AI-2, history appeared to repeat itself. Following a political crisis born inside Congress itself and against a backdrop of serious popular protests against the authorities, a new "Revolutionary Act" was adopted under the pressure of alleged "ferment in the barracks." This was the Fifth Institutional Act (AI-5). The latest "coup within the coup," as AI-5 was customarily known, completed the regime's authoritarian evolution and ushered in the Years of Lead.

As with AI-2, historiography has deemed the "barracks" and the "hard line" responsible for the regime's shift into authoritarianism. Although the new president, Costa e Silva, did not have Castelo Branco's partly affected air of moderation and legalism, most witnesses and participants agree that officers of all ranks applied pressure to have Congress shut down and AI-5 adopted. The political dynamics of this military coercion remain partially obscured, however. In particular, they do not sit well with the depiction of a dichotomy

From March to June 1968, student demonstrations denounced the dictatorship and made fun of the military. On the banner, next to the drawing of the military policeman, is written "More schools, fewer barracks." São Paulo, April 4, 1968. Estadão Conteúdo Archives.

within the intramilitary political space, which saw only the "hard-liners" in major positions of power after March 1967. If this second term enshrined the victory of an undifferentiated "hard line" that favored adopting ever-more advanced exceptional instruments, what power struggles and types of pressure must it have taken to pass AI-5?

In reality, intramilitary politics in the period 1966–68 were more complex than this. Certainly 1966 saw the end of the collision course between a government that showed strong signs of civilianism plus a degree of respect for legality and an "antiestablishment nexus" of middle-ranking officers who were long-term conspirators, protected from punishment by their status as "revolutionaries." "Their" candidate, Costa e Silva, was elected and then took power. In their eyes, "the revolution was being repeated." Moreover, many of them were brought into the apparatus of the state or returned to key prestigious commands, satisfying their sense of responsibility for the "revolution's" second government just as they had felt responsible for the coup itself. At the same time, however, their political legitimacy shrank. The post-coup disorder was becoming a thing of the past, and with it the recollection of their significance in the conspiracy. Furthermore, the strictly military rationale behind the succession brought the rules and precepts of the army institution—hierarchy, discipline, precedence—into the political game. The attempt to depoliticize middle-ranking officers, undertaken by Castelo Branco in line with a distorted ideal of civilianism, legalism, and the "professional army," was maintained by the new government within the new framework of an overtly military regime. Without the representation provided by the generation of colonels, the "opinion of the barracks" paradoxically became a constant but elusive point of reference, to which all players laid claim to justify their own demands.

However, the "hard line" of the colonels did not give way to a "hard line" of generals, claiming to represent the radicalized "opinion of the barracks." While the military elite grew in visibility and political influence, organized actors pursuing their own agenda remained or emerged: the "first hard line," which lived on behind the scenes; the developing agencies of political repression; right-wing paramilitary and terrorist groups; and the captains' generation. Analysis of this complex political game, obscured in historiography by the standardization inherent in the concept of a single "hard line," should make it possible to understand three determining features of the regime's development: the construction of a military consensus around the authoritarian shift of AI-5 of December 1968; the persistence of and changes in the "barracks' protest," which rocked the government in 1969 when AI-5 appeared to have met all radical demands; and once the protest had been quashed, the definitive establishment of a "generals' regime."

A CIVIL–MILITARY CAMPAIGN

After the serious protests at the end of 1965, 1966 was noted for apparent calm in the military. United behind Costa e Silva's nomination, the one-time protestors bided their time in silence. Backing for the war minister was strictly military in the beginning. Moreover, the resistance mounted by Castelo Branco was essentially due to the change in the political base Costa e Silva's candidacy would entail for the government, rather than to the personality of the minister himself—he was a long-standing comrade—or his less liberal inclinations. This is attested by the president in a document distributed to army generals in January 1966, "Aspects of the Presidential Succession." He believed Costa e Silva had been nominated by "certain radical elements in the army" ("some call themselves Hard Liners, others lean towards dictatorship, still others are linked to discontented political circles"), which "wish to hasten succession procedures even if it splits the Armed Forces."[1] To reassert his presidential authority in the army generals' eyes, Castelo Branco let it be known that the succession remained open despite the pressure from the barracks that, he said, "makes me determined not to give in, not to be discouraged, and to be always worthy of my office. I will do all I can not to be a president under pressure, no matter where those pressures come from." Once again he denied the armed forces the legitimacy of an electorate, but that legitimacy now no longer came from the "people" or the "nation" either, as had been the case in speeches during the post-coup months. Now the government relied on (and gained legitimacy from) a majority party, the National Renewal Alliance (Aliança Renovadora Nacional, ARENA), set up under AI-2 and brought into an electoral system that worked hugely in its favor thanks to indirect suffrage, and to the loss of political rights and suspensions of office, which decimated the opposition.

These subtleties concealed the fact that the process of institutionalizing the revolution, a constant theme for Castelo Branco since the early days of the regime, was taking a new tack. To the president's way of thinking, the use of force and measures of exception or even the complete militarization of the machinery of state were not the only way to ensure that the conservative group victorious in April 1964 remained in power and that its "authoritarian modernization" continued. He longed to build a genuine "authoritarian democracy" shored up by a dominant executive and a "revolutionary party."

During Castelo Branco's final months in office, he and his entourage came in for two highly contradictory criticisms from officers eager to see him replaced by his minister. On the one hand, they were portrayed as an ambitious faction hungry for potentially dictatorial power and, on the other, a gaggle of "pseudo-revolutionaries" brimful of legalist and pro-civilian prejudices. This representation of the government as intrinsically usurping power because of its faithful adherence to prerevolutionary thinking (to "petty politics" and all this implied to the military far Right about compromise, personal ambitions, and the absence of an ideal) was mirrored in the banner Costa e Silva opted to raise over his own candidacy, which was to be authentically revolutionary *and* establish fully fledged democracy in Brazil. As a political communication strategy, this was astonishing to say the least. The strong man, the hard-liner, the leader of his troops, unswerving as to the objectives of the "revolution," now combined his image and his speeches with liberal flourishes and promises of immaculate democracy. Indeed, the general's campaign statements were miracles of ambiguity, blending the appearances of democratic continuity with the expectations of the radical officers who constituted his chief political base.[2] It is hard to find any real consistency. What especially mattered was leaving the door open to all expectations, civilian or military, and avoiding open warfare with the presidency. It was partly to this end also that the war minister sought to disguise a candidacy that had been prompted by the barracks as the decision of the majority party, ARENA.

The military leader mounted a civilian campaign, albeit discreetly since it was not aimed at public opinion, and his political statements were restricted until July 1966 by his position in the hierarchy and his role in government. When he finally left office, he already had the backing of most state branches of ARENA. A few days later the need for popular support became less urgent when the Brazilian Democratic Movement (or MDB, the official opposition party, which also came into being in October 1965) decided not to put forward a candidate on the grounds that the election was unfair. The supreme irony and embarrassment was that the MDB ultimately supported the minister's candidacy in the hope that he would keep his endlessly reiterated promises of the "humanization of the revolution" and of "redemocratization."[3]

In presenting himself as the ARENA candidate, Costa e Silva became part of the institutionalized political system Castelo Branco wanted. His lengthy term as war minister and the way in which he became a candidate, meanwhile, clearly identified him as a military leader. The castelista attempt at the "institutionalization of the revolution," together with the imposition of a general by armed forces consensus, inaugurated a new political custom: the intramilitary selection of would-be successors according to an equilibrium that fluctuated between political leadership and hierarchical legitimacy, which was supported by a sham democracy reliant on a majority party subject to the whims of the Presidential Palace.

MILITARIZATION OF GOVERNMENT AND LACK OF POLITICAL DEFINITION

Behind General Costa e Silva's "election campaign" lay the desire to give new direction to Castelo Branco's policies. Far from balking at the new authoritarian instruments for which historiography and collective memory hold the hard-line officers solely responsible, the castelista government exploited them eagerly to put down dissent and to gag Congress. From April 1966 onward, it applied the powers to suspend mandates and political rights (the "cassação") permitted by AI-2. The offensive met with resistance from the Chamber of Deputies in October 1966, when its chairman, Adauto Lúcio Cardoso (ARENA), refused to recognize the cassação of six members of parliament. Congress was then suspended and troops under the tough leadership of Colonel Meira Mattos were sent to surround it in a bid to dislodge the intractable members. At the same time, AI-2 inaugurated an unprecedented phase of legislative business, culminating at the very end of the castelista mandate in the Press Law (Law no. 5250, February 9, 1967), the National Security Law (Decree-law no. 314, March 11, 1967), and a new constitution. These reforms ran up the authoritarian colors of the political system and led to growing democratic opposition to the president, while the pursuit of economic and financial austerity and the fight against inflation triggered discontent in various social groups. As a result, the political class and social elites that had supported the coup were far from associating President Castelo Branco with the legalist moderation historiography has attributed to him a posteriori.[4] Accusations of "continuism" and dictatorial ambitions, bizarrely brandished by the "hard-line" officers, became commonplace. At the beginning of January 1967, shortly after the new constitution was adopted, ex-president João Goulart announced from exile in Uruguay that he was afraid General Costa e Silva would never take office despite having been elected and that Castelo Branco would mount a coup to hold on to his position.[5]

On October 3, 1966, the 294 ARENA deputies in the National Congress elected Costa e Silva on their own since the MDB had abandoned the chamber. In the months prior to his inauguration, which was set for March 15, 1967, the political debate centered on quite different issues to the confrontation that opposed a moderate castelista presidency—in a hurry to restore power to civilians—and the militaristic and authoritarian "hard line" associated with Costa e Silva. There was, in fact, great uncertainty about the new authorities' intentions and this continued throughout 1967. In February, the announcement of the new government's composition was an early warning signal to the disparate front, whose contradictory hopes centered on the new term of office. The majority of the chosen team was military. It numbered eight serving officers and two from the reserve, six civilian technicians, and three politicians, making ten out of nineteen from the military. By comparison, only six of the sixteen initial members of the Castelo Branco government were officers. Journalist Carlos Castello Branco put it like this: "The future government, which, in taking office, had to meet the expectations of those advocating civilianism, armed itself like an army, its columns entrusted to the command of general officers or ranking colonels."[6]

In addition to its militarism, the government brought together established figures from the military "hard line," whether or not they had demonstrated opposition to Castelo Branco. Admiral Augusto Rademaker, one of the five radical "Dionnes," punished for supporting the IMP colonels in July 1965, became navy minister. At the Air Force Ministry there was Air Marshal Márcio de Souza e Mello, another serving officer, identified with the military far Right despite never having expressed his opinions publicly. General Jayme Portella de Mello, one of the president's closest advisers and a committed radical, was appointed head of the Military Cabinet while General Emílio Garrastazu Médici, another uncompromising revolutionary and a future general-president in the "Years of Lead," headed up the National Intelligence Service. Reserve Colonel José Costa Cavalcanti, the brother of Francisco Boaventura Cavalcanti and the Congress spokesman of the "first hard line" under Castelo Branco, was given the sensitive post of mines and energy minister, which played a key role in the economic debates over the ownership of the nation's land and minerals.

It was the new interior minister, General Afonso de Albuquerque Lima, however, who primarily symbolized the entry of the "hard-line" protestors to the corridors of power. Architect of the abortive and rather preposterous uprising of October 1965, he was favored as much by the "first hard line" as by officers associated solely with economic nationalism, as well as the famous ex-tenentes he had mixed with in the 1930s. His swearing-in ceremony was attended by hard-line leaders Sílvio Heck, Osnelli Martinelli, Rafael de Almeida Magalhães, who championed radical positions in Congress, General Justino Alves Bastos, a long-standing supporter of economic nationalism, and Marshal Juarez Távora, a celebrated veteran of the lieutenants' movement and Castelo Branco's one-time transport minister.[7] Albuquerque Lima's networks were in fact the result of a particular professional and political career and were not confined to the conspiracy nexus that became the "first hard line" in 1964. Born in 1909, the son of a Ceará dignitary from a generation between the tenentes (1900) and the hard-line colonels (1920), he entered the Realengo Academy in 1927 where, as a pupil, he became a follower of tenentismo and the friend of some of its leaders. As a very young lieutenant, he joined the 3 October Club (Vargas's shadow cabinet, made up of former tenentes who initially had considerable influence) and took part in building the revolutionary state until the 1937 coup, which he opposed. His subsequent career was very similar to the castelista profile. In 1944, he attended a training course at the U.S. Army Engineer School at Fort Belvoir, Virginia, and then fought in the

Second World War as a major. Opposed to the Estado Novo from its inception, he supported the overthrow of Vargas in 1945 and went on to oppose his return. Despite the virulent anticommunism and antigetulismo that were typical of his military camp, Albuquerque Lima himself championed nationalist economic positions from the end of the 1950s. In 1960, he even gave a series of courses on economic development problems, promoted by CEPAL (the United Nations Economic Commission for Latin America and the Caribbean, tasked with furthering the region's industrial development). Also at that time, he was involved in setting up SUDENE (the Superintendency for the Development of the Northeast or Superintendência do Desenvolvimento do Nordeste, a government agency created under Kubitschek), which was run by the Keynesian economist Celso Furtado.

At the same time, the new government was evincing good will toward the younger officers of the "first hard line" in its transfer policy. Colonel Francisco Boaventura, "exiled" to the State of Mato Grosso in the Amazon because of his tendencies toward rebellion in October 1965 and his public demonstration in November, was given the prestigious command of the São João Fortress at the foot of Sugarloaf Mountain in Rio de Janeiro. Colonel Florimar Campelo, former head of the Intelligence Section of the First Army General Staff and a noted radical, became director-general of the Federal Police Department. As for the somewhat older General Mourão Filho, already a member of the MDB at this stage, he was promoted to head the Superior Military Court, where he was already on the bench, thus boosting his authority within a setting to which dissidents were relegated with honor. Conferring an important office on the early protesters could, however, be a double-edged sword. Colonel Osnelli Martinelli, for example, was tasked in April 1967 with combating coffee smuggling within the Brazilian Coffee Institute (Instituto Brasileiro do Café, IBC), which had caused a scandal under Castelo Branco. He was pleased with the appointment, regarding it as of the utmost significance, and in an interview recounted a brief meeting with the president who was keen to see "the hard line working" in the sector. Martinelli was never brought into the IBC, however, despite repeated promises, and he interpreted this as the inability of a "fine, upstanding" president to withstand the corrupt forces holding sway over Brazilian politics.[8] In fact, it is hard to see the appointment as anything other than his being sidelined.

In addition, the composition of the government bore witness to more complex political balances than merely including the "hard line." The Army Ministry (previously known as the War Ministry) had as its new head General Aurélio de Lira Tavares, who himself was considered a member of the military Sorbonne or had at least been identified as such in 1967. His crucial role in the hardening of the regime at the end of 1968 and during the succession to Costa e Silva in September 1969 makes it difficult to see what this castelista affiliation might have meant in terms of political moderation. Many ministers, reserve officers, and civilians belonged to no far-right factions and showed no trace of far-right politics. If a form of "authoritarian nationalism" came into government with Costa e Silva, it was neither predominant nor uniform in its links to the "first hard line" and military activism. Aggressive nationalism was essentially the preserve of two ministers, General Afonso de Albuquerque Lima and Colonel José Cavalcanti, who had the closest personal ties to the high-profile protesters of 1964–65. Last, the groups within the government were not fixed. Even more than in the wake of the coup, the great uncertainty about the future of the regime and the immense political confusion of March 1967–April 1968 led to officer factions being constantly reconstituted, turning politics in the military institution into an experimental laboratory.

FROM "HARD LINE" TO ORTHODOX

All political players, civilian and military, negotiated their support for the new authorities during the early months of Costa e Silva's presidency. Until May 1967, the MDB assured the head of state of its support in completing the redemocratization process. From April onward, there were rumors of a judicial review of revolutionary punishments or even a political amnesty, a measure backed by the MDB, a few dissident officers and some of ARENA. The presidency remained silent, leaving it to Army Minister Lira Tavares to issue a memorandum to the troop commands, which refuted the rumor.[9] Other general officers came together to reject the move, from Moniz de Aragão to Mourão Filho, despite the latter being an MDB member. The possibility that those who had been expelled might return marked a fault line between the civilians and the military who had united behind Costa e Silva.

During this period, generals were the only officers visible to the public, with commander of the First Infantry Division of the Vila Militar Carvalho Lisbôa, commander of the First Army Siseno Sarmento, and head of the Army Education Department Moniz de Aragão to the fore. The colonels had virtually disappeared from the public stage. The most famous figures in military protest spoke out initially only to shower the new authorities with praise. Colonel

Boaventura, for instance, leaked his speech to the press on the occasion of his taking command of the São João Fortress at the end of May 1967. In it, he defended the fact that the new president would have to lead a revival of the revolution and condemned "the defeated forces of the old regime and their allies [who] are accusing the Armed Forces of usurping power and, on the pretext of a false redemocratization and pacification, are applying pressure or scheming for the return to the national political stage of those to blame for disorder, corruption and subversion" (after the election, there were rumors of the imminent return from exile of former presidents Juscelino Kubitschek and João Goulart). Clearly supportive of the incumbent authorities, he went on to challenge accusations leveled at the government of a militarism running counter to the "democratic tradition of the Armed Forces."[10] Boaventura was speaking as the spokesman of the military institution, which, through him, endorsed the authorities. His comments had a great influence, which was astonishing given his rank. Indeed, his speech was praised at a meeting of the Army High Command (ACE) a few days later, as well as by ARENA senators.

And yet this was the calm before the storm. The following day hard-line colonels issued an anonymous statement of support for the government but wanted it to "get started." They considered it their responsibility to support the authorities they believed they had helped to install, and to ensure calm in the barracks to allow its policies to bed down. At the same time, they feared that a "disarmament mindset" might lead to the exercise of power becoming routine, and thus no longer revolutionary and combative in spirit.[11] From that date on, some of the radical colonels most closely linked to Boaventura launched a campaign to claim power. One of the most high-profile was Rui Castro. Director of the Army Library, where he had scant military influence but greater freedom of expression and more free time, he disputed the very principle of an apolitical military. "The notion of the military consigned to silence is a thing of the past," he said a few days later.[12] In July 1967, he became the first colonel to embrace "hard-line dissidence" publicly.

He was not alone in the positions he adopted. As of the end of June 1967, barely a month after assuring the government of his full support, Boaventura sought an audience with Army Minister Lira Tavares to protest against obstacles to the "hard line's" involvement in politics. In doing so, he rid himself of his hierarchical middlemen, demanding direct access to the president and accusing his immediate superiors of betraying his ideas, even as he acknowledged the ministry's authority. This was embryonic dissidence rather than outright opposition, as previously demonstrated by Boaventura's customary practice of public manifestos published in the press.

The authorities were quick to respond even so. At the end of July 1967, the army minister issued an internal memorandum banning the military from sending individual or collective documents to the government authorities without going through hierarchical channels. Boaventura responded on behalf of the "hard-line colonels" (no longer on behalf of the whole of the armed forces as had been the case a few weeks earlier), by questioning his comrades' enduring submission to Army Disciplinary Regulations. He indicated that the colonels were now ready to assume the tasks of a government for which they believed themselves responsible.[13] This was nothing new, of course. Since 1964, the "hard-line" protesters had constantly presented themselves as responsible for the revolution and the authorities resulting from it. Now, however, they laid greater emphasis on themselves as a generation of colonels, taking up position against the generals in power. The universe of legitimate political players had been reduced to the military world.

In addition, the colonels altered their discourse. They no longer presented themselves as long-standing revolutionaries and followers of Carlos Lacerda but as officers entitled, whatever their rank, to support or to criticize the policies of the increasingly militarized "second government of the revolution." This is attested by a questionnaire distributed a few months later at the Vila Militar, at the instigation of hard-line officers who remained anonymous:

> Comrade in the Navy, Army or Air Force in every post and every rank in all four corners of Brazil: have you already realized the immeasurable responsibility that weighs upon each of us military personnel, and on the Armed Forces as an institution, to Brazilian public opinion and to History for the success or failure of the Second Government of the Revolution, which we all brought to Power [*sic*] by united and coherent action and to which we have confidently entrusted the fate of the Nation?
>
> We are all jointly responsible, and if the ship goes down, will it not damage the prestige of the Armed Forces beyond repair?"

The "responsibility" of the officer corps was collective. It was the responsibility of military personnel, not of revolutionary activists. The questionnaire implicitly encouraged the reader to be critical of the authorities while respecting the chain of command and "to forward [his] view via [his] superiors": "Are you happy with the Second Government of the Revolution? If not, in what do you think it is deficient? (authority, morality, competence, dynamism, imagination, etc.)." "Comrade, You must make the general atmosphere of apprehension that prevails among the people your own. It is not normal to stand idly by. Offer your superiors your sincere and timely cooperation. In this way, if in the future the ship was likely to sink, you would be forced to go down with it."[14] Under the guise of an opinion poll, the manifesto took up some of the favorite themes of the military opposition to Castelo Branco. It insinuated that the president's entourage was corrupt, an accusation that was still low key in 1967 but that blossomed over the next two years. It challenged the government's economic choices although not in great detail and denounced the moderate repression that would leave the door open for the vanquished to return, all set to launch an attack on the authorities. Four days before the questionnaire was released in the press, Colonel Gérson de Pina and Colonel Ferdinando de Carvalho, heads of the ISEB and Communist Party IPMs respectively in 1964–65, publicly voiced their disappointment about the outcomes of the political inquiries that they felt had not enabled punishment of the real culprits.

Among the recurrent subjects of radical dissatisfaction, the government's lack of "economic nationalism" was the one that first rallied the colonels associated with Francisco Boaventura. They began to call themselves "orthodox" rather than "hard-liners," a term they claimed had been perverted by officers who had taken government office—especially Boaventura's own brother, mines and energy minister José Cavalcanti, with whom the former was at odds. Against the background of this family quarrel, the orthodox decided to accompany their move into dissent with a stunt organized by Boaventura. In July 1967, Boaventura, Colonel Amerino Raposo Filho, and Colonel Hélio Lemos taunted Finance Minister Antônio Delfim Netto in his own office, accusing him of retaining the previous government's economic approach. The protesters were quickly defeated in the ensuing show of strength. Under the guidance of General Jayme Portella, head of the Military Cabinet, the government mounted a new operation to disperse and punish the "first hard line," reborn from its ashes. In September, the network linked to Boaventura was scattered across the country. He himself had to leave Brazil as part of a national delegation to the United Nations, while Hélio Lemos also went on a "mission" abroad, leaving the General Staff of the powerful and prestigious Atlantic Coast Artillery. Rui Castro abandoned the Army Library in Rio de Janeiro for a unit in Ijui on Brazil's southern border. Amerino Raposo Filho was removed

```
            ESCOLA  SUPERIOR  DE  GUERRA
               (SUPERIOR WAR SCHOOL)

                  BIOGRAPHICAL DATA

   1.  NAME        FRANCISCO BOAVENTURA CAVALCANTI JUNIOR
   2.  RANK OR TITLE         COLONEL
   3.  SERVICE  ARMY - ARTILLERY    4.  DATE OF RANK  25 AUG 66
   5.  PRESENT POSITION    STUDENT - SUPERIOR WAR COURSE
   6.  DATE AND PLACE OF BIRTH  15 APRIL 1919 - CEARÁ, FORTALEZA
   7.  NAME OF WIFE   MARIA AMÁLIA JANSEN FIGUEIREDO CAVALCANTI
   8.  NUMBER OF CHILDREN    TWO
   9.  NAME OF FATHER       FRANCISCO BOAVENTURA CAVALCANTI
```

Information Report on Colonel Francisco Boaventura in the U.S. Department of State Archives, as an Escola Superior de Guerra graduate. U.S. Department of State Archives.

from the SNI but not given a troop command. He became chief of staff to General Mamede at the Department of Production and Construction before being delegated to the Inter-American Defense College in Washington, DC, a year later. Luis Alencar Araripe was transferred to a remote region in Paraná while Ferdinando de Carvalho, still head of the Communist Party IPM, was removed from that post once and for all and took command of a Reserve Officer Training Centre (CPOR) in Curitiba.

The high-profile protesters in these early months of the *costista* presidency were serving colonels with outstanding careers rather than the "conspiracy professionals" who had once flourished in LIDER. Their proximity to the barracks prompted them to emphasize the collective political legitimacy of serving military personnel rather than that of long-term conspirators and activists as had often been the case immediately after the coup. In addition, they played on this semidissident status and on their "professional" military identity in their protests. Most of their demands were conveyed through the chain of command and we usually have only echoes and rumors of the contents, making it difficult to determine their political plan. Fragmentary sources allow us a glimpse of bitter, disillusioned officers, their anticivilianism radicalized by the ousting of Lacerda, calling for a total political overhaul that was never explicitly defined.

The reforms some colonels began to champion at the beginning of 1968 when their political marginalization was complete are evidence of the interweaving of frustrated personal ambitions and a "revolutionary mystique" in search of new supporters. In March 1968, Colonel Rui Castro stated that nothing was more like the Goulart government than that of Costa e Silva, with the difference that, in the past, it was the sergeants who lacked discipline whereas now it was the officers.[15] Then came something new. Colonel Castro demanded that a hard-line member of the military or a civilian at a maximum age of forty-five years (which would rule out Lacerda, born in 1914) should be put forward to run in the 1970 presidential election. His statement, which earned him five days of disciplinary incarceration, was the first step in the radical dissent of some of the "first hard line."[16]

THE END OF MILITARY LACERDISM

The first year of Costa e Silva's mandate did not then correspond to the coming to power of the "first hard line" nor to the imposition of the policies that those "hard-liners" wanted. On the contrary, the government, without revoking any of Castelo Branco's authoritarian measures of 1966 and 1967, adopted a wait-and-see attitude and continued its predecessor's approaches to the economy and finance. The older conservative officers who held ministerial posts expressed no solidarity with the young generation of activists, which was systematically repressed, remained very low key, and, for the moment, little feared by the authorities. It was Lacerda's revolutionary dissent that troubled the Costa e Silva government most. Loquacious and provocative as was his wont, Lacerda occupied the space of an increasingly "democratic" protest, even as he retained his previous political repertoire, which he shared with the youngest "hard-line" officers who had long been his disciples.

Lacerda's political reorientation distanced him from the radical young officers, without detaching him completely or for good. The ex-governor of Guanabara, skilled in setting the agenda of political debate, was also a networker who strove to build bridges between sectors the government would have liked to pit against one another. Taking the "anticastelista front" of 1966 and the beginning of 1967 as his model, Lacerda set about rallying everyone willing to his "Broad Front" (Frente Ampla) project, a widely based political coalition open to everyone from MDB politicians to dissident generals, including the young and hesitant "hard line" he was constantly reminding of his existence. In doing so, Lacerda helped weaken the ideological boundaries. He also, however, revealed latent affinities with nationalist issues and with the condemnation of a power regarded to be in moral free-fall.

Lacerda's electoral and political ambitions had been substantially damaged by the Second Institutional Act's introduction of a two-party system at the end of 1965. The disappearance of the UDN cost him his place as a presidential candidate. ARENA, which included former members of the Social Democratic Party (center-right getulista, won over to the military), was beyond his control. Moreover, since the early months of 1966, ARENA had supported the "opinion of the barracks" and backed the war minister's candidacy. Lacerda set about forming a third movement in defiance of AI-2, the Democratic Renewal Party (Partido da Renovação Democrático, or Parede, meaning "wall" in Portuguese). Without support, however, the enterprise failed. As a permanent opponent of the incumbent authorities for nearly two decades, he had no intention of joining the yes-men's party, ARENA, where he would lose his special status as a systematic opponent and be compromised by association with the "foxes of the PSD," so much decried by the protesting young officers.

Above all, therefore, the Frente Ampla, which he began to organize in mid-1966, was a tool for political survival. It came into being on October 28, 1966, a few weeks after the presidential elections, solely thanks to Lacerda, who wrote a manifesto calling for free and direct elections, the reform of political parties and institutions, the resumption of economic development, and the adoption of a sovereign foreign policy. Lacerda's strategy was to attract national figures who had been removed from power in order to develop a powerful political alternative. From its inception, the "meeting of leaders" was rooted in opposition thinking and networks. The Frente took off with the "Declaration of Lisbon" of November 19, 1966, signed jointly by Lacerda and Juscelino Kubitschek, despite the former having stripped the latter of his political rights only eighteen months before.

Since August 1966, moreover, Lacerda had supported two dissident generals, Amaury Kruel and Taurino de Rezende, who had joined the MDB in protest over the distortion of the "Revolution." At the time, he had leaked a manifesto in which he condemned the authorities' militarism not to champion civil democracy but because the situation was damaging the armed forces themselves, "abandoned by the Castelo Branco government, a militarist government opposed to the military, at whose expense it was installed, and favoring the defaulters and opportunists for whose benefit it endures." This apparent rejection of a military government prevented Lacerda from backing Costa e Silva since, he said, "I do not believe a change of general is so important for Brazil." Lacerda did not, however, disown the "31 March Movement": "An opposition must be built, which *favors* the revolution Castelo has led astray, a revolution betrayed or misunderstood by those who, in their dotage, deny the sacrifices of youth."[17]

These fine speeches could not, however, prevent a split from the military Right. The Lisbon Pact, signed in November 1966 (a few days after Costa e Silva's "election"), which targeted the abhorrent "return of the vanquished," was one breaking point. General Mourão Filho, despite being just as much a dissident, refused to accept it. The colonels backed off. For some time, however, Lacerda walked a fine line between crying out for a return to civilian democracy and discreet nods to the "first hard line," particularly by brandishing his preference for economic nationalism.

As head of the Frente Ampla at the beginning of Costa e Silva's term, Carlos Lacerda initially adopted the same wait-and-see stance as the colonels. He was a critic, but nonetheless interested in potential government office although this was speedily ruled out by the new general-president. He took advantage of the authorities' lack of political definition and a temporary halt in discussions of the purge, repression, and the regime's institutional development to increase his own room to speak out. He indulged in particular in economic and financial criticism of the incumbent government that had "sold out to foreigners." He was sufficiently vague in doing so that the contradictions between his own positions and the industrialist ideals of most of the military remained under wraps. His gradual break with Costa e Silva's presidency began in June 1967, coinciding with the "hard-line" colonels' first acts of dissent. At the time, the Frente Ampla was putting forward only nationalist demands, while the institutional issue ("measures of exception" as much as the militarization of the authorities) was not discussed.

The unease between Lacerda and his erstwhile followers in the officer corps had been palpable since the creation of the Frente. Events in August 1967 hastened the split. On July 18, 1967, Marshal Castelo Branco died in a plane crash in his home state of Ceará. The following day, Lacerda's friend, the journalist Hélio Fernandes, editor of the newspaper *A Tribuna da Imprensa*, previously a long-standing official mouthpiece of lacerdismo, wrote an editorial that was violently opposed to the legacy and person of the first general-president, describing him as "a cold, pitiless, vindictive, inhuman, calculating, resentful, cruel, and frustrated man, without greatness, without nobility, dry inside and out, his heart a veritable Sahara desert."[18] This onslaught on the memory of Castelo Branco earned him an IPM, immediate imprisonment on

Fernando de Noronha island, and the outrage of all military personnel then voicing their opinions in public, irrespective of faction. Hélio Fernandes, who had opposed João Goulart and backed the coup d'état, had been highly suspicious of the new regime from the outset. His articles constantly denounced the "denationalization" of the Brazilian economy orchestrated by Castelo Branco. The provocative tone of his writings earned him the small matter of twenty-seven lawsuits in the immediate post-coup period alone. Over the course of 1966, he grew closer to the MDB and in November his political rights were suspended for ten years. Banned from the press, he continued writing under a pseudonym and kept up his attacks, always promoting nationalism, during Costa e Silva's term of office.

In July 1967, Carlos Lacerda took his fellow journalist's part, dubbing him "the knight protector of nationalism" under a Castelo Branco government "distinguished by foreign penetration into the national economy." He declared that the "international groups led by ex-minister Roberto Campos" were now attempting to blind Costa e Silva in turn and to silence Hélio Fernandes.[19] For Lacerda, pretending to interpret Fernandes's arrest as an antinationalist act thought up by stateless business circles and for which the armed forces bore no responsibility was a means to avoid alienating "military opinion" in its entirety. When he visited Fernandes, who was then ten days into his sentence, Lacerda declared that, unlike a poorly identified "elite," the officer corps was not angry with the journalist. As evidence, he cited the good conditions in which he was being held and the lack of maltreatment. It was a tortuous strategy. Lacerda implied that torture existed in the regime's prisons and so strengthened his position within the civilian opposition but freed ranking officers from any responsibility in order to win their favor also. General Moniz de Aragão (a friend of Castelo Branco but very well regarded by the radical officers) was the first to criticize Lacerda's campaign on behalf of the armed forces and through him those whom Castelo Branco had condemned as the "serving wenches of the barracks": "demagogues" and "subversive journalists," "politicians," and "frustrated rulers." He reiterated the order given them in the same paper on the eve of the coup to "get their hands off the Armed Forces."[20] Lacerda was drawn in caricature as an amoral and manipulative civilian, the enemy of the military, and, worse still, indifferent to their honor. In the same newspaper a few days later, Admiral Sílvio Heck delivered the coup de grâce, saying that his supporters were disillusioned: "Will Brazil be held responsible if the ex-governor of Guanabara no longer persuades anyone with his verbal trickery and if, with each passing day, he alienates a greater number of admirers who were once elated by his earlier campaigns to promote morality in public life and the union of the Armed Forces?"[21]

Lacerda may perhaps have consoled himself with the fact that August 1967 was not a good time for his strategy. The first conference of the Latin American Solidarity Organization (OLAS), which brought together various of the subcontinent's revolutionary and anti-imperialist movements in Havana, revived the military's fear of the "international communist movement" and left less political space for the disparate front Lacerda wanted to create, which included alleged "subversives." At the same time, the first armed actions by Brazilian left-wing groups were highlighted by some officers, quick to point out objective signs of revolutionary war in the country. This was true in the case of the Caparaó Guerrilla group, promoted by the Nationalist Revolutionary Movement (Movimento Nacionalista Revolucionário, primarily made up of former military personnel, recently dismissed from the armed forces), in the mountains between Minas Gerais and Espírito Santo and disbanded by the Military Police in April 1967.

The second half of 1967 therefore saw a growing gap between the military and civilian elites, while the return of the "subversive peril" was already obscuring the nationalist issues that had been predominant since the start of Costa e Silva's mandate. Carlos Lacerda dealt himself the coup de grâce that cost him his popularity with the radical military youth when he signed the "Montevideo Pact" at the end of September 1967, together with former president João Goulart in exile in the Uruguayan capital. The agreement had been envisaged by Lacerda since the inception of the Frente Ampla, but Goulart had initially put up understandable resistance given that the ex-governor of Guanabara had been a major factor in the media and political destabilization of his government. The pact championed the redemocratization of Brazil and declared the workers to be the first victims of the regime's oppression. The main political demand was a return to direct elections, a point of convergence between Lacerda and the institutional Left since 1965, while the call for "fairer pay" to enable expansion of the domestic market was the common denominator at the economic and social level.

The immediate outcome of the Montevideo agreement was that Lacerda's former followers in the armed forces rejected him outright. Some self-proclaimed "hard-line" officers, acknowledging that "the Revolution had been ungrateful to the ex-Governor" initially hoped he would backtrack and be redeemed, although "if Lacerda continues on that path and does not change his behavior, he will be on his own. The hard line cannot accept him identifying with the past. We have a philosophy and we will not change our principles. We will not merge with what was ousted by the Revolution."[22] A posteriori, the officers of the "first hard line" regarded the agreement as the point of definitive disillusion, as of which "Lacerda ceased to be lacerdista." Lacerda recalled this bitterly a few years later: "In the early days of the Frente Ampla I lost nearly all my friends and political support. The early days were like the time I broke with the communists, especially the fanatics. The more fanatical someone was about me, the more he was disappointed. If someone backed me rationally because our points of view coincided, he at least made an effort to understand. He at least didn't think I'd gone crazy or committed a betrayal. But the so-called chronic, fanatical lacerdistas, they were really outraged."[23] Lacerda did not immediately abandon his charm offensives or the other media stunts that epitomized his way of doing politics. In addition, the criticisms he continued to level at the authorities (accusations of corruption, connivance with the oligarchy, and the government's "America-maniac" tendencies) retained the flavor that had long attracted the military "hard line." The strategy failed. Worse still, the former governor's erstwhile allies became his most virulent detractors. In February 1968, Francisco Boaventura and Hélio Lemos, members of the "first hard line" who had recently been renamed "orthodox," publicly proclaimed that eliminating the Frente Ampla was a priority political objective. It must be said that, in addition to selling his soul to the devil in the Lisbon and Montevideo pacts, Lacerda had castigated the regime as "militarist" or "standing to attention" and had described the "force of bayonets" as the main protector of the corrupt and the "armed forces" as a whole as traitors to the revolution, which was more than enough to confound even those who until then had been his most ardent admirers.

Increasingly labeled an enemy of the military and the regime rather than just the government, Lacerda took up a stance that finally cost him all support in the barracks in March 1968. Brazil's big cities were experiencing growing student disturbances at the time, inspired by the start of protests in Europe. On March 28, 1968, Edson Luis, a school student only eighteen years old, was killed by the Military Police during a demonstration against increased prices in a university restaurant. The killing generated an emotional public response and Lacerda sought to become its mouthpiece through the press. On April 3, a Frente Ampla manifesto was read out in the Guanabara Legislative

Assembly, to which students had brought the boy's body several days earlier. The penalty, adopted under pressure from the "hard-liners," was not long in coming. On April 5, 1968, the justice minister's Memorandum no. 117 banned all Frente Ampla activities without, for the moment, robbing Carlos Lacerda of his political rights.

Throughout 1968, the colonels and Carlos Lacerda each maintained a latent opposition to the government. Their divorce was complete but their positions and words betrayed a common culture and a common past. They shared what they imagined to be a particular "ethic of power," constructed in opposition to a political system deemed sclerotic, decadent, and detached from the concerns of the people and the interests of the nation, issues familiar to antiparliamentarian and antiparty movements in Europe. Faced with these self-serving and degenerate oligarchies, these officers and the former governor were at one in regarding themselves as "pure" idealists, for whom political action was a vocation and a display of personal heroism. For the colonels, it was also a projection of their military identity of rectitude, selflessness, and courage. Their rejection of the system that had been overthrown, a leitmotif and cornerstone of "hard-line" discourse, was based just as much on anticommunism as on contempt for civilian politics and the pluralist parliamentary regime the officers regarded as corrupt and oligarchical.

This criticism of the authorities as eternally betraying the nation was in fact very close to the accusations that had been made against the ousted regime. And with good reason: it was thought that the "revolution" had not achieved its objectives in a military government that reproduced the practices and retained the men of the "system that had been overthrown." Moreover, the generals now running the state were believed to have surrounded themselves with experts without greatness or ideals and inclined to "sell" the country to multinational and U.S. corporations. Lacerda and his one-time military disciples had differing analyses of this "power system." For the former, the coup had led to politics once again being dominated by militarism whereas the hard-line colonels most frequently believed the presidency guilty of civilianism—in other words, of conniving with the oligarchies and petty politicians that had been pillars of the republic for nearly a century.

DIVISIONS AND DISSENT

During the first year and a half of his mandate, therefore, General Costa e Silva failed to meet the expectations of a "hard line" of radical colonels who had thought that their hour had come. Without their mentor Lacerda, they were caught in the vise of a regime whose increasing militarization did indeed bolster general military solidarity against the civilian population; however, this also meant that military hierarchy now trumped revolutionary credentials. Revolutionary or not, a colonel was firmly below a brigadier general or an army general, and could no longer have ideas above his station just because his values and charisma might make him ideal for a top post.

They were not the only ones in the military institution to demonstrate their discontent with the new regime. The political climate of 1966–68 is harder to understand because dissent increased among the generals, who were caught in an uneasy balance between the MDB's moderate opposition and the temptation to support a government that might yet develop, or might yet open the doors of the palace to them. These collaborations between nays, ayes, and undecideds, between getulistas and antigetulistas, conspirators and legalists, ARENA and the MDB, so difficult for the collective memory to process, offer certain keys to understanding what political life under the dictatorship was like, as well as what future reconfigurations of the "opening" (*abertura*) period would hold.

The profiles of the dissident generals vary. Initially supporters of the coup, some moved closer to the MDB at the beginning of 1966 and all in a variety of ways endeavored to resist the government's growing authoritarianism and political repression. General Peri Constant Bevilacqua expressed the earliest and most candid opposition to changes in the regime.[24] He was Superior Military Court (STM) minister from March 1965 to January 16, 1969, when he was dismissed and stripped of his military decorations under AI-5. In the years leading up to the coup, Bevilacqua was already to some extent outside the military's dichotomous view of the world. Firmly anticommunist and opposed to strikes and popular protests, he nevertheless displayed a staunch legalism (hence his support for Goulart's inauguration in September 1961) and championed a nationalist economic policy that, at the time, was suspect to a good many on the military Right. In May 1962, Bevilacqua represented the nationalist tendency in the election for Military Club president, which he lost to General Augusto da Cunha Maggessi, backed by the conservative, anticommunist, and antinationalist Democratic Crusade (Cruzada Democrática). The rise in social tension and military insubordination in 1963 won General Bevilacqua over to the idea of a coup d'état, although he played no part in its planning or staging even so. While he initially took a benevolent view of the

Castelo Branco government, it was not long before he expressed his worries about the political purge and, particularly, the use of legal and Military Police tools (IPMs) against civilians. Already a member of the STM, in 1965 he gave almost systematic support to grants of habeas corpus and political amnesty for the victims of "revolutionary punishments."

These stances isolated him within the STM where, from the moment he joined, he had incurred the wrath of General Mourão Filho who accused him of leniency toward insurrection and the "system that had been overthrown." Nevertheless, at the beginning of 1966, Mourão made a U-turn and the two officers spoke out jointly in favor of the amnesty for those punished by the "counterrevolution of 31 March" and of direct elections at every governmental level. The consistency of General Mourão Filho's political thinking was dubious. He had long been identified with the military "hard line" and called for greater political authoritarianism, while his early rejection of the castelista government was based on arguments identical to those brought to bear by the radical colonels. As of AI-2, however, which he regards in his memoirs (written during the political opening, or decompression, at the end of the 1970s) as the start of "an irreversible phase of deterioration,"[25] he turned himself into the spearhead of political democratization. In January 1967, he stated that the new constitution, the Press Law, and the National Security Law (LSN), the results of "authoritarian *castelismo*," had plunged Brazil into a "long medieval night." He subsequently hoped that the new president, Costa e Silva, would facilitate the repeal of the LSN, a "law of slavery" that killed off public freedoms.[26] This spectacular about-face masked an inept political opportunism. While his "first hard-line" comrades aspired to come to power by intimidating and controlling the future "governments of the revolution," Mourão opted for a head-on challenge. In May 1966, on the basis of a nationalist and democratic speech (condemning an antinationalist economic and financial policy), he declared himself ready to run for the MDB in the upcoming presidential election: "What is the situation two years after the movement? A whole lot of injustices resulting from cancelled mandates, suspended political rights, dismissals and expulsions, without the victims, civilian or military, being entitled to any kind of defense, something that is fundamental in democracies and universally enshrined in the Declaration of Human Rights. At the same time, many of those most guilty of corruption have slipped through the gaps of the legal sanctions necessary to a democracy. Innumerable undoubtedly popular and democratic political leaders have been sacrificed and marginalized."[27] In fact, the background to the liberal and pro-civil government demands belatedly advanced by General Mourão was a confused understanding of the political regime suited to Brazil, which sometimes bore the marks of his integralist past, and at others was suspicious of a strong executive and representatives of the people, who had been badly chosen by a flawed system.

During the same period, Generals Justino Alves Bastos and Amaury Kruel opted to join the MDB as a means of expressing their disagreement with the new directions of the castelista government. Their dissent was born of frustration about the impossibility, given the electoral residence requirement stipulated by the June 1965 "Law on Ineligibility" (Constitutional Amendment no. 14), of standing as ARENA candidates in the state assembly elections of October 1966. They saw the closing of this door by people they considered mere comrades in arms as a sign that the government had lost its bearings, particularly when they believed they themselves had great revolutionary credibility. Indeed, they had been troop commanders at the time of the coup, whereas Castelo Branco and Costa e Silva had held only General Staff or cabinet office. Their discontent swiftly took the form of a challenge to the regime itself. This was evidenced by General Kruel's August 1966 manifesto, timed to coincide with his move to the opposition party. In it, he accused the government of being "armchair revolutionaries": "Disappointingly, [the sources that inspired 31 March] are no longer present in the memory of those who, in power today, deem themselves the only authentic revolutionaries, as if to be a revolutionary it was enough to criticize the government in private, drink whisky in the comfort of a flat, whisper conspiracy into the telephone, and await the victory of fighting forces to take to the streets and enter the race for already vacant key posts."[28] Kruel's attacks also targeted repression by the authorities, which he considered excessive, and called for a return to the secret ballot and to real democracy:

> And what's more, not content with these easy conquests, they take it out on guilty and innocent alike, with a punitive rage unknown in the history of our armed *pronunciamientos*. . . . It is in truth a fully operating system of oppression, maintained by the contrivances of a two-party system that suppresses democratic dialogue since one of the speakers is condemned in advance to play only a bit part or to be sent from the stage. All this show of mystification, imposed on the suffering people of Brazil, is justified by the claim to be seeking democratic improvement.[29]

This dissent—motivated to a varying extent by frustrated ambitions, by a sense that the authorities lacked legitimacy, and by genuine liberal concerns—was played out, we must remember, in a context of great political uncertainty. Until the start of 1968, despite an obviously militarizing regime, redemocratization remained a possible outcome. Adopting a wait-and-see position, the MDB initially took a benevolent view of the candidacy and early presidency of General Costa e Silva. Eventually, the issues of repression and the fight against subversion were temporarily eclipsed in the public arena (until August 1967 at least) and economic nationalism came to the fore, an issue favored by all the dissidents, despite their differences in other areas. Indeed, they had long advocated a shift toward nationalism in both economic and financial policy. This shared demand helped build political bridges, putting profound disagreements on the back burner by comparison. In January 1966 this enabled Colonel Rui Castro to meet Vieira de Mello, head of the MDB group in the Chamber of Deputies, to decide on potential joint opposition to Castelo Branco's economic and financial policy. The following year, when Costa e Silva was president, three opposition deputies (Marino Beck and Henrique Henkin, with close ties to Leonel Brizola; and Raul Brumini, of lacerdista persuasion) went a step farther and set up the "Position Brazil" group (Posição Brasil), open to all "nationalist, idealist military of good faith." The move came several days after "hard-line" colonels had invaded the Finance Ministry. It was clearly an attempt to hijack control of the economic issue.[30]

These ventures were, of course, marginal and did not produce stable alliances. The opposition front, which Lacerda's acrobatics failed to unite, lacked even a minimal consensus. More specifically, Bevilacqua, Kruel, Alves Bastos, and even Mourão Filho, all of them "independent officers" hard to pin down to a particular military faction, disagreed over the interpretation of the political process launched in 1964. While for some the social and military upheavals exacerbated under the Goulart government had simply been brought to a halt, most of the military believed a complete overhaul of the early democratic system was required. As a result, none of these general officers was able to emerge as the leader of an antigovernment, nationalist, and "democratic" protest.

A nationalist leader did appear, however, at the end of 1967, as public life began to revolve around the presidential elections to be held in 1970. He was no dissident, though, and still less a liberal or a democrat. He was General Afonso de Albuquerque Lima, a renowned nationalist with robust legitimacy as a radical after his role in the abortive "power grab" of October 1965. Far from claiming to embody an alternative to militarism, he embraced it by campaigning solely among the military—giving many nationalist speeches at the Vila Militar, for example—and pushing an authoritarian political line. We should recall that at the end of 1967, even before the social protests of the following year, the OLAS (Latin American Solidarity Organization) meeting in Havana and the crushing of the Caparaó guerrilla movement had refocused public debate on the continuing "subversive peril." The context was more favorable to a "blanket crackdown" and acquiescence in authoritarianism than to the dissidents' hesitancy.

On his arrival at the Interior Ministry, the general charmed broad swathes of the military Right with an inauguration speech that was voluntarist, developmentalist, and nationalist. Moreover, he put forward the idea, very popular with the "hard-line" colonels, of the "citizen under arms," endowed with real political legitimacy. He addressed not the nation but his "comrades in uniform" alone, asking for their trust, pledging not to betray their hopes and pointing to his "political and moral idealism: nationalism."[31] The objectives he officially set his administration were to reduce the regional inequalities that stemmed in particular from the economic development of the Amazon and the Northeast, and to fight against poverty and for social justice. In a bizarre parody of the Marxist philosophy of history, his speech made "democracy" the last stage of the "Brazilian Revolution," "which would make the class struggle vanish by acting, together with nationalism, as a factor bringing national forces together." In the background was the ideal of a "great power Brazil" or "Brasil pôtencia," inherited from the authoritarian thinking of the 1930s and promoted in Estado Novo propaganda,[32] that would be economically robust, socially at peace and freed from territorial imbalances and divisions. Albuquerque Lima seemed to base the nationalist policies he favored on more advanced theoretical reflection than the officers of the "first hard line," but he stressed the same features: the restricted entry of foreign capital, national ownership of land and mineral wealth, and support for Brazilian private enterprise, within the framework of a foreign policy that was cautiously aligned with the Western bloc.

The interior minister emerged as a new military leader through an offensive against the government of General Costa e Silva, whom the military Right as a whole now accused of the same "pro-civilian" failings as Castelo Branco: weakness, softness on corruption, and connivance with a decadent political class and the oligarchies inherited from before 1964. Albuquerque Lima, by contrast, was an exclusively military figure, based on two pillars, familiar to the radical officers: nationalist fervor and a demand for more thorough-going repression and authoritarianism. His candidacy marked the end of the military protest's lack of political definition in 1966 and 1967. In numerous respects, it took up the baton of the post-coup hard line and attracted a good many of its members, despite the continued shilly-shallying of a handful (such as Boaventura) when it came to Lacerda. In December 1967, navy minister Admiral Rademaker publicly declared his solidarity with Albuquerque Lima regarding his Amazon policy. The former LIDER leaders, such as Admiral Heck and Colonel Martinelli, who were friends of Albuquerque Lima, welcomed his candidacy while many radical young officers liked the ideas he articulated as much as his manly, charismatic political style. Furthermore, many observers remarked on the parallel between his presidential ambitions and those of the war minister two years before, with the sole difference that Albuquerque Lima was a lieutenant general (General de Divisão) rather than an army general (General de Exército). He had not reached the summit of the military hierarchy and on those grounds ought not to be able to run for the highest office.

1968: GOING TO WAR

At the end of 1967, the anticommunist discourse of the media, the political elites, and the military leaders became harsher. At the same time, "revolutionary war" instruction in the military schools changed. Practical training was now added to the theoretical instruction that had rippled through the hierarchy since the end of the 1950s. In December 1966, a Special Training Department (Departamento de Instrução Especial, DIEsp) was set up at AMAN, the cadet training academy, to run courses in jungle, mountain, and guerrilla warfare, which had previously been led by Vila Militar paratroopers.[33] It began work in 1967. Guerrilla warfare training courses then started to feature in almost all the country's barracks and were toured by Army Minister Lira Tavares in November. The increasing influence of anticommunism in the military could also be seen in "lectures" given at AMAN. These grew in number as of May 1968 and for a year dealt exclusively with "democracy," which had to be protected against the "Marxism" and "communism" that were intent on "world domination." Among the speakers were ECEME colonels addressing "Communist Activities in Brazil," far-right deputy Clovis Stenzel on the foundations of democracy, bishop of Diamantina Geraldo Sigaud (a member of the fundamentalist Catholic organization Brazilian Society for the Defense of Tradition, Family and Property, Sociedade Brasileira de Defesa da Tradição,

Família e Propriedade [TFP]) on "The Church's Social Doctrine and Revolutionary Warfare." Both inside and outside the barracks, the communist revolution was once again a constant concern and topic of public debate. This new focus stemmed from a changing national and international situation but also from the maturing repression and authoritarianism of the regime, which was taking up arms and training its troops for the "warfare" that had justified its creation.

As of May 1968, statements by officers proliferated on two subjects: the condemnation of "rising subversion," sometimes combined with calls for political radicalization, and the stigmatizing of a political class that was preventing the "revolutionary" government from taking appropriate measures. (Indeed, since March, the MDB opposition in Congress had been growing stronger.) An anonymous manifesto published at the beginning of May suggested creating a real "militarist state," supported solely by entrepreneurs and freed from the antirevolutionary burden of civil politics.[34] At this point, political pressure did not come primarily from the historical "hard line" in its low-key manifestation or, by contrast, as the champion of direct elections, constitutional reform, and the partial amnesty of victims of revolutionary punishments (according to an anonymous statement by "orthodox" officers in August 1968[35]). Nor did it come more broadly from the middle-ranking military Right. Rather it was chiefly the higher army ranks of various persuasions who took to the press to share their concerns about ongoing events. The anger and discontent crystallized on June 26, 1968: the Rio de Janeiro's student organizations had chosen that day for a mass demonstration, attended by artists, intellectuals, politicians, and ordinary citizens, which became the March of the One Hundred Thousand (Passeata dos Cem Mil), challenging the dictatorship head on. On the same day, the Popular Revolutionary Vanguard (Vanguarda Popular Revolucionária, VPR) carried out one of the first large-scale operations by an armed group when its activists seized the Second Army Headquarters in São Paulo, killing Mário Kozel Filho, a nineteen-year-old soldier.

To the generals who were increasingly speaking out in public, these two events offered simultaneous proof that the communist revolution was truly under way in the form of both a mass uprising and nascent guerrilla operations. Second Army Commander General Carvalho Lisbôa declared at the time that he would go and "find the communists wherever they had infiltrated, the Church, the schools, the factories, even hell itself. . . . It's a tumor that should have burst. It's something staged by people operating from abroad. We were already expecting attacks. I don't hide under the blankets. I saw it coming, but violence fires me up. If someone slaps me, I don't offer the other cheek. I am not a biblical man. If someone shoots me, it had better be in the back because otherwise I'll make short work of whoever made the attempt."[36] A few days later, Admiral Sílvio Heck joined in the prevailing alarmism. He spoke out on behalf of the navy, which he said was determined to do battle with "the anarchist terrorism that is plunging homes into mourning, causing loving mothers to weep, maiming innocent children, blowing up barracks, targeting officers, and preventing the Brazilian's peaceful labor."[37]

Military anticommunism was not just revived by the political disturbances and cultural ferment of 1968, it changed its tone. Although the destruction of the family, the overthrow of morality, and the damage done by atheist materialism had not previously been central to the military's public statements, these now became obsessive proof of advancing subversion.[38] General Albuquerque Lima showed himself to be particularly concerned about these social issues, which he linked to infiltration of the Church by communist agents. Some of the clergy, associated with the National Conference of Bishops of Brazil (Conferência Nacional dos Bispos do Brasil, CNBB) and the basic ecclesial communities born of Vatican II, were experiencing a cultural and social revolution of their own, which initiated dialogue with socialism and created growing opposition to the military government. Speaking to officers from the Military Circle of São Paulo, General Albuquerque Lima addressed himself to "the communists, priests and bishops of the festive Left, those who claim to be students and are playing into the hands of powerful economic groups and, finally, those who want nothing to do with the new order the Revolution is trying to impose."[39] In doing so, he was reflecting a reorientation in Brazilian (and, more broadly, Western) anticommunism toward greater denunciation of sexual freedom, drug use, idleness, and challenges to the symbols of authority as communism's new brainwashing tools.

The year 1968 in fact saw the reinvention of Brazilian Catholic fundamentalism to counter "communist subversion." It was influenced by the conservative writer and academic Gustavo Corção, who published his theories in the mainstream conservative press (*O Estado de São Paulo*) and his magazine, *Permanência*.[40] Some officers proclaimed these theories in the military space. This was true of General Moacir Araújo Lopes, born in 1918, a devout and puritanical Catholic, greatly concerned about moral education (in 1969 he became the first head of the National Commission on Morality and Civics, a public body championing morality and moral standards, set up in September 1969). The Catholic traditionalist, paramilitary, and sectarian organization TFP, founded in 1960 by Plínio Corrêa de Oliveira, was gaining a higher public profile and contributed to the religious and moralist shift in military anticommunism. Its founder's obsession with the Left's control of the means of communication, of the universities, the press, and the Church, and of all the leaders and shapers of opinion, became part of the military Right's political repertoire and remained there for good.

The resurgence of paranoid, military anticommunism, obsessed with subversive infiltration and contamination, went hand in hand with the rebirth of right-wing political violence, its preferred targets being theaters, publishers, university centers, and the press. Far-right terrorism was not just a sign of anticommunism, however. It was also a rejection of other means of political participation and an act of defiance aimed at the authorities or even an attempt to destabilize them. While speaking out in public in the armed forces became the preserve of the general officers, a type of action returned that was not only contrary to disciplinary regulations but also was secret, criminal, little known to the government, and barely part of the chain of command at all. This radical nexus was thus in transition from the violence of the small pre-1964 civil and military groups toward the political violence of police and military officers at the end of the 1970s. Assassination attempts and acts of violence were evidence of a desire to put pressure on the authorities rather than to become part of them.

The names of far-right movements responsible for acts of violence in 1968 are known: the Communist Hunting Commando (Comando de Caça aos Comunistas, CCC), the Anticommunist Movement (MAC), and the Secret Group (Grupo Secreto)—their composition, connections, objectives, and ways of operating less so. Most of the information available to researchers is journalistic, drawn up on the basis of interviews, piecemeal archival material, and the press publications of the day. All the accounts relate almost the same sequence of events, however: basically, around twenty bomb attacks and some graffiti.[41] At the time, only artists, journalists, and intellectuals incurred the extremists' anger in the form of this "bloodless terrorism," with no deaths to report as yet. "Since the government wasn't doing much and the communists had begun to run the show, we overturned the political situation with the aim of fighting the guerrillas. Who are enemies? The Left! Which is the most vulnerable part of the Left? The festive Left. How does it express itself? In theater, television, newspapers, etc. How can the operation be most easily mounted? It's got to be in the theaters where there is the most agitation and the operation is disguised . . . so, we'll launch the operation in the theaters."[42] Since no inquiry was ever opened, a degree of mystery still shrouds the authors of the attacks. Some witnesses lay responsibility on an enigmatic "Secret Group," uniting officers from the air force, and to a lesser extent the army, with civilian activists, involved in all revolts and power grabs since the second Vargas government (1951-54).[43] This network was linked to Martinelli's section of the "first hard line" although not to the "enlisted officers" close to Boaventura. Born around 1920, these servicemen had often rubbed shoulders at army cadet school before some opted for air force school. Alberto Fortunato, Osnelli Martinelli, Rubens Vaz (who died in the Toneleros Street assassination attempt on Lacerda in August 1954), and Haroldo Veloso (one of the Aragarças leaders) were initially classmates, although only the first two stayed in the army. Shared experiences in the 1950s, particularly the Jacareacanga and Aragarças rebellions, strengthened their solidarity, as did the apparent leadership of air force colonel João Paulo Moreira Burnier, a daredevil as comfortable with mutiny as with beating up opponents or committing other acts of political violence.

Only some in these networks of "long-standing revolutionaries" opted for planting bombs in 1968. Air force major Alberto Fortunato was one such. A veteran of the 1950s uprisings who had been a member of small extremist anticommunist groups before the coup and then of LIDER, Fortunato explained in the 2000s how and why many officers had chosen political violence forty years earlier. He pointed out in particular that the creation of a system of domestic espionage and police repression during this period enabled particularly fervent officers who had volunteered for these tasks to meet one another and work together. As of 1967, indeed, the military dictatorship armed itself against "internal subversion." The Army Intelligence Center (Centro de Informações do Exército, CIE), set up in May 1967, at its inception staffed predominantly by Vila Militar officers, soon became a haven for the "Secret Group." Colonel Luiz Helvécio da Silveira Leite, one of the center's founders, was the prime instigator of interpenetration between what was coming to be known as the "security community" and activist networks. Born in 1923, he graduated from AMAN in 1947 and belonged to a generation scarcely younger than the "IPM colonels" who had formed the core of the "first hard line." He was only a major at the time of the coup. Conspiring actively from the War Ministry in Rio de Janeiro, he taught himself "psychosocial techniques" (interrogation and espionage) early on and in 1966 joined the (second) intelligence section of the First Army General Staff even before General Costa e Silva was sworn in as president. He was at the center of the crackdown on the Caparaó guerrillas, before being transferred to the brand-new CIE in Rio and then Brasília as head of the Counterintelligence Section, just as the "Secret Group" got off the ground.

There is a clear parallel between the practice of political violence by members of the brand-new intelligence and repression agencies, particularly the CIE, and the activism of the IPM colonels in the early days of the dictatorship. In both cases, officers of stated anticommunist convictions and, often, with a past as conspirators and rebels, were appointed to repressive roles, with the sole difference that agents in 1968 and 1969 were more highly specialized and trained for their work than their 1964 peers. Since the coup, the authorities had begun to develop intelligence officer training programs that included courses and placements at centers in Brazil (particularly at the Center for Personnel Studies/CEP in Rio) and the United States. Typically, as well as being far-right militants since their youth, those few officers who undertook acts of violence in 1968 had been trained and brought together by a military government—though one that they nevertheless opposed.

The small groups claiming responsibility for assassination attempts and attacks were only the tip of the iceberg. Several sources told us that as well as the machinery of repression and the intelligence agencies, numerous clandestine anticommunist organizations saw the light of day, about which we know generally very little. There was the Revolutionary Vanguard (Vanguarda Revolucionária), which set itself the goal of "promoting the coming together of supporters of revolution" to counter "the reorganization of communists and the corrupt backed by a faction of the Church and by politicians interested in restoring their privileges, in order to overthrow the Government and the democratic regime that resulted from the Revolution of 1964";[44] the Air Force Anticommunist Movement (Movimento Anticomunista da Aeronáutica), which was highly critical of the government; and the Nativist Spark (Centelha Nativista), set up in Bahia at the end of 1968 or the beginning of 1969. The latter was a kind of ultranationalist sect with fascist leanings, created by paratrooper officers (José Valporto de Sá, Kurt Pessek, Ivan Zanoni Hauser, and one Colonel Jaeger), and teachers from the Salvador Military High School.

Colonel Kurt Pessek recalled that his colleague Valporto wanted its slogan to be "Brazil above all." Pessek then went on to say: "The group called itself Centelha and it had a little magazine called 'The Lure' [*Isca*]. *Isca* and *centelha*. Hah . . . laughs [several times] and now our slogan's going to be 'Brasil acima de tudo' so things are getting complicated. Because there's 'Deutschland über alles' [bursts out laughing]. Valporto . . . hey, we're not going to take everything from them? Valporto liked symbols. He invented symbols. You had to put your hand on your heart. He invented a sort of secret society."[45] The slogan, rituals, symbols, and bodily stance invented by paratrooper major Valporto de Sá were evidence of an attraction to a fascist style, inherited from the integralism and rituals of the Estado Novo. The Centelha Nativista had several incarnations, often poorly recognized both by the intelligence services (like the SNI) and the media. It rose from its ashes in the Parachute Brigade of the Vila Militar a few months later, survived as a nationalist military group courted by part of the civilian Left during Emílio Garrastazu Médici's presidency (1969–74), and formed a pressure group pushing for openness at the end of the Ernesto Geisel government (1974–79). We shall return to these ambiguities and astonishing about-turns in due course.

The spate of small far-right military groups in 1968 reveals that, as well as a few armed actions involving a very limited number of officers, dynamics similar to those seen before the coup were being repeated within the military institution, in a bid to support the authorities or to offset their "omissions" in the fight against subversion. It was no longer a case of guiding the authorities, but of acting behind the scenes in blatant contradiction of the demand that officers be apolitical—which, for its own benefit, the executive had been trying to reestablish for four years. Not all in authority opposed this new activism, however, armed though it was. There was some support within the administration and the ministries. Moreover, these groups gained a degree of protection as well as a reserve of trained and armed followers as the agencies of repression grew stronger.

Only a part of the 1964–67 "hard line" embarked on this route and on violent action, effectively reproducing the practices of the early 1960s within the new context of dictatorial rule. The military or revolutionary nature of the regime is less important to an understanding of this new chapter than its repressive and police aspects. These men no longer had their sights on belonging to the authorities. They no longer sought public recognition of their political legitimacy but rather aimed to terrorize and suppress the opposition, doing it themselves since they deemed the authorities to be too timid or too slow to act. They were part of the machinery of state, but distrusted the authorities, tending rather to regard them as intrinsically corrupting and detached from revolutionary authenticity (as Colonel Octávio Moreira Borba, a member of the CIE with links to the Secret Group, put it: "A minister is like pasta. Put him in a pan and he goes soft"),[46] a discourse they shared with many radical officers who had taken the same paths of dissent.

Military "radicalism" and the actions and excesses of the new "security agencies," together with the suppression of social movements, altered the public image of the army and the regime. An October 1968 scandal involving an air force unit was the last straw. The institution's reputation was tarnished once and for all. It involved the Airborne Rescue Squadron, better known as PARASAR (Paraquedista Search and Rescue), designed to provide assistance at the scene of natural disasters. In April 1968, João Paulo Moreira Burnier, now a brigadier and Air Force Ministry chief of staff, ordered the PARASAR commander to use his unit to suppress the student movement as well as to carry out secret attacks and political assassinations. He wanted to kill two birds with one stone: to incriminate the Left and to rid himself of awkward individuals like Carlos Lacerda, Juscelino Kubitschek, General Mourão Filho, and even Bishop Dom Helder Câmara, one of the leading ecclesiastical voices to oppose state violence. Burnier was just back from the Panama Canal Zone, where he had attended an intelligence course run by U.S. instructors at the School of the Americas. He immediately put his new skills to good use by taking part in the creation of the Air Force Intelligence Center (Centro de Informações da Aeronáutica, CISA), which would become operational a few months later.

The perverse venture dreamed up by Burnier was soon leaked, however, thanks to PARASAR's Captain Sérgio Ribeiro Miranda de Carvalho (known as "Sérgio Macaco," or "Sérgio the Monkey"), who dared to oppose it in public. He appealed to the upper echelons of the hierarchy and secured the support of flight routes director brigadier Itamar Rocha and of highly respected Brigadier Eduardo Gomes, a veteran of the tenentes movement. The affair divided the air force and, before long, the whole of the armed forces into two camps. It ended in the disciplinary incarceration of Captain Sérgio Macaco in September 1968.[47]

Apart from the bloodlust and license to assassinate evidenced by the plan, the date it was revealed to public opinion, October 1968, in the middle of the main political and military crisis of the dictatorship, gave it particular significance. The press, the MDB group in Congress, and Lacerda (who tried to have his military networks denounce terrorism in the army) seized on the story after some in the government had entered into all-out war with the legislature at the beginning of September. There were also signs of deep unease among the students of the military schools.

MILITARY OPINION AND THE MOVE TO DICTATORSHIP

From August 29, 1968, the day on which the Military Police invaded the University of Brasília (UnB) in an outburst of violence, to December 13, 1968, when the Fifth Institutional Act came into effect, the machinery of the military regime tightened its grip on the country. AI-5 went beyond the wildest dreams of both the officers most hostile to any checks and balances on the authorities and to any show of opposition; and of those who favored a thorough-going purge. In fact, its text contained only measures that had been sought or demanded by the "hard lines" that had challenged the regime on the Right, one after the other, since the coup. It appeared to fulfill the program of the military far Right—one that may well have been put forward in disarray initially, but whose demands had clearly appeared recurrently since 1964.

The political and military crisis brought to an end by AI-5 began with two speeches in the Chamber of Deputies at the beginning of September. Márcio Moreira Alves, a journalist known for his opposition to torture (he published the polemical book *Torturas e Torturados* in 1966), and the MDB's elected representative for the Rio de Janeiro constituency, was vehemently hostile to troops going into the UnB. In an initial speech on September 2, he described the Brasília events as an archetypal example of a policy based on repression and torture. He lambasted government leniency toward the torturers and murderers who filled the armed forces, cited instances of maltreatment, and condemned the lack of any inquiries.

The following day, he repeated his attacks on the government:

> Mr. President, Deputies, everyone acknowledges, or says they do, that the bulk of the Armed Forces do not approve of the militarist elite which commits violence and maintains an oppressive regime in this country. I think that after the events in Brasília, the great moment to unite for democracy has arrived. It is also time for a boycott. Brazilian mothers have already protested.[48] All social classes proclaim their rejection of violence. But this is not enough. There has to be a boycott of militarism, especially by women, as has already begun in this House by the wives

of ARENA members of parliament. It will soon be 7 September. The militarist elites are attempting to exploit the people's deep feeling of patriotism and will ask the high schools to march alongside the students' persecutors. Every father, every mother must be persuaded that their children's attendance of this parade assists the beasts who attack and spray bullets in the streets. Let everyone boycott this parade, therefore. It could also—while we're still talking about women—be a boycott by young ladies, the girls who go dancing with the cadets and go out with the young officers. Today, in Brazil, the women of 1968 should imitate the women of São Paulo in the War of the Emboabas and deny entry to their homes to those who sully the Nation,[49] refuse to accept those who remain silent and, in so doing, become accomplices. Disagreeing in silence achieves nothing. Now, action has to be taken against those who abuse the Armed Forces by speaking and acting in their name.[50]

The call for women to strike was transgressive in several respects. By asking women to deny their favors to cadets and young officers, Moreira Alves was threatening to rob the latter of some of the social standing that deemed them "good matches" and thus members of a certain elite. Moreover, his speech attacked one of the pillars of the military institution, the hierarchy, since it asked officers to rise up against the military elite. Then, by suggesting a break between civilians and the military, he shattered the image of a "revolutionary movement" achieved by the latter at the former's request. Last, the allusions to the private lives of new generations of officers were experienced as an unacceptable insult since they related to the holy of holies: military honor.

Moreira Alves's two statements were the starting point of a calibrated military offensive intended to have Congress withdraw the deputy's political rights and mandate (cassação), irrespective of his parliamentary immunity. A tussle with the legislature ensued, in which the latter risked and lost any remaining authority and prestige. For the military Right, these speeches provided a pretext to rid itself of Congress, a stronghold of the "oligarchical political class." Incidentally, Márcio Moreira Alves himself uses the word "pretext" in recounting the event.[51] There were two factors in the effectiveness of this "pretext," both fundamental to the crisis: first, the construction of a military consensus to move to a dictatorship; and second, the identification of the political class as the enemy to be destroyed as a matter of urgency. These two processes took place jointly over the three long months between the deputy's speech and the enactment of AI-5.

From early September, the military voices pressuring the government to take radical measures were not principally recruited among the factions that bore the "radical" label. The old hard line of the colonels, deprived of influence and, in the case of a small number, tempted by opposition lacerdismo, joined the debate in piecemeal fashion, and for two months it was the generals who held sway. The military ministers initiated proceedings by demanding that the president take harsh measures against the deputy. Head of the Military Cabinet general Jayme Portella de Mello took the request to the justice minister. However, the STF could not expel the deputy from the Chamber without the approval of the Assembly, which it declines on December 12, after much procrastination. AI-5, issued the following day, was the direct consequence of this refusal. During these two months of proceedings, other general officers, most often associated by witnesses with radical positions, had also been letting the authorities know that they expected a "revolutionary" solution, and AI-5 was nothing if not radical.

The highest ranks now had the stage to themselves, therefore. Authorized by their position in the hierarchy, they put into words the expectations of the military rank and file, who remained entirely offstage, and without representation by the middle ranks. Only one colonel made the news, Francisco Boaventura Cavalcanti Júnior, just back from a mission abroad. He opposed the new AI from behind the scenes and organized a sort of resistance together with various political circles. Few followed his example. Some of his friends explained his stance as the result of disinformation and personal confusion. According to Colonel Tarcísio Nunes Ferreira who was close to the same group, Boaventura "had not yet felt the pressure . . . he had been taken by surprise, barely returned from his trip abroad and not fully integrated into the context of the revolutionary process."[52] General Jayme Portella's testimony is quite different. He points out that far from commenting briefly and in surprise, Colonel Boaventura spoke to opposition figures on several occasions (particularly deputies Mário Covas and Renato Archer of the MDB, whom he welcomed to his home), and that a small group of senior lacerdista officers followed suit.[53] At that same time, the U.S. ambassador spoke of a "group" surrounding the colonel and hostile to the latest Institutional Act.[54] Last, just before its promulgation, anonymous "orthodox" figures continued to put out strange liberal manifestos suggesting that "the prevailing view was that we should go back to the barracks and hand supreme power to a civilian."[55]

The generals who in November and December 1968 were calling for retaliatory measures against members of parliament and then the assembly itself systematically claimed to be speaking on behalf of the armed forces, which were, allegedly, "at boiling point." Márcio Moreira Alves challenged this image of the "opinion of the barracks" and made it one of the lines of his defense. At parliamentary Constitution and Justice Committee hearings on November 18, 1968, he said he believed that:

> [General Lira Tavares] wanted to present the ministerial initiative as the outcome of pressure from officers outraged by [my] speech. Simply examining the dates shows that this pressure, if it is real, could not have come from many and certainly not a great many officers. Brazil's poor means of communication; the traditional delay in delivering letters and telegrams; and, above all, the poor distribution of the *Diário do Congresso*, with the 4 September issue going out only after that date; and lastly the extremely limited way in which the speech was covered by the press and not even mentioned on the radio, makes it possible to deduce that this much-vaunted pressure from the rank and file is mainly produced by the imaginations of a small group of officers to whom the Minister had access, rather than by the officer corps.[56]

The radical generals were not the only ones to use rank-and-file pressure as the main argument to justify their positions. The opposition did the same, exploiting the uneasiness that had been brewing in the barracks since the start of 1968, and that the repression had increased. From exile in Uruguay, Goulart clearly revealed the hope being placed in the disquiet and dissatisfaction of the military. He launched an appeal designed to encourage an uprising by members of the military "who do not accept the role of guardians of an unjust and inhuman order which humiliates our country, oppresses the poorest comrades, and appalls young people, setting the soldier against the people as if they were meant to be enemies."[57]

The officers who favored an authoritarian shift were also campaigning. In mid-October, the second speech made by Márcio Moreira Alves was circulated in the form of leaflets to all the garrisons in the country. Astonishingly, both camps were arguing for the same things: to defend the honor, dignity, and prestige of the army, in one camp against subversion (journalists, politicians, the "festive Left") and, in the other, against a government acting in such a way that the people could see only torturers behind the uniform.

The eruption of the PARASAR scandal in October, which deeply divided both army and air force, heightened the anxiety of certain sections of the officer corps regarding the damage done to the public's image of the army. This can be seen in a manifesto by hundreds of Officer Improvement School (EsAO) students, made public on November 1, 1968: "The Brazilian Army, which has always been considered the guardian of the institutions, and which is, by historical tradition, one of the most legitimate of democratic consciences, is nowadays regarded by public opinion as a usurper, as privileged and as responsible for our society's reactionary values, be they political, economic, or social."[58] The captains did not claim to have written a political document and said that the army supported the achievement of the government's objectives. However, they spoke of the government as increasingly discredited, because of accusations of "corruption" and the "denaturing of the Army's mission."

The manifesto is interesting for several reasons. Its contents are almost entirely devoted to professional matters: promotion and transfer policy, the failures of the military education system, and low salaries. It is evidence of both genuine professional unease and the myth that the armed forces at the time were obsessed with the political process. Furthermore, its immediate instrumentalization revealed what it represented for the main political players as a compendium of military opinion. Minister Lira Tavares neutralized its antiestablishment aspects by reducing it to the issues of salaries and the young officers' standard of living. João Goulart put forward his own interpretation, believing the manifesto proved that "the vast majority of the military is already persuaded that the time has come to hand power back to civilians."[59]

Military discontent thus became the issue in a symbolic struggle between politicians, generals, and journalists, who took advantage of the gray areas surrounding "military opinion" to make the enemy responsible for the scorn officers felt was aimed at their institution and, therefore, to win the officers' favor. They all took their campaign to an officer corps whose "opinion" had acquired a kind of political sovereignty. Supporters of greater authoritarianism gained the backing of the small far-right groups that had proliferated within the officer corps over the past year and helped win them around to the government's choices.

The campaign vanished amid the ever-more prevalent debates about the presidential succession. General Albuquerque Lima traveled from barracks to barracks with a distinct preference for the Vila Militar, full of nationalism and greatly concerned with the Amazon issue, sometimes to speak up for improving the officers' status; sometimes to promote his own government activities; sometimes to lambast liberal priests; to deny spending time with politicians; or to champion a new Institutional Act or five or ten more years of "revolution." At the end of November, Albuquerque Lima made a genuine electoral tour of the country's barracks. It became the subject of daily press articles and government alarm. At the same time, an orthodox colonel (probably Colonel Boaventura or someone close to him) reiterated his desire to see a civilian stand in the upcoming election "not because the military are incapable but because there has now been enough of making the Armed Forces and, primarily, the Army, responsible for all the country's problems."[60]

The generals, who were putting decisive pressure on the presidency of the republic at the time, spoke out systematically in the name of the armed forces, claiming to defend their honor and their constitutional role. The battle they waged in these final months of 1968, however, was not a war on communist subversion, student disorder, or an armed threat from the Left—despite the obsession with these issues that had been apparent since April 1968. They were pitting one national institution, the armed forces, against another, Congress, and basing their political proposals on an imagined disparity between two moral codes, two forms of patriotism, and two attitudes to politics. Congress was even induced on October 2 to hold a "session of self-criticism," confirming the legislature's symbolic subordination to the military executive. The "enemies of the revolution" targeted by the military offensive at the end of 1968 were, therefore, the parliamentary opposition and dissidents rather than the communists. "The honor of a class" that had been dealt "a disproportionate insult," according to Army Minister Lira Tavares at the beginning of December, had far greater importance in the revolutionaries' demands than whether Congress even existed.[61]

Historiography and the collective memory most frequently allege that AI-2 and AI-5 gradually achieved the essence of a coup d'état between 1965 and 1968, through "pressure from the barracks" and from a "hard line" on the Presidential Palace. Having come much closer to the center of power—if not to its very heart—when General Costa e Silva became president, the most radical wing of the Brazilian Army is thought to have finally succeeded in imposing its dictatorial views in full in 1968. A closer look at intramilitary politics reveals that this dynamic was in fact more complex and that this complexity had an ideological backdrop. The clear-cut hatreds of anticommunism, antiparlementarianism, anticivilianism, contempt for localism, and loathing of political parties were the common denominator of military radicalism that gave rise to AI-5. But they also obscured the ambivalence of all putschists, both civilian and military, to liberal democracy, elections, and the existence of checks and balances. Of course, maintaining a pseudo-democratic institutional architecture created a facade that masked a repressive military dictatorship. The prevailing misgivings, however, were proof of just how poorly defined the "ideals of 31 March" really were—although all those involved, whatever their subsequent careers, claimed to uphold them. The consensus regarding a coup d'état that had been motivated by class fears and concern about the "red peril," together with a vague enthusiasm for a new upright, competent, and patriotic elite, was not easily transferred to a government that was gradually monopolized by a handful of generals. This is evidenced by the lack of definition, the hesitation, and the political uncertainty of 1966 and 1967—although the retrospective gaze (after AI-5 and, especially, after the Years of Lead) has tended to regard these as irrelevant or even lacking in historical reality. Dissenting opinions, apart from a predictable fraternity of those frustrated by the regime that was coming into being, were in fact the traces left by having constructed this military regime without a consensus. Moreover, they would also give rise to subsequent realities, particularly during the period of political opening.

The essentialization of a victorious hard line also concealed the pattern of intramilitary restructurings. Between 1966 and 1968 in fact, the "first hard line" split into two groups. The first, distinguished by a past of permanent conspiracy and revolt, never abandoned the use of violence. With very few exceptions, the Aragarças veterans, the members of anticommunist groups at the beginning of the 1960s, and the authors of several attacks in 1968 belonged to the same militant nexus. This was not true of the serving colonels of a second group, close to Francisco Boaventura. Their "revolutionary" and radical romanticism, as well as their nationalist faith, were related to those of their activist colleagues but they wanted to run the country (as officers rather than activists) more than to implement a clearly defined policy. In this way, the "first hard line" covered two far Rights, one activist, the other military, and they responded in very different ways to the establishment of a regime of older officers.

It was not just a dictatorship, with AI-5 as its cornerstone, that was coming into being but a military regime. This militarization was de facto: under Costa e Silva, most of those in the government wore uniforms, and agencies dominated by general officers (such as the National Security Council or CSN, which assisted the president in related matters and approved the Fifth Institutional Act in December) acquired growing importance in the machinery of state. Militarization was also symbolic. In the discourse of all the players, the barracks gained a kind of sovereignty without, however, being able to enforce it through middle-ranking officers as had been the case immediately after the coup. From the "first hard line," to the exiled representatives of the "overthrown system," and including dissident revolutionaries like Lacerda and presidential candidates like Albuquerque Lima, everyone claimed to be the interpreters and defenders of "military opinion." Control of the latter and the ability to become its credible interpreter guaranteed political authority. The enactment of AI-5 was, therefore, preceded by a media operation seeking to present it as the punishment of the political class that had offended the honor of the officer corps. The latter was said to be in revolt and out of control and it would be that pressure, experienced by some and fueled by others, that led twenty-three of the twenty-four members of the CSN (ministers, chiefs of staff, heads of the presidency's Civil and Military Cabinets, and the SNI) to support the act. Only Vice President Pedro Aleixo opposed it. Symbolically, the barracks had obtained both a monopoly on force and the status of sovereign opinion. Nevertheless, the generals alone were now authorized to proclaim this since the intermediate generation of officers had been gradually silenced.

CHAPTER FOUR

Shaking the Ground
1969

> Faced with modern life, the Army officer ceases to be merely a cog in the machine of war and becomes a citizen, aware of his civic responsibilities to the Nation. He has become an actor with far more deeply rooted nationalist feelings than in the past. He has been politicized in the positive sense of the word so that he is able to face up to the internal and external enemies who are endeavoring to destroy us with their anti-Christian and materialist ideology. He has become a defender of our institutions.
>
> —JOINT LETTER FROM 189 OFFICERS TO GENERAL AFONSO DE ALBUQUERQUE LIMA, SEPTEMBER 6, 1969

In declaring Congress closed indefinitely, AI-5 excluded the bulk of the civilian political class from spaces for debate and participation in politics. Admittedly, only half those in the government wore military uniforms, and most local executives were still civilians, but federal decision-making circles shrank to include only the President's Office and the general staffs of the armed forces. In addition, the imprisonment of Carlos Lacerda on December 14, 1968, followed by the withdrawal of his political rights on the thirtieth, silenced one of the last national-level civilians with a degree of "revolutionary" credit. Last, the burden of censorship increased dramatically, and the population found itself not only robbed of participation in decision-making processes but also of any information about them. Power was now debated, organized, and exercised behind closed doors.

This militarization did not benefit the "military" in general but certain officers, groups, and state agencies. AI-5 had given its blessing to presidential rule. Within the president's entourage, military authorities (the High Commands and staffs of the three armed services, the High Command and staff of the armed forces) and civilian bodies (the National Security Council, the

Meeting of the three military ministers and their staff in Laranjeiras Palace. Rio de Janeiro, September 1, 1969. O Globo Archives.

National Intelligence Service, the president's Military and Civil Cabinets) fought for the role of power behind the throne. Did a military protest movement involving lower-ranking officers survive AI-5 elsewhere? The act certainly seemed likely to assuage the authoritarian thirst of the antiestablishment far Right. The "revolution" had acquired a tool for ridding itself of "representatives of the overthrown system," "oligarchies," and other "outmoded elites." These no longer hampered the military authorities from inside Congress. At the same time, the military Right's paranoia about communists and subversives took on new and concrete expression. As of 1969, the intelligence services of the navy, army, and air force (respectively, the Centro de Informações da Marinha, CENIMAR, 1955; Centro de Informações do Exército, CIE, 1967; and Serviço de Informações da Aeronáutica, SIA, 1968, then Centro, CISA, in 1970) along with the old political police services, the DOPS (Departamentos de Ordem Político e Social), received backup from new agencies in their repressive agendas. The Bandeirante Operation (Operação Bandeirante, OBAN), launched in São Paulo in July, was the first attempt at civil–military collaboration for the sole purpose of combating "subversion." In several states of the federation from 1970 onward, it inspired the creation of Intelligence Operations Detachments (Destacamentos de Operações de Informações, DOIs) and Operational Commands for Internal Defense (Centros de Operações de Defesa Interna, CODIs), which provided the framework for repression in the Years of Lead.

Nevertheless, the hardening of the regime did not mean an end to military protests. Nor did it lead to complete calm in politics within the armed forces. It certainly put a hold on anticommunist terrorism, but political debates and conflicts continued within the officer corps. This is attested by many sources in 1969, which are all the more precious in view of the archives' silence about intra-military political activity that characterizes the Years of Lead.

TWO MILITARY AFFAIRS

To begin with, AI-5 appeared to restore calm in the military thanks to compliance rather than repression. Like the first two institutional acts, it enabled the internal purge of the armed forces to resume by retiring personnel, shifting them to the reserve or dismissing them altogether but it was little used for this end. "Only" 262 met this fate in 1969 and 1970, including 99 officers. The disciplining of officers under AI-5 in the early months of 1969 was rare and intended to set an example. First to be targeted was General Peri Constant Bevilacqua who openly opposed the regime from the STM benches and was forced into retirement on January 16. The third, on April 11, was Captain Carlos Lamarca for desertion and for stealing weapons and ammunition from his barracks at the end of January before joining the armed struggle. The sixth, on May 19, was our old acquaintance, Colonel Francisco Boaventura Cavalcanti Júnior. The reasons for the latter's punishment—which caused a stir in the armed forces—were set out in the "explanation" published with the sentence in the *Diário Oficial* (Official Journal). It deemed Boaventura guilty of "subversive activities and opposition to the Government of the Revolution" on two grounds:

–Failure in the duty of loyalty to his superiors in the hierarchy who had developed a government of exception, led by a person incompatible with the principles of the revolution, from what he himself told the committee;

–He entered into agreements with members of parliament, including Opposition members, showed solidarity with those opposed to authority being granted to indict a deputy for scurrilous and insidious offenses against the Armed Forces, and urged them to vote against this measure.[1]

The second charge refers to Boaventura's opposition to AI-5 and the contacts he established with opposition deputies in the latter months of 1968. The first point is more obscure. It hints at a conspiracy seeking to overthrow General Costa e Silva in favor of Carlos Lacerda. In his memoirs, the latter claims that Boaventura's error was made in a private meeting where he championed the military's return to barracks and Lacerda's coming to power.[2] Other witnesses suggest the colonel went further, contacting General João Dutra de Castilho, a renowned radical, close to the "first hard line" and the commander of the Vila Militar First Infantry Division, to involve him in his plan. The general declined the rebellious colonel's offer, however, refusing the inversion of the hierarchy inherent in the conspiracy. Colonel Gustavo Moraes Rego analyses its failure:

> There are things that belong to the revolution and things that belong to the institution. During the revolution, Colonel Dutra, who was a colonel in Recife, conspired with his subordinates because the process wasn't in line with the chain of command. Generals conspired with colonels, majors with captains and there's the problem, right there. When the revolution's over, there's the problem. I mean Boaventura went to find the conspirator from earlier on but that conspirator had stars on his chest, he was the commander of the Vila Militar and in duty bound to be loyal to his own commander, who was the president of the Republic. He could see no reason to overthrow him for the sake of Carlos Lacerda.[3]

Boaventura believed the existence of an ongoing revolutionary process gave permission to go beyond hierarchical boundaries. He thought his political identity, based on his past exploits, his intellectual value, and "the idealism" of his involvement, should take precedence over his rank in certain interpersonal relationships within the barracks. Indeed, this was the keystone of the colonel's "indictment," whereby "the officer in question has broken with his fundamental duties as a soldier by taking a stance incompatible with his status as a serving senior army officer and with the basic standards of the Armed Forces." Ultimately, AI-5 affected Colonel Francisco Boaventura as a soldier rather than as a dissident or a member of the opposition.

There was barely any press reaction to his sentencing although it caused a great stir in certain parts of the military, despite the fact that Boaventura had seemingly been going it alone for several months in both his conspiratorial ventures and his opposition to AI-5. Looking back, his usual companions are almost unanimous in condemning his choices. Nevertheless, his expulsion from the army provoked a wave of dissatisfaction. The key themes of this irritation were not the penalty as such but the application of a decree intended for the "enemies of the revolution" and, above all, the revelation of the "reasons adduced," which Colonel Moraes Rego regarded as "indelicate, hostile and damaging to the officer's dignity: an irreparable indignity." He went on to make clear that from the small Amazon garrison of Tabatinga where he was serving, having been sent away from the center of power for his castelismo, he and General Rodrigo Otávio (who headed the Amazon Military Command and was moving toward liberal positions) "did their utmost on their part to save Boaventura. But to no avail."

Of the disgruntled officers, it was General Augusto César Moniz de Aragão who signaled his disagreement with the greatest furor. We have met him before on several occasions. It was he who, a few days before the coup, wrote the "Messages to Young Soldiers" in the *O Globo* newspaper and, after the death of Castelo Branco, roundly condemned the journalist Hélio Fernandes's comments about the deceased. Born in 1906 to a father who was a medical officer, he was a little younger than the tenentes and had previously pursued a classic military career, punctuated with long periods as an instructor in the military schools, which was partly the reason for his reputation among several generations of officers. In particular, he had been close to Castelo Branco but also to middle-ranking officers of the "first hard line." Suffice it to say, he was scarcely in the Presidential Palace's good books in 1969. Head of the Military Cabinet, General Jayme Portella regarded him especially with open hostility. In March 1969, Moniz de Aragão just managed to secure his fourth star (attaining the supreme rank for a general officer), but with no troop command. He left the minor Veterinary Services Department for the General Provisions Department (Departamento de Provisão Geral, DPG), handling army logistics. This position allowed him to join the ACE, which was reserved for serving army generals, but deprived him of the prestige and the military and political might of the troops. A few days after Boaventura's sentencing, he sent a letter to the army minister, reporting the unease he claimed the ruling had provoked in the officer corps. He spoke of reactions of "puzzlement and consternation" at the use of AI-5 against an officer who, to his mind, had "an excellent image as a citizen and soldier in the military world." Most of all, however, Aragão took exception to the revelation of the reasons adduced for the punishment since they "contain[ed] demeaning and hostile assessments—unsuited therefore to the serenity that should attend court rulings—and, in damaging the honor of this officer, also redounded upon the feelings of his peers, disturbing and dismaying them. . . . The spirit of the Army is ablaze." And, indeed, many officers did interpret the punishment as an abuse of office by the Presidential Palace and by General Jayme Portella in particular. As a result, it provoked outrage among officers of highly disparate backgrounds and political inclinations, from the castelistas to the "hard-line colonels," as well as generals popular with young, radical officers, such as Moniz de Aragão and Albuquerque Lima, of whom Colonel Boaventura was also a friend. General Aragão did confine himself to his letter of May 22. He entered the letter-writing war against Minister Lira Tavares, which led in June 1969 to his expulsion from the logistics department and the Army High Command.

"The Boaventura affair" did not create a genuine antigovernment front in the way that *anticastelismo* had united civilians and officers with sometimes diametrically opposed political positions and plans in 1966 and 1967. The punishment of the famous colonel and the reaction from Moniz de Aragão did, however, give the protestors two causes to champion: Boaventura's return to the army and a post for Moniz de Aragão. Less than a month after setting out his objections to the handling of Boaventura's case—and, he would later say, without having heard from the minister—General Aragão launched a large-scale revolt, giving rise to the second military scandal of 1969. On June 17, he held a meeting in his department, at which he drew up a list of grievances against the president's entourage. A second letter, sent the same day to Minister Lira Tavares, detailed his complaints. It contained a serious allegation from a prestigious and popular army general and known revolutionary: that the second military government was dictatorial, even totalitarian. Remember, however, that a few months earlier Aragão had been an intimidating advocate of AI-5, the most authoritarian measure adopted by the military regime. Yet now he was condemning the drift toward dictatorship of a government appropriated by the presidential "clan" at the expense of the common good. To the military mind this was the ultimate accusation as it (once again) reduced the exercise of power to politicking rather than a duty or a mission in the service of the motherland.

In his letter, Aragão raised two issues: totalitarianism, a word Brazil's putschists were more used to associating with communist ideology; and amorality in governance (malpractice by some and complicit cowardice by others), which was more usually attributed to civilian politicians. The general's skill, although it would not protect him from punishment, was to play on the ambiguity between a whistle-blowing pamphlet and the legitimate communication of his subordinates' dissatisfaction. It is this that explains the second part of his letter, which caused outrage in the presidential entourage, equal at the very least to the indignation that greeted the first half's allegations of nepotism and dictatorship. This was the first time an army general had been the mouthpiece for the feeling of revolutionary responsibility that was widespread among the young protesting officers:

> The officers of the Armed Forces, because they deem themselves responsible for the revolutionary regime, think they have the right and the duty not only to monitor and assess the actions of the Government—which they regard as their creature—but also to remove it if they disagree with it. Given the Government's confusions, ambiguities and contradictions—real or apparent—in addition to the publicity permitted over the "Colonel Boaventura affair" and exploited in Machiavellian fashion by agents of subversion, the officers have shown themselves to be distressed and anxious, especially the youngest.[4]

General Moniz de Aragão did not explicitly associate himself with this depiction of revolutionary legitimacy but nor did he condemn the officers who supported it, even as he called for the restoration of military discipline. The main danger, he said, was not a rebellion of military subordinates but the exploitation of their discontent by ill-intentioned military leaders, a role he himself would very soon be suspected of playing.

Dozens of copies of the letter were distributed to all the military commands and schools, to Congress, and to foreign embassies. It drew a collective response of support for the minister from the army generals, who demanded Aragão's expulsion from the Army High Command. In the name of the "spirit of authority and hierarchical discipline," Army Chief of Staff (EME) General Antônio Carlos Murici even believed that General Aragão's position was "incompatible [with] the Revolution." Like Lira Tavares, Murici interpreted what Aragão had to say as legitimizing the barracks' collective control of the government. To his mind, it betokened an "attempt to diminish the government's authority," which could only be the work of an "insignificant little group of 'new Christians' of the Revolution," while Lira condemned the desire it displayed to present "Brazilian Democracy" as a "real Military State."[5] On June 30, Aragão was dismissed from his post at the Department of General Supplies (Departamento de Provisão Geral, DPG) organizing logistics and, thereby, from the ACE.

This letter-writing dual between General Aragão and General Lira Tavares reveals far more than merely the rebellion of an influential officer with connections to two factions opposed to the presidential clan (the castelistas and the hard-line colonels). It was a confrontation between two understandings of the relationship between the officer corps and the authorities. Strictly speaking, General Aragão was not in favor of implementing a policy that bestowed sovereignty on the barracks. Like the majority of officers and especially of generals, he was imbued with the hierarchical mindset. He too would have seen giving direct power to his subordinates as a serious attack on military regulations. Nevertheless, for Aragão, the officers' mobilization and dissatisfaction were a political resource in terms of the physical threat they entailed and the political legitimacy associated with them. They allowed him to showcase his qualities as a military leader who listened, represented, and controlled his subordinates. This figure of the leader was a threat to the ministry, which countered it with the ludicrous, nonsensical image of its own government as a pro-civilian and democratic institution, independent of the military. Lira Tavares explained this to the High Command at a meeting held on July 21 to review the "Aragão affair":

> None of us can maintain, especially to the Nation, that the Armed Forces achieved the Revolution without the People, because the work of the PCB consists precisely of stating that the people are against the so-called Military Dictatorship created by the Revolution.
>
> The statement by an Army General that the officers of the Armed Forces have a duty to monitor the actions of the Government and even to remove it from power if they disagree with it, would, as is already happening, incidentally, raise a question that would harm the Revolution: and what about the People? And the Workers? And the Class Unions? And the other Powers of the Republic? Etc. etc.[6]

The effort the minister expended to explain at length to the generals of the High Command that the "Revolution" represented the people rather than the armed forces is evidence in itself of growing confusion about the legitimization of the "military government." The established dogma of the professionalism and legalism of the armed forces was unable to embrace the manifest militarization of the authorities and the recourse at times of crisis to the mantra of "the opinion of the barracks."

PROTEST LEADERS AND "UNEASE IN THE ARMY"

To what extent did the two "affairs" in the first half of 1969 reflect a resurgence of military protest? Personal and ideological, Aragão's ties to the "first hard line" left little room for doubt. The remarks that brought about the general's dismissal (not just his sense of the officers' collective political responsibility but also his condemnation of the personalization of power and the corruption and nepotism of the presidential group) had in fact been part of the protesting colonels' political repertoire since mid-1967. After the upheavals of 1968, which (with very few exceptions) indefinitely delayed any issue other than the "fight against subversion" and the neutralization of inconvenient civilian politicians, the tense lull at the beginning of 1969 put the authorities themselves back under the microscope. Colonel Tarcísio Nunes Ferreira, aide-de-camp to General Aragão, an Aragarças veteran and very much part of the old "hard-line" networks, confirmed the extent of the rumors and dissatisfaction. He spoke of "abuse of authority" by some ministers, of the interference of "corrupt persons" in ARENA, and of the negative influence of the president's wife, Yolanda Costa e Silva, over her husband and his entourage.[7]

Minister Lira Tavares was not taken in, and Aragão's dismissal from the High Command, which was not strictly speaking a disciplinary punishment, was accompanied by sanctions against his young "hard-line" entourage, especially Colonel Tarcísio Nunes Ferreira and Colonel Hélio Lemos. It was during this period that barriers appeared to members of the "first hard line" to impede their rise to the rank of general officer. Of the troublesome colonels who nonetheless had outstanding professional careers, only Ferdinando de Carvalho, who had said nothing since 1967, and Hélio Lemos, who was never given a troop command, did in fact become general officers. By 1969, this network of middle-ranking officers was largely dismantled as a result of successive punitive transfers and of the dissident options chosen by its two leaders, Lacerda and Boaventura. Still in search of a political future and a political leader, they rallied to the candidacy of Albuquerque Lima, who had resigned from the government on January 27, 1969.

In voluntarily exiting his cabinet post as interior minister, Albuquerque Lima opted for a strategy to attain power that went beyond the internal balances of the circle of general officers. Furthermore, he avoided the early move to the reserve that was mandatory after two years away from military office under the December 1965 "Law on the Inactivity of Military Personnel." His return to active service also allowed him to escape criticism in relation to the compromises inherent in exercising power, while reviving his image as one of the men (even though he was given not a troop command but the Directorate-General of Ordnance). Last, he took advantage of his resignation to pull off a minor political coup by blaming it on Finance Minister Delfim Netto and Planning

Minister Hélio Beltrão, the occasional objects of the wrath of the "first hard line" and Lacerda since July 1967. It is also worth noting here the adroitness of General Costa e Silva in appointing as Albuquerque Lima's successor Colonel José Costa Cavalcanti, another champion of nationalist positions in the economy, although his passivity when his brother, Colonel Boaventura, was disciplined a few months later would discredit him among the young radical officers.

Albuquerque Lima's speech at his inauguration as interior minister had positioned him as a nationalist alternative among the general officers. His resignation speech officially launched his election campaign. He conducted it under the banner of nationalism, regional development, and national integration (his slogan was "Integrate in order not to yield" [*Integrar para não entregar*]), and a social justice to be won against the dominant interests. Euler Bentes Monteiro, head of SUDENE and known for his nationalist convictions and defense of certain social reforms (he was nicknamed the Brazilian Army's "Peruvian General," a reference to the officers who had recently taken power there), resigned in solidarity. Albuquerque Lima's speech, moreover, inclined surprisingly toward socialism (with calls for agrarian reform, greater domestic savings, and participation in corporate profits), while his virulent anticommunism was deliberately concealed.[8] Neither nationalization nor potential restrictions on foreign-capital penetration were envisaged, however. The program was therefore a retreat from the nationalism of the hard-line colonels, which was also more anti-American, antiliberal, pronationalization, and procentralism.

The exact place of authoritarian nationalism at the heart of the Brazilian Army in the second half of the twentieth century is an issue not yet settled. Several early works brought to light the importance of economic nationalism within the Brazilian officer corps, and its consequences on the regime's political choices. This is in contrast to Chile, Uruguay, and Argentina, where the military general staffs were more unequivocal proponents of a pure internationalist liberalism.[9] However, much light still needs to be shed on the persistence of this political philosophy between the fall of the Estado Novo and the coup d'état of 1964, while a socially conservative, politically elitist, economically liberal, anticommunist, and pro-American Right affirms its hegemony over the political family and the higher echelons of the military. Meanwhile, the Left, whether or not it believed it was following in Vargas's footsteps, claimed a monopoly on both geopolitical nationalism—rejecting North American imperialism and diplomatic alignment with the United States—and economic nationalism, which it linked to concern for industrial development, the expansion of the internal market, and the well-being of the working classes.

In reality, bipolarization came late and was partial at most, especially in military circles. From time to time, until 1959, Brazil's business circles championed the same nationalist proposals as left-wing intellectuals. The Cuban Revolution and the heightened tensions of the 1960s discredited this conservative nationalism on the Right. It revived the fear of a "communist peril," which would initially take cover behind a nationalist discourse, as had happened in Cuba, and increased suspicion of the masses' inclusion in the political system. The conservative elites rallied en masse to a liberal orthodoxy open to foreign capital.

A dispute between economists was added to this polarization of the political debate at the beginning of the 1960s, over the causes of slower growth in Latin America and how to deal with it. Intellectuals linked to CEPAL, such as Celso Furtado and Maria de Conceição Tavares, believed the crisis occurred because the system of import-substitution industrialization was running out of steam.[10] They thought the economy could be revived by expanding the domestic consumer market beyond the wealthiest in society, which would require "fundamental reforms," agrarian in particular, and massive state investments. At the other side of the ideological stage, liberal economists, like Eugênio Gudin and Octávio Gouvêa de Bulhões, considered economic stagnation the outcome of monetary instability and inflation encouraged by excessive state intervention. Development could not, therefore, resume without stimulating private investment and attracting foreign capital and foreign businesses.

Within the military, where political polarization had led to violent internal conflicts since the 1950s, officers who were nationalist, anticommunist, and socially conservative all at the same time appeared to be in a very small minority and of no significance in the political process. Their place in historiography is minuscule. The 1950s and early 1960s were understood in terms of dichotomies: nationalists versus *entreguistas*, legalists versus putschists, military Left versus military Right. The coup completed the reification of this simple table, its boundaries hermetically sealed. The crackdown on military supporters of the Goulart government confirmed that two camps existed, their mutual loathing seeming to indicate their opposition on all points. In addition, those in charge of economic policy under Castelo Branco—Roberto Campos at the

Planning Ministry and Octávio Gouvêa de Bulhões at the Finance Ministry—and in these same posts under Costa e Silva—Hélio Beltrão and Delfim Netto, respectively—were figureheads of economic liberalism. Furthermore, they implemented a policy of monetary stabilization and combating inflation that was broadly in line with the dictates of liberal stabilization.

Nevertheless, intramilitary politics between 1964 and 1968 attested to the persistence of a nationalist discourse within the military's "revolutionary" camp, little known but endowed with a considerable capacity to mobilize support, as Daniel Zirker has recently emphasized.[11] Indeed, the whole of the Brazilian military Right asserted a degree of nationalism. It was regarded as a pillar of the institutional ethos and was linked to a widely shared ideal of "great power Brazil," which the military government's propaganda campaigns that were made systematic at the end of 1969 would endeavor to inflame. Indeed, successive governments did not conduct a policy that was pro-American in every respect, particularly when it came to diplomacy—far from it.[12] From the mid-1970s onward, under the government of General Geisel, Brazil would even move closer to a sort of nonalignment. Nevertheless, nationalist and pro-nationalization positions on the economy, and anti-Americanism were more strongly held by the protesters, particularly the colonels of the "first hard line" and the dissident generals. They failed to impose their views on the first two governments when it came to economic policy, and liberal orthodoxy remained the primary guideline. Their nationalist discourse remained very popular with the young military, however. Moreover, between 1964 and 1969, the "hard-line" colonels and General Albuquerque Lima were simultaneously the main proponents of far-right economic nationalism and the only actors to justify their political protests on the grounds of their popularity with the officer corps.

The nationalist discourse of activist officers was not, however, simply the product of a strategy for attaining power. Like the nationalism of fundamentalist Catholic groups and that of the heirs of the pseudo-fascist "integralist" movement, it fell within a tradition of interwar authoritarian thinking. It was rooted in a manifestly political antiliberalism that encouraged distrust of all institutions, groups, or social practices likely to divide a fantasy "nation." More complicatedly, it espoused an economic antiliberalism, expressed by rejecting the symbols of international, U.S., or "stateless" financial capitalism, without specifically detaching itself from entrepreneurs and business circles. Unlike the economic and diplomatic nationalism promoted by the intellectual and party-political Left in the 1960s, it was not based on any plan to involve the masses in political and social processes, any mobilization on their part being suspected of "populist" or communist manipulation. Even so, it drew some of its references from the most prolific source of nationalism of the previous two decades—the left-wing economic and social reformism, from which, depending on the actors and the time, came the demand for agrarian reform, concern for the economic development of the Northeast, and the defense of state monopolies or state enterprises.

In addition to this "conservative national-developmentalism," the 1969 protest nexus was united by a common past and shared networks as well as the demand, constant since the coup, for greater power despite being lower down the hierarchy. The latter denied the colonels access to the main circles of power, and stood in the way of Albuquerque Lima's ascent to the presidency—since as merely a lieutenant general (general de divisão), he was one rung below the top of the ladder. Their position as subordinates and eternal challengers encouraged their repeated recourse to the "opinion" and political legitimacy of the barracks where nationalist topics were popular.

There were mutterings in the barracks in August 1969. This is demonstrated in July by the formation of a mysterious Nationalist Military Vanguard (Vanguarda Militar Nacionalista), claiming to have several hundred, then several thousand sympathizers in the armed forces, and calling for the restoration of the rule of law, the repeal of the institutional acts, a "general amnesty," universal suffrage to elect a Constituent Assembly, the lifting of censorship, and an end to political repression.[13] Internal disturbances were also attested by the sudden rise in punishments under AI-5. Of the thirty-three officers affected by the act since it came into force, twenty-one, mainly navy captains and lieutenants, became its victims in August.[14] They had very diverse backgrounds, ranging from young reserve officers who opposed the regime (the future historian Israel Beloch and student movement leader Jean-Marc von der Veid, in particular); to those at higher ranks who had once been in favor of the Goulart government without being activists, such as Lieutenant Commander Dalmo Honaiser. At the time, a new institutional upset was imminent: the president was planning to reopen Congress and pass a new and more authoritarian, more securitarian constitution to replace AI-5 and allow its repeal.[15]

It was in this context of rising tension that the authorities were dealt a blow to the heart—or rather to the head. In late August, General Costa e Silva suffered a debilitating stroke. Although it was hushed up for several days, the evidence could not be ignored: the President's Office was vacant. Under the 1967 Constitution, the vice president was to fill the office for the rest of the four-year term. The vice president, however, was Pedro Aleixo, who served as a reminder of presidential candidate Costa e Silva's liberal campaign promises, and was doubly flawed as both a civilian and the only person in the National Security Council to have voted against AI-5 in December 1968. For an overwhelming majority of the military it was unthinkable that he should become president. Legality did not apply therefore, and no regulation, law, or hierarchy of legitimacies made it possible to determine how a new executive should be appointed, chosen, or elected. Selection procedures would have to be improvised by men and agencies (military and governmental) and, with the president gone, there was no one to decide between them. This improvisation was to reveal or recall a fundamental ambiguity in the Brazilian military regime when it came to the legitimacy of the barracks' participation in politics. Were the political expression and autonomy of the troops a danger to the institution and the authorities, as stated by the precepts of military professionalism, or were they in fact the beating heart of the nation, guardians of its morals and its best interests? The two options corresponded to two legitimate military voices: that of the official commanders and that of the natural, de facto political leaders, whatever their position in the hierarchy.

THE SUCCESSION CRISIS

Between August 31, 1969, the day on which General Costa e Silva was formally removed from presidential office on health grounds, and October 30, when his successor, General Emílio Garrastazu Médici, was sworn in as the third president of the "revolutionary regime," the Brazilian armed forces were in unprecedented political ferment. There was a chorus of debate within the military, which was particularly well documented. Collective bodies (the Army High Command, the Admiralty Council, the Air Force High Command) operated as forums, their documents circulating within the military elite, expressing the views of the various hierarchy groups, although the most senior ranks of army officers sought to impose their own consensus at every stage. At the same time, an "epistolary revolution" was under way,[16] which became a semipublic space for debate in the officer corps, with letters frequently written collectively by lower-ranking officers and forwarded to several recipients by the generals.

General Costa e Silva's stroke had two outcomes. First, on August 31, it temporarily conferred presidential power on the three armed forces ministers. Second, on October 30, it brought Third Army Commander General Médici before a Congress obliged to approve his election as president of the republic. While a lengthy and troubled debate involving major sectors of the military preceded this second resolution, the first was decided offstage. Without even a hint of a debate, a new, Twelfth Institutional Act (AI-12) appointed a three-man "junta" of Army Minister General Lira Tavares, Navy Minister Admiral Rademaker, and Air Force Minister General Márcio de Souza e Mello as the new executive. AI-12 justified the break with legality by stating that Congress had been suspended and could not, therefore, elect anyone and by referring to "the commitments made to the Nation by the armed forces since the victorious Revolution of 31 March 1964." From a legal point of view then, the first "coup within a coup" since 1964 was not the Fifth Institutional Act but the Twelfth, whereby the military ministers took sole command of the nation with no prior legal measure having empowered them to do so. They were acting not on their own initiative but as decided by the Armed Forces High Command (Alto Comando das Forças Armadas, ACFA) although this was in fact nothing other than their own triumvirate expanded to include three generals subordinate to the ministries (the chiefs of the forces' staffs), in other words to the triumvirate itself, along with the chief of staff of the armed forces.

This imposition by the hierarchy created unease among those protesting officers farthest removed from the circles of power. In addition, they transferred onto the junta all the suspicion the presidential entourage and some of the Costa e Silva government had instilled in them. Colonel Tarcísio Nunes Ferreira, who was at the center of the 1969 intramilitary opposition, testified to a feeling that power had been usurped by "the Most Holy Trinity."[17] Nevertheless, the customary nature of this political configuration, the military consensus against Pedro Aleixo, and the prospect of escaping the entirely relative liberalization plans envisaged by Costa e Silva, gave the junta fleeting credibility, particularly with the generals. In fact, immediately prior to AI-12, Albuquerque Lima had distributed a document supporting this solution.[18] In it, however, he set out the rules for subsequently appointing a new government that must be able to rely on the "unanimous approval of the Armed Forces, as represented by their military leaders"—rather than just merely the approval of those at the top of the hierarchy.

General Albuquerque Lima was asking two questions here that were to remain key in debates about the presidential succession. The first was about military unanimity, which all the protagonists highlighted as a priority objective in resolving the crisis. The lack of dissent, as well as being in keeping with the traditional demand for institutional "unity and cohesion," meant politics could be ruled out as a synonym of division, debate, and competition. As long as there was unanimity in the armed forces, they could be regarded as separate from politics to a certain extent. The legitimacy of their voices also stemmed from this consensus since in the generals' eyes it was as an institution that they embodied the people and the "revolution." Representation of this military opinion was the second issue at stake in the internal debates. To Albuquerque Lima's mind, this role was naturally and even by definition taken by the leaders.

Albuquerque Lima was surrounded by general officers from the Corps of Engineers, who were ten years younger than those then in power. This was explained by General Antônio Carlos Murici, army chief of staff at the time:

> Another zone of tension was created in the Army. We already had three: the one made up of those who had been opposed to Costa e Silva even from before; the one with those linked to [Moniz de] Aragão; and the one with those linked to Afonso [de Albuquerque Lima]. The generals from the military Engineers were all very young: Afonso, Rodrigo, Candal. . . . Then, there was a report—I don't know if it's true—that during a discussion they held [some stated] . . . "Fine, at some point in the future, the Army will belong to the military Engineers." There were times when people said: "The Army belongs to the Gunners." It's true, the minister was from the artillery, the chief of staff was from the artillery. . . . There was a time when, like now, it was all cavalry. . . . Each period has its time, then it passes.[19]

Astonishingly, some sources stressed the fairly liberal nature of the group's program, said to have included "the reopening of Congress, a presidential succession ensured by direct elections, a full presidential term rather than an interim mandate, a restored democratic process eventually making it possible for civilian candidates to stand"[20]—all provisions running counter to the general's statements since 1964 and hard to reconcile with the extremism of many young officers who gave him their enthusiastic support. The consistency of this platform was not the focus of the accelerated "presidential campaign" launched by Albuquerque Lima in his letter of August 31, 1969, however. The candidate's personal connections and popularity in the barracks, as well as his reputation as an uncompromising nationalist, were the minimum required for a campaign in his favor. In any case, the immediate challenge was not the political program but the procedures for selecting a future president.

With the militarization of the regime, the voice of the barracks, to which the first president, Castelo Branco, claimed to turn a deaf ear, had gained great legitimacy among "revolutionaries," but to date it had largely provided a clinching argument to the generals, keen to impose their own political choices. Now, in order to decide between potential candidates, more precise procedures were needed for consulting that voice and these ran clearly counter to the requirement for a united military institution.

The precarious nature of the junta's military credibility only came to light because of an unexpected event. On September 4, 1969, the armed left-wing movements, National Action for Liberation (Ação Libertadora Nacional) and the October 8 Revolutionary Movement (Movimento Revolucionário 8 de Outubro, named in tribute to the date in 1967 when Ernesto "Che" Guevara was killed) kidnapped the U.S. ambassador Charles Burke Elbrick. The kidnapping itself and the kidnappers' distribution of a manifesto were thunderbolts that appeared to prove what the military Right had been predicting for over ten years: that there was revolutionary war in Brazil. Although armed left-wing groups had been virtually nonexistent in 1964 and their strategy not yet formulated, the fulfillment of the prediction now bolstered those in favor of greater repression and unsettled the junta, which immediately acquiesced to the kidnappers' demands. Some sectors of the military saw this as an admission of weakness and vulnerability and called all the more loudly for more lasting power than that of the current junta, a power that would have legitimacy in the barracks and thus ensure a firm hand in the fight against "subversion." Furthermore, the release of jailed members of the opposition in exchange for the ambassador's release stoked certain officers' hatred of communism and stirred up their anti-American disdain.

While the imposition of the military junta led to genuine discontent among radical officers, it was the exchange of prisoners that sparked the first military rebellion since the coup. Only certain parachute units of the Airborne Brigade (Vila Militar) were involved: the Santos Dumont Battalion, an elite parachute infantry unit; the Parachutist Instruction Center; and the First Airborne Artillery Group (1° Grupo de Artilharia Aeroterrestre, GAAet). First GAAet commander lieutenant colonel Dickson Melges Grael was the key figure in the small-scale rebellion by some thirty officers on September 6 and 7, 1969. A friend of Colonel Boaventura, who before the putsch had commanded a similar unit, the Airborne Division Howitzer Corps, Colonel Grael allegedly took the initiative (as he himself claims) in a single act of disobedience—refusing to parade past the military junta on Independence Day, September 7. He also took responsibility for actions carried out by younger paratroopers: a vain attempt to prevent the takeoff of the aircraft carrying the freed prisoners and a raid on the National Radio station in a bid to read out on air a manifesto rejecting the military junta and urging resistance. Grael's show of solidarity (he had decided to "regard these actions as a logical consequence of the emotional atmosphere in the Airborne Brigade and as a consequence . . . publicly to declare himself jointly responsible for all the consequences of these attitudes"[21]) earned him two weeks in jail and, shortly after General Médici was sworn in as president, a transfer to the Amazon garrison of Belém (the headquarters of the Eighth Military Region).

On the day he was expelled from the GAAet, Lieutenant Colonel Grael issued an Order of the Day giving his own account of the affair.[22] In it, he maintained that the transaction had been unanimously opposed by all military ranks in the Vila Militar. There was a consensus first among "its officers, sub-lieutenants, and sergeants, whom he consulted in person, giving them the opportunity to express disagreement." There was a consensus too among his superiors in the chain of command, with Airborne Brigade commander general Adauto Bezerra de Araújo in particular saying he was "stunned" by the "cowardice" of the junta, which "could not carry on any more." Only in this context of consensus would he have made the decision "not to parade at attention past authorities that had failed to find a fitting solution to a problem created by the communists." The insubordination of these parachute officers had the distinction of genuinely being viewed benevolently by some Vila Militar generals, long-term leaders of the "first hard line," like Siseno Sarmento and João Dutra de Castilho. It was their opinion that was trusted by those of the officers who invaded Galeão Airport (Rio de Janeiro) on September 6 in the hope of preventing the banishment of thirteen out of fifteen prisoners being flown out of Rio.

The thirty rebel captains, all sentenced to disciplinary incarceration at the end of their escapade, were led by Captain José Aurélio Valporto de Sá, already encountered as the founder of the small far-right nationalist group, Centelha Nativista, in Bahia a few months earlier[23]; as well as by Captain Francimá de Luna Máximo, editor of the group's newspaper, *O Farol*, and Captain Adalto Luiz Lupi Barreiros.[24] From ten to fifteen years younger than the "hard-line colonels" (they were born in 1939, 1936, and 1937, respectively), they lacked and indeed never acquired the academic distinction and honors of their elders. Their rank was the result of their specialization as paratroopers or of their having fought the guerrillas. Of the three, Luna Máximo had not even attended the Staff School (ECEME). He was also the one who, as a lieutenant colonel, ended his career with the lowest rank. None of them rose as far as general officer, studied abroad, or won any medals, other than the frequently bestowed Peacemaker Medal. This made their military background very different from that of the protestor colonels who had held center stage in intramilitary politics since the coup. They had links to the latter even so. Adalto Barreiros began his career as a first lieutenant in the Airborne Division Howitzer Corps, under Colonel Boaventura's command. In a later testimony, he indicated his solidarity with his one-time commander whose punishment he viewed as "another striking example of the self-devouring vampirism that came to prevail, and claimed many important figures in the revolutionary effort of 1964 as its victims."[25] These captains were also linked to the "hard-line" colonels through Major Tarcísio Nunes Ferreira, born in 1930, and Kurt Pessek, born in 1934, who were from a generation closer to them.

They were clearly amateurs: they were late turning up at Galeão Airport and missed the military aircraft's takeoff. Their abortive attempt at the airport, the raid on the radio station, and the refusal to parade saw them rounded up and arrested on September 8. Everyone was aware that the rebellion and the presidential campaign were connected. Furthermore, Lieutenant Colonel Grael himself wrote, "contact was made with Albuquerque Lima, who was at loggerheads with General Murici who accused him of being responsible for events."[26] The operation involved the airborne group GAAet, which was put on a state of alert, and the Santos Dumont Battalion, whose commander (Colonel Sarmento) issued an ultimatum to the junta giving the military ministers until September 9 to resign. After that, the paratroopers would take to the streets. The operation came to nothing, however. The ultimatum had no effect despite the promises and support of some commanders, such as General Castilho. The main reason was the confirmation of Albuquerque Lima's candidacy, which gave the protest a political outlet. To begin with, the rebel captains did not appear to favor any particular candidate very much. It was the support of "hard-line" generals from the Vila Militar Siseno Sarmento and Dutra de Castilho for Albuquerque Lima that prompted the younger officers to back the former interior minister. It also snuffed out the rebellion. Pressures and influence did not move only in one direction, therefore. Subordinates in immediate command of the troops might pose a threat to their superiors but they were also prepared to follow those same superiors' political choices.

From the very first day of Lieutenant Colonel Dickson Grael's disciplinary incarceration, General Castilho and Colonel Boaventura went to visit him in a show of solidarity with the protestors and in a bid to give political meaning to the ongoing disturbances. Colonel Boaventura even communicated a set of "Recommendations . . . for Colonel Dickson and other parachute comrades," in which he endeavored, with a view to the presidential succession, to promote a political strategy among his own group, which was now supported by the turbulent officers of the Vila Militar. Boaventura began by aligning himself with the positions taken by Albuquerque Lima on August 31, in the belief that Costa e Silva would never be able to complete his term of office, and that a new president should replace the junta as soon as possible. He pointed out that he declined to entrust the post to the vice president "on the grounds of his incompatibility with the Revolution."[27] Like his former mentor Lacerda, the colonel was not averse to contradicting himself: he fully endorsed the categorical refusal to confer presidential power on Pedro Aleixo, despite the fact that the latter's main defect by "revolutionary" standards was having opposed AI-5— just like Boaventura himself, in fact. He went on to set out the principals that should govern the choice of a successor:

> The name ultimately put forward to take on presidential office must have the general agreement of the Three Forces (*at the top and bottom—important*). This is the sole condition for securing sufficient support for the President to be able to govern. The support of the bases is necessary not to legitimate the future president but so that he can govern. Just as we refuse imposition from the top so imposition by a small fraction of the base will not provide sufficient conditions for the President to achieve a revolutionary Government in terms of healthy nationalism, as we have advocated.

For Colonel Boaventura then, this was not about conferring political legitimacy on the officer corps as a whole but about allowing officer participation in order to ensure that the new authorities had a sufficient base in the barracks. Giving "military opinion" a hearing was a necessity therefore. Even so, the colonel was tacitly pointing out that this guaranteed a "healthy nationalism" on the part of those in power. It was a perfect expression of the ambivalent mindset that placed the barracks somewhere between a physical threat and the moral conscience of the nation.

The term "head and base" was a recurrent one in the succession debates. It had already featured in a letter sent by Albuquerque Lima to General Murici on September 5.[28] In it, the ex-interior minister placed himself clearly in the opposition front organized in 1969, denouncing in veiled terms a dictatorship of profiteers; and demanding General Aragão's return to his post and to the High Command, as well as the quashing of Colonel Boaventura's sentence. He said the same, in a more friendly and moderate tone, to Army Minister Lira Tavares, even as he tried to win him over to his political project for a "Constructive Revolution," a "Revolution [that] would mean not only punishment, withdrawal of rights, and expulsions but far more the expectation of renewal, of bold changes to archaic structures, of the gradual elimination of inequalities between regions, and the elimination of the economic lobbies' influence on government decisions."[29]

Albuquerque Lima's popularity with the young officers of the Vila Militar, the networks he maintained there, and the hopes he aroused are established in numerous letters and testimonies. On September 6, when the parachute brigade was still in ferment, nearly two hundred middle-ranking officers sent him a joint letter that smacked of a manifesto. "Faced with modern life, the Army officer ceases to be merely a cog in the machine of war to become a citizen, aware of his civic responsibilities to the Nation. He becomes an actor with far more deeply rooted nationalist feelings than in the past. He has been politicized in the positive sense of the word, to be able to face up to the internal and external enemies who are endeavoring to destroy us with their anti-Christian and materialist ideology. He has become a defender of our institutions."[30] This new role for the officers flattened the hierarchy even though the manifesto writers were appealing to a general's leadership and not seeking to exercise power directly. The return to the "real ideals of 31 March . . . to exterminate the vile enemy, put morals into politics, restore democracy with a capital D," they said—was once again the prime justification for political engagement: "We have not seen its colors as yet, and especially of late, there has been nothing to say that '64 is still in force. What we have seen is compromise by the authorities, all-powerful politicking, and persons known to be opposed to our position openly leading the country." Contemporary criticisms of the policies conducted since the coup were both vague and familiar. On the one hand, they suggested "antinationalist elements" had been brought into the heart of government—this by the advocates of economic liberalism and the opening of the country to foreign capital. On the other hand, there was condemnation of a compromise with the political class and the appropriation of its corrupt and accommodating methods. The final part of the letter was an appeal for General Albuquerque Lima to "assume leadership."

Given the rebelliousness of certain junior officers and the political participation demanded by others, and given that retired colonel Boaventura was acting like an undercover civilian and that there was a three-star lieutenant general reminiscent of the pre-1964 "generais do povo" to deal with, the highest-ranking military had good reason to worry. The captains' generation (many of them engineers, along with a handful of paratroopers) now led the protests. That of the colonels had faded from the scene. The "first hard line" had been broken up and moved out of Rio, where the main political choices were made. The rank and professional standing of the protesting captains were too low for them to attain the political legitimacy of their elders. Nor was it the case, as it had been with the colonels, that a few of them claimed to be the interpreters of the armed forces. Rather they spoke en masse. They *were* the opinion of the military. Of their number, officers opting for outright insubordination were in a very small minority, members of the elite corps of paratroopers, who were highly politicized, militant, nationalist, and on the far right. The rebellion of this small number on September 7 did not have the intended consequences. The exchange demanded by the communist activists went ahead and the military junta was not forced into an immediate retreat.

Nevertheless, the image of the Vila Militar as a "powder keg" once again, along with General Albuquerque Lima's obvious campaigning in the barracks hastened the senior military authorities' development of a political solution to the succession. This was the mission the Army High Command set itself when it convened on September 15. At that point, the danger to the hierarchy came not so much from the extremist turbulence of the radical young officers as from specific military leaders. They were not explicitly campaigning for the individual's right to political participation within the armed forces. Rather, they mobilized thinking common to the majority of the military, including its elite: the need for consensus among the armed forces as guarantors of the revolution, the importance of keeping the barracks calm to ensure stable government, and the validation of senior military leaders displaying charisma and concern for their subordinates. As such, a "consultation" of the officer corps to decide on a successor to Costa e Silva was not really a victory for Albuquerque Lima's supporters. It was the only legitimate option in a regime whose militarization brought with it an ever-greater recourse to depicting the military as a whole as the soul of the nation and the "revolution." Behind these largely consensual principles, however, the practices tolerated diverged. How could the ballot required to find a "military consensus" avoid becoming an unacceptable election? Because, as all the protagonists agreed, the opinion of a corporal could not weigh as much as that of an army general, how could rank, the number of troops commanded, and military prestige be weighted in determining political legitimacy? At what rank could someone represent his subordinates and thus express an opinion rather than being represented?

THE "ELECTION" OF 1969

The last two weeks of September saw the discussion, decision, and holding of the armed forces consultation that led to General Emílio Médici's nomination for president of the republic. Congress, which was reopened for the occasion, was tasked on October 22 with formally validating the general's accession as head of state. ARENA approved the choice unanimously while the MDB, considerably in the minority, abstained. Médici was inaugurated on October 30 for an extended term of office, which would last until March 15, 1974, seeing out the remainder of Costa e Silva's mandate, plus a four-year presidential term.

It was a remarkable event insofar as it credited the officer corps with a collective political responsibility of a sort. The military regime, installed on the grounds that it would restore the discipline and apolitical nature of the armed forces, thus resolved its first major crisis by triggering the military's active participation in politics. In practice, the consultation was organized and largely controlled by a single body: the ACE. In other words, a council of the eleven army generals took priority over the presidential entourage (especially the head of the Military Cabinet Jayme Portella) and the Navy and Air Force High Commands. The presidential circle linked to Portella, which since the beginning of September had favored prolonging the interregnum in the hope of remaining at the center of government, grew weaker, as the need for a lasting solution became ever-more urgent. On September 15, the ACE went to the trouble of entrusting an ad hoc commission with the task of suggesting the procedures for the consultation. It was dubbed the "3Ms" from the initials of its members, army generals Jurandir de Bizarria Mamede, Emílio Garrastazu Médici, and Antônio Carlos Murici, all three of whom were members of the ACE and respectively head of the Department of Production and Construction (Departamento de Produção e Obras), commander of the Third Army, based in the south, and army chief of staff.

The proceedings of the High Command meeting give no indication of the reasons for appointing these three men in particular to initiate the thinking process.[31] Two days later, the "3Ms" submitted their plan to the ACE, stating that a successor should be appointed as a matter of urgency, who would meet the unanimous approval of the High Commands of each of the three service arms and of the Armed Forces Staff (Estado Maior das Forças Armadas, EMFA). Nothing was said about the details of the consultation. That was left to the High Commands that had, therefore, to decide on an electorate, constituencies, voting procedures, and a voting system, which could not be called an election. In making the highest military bodies the masterminds of the ballot, the commission merely extended the logic of the junta, while conferring on it the collective character that made it possible to avoid disputes.

It quickly emerged, however, that the names put forward by the Admiralty and the Air Force High Command would carry little weight compared to the choice of the politically and militarily dominant force, the army. Officially, the consultation took place in each force and their hierarchical elites were to provide the Armed Forces High Command (ACFA) with the names that reached the "final." Unofficially, however, it was established that only army generals could be named rather than admirals or air force generals. No argument was forthcoming to justify the minority position given to the navy and the air force. It stemmed from tradition as well as the balance of power between the three forces. More broadly, this intramilitary "election" had two rationales, the first to build a consensus about legitimate political participation and representation in the armed forces, and the second to enforce procedures enabling the appointment of the Army High Command's candidate or, more accurately, to prevent the appointment of the candidate who was not to the ACE's liking: General Afonso de Albuquerque Lima.

Many issues became the subject of debate or even conflict. Most army generals condemned the "consultation" of the entire officer corps, all ranks combined, as the utmost in military anarchy. It was a view shared by an anonymous officer in a letter, written after the vote, to General Albuquerque Lima who was accused of wanting all ranks of officer to be heard:

> As for consulting the base, . . . this does not seem to me to be the best procedure to use in a military organization reliant on hierarchy and discipline because the

Commanders—the real Commanders—are at all times, and especially in times of crisis, the repositories of the trust of, if not all, then of the great majority of their subordinates. To state the contrary would be to concede that, before deciding to go into battle, the General-in-Chief would have to consult thousands or millions of soldiers.

The situation is the same when transposed to the political field. There, I think and believe that hearings should go no further than the Generals who are the Commanders responsible for everything their great units do or do not do.

Otherwise, the hierarchy would be turned upside down and discipline subverted. We would then be back at the end of 1963 [with] JOÃO GOULART's Sergeants and the "People's Generals."[32]

General Murici was of the same opinion and believed that to go outside the general officers would be to cross a dangerous frontier. "If this goes on, we'll end up at the corporal. We will hear the corporal because he also has the right ... to have an opinion on the national problem."[33] In addition, the information available at the time (notably a survey circulating among the general officers) suggested that a consultation of this kind would favor General Albuquerque Lima, who was popular among young officers. [34]

While the ACE never seriously contemplated taking the direct consultation of officers outside the circle of general officers, the weight that the vote should give to a general's stars was subject to debate. General Moniz de Aragão, for example, wanted all general officers to make up the electoral college, irrespective of rank.[35] There should, he said, be no "exaggeration on the grounds of hierarchy or profession." "The future President must be a military man who should not be chosen for his length of service, or his office, nor for the value of his command but for capacities which have already been proven—or which he seems to possess—to run and to govern the Country. He will have to be elected by all the general officers and not by four-star generals alone. The preference so expressed would be more authentic and better accepted by everyone." For the members of the High Command, this solution was all the more unacceptable since one of the criticisms of the man to be beaten, Albuquerque Lima, was precisely that he had only three stars on his chest. He was, to use the approximate U.S. equivalents, a lieutenant general (General de Divisão) rather than a general of the army (General de Exército). Above all, however, his popularity in the First Army, which had no shortage of general officers, suggested that an "egalitarian" ballot would sweep him to power.

In the end, the ACE went for a complex and so poorly standardized ballot that generals with local influence could largely interpret it as they liked. Each of the eleven army generals was given an electoral constituency in which only general officers could vote (i.e., 114 officers). Each constituency was to provide the ACE with a list of three names in no order of preference and without showing the number of votes obtained. The officer most frequently put forward won the nomination. This list system awarded a bonus for consensus. To be elected, the candidate had to attract no hub of opposition, and had to be known everywhere—at the risk of not being particularly popular anywhere. This was true of General Médici, a remote individual with a sound reputation both as a man familiar with the apparatus and secrets of the state after several years as SNI chief, and as a "revolutionary." He had won the AMAN cadets' loyalty to the coup, thereby halting any tendencies toward resistance among the troops of the First Army. Nominated by ten of the eleven constituencies, he finished well ahead of Albuquerque Lima with his mere five nominations, and won the "election" hands down.

THE PROTESTING OFFICERS' LAST STAND

There was no revolt even after this odd election, although almost all the officers who had protested in public since the coup had seen their leader lose. The few challenges from within the military that followed the selection process tended to demonstrate the omnipotence of the Army High Command. None of them queried General Médici's appointment or undermined his validation by the Armed Forces High Command on October 6 and by the specially reopened Congress a few weeks later. On October 2, General Albuquerque Lima notified the Army Ministry of his dissatisfaction at the "methods adopted" and what he regarded as "irregularities" in the election.[35] He belatedly condemned the lack of precise and uniform standards; voiced his approval of the procedures carried out in the First Army where "the general officers [had] listened seriously and with dignity to the grassroots" and where the vote had gone his way; and criticized the imposition of the hierarchy's choices elsewhere. The response from Lira Tavares was also very much as expected. He rejected any idea of "the bottom overtaking the top" and the notion of an "election, involving every level of the military hierarchy, because our Institution is not a political party."[37]

After their leader's failure, the mass of general and senior officers who supported Albuquerque Lima kept a low profile. While most admirals had backed him for president (he secured thirty-seven of their sixty-nine votes[38]), only one, the well-known and far-right Ernesto de Melo Batista, risked a public manifesto. On October 2, his "Appeal to the Government and to Public Opinion" denounced the introduction of a system in which "the army generals [make up] the Country's one electoral college."[39] This manifesto was the only conspicuous challenge to the succession process from an officer with a general's rank. It was to earn him extraordinary punishment: he was the sole victim of a new Institutional Act, AI-17, decreed by the junta on October 14, 1969, and designed to have military "revolutionaries" who had been carried away by their antiestablishment fervor temporarily suspended from active service. The transgression punishable under the act was violating "the cohesion of the armed forces by straying, for short-term reasons or political objectives of a personal nature, from the basic principles and vital goals of our constitutional mission." The measure had great symbolic importance. It was a tool specifically to manage military dissent and was justified by the apolitical nature and disciplinary principles of the armed forces. It gave the presidency an immediate means of setting the acceptable boundaries of political participation within the military institution while, perhaps, sparing it the scandal of punishing "revolutionaries" under the tougher and more dishonorable AI-5, and any repetition of "the Boaventura affair." General Adolfo João de Paula Couto attested to these intentions by explaining that "the act was prompted by a resurgence in demonstrations by the so-called hard line within the Armed Forces. The instituted punishments are temporary, giving those punished a chance to return to active service once their antiestablishment fervor has abated. It was implicit in the measure that it recognizes the professional merit of many of those punished."[40]

This instrument to rid the officer corps of revolutionary politics was regarded by the EsAO captains as the ultimate betrayal and on October 25, 1969, they wrote a "Protocol" to refute the turn taken by the regime. Their manifesto was the most developed and sophisticated form of demanding collective officer participation since the coup. It was written and distributed, however, after Congress had approved General Médici's appointment as president of the republic and the die had already been cast. Without calling for a revolt or even issuing catastrophic prophesies about the consequences of this "closing in" of the authorities on themselves, the captains confined themselves to pointing out their discontent at what they considered a power grab by a "delusional group," which they claimed had succeeded in transforming the noble "ideals of 31 March" into an "Absurd Revolution."[41]

The captains took up the theme of a revolutionary government usurped by a small group. Unlike their elders, however, they refused to accept the principles of discipline and submission to the hierarchy once national issues or even "politics" were at stake. It is there in writing:

> Aware of national problems, we will not let ourselves be taken in by the trickery introduced in the zones of command. We think that the principle of authority taken as the sole and absolute criterion of truth in analyzing, interpreting, and resolving eminently political issues is not only false but denaturing too. It is in fact the absolutism of a group, disguised as hierarchical discipline, in which a delusional government attempts to impose solutions. . . .
>
> Because we do not accept in the political sphere the "perinde ac cadaver" way of doing things,[42] which St. Ignatius of Loyola prescribed for the Jesuits as the essence of passive, absolute, and submissive obedience—a genuinely corpse-like discipline—we reserve the right as authentic revolutionaries to express our point of view with idealism and in the name of Brazil's future, which belongs to us thanks to the whims of Time and Fate.

The captains claimed to have acquired this political legitimacy—and this was not a new idea—by being the ones who had in actual fact carried out the revolution, and also by having taken part since then "in a revolutionary dynamic, acting in particular against CORRUPTION and COMMUNIST SUBVERSION," while "our efforts are systematically and wholly neutralized and our actions often misunderstood." This line of reasoning had already been used in the months after the coup by the IPM colonels in charge of the "revolutionary cleanup." Now, it was brought to bear by ordinary regimental officers, describing themselves collectively as responsible for the counterrevolutionary struggle.

These young officers claimed to be responsive to a "global situation" that, beyond the Cold War and its fight to the death against communist subversion, encouraged new players in the developing countries to work toward a "national reconstruction" that was sometimes placed under a revolutionary banner. It is difficult to know which national experiences the captains were referring to here. Since the coup, manifestos and protest pamphlets had been very Brazil-centric and this idea was barely developed. Nevertheless, it is evidence of the meaning this generation of officers attached to the 1964 "revolution," understood as a collective work of national regeneration. It is worth noting that their own words made no reference to the revolutionary or reformist role of past protests by Brazilian officers. In particular, while they claimed to embody a generation and a rank (of captain), there was no mention of the lieutenants of the 1920s, who were now the generals they accused of usurping the revolutionary government.

The captains' reluctance, however, does not appear to have been shared by their comrades, the majority of whom accepted the appointment of the new general-president without a murmur. That AI-17, the final revolutionary act decreed by the military regime, had to be used only once indicates the overwhelming triumph of the 1900 "generation of the century," which locked another presidential succession so much into its own rank of generals that it deterred all challengers. The most activist regimental officers on the ultranationalist Right, the captains who were devotees of General Albuquerque Lima, and the ashes of the first hard line all ultimately fell into line behind the "third government of the revolution."

The 1969 presidential succession has been described and interpreted as the definitive advent of a particular kind of military regime, a "hierarchical" or "generals'" regime which kept the lower officer ranks out of big political decision making without personalizing the military government.[43] In fact, the transfer of the presidency to Médici created a precedent: the High Commands of the three armed forces, with the army in pride of place, were able to decide who ran the state on their own, almost without any reaction from the barracks and with the approval of a chastened Congress. The handful of army generals appeared to have sufficient political, military, and symbolic strength to govern the country without any checks and balances and, when necessary, against the opinion of the majority of the military itself.

Yet this victory of the "hierarchical regime" was not achieved either by a largely mythical tradition of distance from politics or by a culture of discipline and professionalism peculiar in South America to the Brazilian Armed Forces. Admittedly, the establishment of the "generals' regime" brought to bear the mindset of the professional, apolitical, and hierarchical army: if politics were evil, then only having generals involved was a lesser evil. The system that legitimized this regime was fragile, however. The simple fact that an election held solely within the armed forces was imposed as the only acceptable way out of the impasse revealed the ambivalent thinking about the military's involvement in politics. When it came to speaking out in the political domain, other symbolic hierarchies competed with the chain of command: a reputation and a past as conspirators, the extent of involvement in the fight against "subversion," authority, and reach within the barracks. Everyone, including the generals, used all the available options, highlighting one or another social identity. Only given the great ambiguity of political representations was this strange presidential "election" of 1969 possible.

CHAPTER FIVE

At the Heart of the System
1970–1977

We felt we were the victims of an injustice. We had risked life and limb while the majority were sleeping peacefully, benefiting from what we were doing, in all the safety they enjoyed as of then. We on the contrary had nothing but struggles, braving that whole wave, some colleagues braving gunshots and other dangers. We felt we were the victims of an injustice. Right or wrong, what's important is what we felt, isn't it? And analyzed by many of us, the responsibility for that injustice lay with thwarted interests, of course, but mainly with the weak, those who were still positioning themselves politically for personal gain, for their families, etc. By which I mean the politicians we have in this country. In our eyes, they equate to the line of those who are weak in the head, weak in everything, the "soft line." The line we opposed it with, fiercely, was "hard."

—Colonel Cyro Guedes Etchegoyen

A door closed when General Médici became president at the end of October 1969. The new government, "elected" in such turbulent circumstances, quickly prevailed over all its detractors, no matter what their rank, faction, or personal allegiances. Bar a few divisions, the military regained its cohesion as it confronted what was now a very real enemy, dozens of armed movements, made up of students driven onto the paths of resistance and communist revolution as the regime closed in on itself at the end of 1968. Several thousand army officers, sergeants, soldiers, firefighters, as well as military and civilian police officers were involved in a violent political crackdown experienced as a no-holds-barred "dirty war," in which torture was taught, systematized, and supported in high places, and where the authorities covered up the murders and disappearances of opposition members. Over four hundred activists died

General-President Emílio Médici (right) meeting his future successor, General Ernesto Geisel, then chief executive officer of the petroleum company Petrobrás. June 1973. O Globo Archives.

within the space of a few years and their organizations were decimated. Brazil sank into the "Years of Lead": a period of crushing repression in which political time was suspended. It had become an authoritarian, militaristic, and police state—buttressed by legislation that no longer set a time limit on its validity, and by a tentacular and repressive law-enforcement and state security apparatus—a state that was no longer being formed and re-formed in reaction to its own fragmentation and internal conflicts. As in the rest of South America, the "revolutionary" and dictatorial structure seemed complete.

This suspension of time would last only five years, however. In 1974, Ernesto Geisel, a new general-president labeled a castelista, began the fourth mandate of the "revolution" and, a few months after being sworn in, promised to take the country, if not into the liberal democracies' camp then at least away from the yoke of authoritarian regimes. Since all his predecessors had made the same promise, this was greeted with skepticism, to say the least. And yet the "slow, gradual, and sure détente" Geisel announced soon gained political content. During his presidency, media censorship was substantially reduced, while the excesses and operational autonomy of the law-enforcement apparatus were curbed. Last, a constitutional amendment in October 1978 put an end to the state of exception, repealing all institutional and complementary acts, including AI-5. After the stagnation of the Years of Lead, Geisel "brought temporality back into the political process."[1]

This lessening of authoritarian pressure initially occurred without direct public participation. For that matter, the fact that the political transition in Brazil was effectively gifted by the authorities conflicted with the democratic understanding that dictators relinquish power only if forced to do so. This causes serious difficulties of recollection. Whereas Argentina's military regime, stripped of legitimacy by its defeat in the Falklands War (June 1982), collapsed under popular pressure in less than two years, the Brazilian generals spent more than a decade gradually accustoming the people to the political instruments of a return to democracy. As they did so, they retained spaces of autonomy for themselves within the machinery of state and guaranteed themselves protection from legal sanctions for their wrongdoings. One of this strategy's main achievements was the unprecedented "national reconciliation" solution devised by the Brazilian military, its two-pronged amnesty of August 1979, which extended to the victims of political persecution as well as their torturers and killers.

One of the great difficulties encountered by the architects of "détente" (*distensão*) was keeping it under their control. Many sectors of Brazilian society made freer use than expected of the democratic tools returned to them, voting "badly," holding demonstrations, and challenging authoritarianism in the press as soon as the lifting of censorship made it possible. This was only one of the oppositions the Geisel government was facing, however, and not the most hostile at that. The general had first and above all to face his own camp of powerful military networks, which were highly antagonistic toward any lessening of the pressure of repression and any challenge to the authoritarian state. Between 1975 and 1981, the military government had to contend with a "second hard-line" offensive, subordinate to the agencies of political repression, opposed to a controlled opening, and inclined to take up arms to preserve the existing order.

Everything appeared to contrast the Médici and Geisel governments. A "tough" president was succeeded by a castelista; and a peaceful and lethargic military was replaced by the resurgence of a familiar conflict between, on the one hand, a Presidential Palace with liberal leanings and, on the other, groups of "fighters against subversion" raising the eternal specter of communist revolution. At the heart of both presidential terms, however, stood a single player, already known as the "intelligence community" (*comunidade de informações*) or "security community": officers, subofficers, and soldiers selected and trained to serve in the agencies of political repression. Their prestige, their community's internal solidarity, and its operational autonomy developed in the Years of Lead. Since then it had developed into a new, yet still dormant faction. The proclamation of détente in 1974 revealed its political dimension and its substantial capacity to harm the authorities, for which it would become a new "hard line." It took up position in an intramilitary game in which some of the players and some of the rules had remained the same. As always, it was a question of discovering how to make the numbers involved matter despite their lower place in the hierarchy; of rallying supporters by defining the boundaries of the "real revolution" while placing their opponents on the side of treason and compromise with civilian politics; and of banking on the good general so they could make him their "leader." All these objectives are familiar by now but they were given a new lease on life by the very different context. The protesters no longer wanted to change politics or participate in government, they wanted to maintain the status quo, a system of which they were the core.

A LEADEN SILENCE

The Médici presidency corresponded to the most repressive years of the dictatorship, during which the civilian political class had the least influence, censorship was at its worst, and secrecy at its most oppressive. There are very few sources from which to study the intra-military politics of these five years. After a reprieve for archive activity in 1969, a "leaden silence" effectively descended on political life, particularly within the military. The censorship expedited by AI-5 was boosted in 1972 by specific prohibitions relating to the possibility of a democratic opening, the presidential succession, the government's economic approaches, and the actions of the intelligence and law-enforcement services.[2] As a result, the press was horribly silent and while well-informed journalists retained their access and contacts, they kept their information to themselves. SNI bulletins and reports provide no more specific data about life in the barracks at the beginning of the 1970s than documents from other civil agencies (such as ministerial intelligence divisions). Nor is there anything to be gleaned from the Presidential Palace, since General Médici placed no boxes in the archives, unlike his predecessors, Castelo Branco and Costa e Silva, or his successor, Geisel.[3]

The Years of Lead are also those about which the protagonists had least to say. Repression and its attendant taboo on speaking out prompted witnesses, who were sometimes verbose when relating and justifying the coup, to dispense with this period in just a few words. Those who agree to talk, however, are unanimous in describing a post-1969 officer corps that was calm and submissive to its hierarchical superiors and to government authority after the recurrent disturbances of the first two military governments. Several elements could help to explain what seems, plausibly to our mind, to have been a mass stand-down by the officers. First, the "dirty war" against the armed Left united the military against a common foe and reduced the space available for internal disagreements. As in the past, they closed ranks against the enemy. Furthermore, there was genuine satisfaction with government activity, and not only among the military. Médici appears to have been very popular with the public at the time because of strong economic growth that temporarily masked social tensions even as it deepened inequalities. The campaigns of the government's brand new propaganda agency, the Special Public Relations Office (Assessoria Especial de Relações Públicas, AERP), were in full swing. It was the AERP that came up with the notion of "great power Brazil," a key concept in the military imagination, symbolized by large-scale construction works: laying the Trans-Amazonian Highway and building the Itaipu Hydroelectric Dam on the border with Paraguay. These great achievements and the genuine nationalist claims underpinning them no doubt helped to strengthen Médici's military base despite the disappointment for some young officers when General Albuquerque Lima was defeated in the 1969 election. The media presented the image of a simple man, loved by the ordinary people, and close to their concerns. Médici's love of soccer and his stadium appearances are famous and often mentioned by the military. The collective euphoria after Brazil's 1970 World Cup triumph made these images all the more effective with public opinion. His popularity seems to have enabled the "revolution" to reconnect with the imaginary "people" supposed to have carried it out.

The peace and quiet Médici enjoyed also stemmed from the fact that he amassed a unique political base, the infamous "intelligence community," made up of the staff of civilian agencies (although they might be officers, as in the SNI), military agencies (in the army, navy, and air force intelligence centers, CIE, CENIMAR, and CISA, respectively) or a combination of the two (OBAN and then the DOI-CODIs). It was not a united community. Real collaboration was impeded by service rivalry, hierarchical dependency (on the presidency, the ministry, the zone commander), and structural dependency. Its officers identified with a specific profile, however. Despite the rotation of posts, during the dictatorship "intelligence" in the military mind acquired the symbolic, albeit unofficial status of a combat arm, like the infantry or artillery. The development of specific training, run by the National Intelligence School (EsNI) as of 1971, promoted the specialization and isolation of these agents, regarded as an elite in terms of character and status, but also subject to extreme pressure that might potentially alter their personalities.[4]

Partly because of the lack of an easily accessible archive, the composition of the machinery of repression has not yet been scientifically studied (sociological profiles, means of recruitment).[5] Fragmentary information is to be found in the testimonies of a few former agents but these are rare and often merely touch on these issues. General Agnaldo del Nero, successively a member of the DOI-São Paulo (1970-71), the SNI (1971-72), and the CIE (post-1976), talks of his "entry into the intelligence sphere" as a promotion.[6] As a captain straight out of the ECEME, which he left with very good grades, and a trainee at the second (intelligence) section of the Second Army Staff in São Paulo, the standard of one of his reports on the progressive clergy brought him to his commander's attention. His age (he was thirty-five) was an asset. He claims that the best candidates for DOI entry were the youngest officers of the staff's second section. Entry into the intelligence sphere was then a professional and social promotion that he owed, as he himself says, to his own excellence rather than to personal choice. This was not true for everyone. Specifically, some officers known for their anticommunist militancy, such as Colonel Burnier or Colonel Silveira Leite, volunteered to set up and then run these agencies.[7]

Those responsible for police repression are seen as men apart, with different backgrounds and morals to regimental officers. Their appearance singled them out. They did not necessarily wear uniforms or have short hair, and the hierarchy weighed less heavily in their relationships with their colleagues. The material or symbolic benefits and remuneration they enjoyed, which some say were a source of envy and resentment, are a controversial matter. The majority of officers who were themselves involved in repression or who used state violence unreservedly during the Years of Lead vehemently deny any favoritism, whereas the civilian Left frequently highlighted facilitated military careers, the later acquisition of a military attaché's position abroad, or various bonuses, such as military decorations, made possible by time spent at the SNI, CIE, or the DOI-CODIs.

As a whole this community was content with the guarantees offered by the authorities: ever increasing resources, great operational autonomy (meaning agents were never answerable to superiors outside their own agency), and a highly favorable legislative framework unchanged since AI-5. Indeed, unlike neighboring countries (Argentina, in particular), Brazil followed legal procedures in most instances of persecution. The legislation substantially increased the prerogatives of military jurisprudence (which now largely took orders from the executive), drastically reduced the rights of the accused, allowed very long preventive detentions and easy convictions. Nevertheless, it did provide thousands of opposition members with a degree of structure for their arrest and detention. It often enabled families to be told about charges and places of imprisonment after some weeks, and prisoners to benefit on occasion from the services of a pretrial lawyer and, above all, to be kept alive despite being held in appalling conditions and systematically tortured, sometimes over several months.

The retention of a legal framework and procedures most probably made the Brazilian dictatorship less deadly. It did not, however, prevent the mass and systematic use of torture or the existence of secret detention centers, the "houses" (*casas*) that barely anyone left alive. None of these activities was unknown to the military and political hierarchy, and none of its officials appear to have been investigated. The climate suited them. Even one-time protestors, particularly the members of the militant wing of the "first hard line" (most closely linked to violent anticommunist organizations and the most involved in the revolts that preceded the coup) who packed the law-enforcement agencies, were happy with their new roles and with the status quo.

The exception that proved the rule came at the beginning of 1972, when there was a head-on clash between the President's Office and "radical air force colonels" João Paulo Moreira Burnier (then head of the CISA), Roberto Hipólito da Costa, Carlos Affonso Dellamora, and Márcio César Leal Coqueiro. In keeping with the failed terrorist operations that gave rise to the PARASAR scandal of 1968, these officers conducted political repression not just in bloodthirsty fashion but also more independently than other officers engaged in the same activities. They were willing to answer only to air force minister general Márcio de Souza e Mello and enjoyed his protection. On

March 15, 1972, after the particularly barbaric murder of guerrilla fighter Stuart Angel on CISA premises, seven air force officers, including the above-mentioned four, were removed from active service and the minister dismissed. This was partly to improve the regime's image abroad after an international campaign to discover how the young man, son of a famous Brazilian fashion designer and a U.S. businessman, had died. Burnier interpreted this punishment as the start of a "betrayal of the revolution," which revealed "a veritable turning point in the approaches of the President of the Republic to the Air Force's revolutionary officers." "It was there," he said, "that the collapse of that section of officers, which took part in the Revolution of '64 and had started to be overlooked for promotion, really began. . . . Gradually, the objective of provoking my departure and that of other officers who had secured priority promotion to the rank of general under General Costa e Silva became clear. It was easy to see. . . . It was a way of getting units with any military power whatsoever out of my hands, out of the hands of revolutionary officers."[8]

The ouster of "genuine revolutionaries" by a regime that had betrayed its ideals was the very argument used by the army colonels who had found themselves punished and marginalized by the authorities under the first two military governments. The indiscipline of their Air Force counterparts was of a different kind, however. It was not a show of politics banned by the disciplinary rules, still less a desire to be included in leadership circles. Rather it was a demand for complete autonomy in the use of repression. Certainly the "first hard-line" colonels who headed the IPMs had also exploited their police functions to demonstrate their strength to the president, but in doing so they sought to force the government to adopt a different policy. The situation was different during the Years of Lead. The bulk of the officers, even the most radical, were happy with the regime. The issue was no longer participation in state power but complete retention of the operational autonomy they enjoyed, together with the political system that made it possible, in order to pursue the physical elimination of the opposition.

During Médici's term of office, few had misgivings. Furthermore, Burnier and his acolytes had no support. Colonel Ibiapina, a veteran of the protest networks from their inception, told the U.S. military attaché that they were on their own and that the "hard line" was "weak and disorganized."[9] Disagreements remained but they were muted and, most important, affected only the circle of generals. Initially, for instance, there was tension between the Presidential Palace and the Army High Command, the latter transformed by the political and military crisis of 1969 into a sort of supreme authority of the nation.[10] Nevertheless, little by little, the President's Office, its cabinets, and the government gained the upper hand. The strong personalities of Army Minister General Orlando Geisel (brother of Ernesto, president from 1974 to 1979) and head of the Military Cabinet General Figueiredo (president between 1979 and 1985), helped assert this authority. The "regime of the generals" was moving toward "a military presidential regime"—a development General Ernesto Geisel would endeavor, with difficulty, to strengthen.

The best proof of the political pacification of the military and the supremacy of the executive was the succession process of 1974. In June 1973, Médici nominated Ernesto Geisel as the ARENA candidate for the October presidential elections. Geisel, younger brother of the army ninister, was then head of the Petrobrás oil firm, a comfortable relegation for a retired general, identified as a castelista. He had been chief of Castelo Branco's Military Cabinet. The ACE was not invited to take part in the decision. As if it were not strange enough that a president labeled "tough" chose a member of the "Sorbonne" as his successor, neither the revelation of Geisel's nomination, nor his "election" by a handpicked electoral college, nor his inauguration on March 15, 1974, appeared to provoke the least controversy or resistance in the military. Adyr Fiúza de Castro, an officer impossible to suspect of castelista sympathies—he opposed any kind of letup in authoritarian pressure—stated that he, his circle, and the hierarchy as a whole had rallied to the president's choice with the exception of Albuquerque Lima's entourage, a group he believed to be "very small."[11] The senior hierarchy and most officers accepted the president's choice without the slightest display of bad temper.

The 1973–74 succession remains one of the great mysteries of the dictatorship's political development. Specifically, it is one of the events that cannot be explained solely in terms of the classic castelista/hard-line dichotomy since Geisel was identified as a castelista himself. It characterized his entourage as well as his time at the Military Cabinet between 1964 and 1967. In particular, he was very close to General Golbery do Couto e Silva, éminence grise to Castelo Branco and head of his Civil Cabinet. The label would allow him to crystallize a certain number of expectations. Indeed, since the 1970s began, there had been calls for a reduction in authoritarian pressure, the removal of law-enforcement duties from the armed forces, and greater civilian participation in the affairs of state. The preferred platform for these calls had been the Superior War School (ESG), the bastion of the Sorbonne, since March 1970 when General Cordeiro de Farias spoke there, offering blistering criticism of AI-5 and the excesses of authoritarianism.[12] In the years that followed, several officers of indisputable "revolutionary" credibility followed suit. At the same time, the school's doctrine moved toward greater acceptance of certain democratic principles.

Could Geisel, an out-and-out castelista, perhaps even have an "'abertura' mandate?" How then to understand his nomination by Médici in the thick of the "antisubversion" struggle and the consensus that went with it? In reality, General Geisel's background and his plans were not quite so crystal clear. Of the characteristics of the "military Sorbonne," he could boast academic excellence, attendance at a U.S. military establishment (albeit only for a short placement at Fort Leavenworth in 1945), and, above all, having joined the Superior War School's permanent staff in 1952. Unlike many officers close to Castelo Branco, however, his career was not that of a professional legalist. In particular, he had backed the Revolution of 1930, then joined and supported the Vargas regime. Also, he was far from sharing all the castelistas' positions in either economics—since he championed more nationalist positions than the technocrats who surrounded Castelo Branco—or politics, having often leaned toward more authoritarian options in the years immediately after the coup. Nor, above all, had he been associated with any plans for political liberalization before he took office. He himself denied having made any pledges of that kind or having given the subject real consideration before his election. For him, it was Golbery do Couto e Silva, head of his Civil Cabinet, who was the main theoretician and instigator of détente.[13]

Geisel's castelismo affiliation was nuanced, therefore, but what made for consensus was not so much the ambiguities of his political profile as the strength of his military networks.[14] Ernesto Geisel's greatest asset was, in fact, his brother, Orlando, the powerful army minister, former chief of the Armed Forces Staff (EMFA) under Costa e Silva (1967–69) and strongman of the Médici government. At the time, he had an incredible institutional authority, linked to his image as a tough, inflexible man who frightened his enemies and entranced his fans. A shadowy and little-studied individual, he played a key role in both the political repression of the Years of Lead and the interplay between military factions during that time. Since the mid-1950s, he had taken a different line to his brother, Ernesto. They were neither allies nor close but family solidarity and, probably, the hope of retaining his influence prompted Orlando to support his younger sibling's nomination.

The context of 1972–74 placed particularly the Geisel brothers' authority beyond doubt. Since April 1972, the Brazilian Army had been facing rural guerrillas in the Amazon region of Araguaia within the states of Tocantins, Maranhão, and Pará. Since 1968, Brazil's revolutionary Left had confined itself to experiments in urban guerrilla warfare designed to raise funds and weapons and to encourage urban populations to take up resistance and revolt. At no point, whether it was in their plans or not, had groups found themselves in a position to establish a revolutionary *foco* in a rural area as advocated by Guevara throughout the 1960s. In 1972, the Maoist Communist Party of Brazil (Partido Comunista do Brasil, PCdoB), took the plunge.[15] A number of offensives involving the Military Police of the states concerned (special parachute forces, ground troops, and the Army Information Center [CIE]) were carried out one after the other against 150–200 guerrillas, often welcomed and supported by the local population. It took the authorities two and a half years, until October 1974, to wipe them out. The vast majority died in the field and are still regarded as disappeared today. The debate about Médici's succession, the choice of Geisel, his election, and his inauguration took place in a climate of great political and military tension therefore. These distant and unprecedented battles, in which the guerrillas were long undefeated, tended to quash internal turbulence and, particularly, challenges to the army minister who was heading operations.

In reality, General Ernesto Geisel's rise to the President's Office was not the result of victory by one part of the military over another and it is difficult to understand if viewed only through that lens. Factional membership was not the only element deciding the attribution of posts nor did it sum up the way in which the military envisaged the distribution of political legitimacy in their own corps. Professional prestige, an officer's personality and reputation, his political past, his personal and family connections, and, of course, his position in the hierarchy were all vital features. Geisel was acknowledged even by his opponents as an outstanding officer. His image was that of an austere and unlikable man, authoritarian but honest, as evidenced by his nickname "the German" and the systematic mention of his Protestant faith in military testimonies. In 1974, he was an army general at the very top of the hierarchy, albeit in the reserve. The consensus was completed through his own and his powerful brother's remarkable ability to connect with people within the military institution. Links of friendship and, in this case, blood played a leading role.

Once elected, however, the new president opted to do things his own way and to appoint someone else as army minister, casting a veil of uncertainty over the country's political fortunes. As soon as he was sworn in, the rumor of "détente" spread like wildfire. Justice Minister Armando Falcão denied it a few days later. Geisel himself delivered an inauguration speech that fell far short of the democratic pledges made by General Médici when he came to power, although these seemed bitterly ironic in hindsight. While the wind of democracy was blowing in the Portuguese motherland as signs of the Carnation Revolution made themselves felt and even reached the Brazilian press, the new president guaranteed in his speech that he would continue the work of another revolution, the one begun in Brazil by the coup of 1964.

RELATIVE DEMOCRACY

The mark Geisel and his government left on the collective memory has generally been kindly treated by retrospective consideration of the political transition. Since democratization occurred, the general who took the initial measures has been painted as a democrat or, at least, as an opponent of the authoritarian and military regime's survival. Systematically separated with the castelista wheat from the radical chaff, Geisel was able also to claim a comparative advantage over General Castelo Branco in the form of his success against the "hard line," which was kept to the political margins to some extent, whereas the first president had been unable to prevent its rise. Positive depictions of Geisel the statesman, accompanied by the master strategist, Golbery, the head of the Civil Cabinet and his right arm, flooded the media, journalism, and some academic output. Books by the journalist Elio Gaspari, published in the early 2000s, did a great deal to entrench this representation. Their dominant theme is precisely these two men, Geisel, the "priest" (*sacerdote*), and Golbery, the "wizard" (*feiticeiro*), makers and breakers of the dictatorship, each of whom evoked the author's evident fascination. Without going so far as to suggest there is a hagiography of General Geisel, it is worth noting that the ambiguities in how he is remembered equate to those surrounding the castelista military, whose authoritarian ideal was eclipsed by that of others, more radical than themselves.

Did Geisel have plans for democratization when he came to power? That would imply, on the one hand, that his team had clear objectives or even a model of the regime to be built and, on the other, that it was motivated by democratic ideals. The "détente," however, was partly improvised. It was not a negotiated and gradual return to the precoup situation; nor a cancellation of the dictatorship, as the opposition hoped, given the words used by the authorities themselves ("opening," "detente," "decompression"). In fact, Geisel's policy was more an attempt at the "institutionalization of the revolution" according to authoritarian ideals than a democratization.[16] It was an old authoritarian project of conciliation with the liberal reforms, which General Castelo Branco had already tried to implement: the development of a hybrid security-based, elitist political system, which borrowed a few elements of legitimization and effective functioning from representative democracy. The Constitution of 1967 should have laid the first stone of this building. The hardening of the regime and the relegation of the castelistas disrupted these plans, which could now be implemented thanks to the prosperity of the "economic miracle," the end of the armed struggle (the wiping out of the Araguaia guerrillas at the end of 1974 put a stop to any attempts at armed resistance to the regime), and the pacification of the barracks.

Geisel's "detente" highlighted typical castelista concerns, such as placing greater value on the two-party system—the general became involved in ARENA campaigns, for instance, in a way no previous president had done—and aiming to emerge from the state of exception, in other words, ensuring that discretionary acts were made part of the law and the constitution. The idea was to build a lasting political system. In July 1974 Geisel's secretary, Heitor Ferreira, in a note on an election timetable, took it forward as far as 2004.[17] The president's entourage at the beginning of his term was, then, engaged in reflection on an "ideal political system" that was destined to last, and that would allocate a prominent place to the military. Even so, its development was adjusted in keeping with election results and political and military pressures. It was partly improvised.

"Détente" was announced in a speech delivered in August 1974 to the chairmen of ARENA's local branches. Collective memory has retained only the notion of easing authoritarian pressure and the promise of generously interpreting one of the putschists' slogans, "Security and Development," to seek "the greatest development possible—economic and social but political too—with as little security as necessary."[18] And yet Geisel was above all presenting his ambition for an "objective and realistic institutionalization of the ideal of the '64 Revolution." It would include retaining the two-party system, since the existence of too many parties was thought to allow the corruption of politicians to flourish, and instruments of exception until the "creative political imagination" established "at the proper time, effective safeguards and solutions appropriate to the constitutional framework." Geisel's discourse conveyed the desire to keep democracy within a rigid legislative framework in order to mitigate the flaws and defects of the political class, as well as the people's incompetence and lack of insight—although the latter was not explicitly stated.

There were many unknowns behind this objective, particularly when it came to just how elections would be held, as demonstrated by the government's fluctuating stance from one election to the next. Political opening was announced at the same time as the start of campaigning for the legislative elections of November 1974. These entailed a degree of freedom for the MDB, especially when it came to electioneering, which brought it remarkable gains, although not a majority. It was a political earthquake that the authorities pretended to accept "without resentment," while intending to prevent it from happening again. Hence the "Falcão Law," named after Justice Minister Armando Falcão and adopted in July 1976 with a view to the municipal elections in November. It drastically restricted parties' and candidates' access to the media in order to confine the vote to the most local level possible, which did indeed ensure a clear success for ARENA and the authorities. These restrictions were extended to other elections by a package of laws in April 1977, enacted at the same time as the temporary closure of Congress, the extension of the presidential term to six years, the introduction of increased presidential control of the executive at all levels of the federation, electoral reforms favoring ARENA, and so forth. The "April Package" (*pacote de abril*) has often been interpreted, wrongly, as a backward step in the opening process. It was in fact a milestone in the political reform the authorities were seeking, the forms and pace of which depended directly on immediate issues.

In the wake of the pacote, Geisel stepped up proclamations about "relative democracy." The term appeared for the first time in an interview given to French journalists:

> When they talk about democracy, many people think about democracy in an absolute sense. That kind of democracy, I don't think exists anywhere. Everything in the world, except God, is relative. So, the democracy practiced in Brazil cannot be the same as the one practiced in the United States, in France or in Great Britain. Brazil has two problems which must make progress with politics: problems linked to economic development and problems linked to social development. There can

be no thought of a perfect democracy without a certain economic standard or a certain social stability. So, Brazil is undoubtedly a country where democracy exists, where liberty exists, but that democracy cannot be the same as the democracy of other countries. It has to take the economic and social conditions we live in into account. But I think that, in a general sense, our democracy is effective. It is functioning with certain problems and in certain circumstances, but it is functioning.[19]

Geisel was defining the regime that his "revolutionary institutionalization" was purported to produce: a democracy suited to the developmental delays and imperfections of Brazil. This is a classic theme in the history of authoritarian thought in Brazil and of Latin American conservative thinking in general: the impossibility of applying liberal precepts from Europe or ones devised for more developed nations to a fragmented, poorly educated, and underdeveloped society, with a people lacking political awareness and a political class lacking a sense of morality. Under the Estado Novo, this representation of relations between society and the traditional elites became state thinking and was used to justify the imposition of authoritarian rule.[20] Consequently, it was necessary to invent a political system suited to Brazil. It would be a less liberal system until such time as Brazil caught up with the rest of the world.

In the months and years that followed, Geisel made relative democracy a recurring theme of his utterances and it became omnipresent in the public domain. He often set liberalism, the Enlightenment's "pure ideal type, beyond reach and therefore utopian," against the pragmatism it took to wield political power, constantly trying to find "the balance, barely stable at that, between the responsible citizen's freedoms and the responsible authority of the state, between the objectives of each individual and the social values and interests of the national group."[21] In some respects, the degree of opening and political liberalism actually declined between November 1974 and the end of 1977. Throughout that time, the president had very frequent recourse to AI-5, stripping citizens of their political rights and elected officials of their posts—for corruption, to be sure, but also for political dissent. As a result, Geisel's détente created great uncertainty about the regime's development for all actors, civilian and military.

Castelismo then was not a form of liberalism. Just as the first government was not the government of the putschists "malgré nous," so the détente promoted by the fourth government did not correspond to a plan for a return, pure and simple, to civil and liberal democracy. Furthermore, Geisel did not fit the intellectual and political mold of castelismo in two areas: economic and financial policy, which was steered in a clearly nationalist direction; and foreign policy, conducted under the label of "responsible pragmatism," which meant abandoning an exclusive relationship with the United States and the Western camp. Médici certainly gave his economic choices nationalist features, but he did not set limits on foreign capital penetration and allowed considerable growth of foreign debt. Proactively supported by his industry and commerce minister, Severo Gomes, and despite the reluctance of his finance minister, Mário Henrique Simonsen, Geisel set about boosting state intervention in the economy and attempted to stimulate the domestic market and domestic investment. The worsening economic situation after the first oil crisis was to temper the authorities' ambitions, however. Geisel's foreign-policy volte-face was even more impressive. From his inauguration onward, the new president displayed the desire to diversify commercial, military, and technology partnerships to go beyond ideological conflicts. Among other symbolic decisions that were not to the liking of the most fanatically anticommunist officers, Brazil was the first country to recognize the new Portuguese government resulting from the Carnation Revolution. Still more controversial was its recognition of the People's Republic of China in August 1974 and then the government of Angola, brought into being by the victory of the Popular Movement for the Liberation of Angola in November 1975.

General Geisel's policy was not as understandable for people at the time, therefore, as hindsight might suggest. It was anything but a linear and controlled liberalization process. It overturned certain conventions when it came to economic policy, and broke so far away from Brazil's U.S. ally as to flirt with nonalignment. Many political protagonists were unsettled by this uncertainty. Staff of the machinery of repression soon interpreted it as the decline of the authoritarian regime, the abandonment of the strategy of out-and-out repression, and therefore as a personal danger, both professionally and legally.

The hostility Geisel provoked in the "intelligence community" was all the greater since one of the key elements in the decompression of the authoritarian regime was the president's war on the excesses and indiscipline of that very community. During the five years of his mandate, he effectively endeavored to curb overzealous repression (in particular summary killings and torturing to death, although he did not oppose torture on principle) and the autonomy of the security agencies. This was not always a symptom of liberalism or humanism. He also and perhaps above all saw in it, in his own words, the restoration of military discipline and the authority of the state rather than the sign of an opening of the regime. The hostility toward his government that some of the officers involved in repression began to display at the beginning of 1975 corresponded to a desire to retain their own operational independence. For these activists, it was not only a matter of political resistance to the change of regime but an attempt to continue freely the "personal war" they had been fighting since the Years of Lead began.

Last, the growing hostility and resistance of these men to the authority of the dictatorship's fourth general-president occurred within the very specific international context of deepening repression in the rest of the Southern Cone and the establishment of a multilateral police cooperation accord from the end of 1975, known as "Operation Condor."[22] The Chilean, Uruguayan, Bolivian, and Paraguayan dictatorships were at the height of their own repressive ventures. In March 1976 Argentina, already affected by legislation that was increasingly prejudicial to human rights and by extreme police violence, acquired a military government. The Condor Plan was in perfect keeping with the internal dynamics of these countries. In Brazil, it appeared to contradict the nascent strategy of opening and, especially, regaining control over the "security community." Nevertheless, Brazil was one of Condor's founding members. SNI chief and future president João Batista Figueiredo received a personal invitation from his old acquaintances Colonel Manuel Contreras and Colonel Mário Jahn, the director and deputy director, respectively, of Chile's National Intelligence Directorate (Dirección de inteligencia nacional). Figueiredo did not go to the founding meeting in Santiago but Army Minister Sylvio Frota and head of the Army Intelligence Center (CIE) Confúcio Danton de Paula Avelino—who, we should note in passing, were not themselves especially enamored of the Presidential Palace's plans for détente—sent two agents from the CIE to formalize Brazil's membership. The latter would be confirmed in the years to come. For those of the Brazilian military who wanted to maintain harsh repression, participation in Operation Condor increased the feeling that their government's approach had gone awry, was at odds with the spirit of the times, and out of step with the struggle against a subversive threat that clearly still remained.

THE SECOND HARD LINE

As of 1975, there appeared to be a repeat of a familiar stand-off. On the one side, we had the Presidential Palace—which it would be wrong to consider democratic or even liberal but that, nevertheless, evinced a degree of discomfort vis-à-vis police violence: it valued the party political system, agreed in good part to abandon censorship, and, above all, looked ahead to an end to the state of exception. For that matter, it was a palace once again staffed with officers close to Castelo Branco and kept out of public life since 1967. On the other side, there were the military members of the machinery of repression who, like their IPM elders, raised the eternal specter of communist revolution, which their weak and corrupt government would prove unable to face.

Was history repeating itself? With the same ideas, the same behaviors, the same actors? The application of the moderates/hard-line dichotomy to the whole of the dictatorship has tended to essentialize the military factions—in other words, to render them unchanging over time. With reference to the "hard line" in particular, this has masked the fact that the military networks varied a great deal.[23] At the end of the 1960s, the "hard line" as collectively expressed since the coup was clinically dead. With the group much weakened by repeated relegation to backwater posts and by strategic differences among themselves, the 1969 presidential succession dealt the final blow, particularly to the colonels at the heart of the protest. Many officers, as we have seen, did become part of the "intelligence community" that was being put together as of 1967-68, but these were moves by individuals or "clusters" of micro-networks. In no way was it the transposition of the disbanded network of the first hard line into the machinery of repression.

In addition, the protest the Geisel government faced between 1975 and 1981 had a very different appearance from the "first hard-line" protests. No longer generational, it was now linked to membership of specific military agencies, in which sergeants, captains, and colonels were all mingled together. Its legitimacy was no longer historical, linked to the recurrent conspiracies and revolts of the 1950s and 1960s and the coup itself, or intellectual as had been the case for some "hard-line colonels." Now it was born from the ordeal of "combat," meaning police repression. This justification was not entirely new. It had already surfaced in speeches by the IPM colonels in 1964-65 or the EsAO captains in 1969. Now, however, it was the only one. The protesters no longer had a past. The revolution they championed was no longer an old ideal for which they had long been fighting, but rather the authoritarian and repressive status quo, of which they were a central part. Finally, this activism now included acts of political violence and became anonymous.

The latter feature makes it very difficult to identify actors of the second radical wave or to differentiate them clearly from the "first hard line." The few lists of "hard-liners" of the 1970s that have been drawn up by witnesses highlight names that were slightly or not at all visible in the previous decade, often leaders of the CIE and, to a lesser extent, other repressive agencies.[24] First there was Adyr Fiúza de Castro, born into an old military family in 1920 and the CIE's first commander before heading the Rio de Janeiro CODI. A lieutenant colonel in 1964, he served in General Costa e Silva's entourage during Castelo Branco's presidency. At the Army Ministry, he rubbed shoulders with some of the key figures of the military far Right but never took part in any protest actions. He will be one of those loyal to General Sylvio Frota, the unruly army minister between 1975 and 1977. General Milton Tavares de Souza ("Miltinho"), born in 1917, succeeded him at the head of the CIE in 1969 and remained there until the early days of the Geisel presidency. A conservative and committed anticommunist, marked by his participation in the Intentona crackdown (1935), at which time he was a mere soldier, he had never taken part in uprisings or political protests before or after the coup. His deputy at the CIE was José Luiz Coelho Netto, born in 1921, also regarded as a radical, who became head of the SNI Central Agency. General Antônio Bandeira, born in 1916, had a relatively classic military career like his comrades, of which the inaugural experience was also the suppression of the communist revolt of 1935. A staff officer, unconnected to the conspiracy networks other than in the months running up to the coup, he earned his place as an extremist leader in the fighting against the Araguaia guerrillas between 1972 and 1974. He commanded regular army troops before the CIE under Milton Tavares completed the guerrillas' elimination.

These officers were all from the same generation as the colonels of the "first hard line" if not a few years older, although their low profile in the intramilitary political space of 1964–69 gives the impression that they were younger. The initial self-effacement and lesser political ambitions of the 1970s "hard-liners" allowed them to avoid the ostracism to which the so-called "hard-line colonels" fell "victim." In this way, they were able to reach the most important positions in the security apparatus and many attained the rank of general.

These previously low-key officers and some dozens of their colleagues first came out in opposition to the military government in the mid-1970s. They met and organized in all the intelligence and law-enforcement agencies, but the CIE was the focus of their protests. General Geisel is said to have attempted to use the SNI, directly subordinate to the President's Office and run by General João Figueiredo, who had the president's trust, to keep the CIE and the DOIs under control.[25] Hierarchical obedience was the key issue in the problem raised by these agencies and their staffs. The CIE was directly subordinate to the army minister rather than to the regular, territorially structured chain of command. Furthermore, General Sylvio Frota, the minister at the time, increasingly displayed a desire for autonomy from Geisel as of 1976. The problem the CIE posed for the administration within the state apparatus was organizational and disciplinary before it was political. Testimonies point to certain CIE officers' involvement as of 1968 in the far Right attacks that proliferated in Brazil's major cities, especially Colonel Luiz Helvécio da Silveira Leite, who ran the center's counterintelligence during the Years of Lead and was in the reserve from 1973 onward.[26] According to his own testimony, the "Secret Group" resumed its activities at the time of political opening. For example, Colonel Helvécio and Colonel Alexander Murillo Fernandes, a parachute officer and one of the founders of the center, were involved in distributing pamphlets within the military as of 1975 as well as in subsequent attacks. The "Group" is thought to have consisted of a handful of civilians and military personnel from various agencies of repression (DOPS, DOIs), a great many of whom had been part of the intelligence agencies and machinery of repression since their inception. Those officers who were members of the Group claim responsibility for some of the pamphlets distributed between 1975 and 1981 and for almost all terrorist attacks.

The testimonies of the small number of officers who took part in the "Secret Group" offer only a restricted view of political activism within the security apparatus, however. Behind the few high-profile activists was the entire machinery of repression, a breeding ground of opposition to the liberalization of the regime and to any political approach considered suspect from the point of view of an obsessive and obtuse anticommunism. The rationales for action and sense of political legitimacy of the agents carrying out this repression were very different from those of the "first hard line," and were the direct result of their isolated and prestigious position within the state apparatus and the military institution. Despite elements of continuity and personal links between the members of these different networks, therefore, a new hard line began to express itself during the 1970s, which was at the heart not of the army but of the apparatus of what was by now a police state.

TORTURE, PAMPHLETS, AND BOMBS

It is even more difficult than in the postcoup years to calculate the number of the military involved in these protests and to assess their reach within the institution. While anonymity is obviously to blame, so is the nature of the actions undertaken, for which it can be difficult to draw a line between what belonged to politics and what was law enforcement. One tool of resistance to détente was deadly police action, no matter the victim's standing. Once largely tolerated, these crimes were now an embarrassment to the authorities. How then can what constituted a protest, conceived in this way, be determined? Another practice alerting the historian to the existence of a political movement hostile to the government was the circulation of pamphlets. Unlike the public manifestos of the 1960s, these were lampoons distributed strictly inside the armed forces or, in the case of the earliest, to the "intelligence community" alone. This completed the change already discernible between 1964 and 1969, as protesting officers' utterances gradually vanished from the public arena. Stronger disciplinary constraints and media censorship do not alone explain this confinement to the internal military space. The rationale behind the protesters' actions was also changing. Their documents now aimed both to recruit activists willing to take up arms for the cause and to find supporters in the senior hierarchy rather than to win over public opinion in an ideological battle. Here too, however, the boundary between protest and professional action was tenuous, as many reports and briefing notes from the agencies were in fact political tracts designed for widespread (and legal) circulation within the institution. As a result, it is hard to demarcate the group within the intelligence community. It is the political participation of a far less well-defined and -identified, and even less well-counted group that we are going to describe and come to understand. It was also less visible, and intentionally so.

"The security agencies will remain active, therefore, persevering in the struggle, rigorous but without reprehensible excesses and tough but without unnecessary violence, because they are duty-bound to act to safeguard the institutions and public order." In these terms in August 1974, Geisel made it part of his distensão project to bring the machinery of repression into line. It is true that at the time, the security forces, especially the CIE, were still wreathed in the glory of having wiped out the Araguaia Valley guerrillas. Yet because no one knew at the time that this would be the last such guerrilla insurgency, the armed struggle did not appear to anyone to be over. On the other hand, the number of political prisoners killed, most often tortured to death, had fallen sharply since 1972 and even further since 1974. The initial reason for the decline was the eradication of the movements of the armed Left, which had been brutally suppressed since 1969. A few returning exiles and exposed clandestine figures were now the only prey for the agents of the security community. At the beginning of 1975, therefore, the latter set their sights on the Brazilian Communist Party (the Soviet-aligned PCB), clandestine but utterly opposed to guerrilla warfare and working behind the scenes with the MDB to find a democratic way out of dictatorship. The opposition's surprise triumph in the November 1974 legislative elections, together with a machinery of repression with little to do, gave rise to a new obsession on the military Right: the fight against the PCB, once again regarded as the source and mastermind of all subversion.

The offensive became official on January 31, 1975, when the printer producing the Communist Party's official mouthpiece, *Voz Operária*, was shut down. Right from the start, the frenzied crackdown on the party had government encouragement from justice minister Armando Falcão. In addition, a few days later, he released a report that gave the security community carte blanche. Following requests from families and civil-society organizations about twenty-seven disappeared persons, he cynically gave the fate of twenty-six opponents: "seven are free, six have fled, the whereabouts of four are unknown, four are unregistered, two are in hiding, one has been banished, one has been found, and one is dead."[27] The members of the machinery of repression, while not perhaps given a blessing, were clearly viewed with indulgence as they led some ten or so PCB activists or sympathizers to an identical end in the months that followed, torturing them to death at the São Paulo or Rio DOI, or on the premises of the CIE. The "security forces" also had support in the upper reaches of the military chain of command. General Eduardo d'Ávila Mello, commander of the Second Army (São Paulo), was their most visible supporter and champion in the press.

The media climate was changing, however. Political disappearances and especially torture became ever-present topics in a press that was increasingly critical of the agencies of repression and felt more comfortable in doing so with the gradual lifting of censorship as of February 1975. At the same time, politics as a whole was restructured with a view to a "détente," some MDB members even expressing support for the president on several occasions. Even though Geisel did not repeat his public pledges of authoritarian decompression, rumors, and anxieties in the military proceeded apace. They were echoed by General Hugo Abreu, head of the Military Cabinet, in March 1975. In a memo to Geisel, he emphasized concerns over low pay, threats to the security community, communist infiltration of the MDB, and government weakness.[28] Abreu identified the release of the first copies of a series of pamphlets titled "A Saga of Betrayal" (*Novela da Traição*), as a symptom and factor in that "anxiety" in the highly prickly Parachute Brigade of the Vila Militar, which he himself had commanded during the Médici presidency. Between February and July 1975, twelve issues in this venomous series attacked government policy and, above all, the influence and character of General Golbery do Couto e Silva, head of the Civil Cabinet. They were distributed first within the intelligence community and then in various garrisons and military schools.[29] Their authors were members of the "Secret Group," particularly Colonel Alberto Fortunato and Colonel Octávio Moreira Borba.

Neither the SNI bulletins of the first half of 1975, nor a CIE Periodic Intelligence Report in March 1975 credited the protesters' activity with very much influence.[30] However, there was often a case in these documents of acting both as judge and defendant at the same time, as shown, for example, in a so-called report, "Studies and Assessment of the 1964 Revolution." In fact, it was more like a political pamphlet. Dated June 1975, it took very militant stances on various issues, and issued an open call to conspiracy, while condemning the United States' loss of influence and the Western world's capitulation in the face of advancing communism. The report's author remained anonymous but it was the head of the CIE himself, Colonel Confúcio Danton de Paula Avelino, who ensured it was distributed. In this way, our source of information on these "conspirators" is written by the "conspirators" themselves, and it is thus difficult to extract any meaningful information from it.[31]

The protest grew between March and June 1975. The transfer of political prisoners held in an island jail on Ilha Grande to mainland prisons after they went on hunger strike and released a manifesto gave rise to a great surge of discontent inside the machinery of repression. SNI agents joined the chorus of dissatisfaction. Other pamphlets hostile to the government were reported in the First Army in Rio de Janeiro in July.[32] Finally, in September an SNI report made first mention of the threat posed by the "members of the Radical Right" responsible for the "distribution of anonymous pamphlets" and deemed to be the "greatest threat to the cohesion of the Armed Forces."[33]

Another event during the same period inflamed the passions of the military personnel most fanatically engaged in the "struggle against subversion." This was the discovery in August 1975 of a "communist nucleus" within the São Paulo Military Police (PM). Dozens of police officers were arrested and interrogated. Two were tortured to death. These police offensives were media and political operations. They sought to provide public opinion and the government with concrete proof of an enduring communist threat or even of growing infiltration of strategic sectors, such as the police, or those traditionally targeted by the military Right, such as journalists, academics, and intellectuals in general. In October 1975 a final operation was staged. It began by leaking the PM affairs to the media and continued in a wave of arrests in intellectual circles. Among the accused was Vladimir Herzog, a well-known journalist, playwright, and PCB activist, tortured to death by agents of the São Paulo DOI on October 25. His death, poorly disguised as suicide by hanging, sparked considerable emotion in civil society and a degree of unease in the Presidential Palace.

All this despite the fact that Geisel had refrained from criticizing the agencies of repression in the preceding months. In August 1975, he even appeared to be omitting them from a plan for détente that was in marked retreat from the suggestions of the previous year: "The security agencies will persevere with measures to prevent machinations, including those still in preparation, which might contribute to internal subversion. . . . The intelligence services are closely following communist infiltration of the communication agencies, class organizations, and the political administration, particularly in education, as well as in the political parties."[34] Throughout 1975, security apparatus staff were in a position of strength, therefore. They had staunch supporters in government, particularly in the Justice Ministry and the Army Ministry, and in the military hierarchy, they retained their autonomy in law enforcement and faced no outright attacks from the President's Office.

The Herzog affair, which has gone down in collective memory as a symbol of state violence and its impunity, was in fact a one-off event and a turning point in the history of the dictatorship. Even if it was not the first killing of an opponent in the regime's jails since Geisel's election, the murder of a well-known individual was the first clear act of provocation by members of the machinery of repression. It coincided with a greater use of police action as a political manifesto, even at the risk of scandal. Public discontent destabilized the government. The press widely debated the circumstances of the tragedy and a mass celebrated in São Paulo by Bishop Dom Paulo Evaristo Arns, who was highly critical of persecution by the regime, seemed like an immense opposition demonstration. Geisel was obliged to take a stance regarding the activities of the agencies of repression. The latter showed unfailing solidarity, nevertheless. When the journalist was buried, SNI agents distributed a report to the press defending the intelligence community. Despite the reluctance of some in his government, notably Army Minister General Sylvio Frota, Geisel had an IPM opened into Herzog's death. The military far Right had no difficulty taking control of it, however, and it was Colonel Alexander Murillo Fernandes, one of the founders of the CIE and a long-term member of the "Secret Group," who was given responsibility for the inquiry. Unsurprisingly, it reached a verdict of suicide. General Ednardo immediately claimed victory, declaring that the Herzog IPM was "the best response to the red Nazis."[35] Nor did a coincidence of timing count for nothing. Herzog's death, the launch of the inquiry, and its abortive outcome coincided precisely with the weeks in which the Condor Plan was drawn up in Santiago, Chile, an episode that appeared to validate increasingly unfettered repression and lauded its perpetrators to the skies, particularly CIE agents.

As a result the security community and its sycophants emerged triumphant from the Herzog affair. It was nevertheless their swansong. A repeat of an identical scenario less than three months later drove the president to wage war on his most fanatical agents. On January 17, 1976, trade unionist Manuel Fiel Filho died under the same circumstances and within the same walls as Vladimir Herzog, those of the São Paulo DOI. His murder was also disguised as a suicide by hanging and this was confirmed at an autopsy performed by the same doctor, Harry Shibata. The case was aggravated by breaches of the rules of hierarchy in informing the president. It was São Paulo governor Egydio Martins in fact rather than the military leaders who informed Geisel of the prisoner's murder. Serious penalties were not long in coming. The following day General D'Ávila lost the command of the Second Army and Colonel Confúcio Danton de Paula Avelino that of the CIE. Geisel made this two-pronged decision without alerting his army minister, General Frota. The president's message was crystal clear: as of that date, political killings by staff of the agencies of repression would no longer be considered misdemeanors that could be blamed on unruly subordinates. Those higher up in the hierarchy, right to the top of the chain of command, would be held responsible.

The effect was immediate. No political prisoner was tortured to death in Brazil's prisons after Manuel Fiel Filho.[36] The regime's machinery of repression still killed members of the opposition but in different circumstances. A last police offensive was launched in December 1976 against PCdoB headquarters, in which three activists were shot dead in the street. The offensive, in which Colonel Carlos Brilhante Ustra, ex-head of the São Paulo DOI and Police Officer Sérgio Fernando Paranhos Fleury, a member of the same state's DOPS and regarded as one of the most barbaric torturers of the Years of Lead, is known as the "Massacre of Lapa" (*Chacina da Lapa*). In 1977 and 1978, no more murders or political disappearances of Brazilian citizens on national soil were recorded. As of 1979, with the revival of the social movement, it would be at the picket lines of strikes and at workers' and peasants' demonstrations that the regime would claim its final political victims.[37]

This sheds new light on the problem of the operational autonomy of the agencies of repression. As soon as real political will was imposed through the military hierarchy to put an end to the most outrageous human rights violations, they were halted even in a context of great animosity toward the authorities. This did not contradict the fact that these services had functioned largely independently of the chain of command and heedless of the rules for the past six years. However, the hierarchy's scant control over the actions of these men was in itself a political choice. For many years, the military authorities had opted not to control their own machinery of repression.

Also in 1976, although political prisoners were no longer being killed, the security community was anything but calm. On the contrary, the production and distribution of pamphlets skyrocketed. On February 2, an SNI report stated that a "small group" of the "Radical Right" was intent on taking advantage of the previous month's events.[38] The activists linked to the "Secret Group" continued their agitation and the writing of satirical tracts constantly focused on lampooning the Geisel–Golbery duo. As one of the most fanatical members of the group, Colonel Borba, stressed: "The objective . . . was to be rid of Geisel because he had shown himself to be a 'traitor.' As soon as we found out that he was a 'traitor,' we started to let everything hit the fan. The other target was Golbery and everything that had to do with antinational interests."[39]

The so-called "Secret Group" was no longer the only one to be promoting far-right agitation. A new group emerged, the Brazilian Anticommunist Alli-

The bombing attempt on the Riocentro concert hall, on May 1, 1981, in Rio de Janeiro, is the last terrorist attack of the "second hard line." Undated. Carlos Chicarino / Estadão Conteúdo Archives.

ance (Aliança Anticomunista Brasileira, AAB), its name clearly inspired by its Argentinean counterpart, the murderous "Triple A," responsible as of 1973 for the killings of hundreds of left-wing militants. The AAB was responsible for the return of political violence in Rio. On August 19, bombs were planted at the Brazilian Press Association (Associação Brasileira de Imprensa, ABI) and the Order of Attorneys of Brazil (Ordem dos Advogados do Brasil, OAB). Only the first exploded and there were no casualties. On September 22, the home of journalist and press baron Roberto Marinho was the target of a bomb attack, while the bishop of the Rio suburb of Nova Iguaçu, Dom Adriano Hipólito, was kidnapped and subjected to abusive and degrading treatment. On November 15, municipal election day across the country, terrorists destroyed first the head office of alternative newspaper Opinião and on December 6 that of the Civilização Brasileira publishing company. Some of these had already been targets of the military Right in 1968: journalists, publishers, the progressive clergy. Hatred of these progressive social groups was revived as they rallied once more in 1975 against ongoing police violence and in favor of the amnesty and a return to democracy.

The AAB were trailblazers. A multitude of anticommunist groups, often focused on violent action, thrived or gained a new lease on life between 1979 and 1981. The Anticommunist Movement (MAC) and the Communist Hunting Command (CCC) emerged from a decade in hibernation, while the new Delta Commando (named in honor of the French OAS execution squads[40]), the fascistic New Fatherland Phalange (Falange Pátria Nova), and the Moralist Brigades (Brigadas Moralistas) would be the most involved in acts of terrorism.

Apart from differences of form and tone, the pamphlets circulating within the armed forces in 1975 and 1976 were far more ideologically consistent than the manifestos of the "first hard line." In particular, an obsessive idea featured in the documents that the incumbent authorities were not only weak and cowardly regarding the presumed resurgence of "communist subversion," but encouraged, incited, and supported it. The military protestors claimed that, in their plan for opening or détente, President Geisel and his loyal sidekick, Golbery, had revealed the secret ambition of the whole military "Sorbonne" since before the coup: that Brazil should join the socialist camp.

None of these topics was completely new and, in this sense, throughout military rule there was real continuity in hard-line mindsets, which were largely heirs to the antiliberal conservative thinking of the interwar years and then the Estado Novo. The political class was deemed unsuited to exercising power, which was seen as intrinsically corrupting. Communism posed an inherent threat to Brazil's history and social reality. It was characterized by changing faces and a capacity for dissimulation and infiltration. The "Revolution" and the "Ideals of '64" were constantly referenced, never explained, and eternally betrayed.

The protesters of the 1970s stood out in several respects in their discourse and political practices, however. Satirical tracts often targeted individuals, particularly Golbery do Couto e Silva—the "Saga of Betrayal" was dubbed a series of "anti-Golbery pamphlets" by one of its authors[41]—and, before long, Geisel himself. While conflicts between factions within the armed forces had formerly retained a degree of camaraderie, the main people wielding political power were now clearly identified as enemies. Presidents Castelo Branco, Costa e Silva, and Médici had generally been spared even by the harshest critics of their policies. Geisel was the first whose image was tarnished and who suffered personal attacks by the malcontents. It was Figueiredo who won all the laurels when it came to the radicals' loathing, however. Colonel Cyro Etchegoyen said of him: "João Batista Figueiredo is the greatest of all the traitors to the Revolution. He was not the first but he was the greatest traitor to the

Revolution and the leading revolutionaries."[42] As a corollary of this representation of the authorities, the malcontents set themselves up as "resistance fighters": they did not organize or protest, they conspired. Furthermore, the ways in which pamphlets were distributed was far more reminiscent of the intramilitary propaganda that preceded the coup than the manifestos published in the press that followed it. The documents were dispatched in small consignments, anonymously and from different post offices.

All these tracts linked Golbery do Couto e Silva to the characteristic features of the enemies of the revolution, the armed forces, and the nation. In the most aggressive documents, he was frequently given nicknames, most notably "Gregório the White," a reference to Gregório Fortunato, Getúlio Vargas's henchman, who was black, and presumed guilty of the August 1954 assassination attempt on Lacerda. The name branded Golbery a murderer, and a traitor to his duties, while simultaneously slotting the protesters' attacks into a long history. Golbery was also regarded as a traitor to the national cause, self-interested, amoral, and sold out to foreigners. There is a clear parallel between these features and those that anti-Semitism traditionally attributes to the Jews, with Golbery also demonstrating Machiavellian duplicity and a love of money. He was accused of being the éminence grise of the President's Office, pulling the strings behind the scenes and benefiting, to the detriment of the national interest, from "international big capital" as president of the Brazilian branch of the U.S. firm Dow Chemical. A March 1976 pamphlet, very probably written by the people who wrote the "Saga of Betrayal," lamented the fact "that our Fatherland is the great victim, defenseless and burnt on the altar of Geisel's vanity and the insatiable greed of Golbery do Couto e Silva, this hawker of Brazil and of national dignity itself! We can all see and feel in our flesh the evil spells of this murky business called distensão, détente,[43] or opening—a euphemism invented by the manager of Dow to bamboozle the unworldly."[44] Geisel was initially seen as a weak and cowardly victim. The real culprit was Golbery:

> Geisel, you still have time to free yourself from this new Rasputin, a Machiavellian traitor who, if he continues his lies, may lead you, like Getúlio, to suicide.
>
> There is still time to free yourself from the pernicious influence of this little worm who, as he flatters you, is filling his pockets with petrodollars, illegally making himself and his numerous gang rich.
>
> Geisel, we ask you by all that is holy to rid yourself of this wretched man and his one eye.

According to the protesters, the ministerial team's moral decay and antipatriotism had led it to the supreme betrayal of subscribing to communism. The expression "communo-corrupt" was not meaningless invective. Rather, it was how the military Right saw the getulista camp and, more specifically, the members of the Goulart government, simultaneously morally decadent and sympathetic to the communist cause. The comparison between the president's team and Goulart's were legion, as were the parallels drawn between the advance of subversion under the two governments. A pamphlet written by members of the CIE in May 1976 says: "When we raised our voices here to inform the nation of the full extent of a sinister plan of betrayal hatched by the corrupt lackey of Dow Chemical—the wretched Golbery—ally of communists, *janguistas* (Goulart's supporters), *brizolistas* (Brizola's) and so many other amoral persons, we thought that, with the Teutonic naivety of a great big gullible colonist, General Ernesto Geisel had been hoodwinked but then, gradually, time saw to it that all the members of that squadron were revealed as traitors to the Movement of March 1964."[45] The government's real plan was said to be to support the new and peaceful strategy the Communist International had drawn up to seize power. The members of the military Right could not envisage that the breakup of left-wing armed movements, which, incidentally, they believed incomplete, could mean the end of the "subversive threat." The communist strategy was a global one. Its divisions were superficial, even the lines between Soviet, Chinese, and Cuban, since the all-knowing and far-reaching communist movement had plans for the long term. The end of urban and rural guerrilla warfare was merely a change of strategy, a move from armed struggle to mass politics.

From this point of view, every sign of a reawakening civil society was proof, put to good use in the military's pamphlets, of the advance of communism—through the ballot box since the MDB was systematically discredited as bursting with subversive agents, through the student movement, and through organizations engaged in the human rights struggle, the battle for an amnesty, and the abolition of measures of exception, such as the OAB, dubbed "Moscow's dog" by the AAB, which had attempted to blow up its headquarters.[46]

The notion of the enemy switching strategy and an anticommunist paranoia verging on insanity over widespread infiltration and the culpability of the PCB alone were well-established at the time of political opening. The same theories were expounded in the press by Democratic Renewal Action (Ação Democrática Renovadora), an organization of conservative officers, and at lectures given at the military schools. Officers, authorized to speak in public and the vast majority of them generals, were able to convey and enlarge upon the security community's warnings about the survival, even resurgence, of the subversive threat. The military protesters added, however, that the government was not content merely to support this "communist upsurge": since the beginning of the 1960s, the ESG itself had allegedly set the establishment of a socialist government as a "Permanent National Objective" (a term from National Security Doctrine jargon). This theory was most clearly set out in a 1976 document interpreting the legalist hesitations of Castelo Branco as the result of "his ideas and plans to introduce socialism," although "the time available and the prevailing pressure" were said to have prevented completion of the project.[47] Geisel, the first president's dilettante disciple, was alleged to have set about implementing the objective in 1974, the key proofs being his leanings toward diplomatic multilateralism, the "dialogue with the Left"—in March 1977, the president gave ARENA Senator Petrônio Portela, chairman of the Senate, the mission of setting up a platform for negotiations between the MDB and ARENA—and an economic policy of state control.

In this way, Geisel's policy, in many respects more "nationalist" than that of his predecessors, was accused of a socialist bent inasmuch as it moved away from the dogmas of economic liberalism (were very much entrenched in the Southern Cone as of the mid-1970s under the influence of the Chicago Boys) and strict alignment with the Western bloc. Nationalism was no longer a priority objective for the "second hard line" although they retained all their contempt for the multinationals with which they associated Golbery. All political choices were now measured, as they had been in the run-up to the coup, in terms of the danger of a communist revolution, with the military government itself seen as its architect.

The security community was said to be the only barrier to this venture to "bring about socialism." It was sufficiently adept and well-informed to be aware of it and strong enough to attempt to block it. From this came a new obsession in the protesters' minds: the government's desire for the "destruction of the Intelligence and Security System or the suppression or removal of its members."

> As a consequence, the media has begun openly releasing names and drawing up harsh criticisms and condemnations. Lists and names have been sent to the [presidential] PLANALTO PALACE and *have been well received there*. The pro-

cess is under way and the socialists are delighted. Every support will be given to the PRESIDENT in search of a shared objective: creating a socialist BRAZIL....

The Security and Intelligence Agencies have been neutralized and prevented from operating effectively, giving the socialists free rein for actions of their own.[48]

The document's authors were alluding to the first condemnations of cases of torture and political killings, which were beginning to be made by prisoners, their lawyers, and their families.[49] The word "revanchism" had not yet appeared but it was these officers' written words that gave birth to an idea that would be omnipresent in the military discourse about the dictatorship for decades to come: that the defeated were seeking revenge in the media, in memory, and in the courts. Ultimately, however, no justice at all was served.

In this way, the "second hard line" of the 1970s, largely born out of the regime's security agencies, constructed its own discourse about the betrayal of the revolution. In the early days of the regime, the military governments were primarily accused of compromise with the civilian political class; leniency in the purge they were carrying out; legalist scruples about adopting authoritarian instruments; and an insufficiently nationalistic economic policy. Whereas now, the discourse of protest was simpler, more aggressive, and more consistent. Its venomous anticommunism, shored up by the practice of repression, became the only way of interpreting the "revolution," and helped reinvent ideological oppositions between military factions. The Sorbonne and the ESG group were classed as on the Left. Symbolically excluded from the revolution's camp, they came to represent its opposite—a communist dictatorship.

The age of the ill-defined revolution was over. The military far Right was now defending not its own interpretation of the revolution but the "System," and its own position in it. If the word "revolution" remained omnipresent, it was no longer used to designate any particular project of social and political reform, however authoritarian, or even the memory of the coup. It signified a dictatorial status quo, of which the sole dynamic was the ever-more intensive persecution of the social and political movement of the Left.

The whole discourse these officers held sought to justify maintaining the machinery of repression and the structure of dictatorship on the grounds that the war on communism was not over. Since to their mind the subversive threat was eternal, so was the legitimacy of a military and police regime. Furthermore, the way in which the protesters presented and pictured their political identity was connected to the evolution, since the coup, of legitimate political roles within the armed forces. Indeed, unlike the "first hard line and its power-hungry officers," that of the 1970s was not looking for increased influence within the state apparatus. The notion of the collective responsibility of the armed forces or the "real revolutionaries" was rarely emphasized. This new generation of the military far Right appears to have accepted the imposition of a "generals' regime."

Nevertheless, the difference in political practices between the militaries of the two "hard lines" does not imply that the regime had profoundly altered military behavior. The increased indiscipline, intramilitary power struggles, and the demand for greater political participation, in the years after the coup, were not the norm. This was an answer to a one-off situation: the "postrevolutionary" climate. In addition, some militant networks, in the sixties, were already maintaining a rationale of protest or resistance rather than one of demands and participation. This was true of the "Secret Group," active in 1962–64 and 1967–68: it was more akin to the anticommunist activist movements and subscribers to "permanent conspiracy" of the 1950s and 1960s than to the handful of colonels asking to be included in running the state after the putsch. Not surprisingly, many 1975–77 activists, members of the law-enforcement apparatus, had links with these protesting and violent networks of the previous decade. The "generals' regime" neither depoliticized, nor demobilized the military institution: it imposed the hierarchical order as a condition for speaking out in public and accessing the highest political posts, but at the same time opened up a strategic space at the height of the state apparatus—the agencies of repression—to highly politicized officers of all ranks.

THE PRESIDENT AND THE MINISTER

As well as the vociferous discontent of law-enforcement personnel, Geisel also had to face dissent from another quarter, his army minister, General Frota, who was beginning to unite the malcontents, irrespective of their position in the hierarchy. Frota was not known as a radical, still less a potential troublemaker, when he was appointed army minister a few weeks after Geisel's inauguration.[50] Admittedly, he had strong ties to the intelligence community. He was chief of staff to Army Minister Lira Tavares between 1967 and 1969 and was involved in setting up the CIE before finding himself at the center of the political crackdown on the Rio–São Paulo axis as commander of the First Military Region (Rio de Janeiro) and then of the First Army.

Even so, in 1974, his image was that of an officer committed to military discipline and the rules of hierarchy, and even sufficiently respectful of military regulations and customs as to condemn torture—although there is serious doubt about this reputation. Frota was certainly a man who cared more about hierarchical rules and precedence than the charismatic military leaders who preceded him did. In 1976, when protest in the security agencies was growing and he became its hero, Frota never let himself be seen in the company of junior officers, unlike, for example, General Albuquerque Lima who was always being greeted by hordes of captains during his travels in 1969, or even General Costa e Silva to a lesser extent, who was acclaimed at the Vila Militar at the end of 1965. Frota, by contrast, traveled with a bevy of generals, as when he visited Congress on the national holiday in 1976.[51] His obsession with discipline was expressed particularly in the reform of the army's Disciplinary Regulations, which on June 19, 1977, made the reserve military subject to the same ban on political statements as serving personnel. Last, General Frota used his institutional authority to influence the balance of power with the President's Office. He used the Army High Command (ACE) as his main political resource, endeavoring to unite it around his own positions. For that matter, he held far more frequent meetings of the ACE than Orlando Geisel, army minister under Médici, who had summoned the generals' council only three times a year whereas his successor did so nineteen times in 1974 and 1975 alone. The ACE meetings marked the rhythm of his gradual departure from the president's line, therefore, even before he genuinely embarked on dissent.

At the time, the political role of the generals' councils, particularly the Army High Command, had not been codified. All the presidents had come up against its customary authority, which was buttressed by the association of the "revolution" with the "armed forces." For General Geisel, gaining the approval of his peers for his distensão project was at least as important as reining in the intelligence community. When he came to power, however, the new general was confident of his own authority over the senior military hierarchy.[52] It is important to recall that he belonged to the "old generation" from before 1910. He had been in the reserve since 1969. Unlike his predecessors as head of state, he was faced with army commanders and heads of military departments who were much younger than he, making it easier to assert his authority. It was his dissident army minister, seeking to make the generals and especially the ACE his main political resource, who triggered the opposition between the Presidential Palace and some members of the senior military hierarchy.

The political embarrassment Frota caused Geisel came early on in his time at the ministry. He often publicly defended the activity of the agencies of repression, particularly against media "libels," and privately informed the president of clear differences of opinion regarding foreign policy, economic choices, and relations with the MDB. The positions he adopted were systematically in keeping with the line of the "radical Right" but he displayed a surface loyalty to the president until the end of 1975. The tensions were only exposed on the deaths of Vladimir Herzog and Manuel Fiel Filho. The minister, despite his alleged hostility to the violent treatment of prisoners, unreservedly backed the torturers who killed the two men. Shortly after Herzog's death, opposition deputy Francisco Leite Chaves took exception to the practices of the agents of repression and ventured a comparison between the Brazilian dictatorship and Nazi Germany. Of the abuse, he said that "even Hitler didn't use the Reich's Army—for that he created the SS." Frota then informed Justice Minister Armando Falcão that he demanded "reparations" and to this end he summoned the ACE. It was a breach of the chain of command since he had given the president no advance warning. When, a few months later, Geisel relieved General Ednardo D'Ávila Mello of the Second Army Command and dismissed Colonel Confúcio Danton de Paula Avelino as head of the CIE, Frota once again convened the High Command to discuss the president's decision but the incipient protest was rapidly aborted because of objections from General Reinaldo de Almeida, STM minister and Geisel's close associate, who stressed that it was not the ACE's mission to oppose the executive's measures.[53]

Indeed, Frota behaved like the head of the army and its representative to the authorities. He claimed to be defending its "rights," its political rights in particular, rather than imposing the president's wishes and decisions. He said so himself:

> Nor was it a secret anymore that I considered myself to be representing the Army to the president so as to fight for the greatness of the institution and the well-being of its members. The Army's missions had been set out in the Constitution and would be accomplished with discipline and rigor. I did not, however, like the idea of acting as the president's submissive representative or emissary to the Army, issuing opinions that favored certain political pretensions to the detriment of the ideas and interests of the collectivity I led. The president was entitled to accept them or reject them but it was vital that he knew about them.[54]

In this way, Frota was, to a certain extent, defending the political system that seemed to have been installed in 1969 and that the reassertion of presidential authority by Médici and then Geisel had soon changed: the political sovereignty of the army, represented by its chiefs. He frequently brought this to Geisel's attention, long before he openly revealed his dissent: the president was only a delegate of the "Revolution" and the revolution was the armed forces, represented by their chiefs.

This depiction of the legitimacy of power is vital for an understanding of the dynamics of the political and military crisis that developed in 1977. At issue was a successor to Geisel, who was attempting to repeat his predecessor's achievement and appoint an heir in the corridors of the palace in a very monarchical understanding of the generals' regime. Geisel made no secret of it. On the pretext of the necessary separation of the armed forces from politics, he banned officers with a general's rank in all three services from involvement in politics and political debate. He said he was "sure that no ambition or reaction would come from the Armed Forces that would compromise the always delicate process of the presidential succession, which it is incumbent upon me—by virtue of the office I hold and the responsibility it bestows upon me—to conduct when the moment comes."[55] Since the armed forces, including their very highest ranks, had to steer clear of dirty political competition—all ambition and self-serving manipulation as it was—the Presidential Palace chose to make the selection of a successor a private affair.

In fact, the campaign had begun at the end of 1976. The army minister's visit to Congress at the start of September was effectively the launch of his own campaign. Frota was mindful not to make the same mistake as General Albuquerque Lima, who had lost civilian support. On the contrary, he cultivated friends and clients in ARENA throughout 1977 until there was a genuine "frotista" group in the assembly, supporting his nomination. It was made up of deputies clearly positioned on the far Right, such as Marcelo Linhares, the brother of "first hard line" Colonel Heitor Caracas Linhares, Dinarte Mariz, or Sinval Boaventura. Frota presented himself, including to his civilian supporters, as the senior military hierarchy's preferred candidate against "the personal power of Geisel," whose preference for SNI chief General João Batista Figueiredo was common knowledge. His reasoning was reinforced by a key fact, that Figueiredo had only three stars and, in keeping with the sequence of promotions, would secure the last one long after the November 1978 presidential elections. This hierarchical shortcoming created an unease among the senior military hierarchy, which was exacerbated by his accelerated promotion, permitted by Geisel via numerous *caronas*, in other words, by leaping over major generals who had spent longer in that rank.

Without making an issue—still less a project—of his beliefs, Frota campaigned in the army and in civilian political circles in the name of the generals' regime as it appeared to have been defined in 1969, and against dictatorship by a "small group in the palace." At the beginning of October 1977, the minister's dissent reached the point of no return. The frotista group launched an offensive in Congress, monopolizing the floor in increasingly less veiled opposition to the government. Rumors of a manifesto signed by civilian and military figures favoring the minister's candidacy were doing the rounds, thought to have been masterminded by General Odílio Denys, General Jayme Portella de Mello, and Admiral Rademaker, all long-standing "radicals."

For Geisel, this was the last straw: Frota's insubordination and attempts at subversion had gone too far. The President's Office appears to have realized the military threat inherent in Frota's removal, which is thus shrouded in safeguards. In particular, the decision was announced on October 12, 1977, a holiday, making troop mobilizations more difficult. Head of the Military Cabinet General Hugo Abreu was tasked with securing the support of major unit commands, especially in Brasília and Rio's Vila Militar. Frota lacked the wherewithal to resist. The generals let him down, which left him with an eternal grudge against them and a feeling of "betrayal." He was unable to summon the Army High Command. Geisel got there first. Those who appeared to have given Frota their unfailing support declined to back his resistance. The power grab would not take place.

The epilogue to this affair of state was the leaking to the press of a virulent antigovernment manifesto written by Frota.[56] In the belief that it would fully expose his former minister's folly, Geisel did not prevent its publication. Prepared far in advance and sent by telex to every garrison in the country on the same day that Frota was dismissed, the document aimed to incite a widespread revolt of troop commanders against the incumbent authorities. It was a failure, and two weeks later an SNI report stated that the barracks were calm.[57] It did cause a great stir, but not so much in the barracks as within the political class, which appeared not to have realized until then the radical nature of Frota's positions, echoing those of the security community's protest pamphlets point for point. It condemned "certain deeds and behaviors, unsuitable to revolutionary conduct"; a foreign policy indulgent toward communist regimes; "the existence of a process of placing the national economy under close supervision by the State"; "criminal indulgence of communist infiltration and the leftist propaganda that appears every day in the press, in student circles, and in government agencies themselves," and, most of all, "the constant encroachments aimed at destroying the national security structure or rendering it harmless.... They call their areas of competence into question, they suggest doctrinal modifications, and they allow themselves foul smear campaigns against the intelligence and security agencies, seeking to present their members as bestial torturers in order to discredit them in the eyes of the nation." According to Frota, the regime's drift to the Left was accompanied by "a clear intent to distance the Armed Forces from the country's decision-making processes, monopolized by a small group embedded in the Government." Frota urged the military masses "from the highest-ranking chief to the young recruit" to resist this "marginalization" and the communization of the country. "And should fate determine otherwise, when the oppressive manacles of totalitarianism bead the pale brows of your wives with the sweat of bitterness, I do not want you in your wailings of despair to accuse General Sylvio Frota of any omission or of failing to alert you to the impending danger." Repeat patterns occurred in politics within the Brazilian armed forces throughout military rule: a President's Office with liberal-authoritarian plans versus "barracks" made fanatical by anticommunism and repressive zeal; a minister who became the leader of young malcontents; presidential successions almost systematically entailing crises or politico-military tipping points. As a result, the years of political opening can seem like the mirror image of those of the Castelo Branco government: the Presidential Palace, imbued with a degree of "moderation," even seemed to defeat the same "hard line" that had annihilated the first general-president, by dismissing the minister who was the radicals' chosen candidate.

In several respects the intramilitary domain did indeed show real continuity, mainly in its political mindsets. This is clear as regards "castelismo," despite the different political shades of the 1964–67 and 1974–79 governments. As for the "radical Right" of the 1970s, to some extent it took various key ideas of the 1960s' "hard line" to the extreme. Its antipolitical position induced it to exclude civilians from power altogether, never envisaging their return. Ultimately, the agents of repression merely systematized "the cleanup operation" clamored for after the coup and pushed it to its limits. The simplistic, black-and-white view of politics came to apply to intramilitary conflicts within the "revolution" itself: whoever was not an ally was a communist. Freed from the postcoup confusion and unconstrained, the military far Right would follow its authoritarian and repressive path to its very limits throughout the 1970s. Moreover, intramilitary conflicts remained constantly focused on the same question: in whom is the real sovereignty of the "Revolution" invested? In the "legitimately elected" government? In the armed institution represented by its chief, that is, in the generals' councils? In the opinion of the barracks? In the key players of the revolution, who enact its ideals, notably by reshaping Brazilian society via political repression? There was also a degree of continuity in the individuals involved, since some long-standing conspirators of the 1950s who were anticommunist activists in the 1960s appeared also in the machinery of repression during the Years of Lead. They were the most virulent, most violent, and most visible detractors of political opening and the easing of repression.

Even so, the "right-wing military protest" of 1974–77 was in many ways the product of the hierarchical and police version of the regime itself. In the early years of the dictatorship, middle-ranking officers seeking greater involvement in government were held back. This "first hard-line" movement was defeated and disbanded at the very time that an increasingly authoritarian and repressive regime was being built, which in fact met the protesting officers' initial demands. The regime became "military," in keeping with the ethos of the organization, particularly its strict rules of hierarchy and the lack of political involvement for junior officers. It would be not a "regime of the military" but a "regime of the generals." Having dealt with that ambiguity, the regime now faced another: the state structure of civilian democracy (a president, government, and congress) was retained, thus leaving the generals' government as a matter of custom rather than rules. The army's hierarchical elite had no institutional role. It used its influence in a constant power struggle with the official wielder of power, the Presidential Palace. It was this never-resolved ambiguity that gave rise to the real threat to political opening that was Army Minister General Frota's dissent. The champion of the "generals' regime" against a President's Office condemned as dictatorial, he turned himself into the system's man against the threat of change, the champion too of the machinery of repression, from which came his main supporters.

The "second hard line" or "radical Right," enmeshed as it was with the intelligence and security community, was not of course formed intellectually and politically only by its experience of repression. The agencies attracted officers already enthused by the fight against subversion, and in some cases already involved in small, militant, even terrorist groups. But the regime gave them a place and a system to defend, as well as a new political identity. As Alfred Stepan was already suggesting in 1986, the experience of repression and the fear of serious repercussions against themselves and their organization if there were to be a democratic opening, played a huge role in the political radicalization of these men.[58] Many of these "fighters of the revolution" believed, among other things, in the undying threat of subversion, to which there was but one response: that the Years of Lead last forever.

CHAPTER SIX

The Final Campaign
1977–1978

> I can say with equanimity that I stood for election in order to help the Armed Forces leave the political stage. This move, I am sure, is the prevailing desire of my professional comrades. It is why I was a candidate of the party of opposition, of opposition to the authoritarian continuity that is now compromising the military's prestige. . . . It is essential that the Armed Forces as permanent institutions take themselves out of the political process. Not as the vanquished but as victors.
>
> —GENERAL EULER BENTES MONTEIRO

For the Geisel government 1978 had the air of an epilogue. With Frota dismissed, the official candidate, General Figueiredo, was rid of his main rival. The protesters in the security apparatus had lost their hope of political power with the departure of their spokesman and protector in government. They had proved that they exercised little influence over the military when, in October 1977, neither barracks nor serving generals in command posts gave the ousted minister the slightest support. Head of the Military Cabinet General Hugo Abreu was tasked with releasing the memorandum that made Frota's dismissal official. In it he denied any connection to the presidential succession.

Frota's replacement was cleverly chosen. General Bethlem, then commander of the Third Army (based in Porto Alegre in the south of the country), had a reputation for championing positions as radical as those of the officer he succeeded. In September 1977, he leaked a "report" on the situation in Brazil that was every bit the equal of the radical right's pamphlets in terms of anticommunist paranoia and hostility to democratization.[1] The President's Office intended this choice to defuse the right-wing opposition, which seemed at the time to be the only barrier in the armed forces to the president's plans. For its part, civil society was only just beginning to remobilize and some political

General Euler Bentes Monteiro epitomized internal army disagreement with the dictatorial government. He stood in the 1978 presidential election as an opposition party candidate. Here he addresses Congress in October 1978. Orlando Brito / O Globo Archives.

reforms, notably the laws of April 1977, promised to guarantee comfortable victories for the government party, ARENA, in the upcoming elections.

For the government, the military crisis of October 12, 1977, was supposed to end rather than postpone intramilitary presidential campaigning. Furthermore, although deliberations were officially due to start in January 1978, the President's Office announced on December 29, 1977, without any kind of consultation, that the "candidate of the revolution" would be SNI chief General Figueiredo. From February onward, the press frequently called him "the president," with a degree of derision, while a recent relocation of the SNI managers had placed him in the Planalto Palace itself, just a few hundred meters away from the president's offices. The Electoral College had already been composed, mostly from ARENA councilors. The October 15, 1978, vote appeared to be a foregone conclusion. Consequently, historiography has devoted very little space to the presidential campaign of 1978 and the intramilitary politics of that year. The few books that do exist are journalistic, many written at the height of events.[2] Concerning the end of General Geisel's rule, researchers have focused more on the rebirth of civil society, the precursor of the great social movements that blossomed at the start of Figueiredo's mandate.

Yet the political remobilization affected the officer corps too and had a greater influence on the course of history than the final result might suggest. Discernible in some archive documents from the inception of the Geisel government, it reappeared in the press and the public domain in 1978 when the presidential succession was at stake. The imposition of an heir by the President's Office had the opposite of the hoped-for effect. A few days after it was announced, the succession problem became the intense focus of officers unhappy about seeing the palace impose its wishes on the armed forces and on public opinion. The signs of this military engagement in the campaign were not long in coming. On December 29, 1977, Reserve Colonel Iese Rego Alves Neves raised the possibility of an alternative military candidate—Army General Euler Bentes Monteiro, a member of the High Command just a few months before and only recently transferred to the reserve. A few days later, General Hugo Abreu, head of the Military Cabinet, tendered his resignation to the president on the stated grounds of his disagreement with Figueiredo's nomination. In his memoirs, he says that this was when he decided to "go to war" against the president and his entourage, who both stood accused of immorality, corruption, and dictatorial inclinations.[3]

From the beginning of 1978, a genuine political movement came into existence in the officer corps and opposition circles to offer an alternative to the government-designated successor. Its forms and ultimate aims were unprecedented under the military regime. For the first time, officers claiming to belong to the " 31 March Revolution" were joining forces with the institutional civilian Left that was part of the political system, in other words with the MDB, in order to challenge the authorities and to take power. Dwindling media censorship and the greater freedoms afforded the opposition gave this movement a high profile, even though the demand that the military keep out of politics, intensified by a decade of dictatorship, forced most of the actors to remain secret and anonymous. The political game over the presidential succession broke away from the moderate/hard-line dichotomy completely. The opposition to the military government followed a more democratic and liberal line than the government itself, despite settling on a candidate who fitted the profile customarily demanded by the regime in every respect. In other words, he was a four-star general. Moreover, Euler had the backing of long-term dissidents, many of them members of the "first hard line" that had called for a "collective and radical revolution" in the years after the coup. This last about-face by radical officers has largely been forgotten by works covering this period, sometimes on purpose—because it upsets a certain memory and representation of the political scene that define themselves by constants and dichotomies.[4]

The history of the dictatorship has largely forgotten the formation of a military "anti-candidacy" in 1978, because of its marginality—since General Euler was defeated—and because it seemed eccentric if not incomprehensible in the classical representation of the military political stage of the dictatorship. The defeat of the "General of the MDB" was not as great or secure as the previous presidential vote, however. Whereas Geisel won with over 84 percent of Electoral College votes in 1974, Figueiredo won with only 61 percent. The ARENA members of parliament did not join the dissidents as Euler's supporters had hoped. It was not unthinkable, however, since it was a split of this kind that, six years later, would enable the election of an opposition candidate as president and thus the end of military rule. Euler was not so very far from coming to power. Nor was his candidacy a complete anomaly in the history of the dictatorship. Admittedly, it was the outcome of this specific context of political opening that helped some officers take their activism out of the barracks and into party and electoral politics. At the same time, it marked the end of the dissident careers of certain officers of the "first hard line." Their action was no longer driven by the ambition to take part in a movement they interpreted as a revolution or, like that of their counterparts in the "security community," by the hope of preserving a repressive system. On the contrary, they wanted to bring down a regime discredited by the monopoly it had conferred on a handful of generals and technocrats whose aim was believed to be to hold on to power.

What appeared to be a political about-face by these actors and a delicate, if not compromising, partnership for the MDB nevertheless had a key element of continuity: the call for an individual political role, which these "first hard-line" officers had constantly made. In addition, it was still in the name of the revolution that they took to the political stage. Paradoxically, the same body of words and references used in postcoup manifestos and pamphlets was now put to use to defend what was effectively a democratic program, centered on convening a constituent assembly, direct elections, a political amnesty for opposition members, and a return to civil rule. What seems at first sight to have been the pinnacle of political hypocrisy for actors eager since the coup to draw nearer to power and then avenge themselves on those who had denied them access is in fact spectacular proof of the malleability of their political identities. This unexpected behavior also revealed the diversity of "hard lines" under the military regime in terms of the courses and legitimations of their political actions.

DÉTENTE AND THE OFFICER CORPS

Once again, visible political mobilizations concerned only several dozen men. An attempt to understand what was happening in the background, in other words to try to grasp the stance of thousands of serving officers, is necessary so as to make sense of these political moves. What did the barracks think about the détente engineered by the Geisel government? From the sources, the military opinion of the day is difficult to understand. It remained a factor of political legitimization and thus a key issue for the protagonists, and as a result testimonies about it conflict. Nor do the actors always put the barracks on their own side. If the detractors of detente talk of a "unanimous opinion" in the armed forces that "took a very poor [view]" of political opening,[5] the castelista officers place far greater emphasis on weak politicization than on mass support for government strategy. Colonel Moraes Rego, who was close to Geisel and replaced Abreu as head of the Military Cabinet in January 1978, puts obedience, linked to a degree of caution about the potential consequences of change on the armed forces, at the center of the military's behavior: "They were honest but anxious—after all, support is far more than simple obedience. They could sense, which is very important, the president's great responsibility and trusted him as a child trusts his father. Those who really were sincere supporters were few in number. I think there was always a fear of revanchism, many had that fear. Belief in the army as an institution, often, encouraged people to disregard the fear of not being deemed revolutionary."[6] The few available archives confirm that even as late as 1977 the officer corps was not the setting for major protest movements. Debates about the controlled political opening, if they took place at all, did not elicit the concern of the government espionage services. For example, under the entry "Military Arena," SNI reports in 1974 and 1975 mention only signs of professional discontent regarding low pay and, to a lesser extent, military career progression.[7] Admittedly, the authorities did worry that these issues might fuel disaffection for the regime and greater sympathy for the opposition that since mid-1975 had been campaigning for higher military pay. The rapprochement between the serving military and the civilian opposition was initially only a minor concern for the

President's Office, however. It was primarily troubled by the radical Right in the law-enforcement agencies and their spokesman, Army Minister Sylvio Frota.

Nevertheless, sectors of civil society weary of military rule placed great hopes in the younger generations of officers as of 1974. This is attested by the extensive media coverage of the Carnation Revolution in Portugal at the end of April that year. The publication in full of statements by Portuguese officers and the comments and even comparisons that accompanied them had the thinly veiled goal of arousing the same feelings in Brazilian officers. The Portuguese revolutionaries' lines of argument certainly recalled the "costs of authoritarianism," which those of the Brazilian military who favored détente believed would also be borne by their country's armed forces. Indeed, the three manifestos behind the April 25 uprising, which appeared on the front pages of all the major Brazilian newspapers, condemned the separation of the armed forces and the nation and stressed the need to restore the military institution's lost prestige. The exile to Brazil of Portugal's ousted president, Marcelo Caetano, and the return of Carlos Lacerda to the public stage as the interpreter of the Portuguese Revolution fueled parallels between the Salazar regime and Brazil's dictatorship.

In fact, despite very little media coverage of a phenomenon that concerned only a small minority and was inevitably kept secret, some young Brazilian officers had been organizing since the beginning of the Geisel government to support or even radicalize the abertura (opening) strategy. A planned Nationalist People's Movement in Support of the Geisel Government (Movimento Nacionalista Popular pro Governo Geisel, MNPGG) was reported in an SNI document dated October 1974.[8] Its origins went back to the end of 1973 but it was only a year later that contacts began to be made between opposition politicians—whether or not "revolutionary" measures had stripped them of their mandates—and young serving military personnel. They called for the "gradual normalization of Brazilian life; a realistic economic and financial policy; an end to torture in the barracks; broad freedom in the election campaign; a realistic foreign policy." The captains' generation, the most numerous in the officer corps, appears to have been the pivot of this movement and, as a generation, displayed genuine resentment of the generals who were in power. According to the anonymous officer who wrote the document, "The recent events in PORTUGAL, in GREECE, and in AFRICA have prompted reflection within the Brazilian officer corps." They confronted the young generations with the problem of their own political role, of their opinions about foreign and economic policies, and, more broadly, about anticommunism as the only lens through which to view the world. MNPGG members regarded themselves as anti-imperialists and nationalists. They said they feared "the reaction of imperialism, the multinationals, the Brazilian reactionaries and fascists, the military right and the corrupt centered in São Paulo who, united, would plot the overthrow of the Geisel Government." Economic nationalism was then clearly linked to a democratic ideal, recalling the positions of the military getulistas, driven out of the armed forces in successive waves since the coup. Furthermore, the document spoke of meetings between this network, on the one hand, and General Hélio Lemos and the colonels Francisco Boaventura, Rui Castro, Amerino Raposo, and Sebastião Chaves—all former "first hard-line" militants—on the other. It did not indicate clearly whether they backed the plan for an MNPGG or whether they were merely making contact. Nevertheless, the creation of this nexus of dissidents and political opponents, united by nationalist issues and rejection of a continuing regime of exception, was a unique phenomenon since the start of the dictatorship in 1964.

It is difficult to establish the objective these officers were pursuing. What attitude did they plan to take toward the new government? One of collaboration, pressure, opposition? It was a question that faced the generals as well, who opened a dialogue with the MDB as of 1975. The most active and most visible was General Cordeiro de Farias, who had made his commitment to a return to civilian rule clear since the Years of Lead. His main reason was the damage done to the armed forces by the exercise of power and above all of police functions. A few years later, in the middle of the presidential campaign to find a successor to Geisel, he said:

> What do we have nowadays? A few privileged persons who are standing for election. A few, a very few. They are the army generals. In my day there were eight. Now there are 12. Can it be possible that the Brazilian elite eligible for the presidency is made up of only 12 people? This country of 120 million inhabitants has a choice of only 12? . . .
>
> Further, I am concerned about another distortion of military service: the Army is in the process of becoming the police. The Army has to count on all its forces to preserve its noble and irreplaceable duties. But acting as the police? Entering houses at night and arresting people is not the Army's duty and does it profound damage. It loses the wholesome nature of its personality and sets a negative ex-

ample to future military staff. Now, in this context, I would prefer not to be a soldier.[9]

Born in 1901, Cordeiro de Farias was now an elderly general and had been involved since his youth in uprisings and revolutions and in elected or executive office. He was the archetypal military leader with a lengthy service career, of the kind Castelo Branco wanted to see disappear. He was not a "liberal," he said, and he had no intention of appearing to be. He agreed with the castelista plan for strong, elitist government, the "relative democracy" Geisel claimed to be building at the time. To his mind, however, this entailed reestablishing control of the police apparatus and taking law-enforcement tasks away from the armed forces to restore the latter's image as the sentinels and protectors of the nation. Since 1974, he had criticized certain cases of torture and political killings to his colleagues. Victims' families identified him as a possible contact. The famous fashion designer, Zuzu Angel, sent him many letters throughout 1975 when she was looking for her son, Stuart, tortured to death on CISA premises in 1971.[10] And yet this behavior did not make him a dissident or an opponent of the government. Families also contacted Golbery to find out what had happened to their relatives. In addition, the contacts Cordeiro de Farias made with the MDB as of February 1975 were authorized and encouraged by the authorities. Nevertheless, it emerged in the press that Cordeiro aspired to enter into agreement about a civilian standing in the next presidential election. This was not the plan of the president who had expressed his concern on several occasions about contacts between the MDB leaders, particularly Thales Ramalho and Ulysses Guimarães, and certain sections of the officer corps.

Alongside Cordeiro de Farias was General Rodrigo Otávio Jordão Ramos, former Amazon military commander and a long-term supporter of a liberalization policy, who had made an increasing number of statements favoring a return to "constitutional rule" since the beginning of 1976. The profiles and political strategies of the generals differed widely. Some were inclined toward genuine collaboration with the government, like Cordeiro, who in 1977 was part of an official mission to talk to the MDB (the "Portela Mission") and civil society associations. Others were set on dissent. Some had been critical of the excesses of military authoritarianism for many years, such as Brigadier Eduardo Gomes, General Rodrigo Otávio, General Cordeiro de Farias and, far more forcefully, General Peri Constant Bevilacqua, dismissed from active army service in January 1969 and very much involved in the growing movement for a political amnesty. In February 1978, for example, he took part in setting up the Brazilian Amnesty Committee. Others whose pasts were far from liberal, had gone into opposition after a fall from grace or out of frustration at never being part of the leading circles of power.

In their bid to make themselves heard in the public arena, many of these officers opted for the same strategy of dialogue, or even collaboration, with the opposition party and, to a lesser extent, with civilian organizations fighting to restore the rule of law. Some even entered the elections game themselves. Such conduct had already been displayed in 1966–67 before the hardening of the regime completely obliterated the MDB's potential for harm. Effective détente therefore brought the policy of the barracks into the public domain. Intramilitary activism revived as civil society remobilized, providing the officers with intermediaries, together with a political outlet. Nevertheless, until 1977, these practices were confined to a handful of generals and not clearly identified as genuine opposition to the government.

Two events transformed these scattered voices into a military protest movement against the government: the April 1977 "package of laws"; and General Figueiredo's nomination as the official candidate for the upcoming elections, which had been an increasingly less well-guarded secret until it was leaked by someone close to the Presidential Palace in July 1977. These decisions exacerbated doubts about the sincerity of the government's liberal intentions. Some sectors of the MDB then embarked more clearly on a strategy of opposition with their sights on the presidential election. At the same time, the isolation of the palace group caused great discontent in some parts of the military whether or not they approved of the process of political détente. The president's entourage was accused of arranging to remain in power and of exercising that power without any consultation whatsoever with the senior military hierarchy or "revolutionary" political circles. General Figueiredo's lack of popularity with the military elite completed the alienation of the malcontents.

Figueiredo was the first official candidate of the "Revolution" not to belong to the 1900 generation. On the contrary, born in 1918, he belonged to that of the "hard-line" colonels. He was a mere lieutenant colonel at the time of the coup. Before 1964, he made a name for himself as an outstanding officer, joining the permanent staff of the Superior War School at a very young age. He went on to work for Golbery at the National Security Council and won his trust. During Goulart's presidency, he proved himself a very active member of the opposition. An instructor at the ECEME, he helped make the school one of the main hubs of the conspiracy. As a colonel under the military regime, Figueiredo became an intelligence officer and the apparatus's man. Golbery made him part of the recently created SNI although he did not take on the "castelista" label. He briefly returned to the troops under Costa e Silva before being removed from their command once and for all. Médici made him head of his Military Cabinet and Geisel appointed him to head the SNI. Although he had links to a variety of factions and was appreciated in high places for his cheerfulness, he had held few command posts, which diminished his reputation in the barracks. His detractors criticized his transformation into a bureaucrat and his lack of leadership of the officer corps. In addition, according to established custom, his mere three stars invalidated him as a candidate of the "revolution."

The first open demonstrations of discontent came in 1977. The military protest movement, which claimed to be the adversary of the government and the regime, was still very marginal but it now affected the lower ranks of the officer corps, primarily lieutenant colonels and colonels. To begin with, it was clandestine. At the beginning of 1977, a Democratic Constitutionalist Military Movement (Movimento Militar Democrático Constitucionalista, MMDC) was set up by about ten colonels, serving mainly in Rio de Janeiro.[11] The group set itself the objective of supporting an opposition candidate in the upcoming presidential election, first Senator Magalhães Pinto (ARENA/Minas Gerais), one of the civilian leaders of the "revolution," who had made no secret of his presidential ambitions since the end of 1976. The MMDC drew up a list of clearly democratic demands: the summoning of a constituent assembly, an amnesty for political crimes and offenses, the restoration of the judiciary's prerogatives and habeas corpus, the repeal of AI-5 and other measures of exception, and the installation of a provisional government. The members of the MMDC in no way disavowed the "revolution" of March 31, however, and placed the emphasis on an argument well-known among revolutionary officers: that a military government had been brought into disrepute, having betrayed the armed forces, which had been transformed in spite of themselves into the "Praetorian guards of technocrats" who were believed to have perverted the revolution.[12]

There is an obvious similarity with the arguments the "radical right" used to denigrate the government, in particular the image of a government of technocrats as a usurper and "traitor to the revolution." It took up the traditional elements of the military's apoliticism, attributing to the presidential group the worse defects of party politicking (*politicagem*), ambition, love of power, self-interest and corruption, and detachment from the people. This depiction of the enemy was far more the common denominator of the military opponents of General Figueiredo's candidacy than their fluctuating and, in some cases, largely superficial "political liberalism."

The MMDC was a secret organization that did not aim to inform public opinion. Its one public appearance, when a few individuals held a demonstration, took place at the Vila Militar on March 31, 1978, during a commemoration of the coup attended by Geisel. It was from precisely this date that the existence of a growing military protest movement calling for more rapid liberalization and opposed to the imposition of Figueiredo's candidacy was fully revealed.

Admittedly, some officers had taken this stance in public since mid-1977. These were the colonels of the "first hard line," active in the years that followed the coup and familiar with public statements and disciplinary sanctions. In July and August 1977, Colonel Rui Castro, Colonel Francisco Boaventura Cavalcanti, and General Hélio Lemos sent the senior military hierarchy letters in favor of "the military returning to the barracks" and an "end to exceptional rule." All three were in the reserve. Rui Castro left active service in 1972 at the same time as General Moniz de Aragão, to whom he was chief of staff. Boaventura was sanctioned by AI-5 in 1969, while the regulations forced Hélio Lemos into the reserve in 1975 as a brigadier general whose sole command had been the Army Documentation Center in Brasília. Nevertheless, they were all subject to disciplinary regulations as reserve officers under Frota's June 1977 reform (Geisel only abolished the measure by decree in July 1978). Rui Castro was the only one to make public the letter he sent to all the High Command members. In it, he said that "political engagement damages the armed forces in the eyes of the people, disrupts their training and the performance of their administrative and command duties, and distances them from the fundamental military values of their hierarchy structure."[13] He claimed that the 1964 emergency had justified a stranglehold on state power that, in the interests of the armed forces themselves, could not continue: "Let us set them free so that the nation can set itself free." For the colonel the sole solution was the "summoning of a constitutional assembly, elected by clearly free and direct suffrage, under the watch but without the intervention of the Armed Forces which, also free, will be able once again to take action should an exceptional situation regrettably recur." He denied any personal involvement in the succession process on the grounds that he had long called for a return to civilian rule. Since the beginning of the Costa e Silva government, the idea had been championed on several occasions by the so-called "orthodox," of which he was one. Boaventura and Lemos declined to support Rui Castro, however, or to give any political dimension to their own letters, the contents of which they kept secret. Castro alone was sentenced to two weeks in jail. The first signs of protest fizzled out.

It was only in March 1978 that the disparate coalition opposed to the imposition of General Figueiredo took on real significance in the media. The trigger may seem trifling. It was a speech delivered by the commander of the Thirteenth Armored Infantry Battalion in Ponta Grossa, Paraná, to the members of the local Lions Club.[14] Titled "Participation and Responsibility," it was a set of thoughts about politics, freedom, and democracy and constituted an indirect attack on the regime. Its author's identity enhanced its political influence. It was written by Lieutenant Colonel Tarcísio Nunes Ferreira, veteran of the Aragarças revolt and a conspirator since the early days, later affiliated to the "hard line" linked to Colonel Boaventura. A low-key activist in the years after the coup, he still had considerable prestige in the military and publicized his comments widely. In his speech, the lieutenant colonel defined democracy as the nation's "natural" leaders taking control of the country's destiny. The military government was implicitly accused of "totalitarianism" because it deprived society of political participation and organization and thereby helped "the state take control of life . . . [which] means initiative paralyzed by bureaucratic centralism, the economy disorganized by inconsistent experiments, authorities without a sense of responsibility because of excess power, the masses manipulated by official interventionism.. . . Society has to live for the State; man for the machinery of government." Although Tarcísio Ferreira did not accuse the government of colluding with "subversion" as protesters on the radical Right did, he, like them, exploited the anticommunist mindset of officers and conservative civilian elites to denigrate it.

The lieutenant colonel was initially given only a symbolic sentence of two days' house arrest. The Lions Club speech, however, was merely a trial balloon. A few days later, Tarcísio gave a lengthy interview to journalists, in which he took a more openly dissenting position.[15] Like the manifesto of the Democratic Constitutionalist Military Movement, the lieutenant colonel condemned the separation of the armed forces and the executive, as well as the latter's dictatorial inclinations. In his opinion, extending the presidential term to six years, a measure included in the April 1977 "package," had the dangerous consequence of giving the head of state the opportunity and the time to replace all the four-star generals and so nip in the bud any leanings toward protest or resistance within the military hierarchy. Tarcísio urged his comrades to speak out on politics—preferably the generals, for he was not free of the requirements of hierarchical thinking—but if they chose to keep silent, their subordinates: colonels, majors, and junior officers.

Tarcísio was in fact defending the principle of a "break with discipline" in "extreme situations" where legitimacy took priority over legality. It was how he justified both the coup and the political action of individual officers. At the time he was very much involved in the campaign supporting Magalhães Pinto, who was challenging General Euler Bentes Monteiro for the role of anticandidate to General Figueiredo. The issue kept the press busy throughout March and April 1978. Many articles correctly stressed that no superior officer, colonel or lieutenant colonel, had spoken out in public for a decade. The interview on March 11 earned the colonel the highest penalty for disciplinary infractions: thirty days in jail and dismissal from his command. Testimonies of solidarity poured in. Magalhães Pinto and Ivo Arzua, former agriculture minister in the Costa e Silva government and now chairman of the Ponta Grossa Lions Club, made them public, while Colonel Rui Castro visited Tarcísio in his prison cell. The MDB took up his cause and on March 16 organized a one-and-a-half-hour debate about him in the Chamber of Deputies. Leaving prison on April 12, Tarcísio reiterated his earlier positions: "Ideas cannot be jailed."[16] A Military Police inquiry was launched, its progress closely followed in the press for more than a year.

Lieutenant Colonel Tarcísio Nunes Ferreira's statements, the supporters he attracted, and the media audience he gained provoked a counteroffensive from the government that appeared to interpret the affair as the sign of a strong movement in favor of an accelerated political "opening." Looking back, Tarcísio saw it differently: "They thought it [was] a rallying sign for a violent pro-opening movement. But no. I hadn't plotted it with anyone. Not even when I was dismissed from my command. When I gave my departing speech, the troops played the 'Carrier Pigeon' (*Pombo Correio*) tune. So then they told themselves 'carrier pigeon' was a signal telling everyone I'd sent a message. But it was nothing of the kind."[17] On March 31, Geisel's speech no longer targeted the excesses of the military far Right but "rabble-rousing, hypocritical, and irresponsible populism" as well as the "utopians of complete democracy" and of "outmoded liberalism."[18] The government seemed, for the first time, to be attaching importance to the expectation among certain sectors of the officer corps of a return to civil democracy, which might undermine the official candidate.

THE SENATOR AND THE GENERAL

The new political climate could be seen during Geisel's presidency in the early and spontaneous emergence of a civilian candidate to run in the presidential elections of October 1978, Senator Magalhães Pinto. A prominent ARENA leader, wreathed in the prestige of the long-term revolutionary, he claimed from 1976 onward to consider himself a potential successor to General Geisel, the policy of détente making a civilian candidate conceivable. He did not identify with the opposition at that point and until September 1977 maintained that he hoped for the backing of Geisel and ARENA. From then on, however, the main displays of solidarity he was shown, particularly when he spoke out in favor of redemocratizing the country, came from the civilian opposition, and in the final days of 1977 he lost all hope of becoming the president's preferred candidate. In addition, a competitor emerged in the opposition camp, in the person of Army General Euler Bentes Monteiro, a low-profile officer in the engineers, who joined the reserve in March 1977, and was known for his nationalist convictions in economic matters.

Euler did not initially confirm this speculation. Nevertheless, his candidacy was already sufficiently likely for SNI agents to take an interest. A report dated January 1978 drew up a list of the general's supporters.[19] The civilian side mentioned Severo Gomes, a former Geisel minister and the architect of a nationalist, interventionist economic policy, who was dismissed from government in February 1977 when the President's Office performed a liberal about-face. "Left-wing intellectuals linked to CEBRAP," the Brazilian Center for Analysis and Planning, were thought to support Euler because of these same nationalist affinities. The general, who was born in 1917, belonged in fact to a group of engineer officers united in a sort of "national-developmentalism" but divided by their unequal hankering for political authoritarianism. The group also included generals Afonso de Albuquerque Lima, Rodrigo Otávio Jordão Ramos, and Arthur Duarte Candal da Fonseca. Major Euler Bentes had appeared on the nationalist list headed by General Estillac Leal in the Military Club's 1950 election campaign. A little later, he submitted his resignation from the Military Club's Deliberative Council at the same time as Captain Francisco Boaventura, after the club's governing bodies condemned U.S. intervention in Korea. Strongly anticommunist, he nevertheless adopted a legalist stance at the time of the coup, in which he did not take part. He was not punished or ostracized by the military government, however, and in 1967, Interior Minister Albuquerque Lima appointed him to head SUDENE (the Superintendency for the Development of the Northeast). In January 1969, he stood down in solidarity with Albuquerque Lima when budget cuts introduced by Finance Minister Antônio Delfim Netto, slashed SUDENE's resources. His friendship with the two Geisel brothers spared him disgrace after the military-political crisis of 1969. Nevertheless, he gained his fourth star only after the new president was inaugurated in March 1974. He then went on to head the Army Services Directorate and later the Ordnance Directorate, which gave him entry to the ACE.

The same SNI report of January 18, 1978, believed that General Euler had two main supporters in military circles, the group formerly linked to Frota, and the "Nativist" group linked to General Hugo Abreu, who resigned from the Military Cabinet at the beginning of the month. They were an unlikely combination, to put it mildly. Not even economic nationalism united them as it had the "opposition fronts" of 1966–67 since General Frota was not identified with these positions. All that brought them together was their rejection of Figueiredo's candidacy and, more broadly, of a successor being imposed by the president's entourage.

It was not long, however, before General Euler exposed the ideological boundaries that the disparate character of his supporters helped to blur. At the end of January, he came out in favor of restoring the rule of law, allowing direct elections, and offering a political amnesty—but not of holding a constituent assembly. He also claimed that he wanted no part in the presidential succession. This defined political stance distanced him from the *frotista* deputies (they declared their support for Figueiredo the following day) but awoke hope among others, particularly in the MDB, who began to suggest Euler as a possible candidate. The military were first to put him forward, however, led by Hugo Abreu, who, since resigning from the Military Cabinet, had made Figueiredo's electoral downfall his prime objective. Born in 1916, General Abreu had had an outstanding professional career, comparable to some of the "hardline colonels" of his generation. He saw combat as an infantry captain in the Brazilian Expeditionary Force and had a brilliant academic career, taking him to Fort Benning (1951) and ultimately to the ESG as a lieutenant colonel in 1962. During the conspiracy and the coup, he was part of General Moniz de Aragão's entourage. As such, he was identified as a castelista in the years after the coup. Even so, as commander of the Parachute Brigade of the Vila Militar throughout the Years of Lead, he was at the heart of the most unbridled repression both in Rio and the Araguaia jungles where he sent in special forces. Appointed head of President Geisel's Military Cabinet in 1974, he rejoined the castelista networks at the very top of the state.

General Abreu's political beliefs, networks, and loyalties are a complicated matter. Admittedly, he gave loyal support to the president's policy of political opening to the extent of backing him when Frota was ousted. Nevertheless, his two books of memoirs, *O outro lado do poder*, covering 1974–78, and *Tempo de crise* about the 1978–79 presidential campaign, indicate above all an obsession with the amorality and harmfulness of the "palace group" centered around Golbery and Geisel's private secretary, Heitor Ferreira, whom he believed had drawn the president into their unwholesome thirst for power and money.

> What is very clear in this inglorious struggle, which the spokesman for the palace group has the habit of calling the "first and second world wars," is the *presidential groups'* petty conflict of interests over taking power. . . . All of it waged in the margins of the Nation as if it had nothing to do with the choice of its supreme leader. This group war even brings to mind the infamous wars between members of the Mafia, united under the command of one or other of its godfathers. The "first world war" is said to be the choice of a successor to Castelo Branco, which was lost by the current presidential group; that group emerged victorious from the "second world war," meaning the choice of a successor to Geisel, by managing to impose on the defeated nation the candidate most beneficial to the oligarchy's interests.[20]

Abreu did not target the whole of the "military Sorbonne" since he spared General Castelo Branco, whose memory he cherished, and, for a long time, General Geisel, before eventually acknowledging his compliance with the strategy of his entourage. Loyalty to the castelista "good kings" did not, however, prevent General Abreu from nurturing a hatred that embraced all those close to Golbery, a hatred he shared with the military right and their then spokesman Sylvio Frota. Abreu's view of Frota himself was fairly positive. In his memoirs, he constantly justifies, even apologizes, for having a hand in ousting the latter and makes great play of Frota's bravery and moral rectitude. General Abreu's networks once he joined the Military Cabinet showed the signs of his years as head of the Vila Militar Parachute Brigade from 1970 to 1974, which was in a state of virtual insubordination at the time of Medici's inauguration. Hugo Abreu said he gained a twofold reputation from the experience. He was "the man who pacified the paratroopers" and "a tough, aggressive [officer] who had taken part in actions [crackdowns]."[21] He also retained the loyalty of the men he commanded, as well as many friendships, particularly that of General Orlando Geisel, then army minister, who, he claims, recommended him to his brother in 1974 for the role of head of the Military Cabinet.

As head of the Parachute Brigade, General Hugo Abreu became close to the "Nativist Group" or "Nativist Spark," which incited activism in the Vila Militar and was led in particular by Parachute Brigade Captains José Aurélio Valporto de Sá, Francimá de Luna Máximo, and Adalto Luiz Lupi Barreiros (Major Kurt Pessek, having been one of the founders, left a few months later). The brigade's farewell message, written by Abreu, in March 1974, ended, moreover, with the nativist slogan: "Brazil above all" (*Brasil acima de tudo*). In addition, two "Nativist Group" militants, or former militants, followed him to Planalto: Major Kurt Pessek, who became his assistant secretary, and Captain Adalto Lupi Barreiros, who joined his cabinet and was appointed to the presidential press office.

Abreu and his entourage of nationalist and radical ex-paratroopers played a central role in constructing the political alternative embodied by Euler Bentes Monteiro's candidacy. In May 1978, the general's agreement to stand in the election was obtained although for several months the opposition party's preference was not official. It was in a ferment of debate. General Euler Bentes and Senator Magalhães Pinto campaigned jointly within the National Front for Redemocratization (Frente Nacional de Redemocratização, FNR), also set up in May. The FNR's political approach was revealed in a communiqué signed by both men and released on May 29. The text was very vague. It called for "the union of all movements involved in the redemocratization of the country," for the "consolida[tion] of the basic aspirations of all the democrats, by structuring them around shared political objectives."[22] As the months went by, General Euler's popularity and amount of support in the party increased, while Magalhães Pinto's appeared to decline. In August, Magalhães Pinto left the FNR, a month before officially rallying behind Figueiredo. The defection obviously weakened the coalition, while the Presidential Palace sought to destroy the military team through a series of sanctions. Beginning in May 1978, General Abreu lost his two key assistants, Lieutenant Colonel Kurt Pessek and Major Adalto Barreiros, both reassigned to garrisons far away from Brasília.

Abreu himself was only belatedly affected after sending a circular letter to the army generals at the end of September, extracts of which were leaked to the press. He was sentenced to twenty days' incarceration for a disciplinary infraction. By robbing General Euler of one of his primary campaign officials a few days before the election, the punishment effectively scuttled his bid. On October 15, 1978, the sympathies the FNR had attracted in ARENA were not enough to win the backing of the party's electors, the majority of whom voted for Figueiredo, sworn in for a six-year term on March 15, 1979.

In terms of the presidential election campaign, the MDB had been overshadowed by the FNR since May 1978. The two FNR figureheads, Magalhães Pinto and Euler Bentes, thus came to represent the only opposition alternatives to the military government even before securing their party's official approval. Moreover, the former's long-term putschist identification and the latter's membership in the army hierarchy's elite sited the opposition *in the "revolution."* The gradual imposition of the general's candidacy to the detriment of the senator's further strengthened the symbolism whereby the revolutionary government after the coup soon came to be identified with a military government. A consequence of numerous dissident officers embarking on an opposition electoral strategy was the imposition of the "revolutionary" norm on the MDB, whereby the presidential nominee should hold the top position in the chain of command. Euler himself, however, showed a degree of unease with the paradox of his own candidacy, purporting to be putting an end to a regime while epitomizing the continuation of its practices, returning the country to civilian democracy while exploiting his general's rank and surrounding himself with campaign staff who were mainly military officers. Moreover, he constantly maintained that his candidacy was not a military one, that he was in the reserve and so an ordinary citizen once again, and that he refused to make great play of his support within the armed forces.

Incorporated into the MDB campaign, the issues championed by the dissident military sat alongside the entirely democratic utterances of General Euler, which were ultimately hostile to military involvement in politics. He was a constant media preoccupation from January to October 1978, and he traveled up and down the country, reiterating the same pledges of effective democratization, a political amnesty, the restoration of basic freedoms, the repeal of exceptional rule, and the "auto-reinstitutionalization" of the nation through the meeting of a Constituent Assembly, elected in a direct, secret, and universal vote. He also highlighted his social justice objectives, insisting that the valid indicator of a country's development should not be per capita income but income distribution. Last, he alerted public opinion to the country's growing external dependence.[23] These pro-state intervention and nationalist remarks delighted the "first hard-line" officers who made up the bulk of his team as much as they did the MDB elected officials who constituted his political base.

During this same period, General Figueiredo substantially altered his discourse. From the very measured political liberalism of the early days, very much centered on the "relative democracy" dear to President Geisel, as of July 1978 the official candidate began to promise a democratization very similar to the one to which his rival had committed himself. The protection of human rights, the restoration of habeas corpus, and the granting of an amnesty began to crop up in the general's statements. Even his physical appearance, as shown to the media, changed. He abandoned his uniform, dark glasses, and air of severity for a suit and the smiling face of a youthful, athletic, and suntanned man in his sixties. The race toward democratization gathered speed at the end of August when Figueiredo promised more rapid reforms than his rival, claiming that he would not wait three years to implement them but would introduce them "the day after tomorrow."[24] "The gradual, safe détente" Geisel wanted, designed to retain certain benefits of the "revolution," would in fact escape him. This loss of control was not solely down to the revival of social protest or to the disaffection of the political class, as is often said. It was also the result of a balance of power partly internal to the armed forces, in which the "opinion of the barracks," real or imagined, and the support of prominent officers were vital resources. Certainly, the distensão survived the resistance of the most politicized and fanatical sectors of the "security community." However, if it was no longer under government control, this was because the authorities' military base had crumbled and certain of the sectors most involved in the "revolution" continued to dissent.

The "second hard line," however, was able to distinguish very clearly between the candidates. The rejection Figueiredo encountered did not prevent an aggressive anti-Euler campaign from emerging. He was accused of left-wing inclinations, or even—and this came as no surprise—of communist sympathies. The hostility some law-enforcement personnel reserved for the "palace group" and the authoritarian imposition of a successor to President Geisel collapsed in the face of hatred for a part of the opposition accused of being a communist Trojan horse, and for fear of more entrenched "revanchism" if government slipped out of the hands of the incumbent team. General Sylvio Frota himself came to support Figueiredo's candidacy, despite his liking for the position of General Euler Bentes who was "there to overturn the palace men's predictions of certain victory.... An intelligent man of very good character, unimpeachable honesty, [with] an exemplary private life, and an excellent administrator, General Euler did not, however, have the sympathy of the revolutionary movement of 1964, a movement to which, moreover, he had barely subscribed.... Furthermore, political ideas from what is known as the ideological left were attributed to him."[25]

In spite of détente, accusations that the "palace group" was isolated and reservations about Figueiredo's character and fast-track promotion, the official candidate appeared to the second far-right generation to represent a particular system and, in doing so, to be the lesser evil. This was not true for one part of the "first hard line," which, on the contrary, committed itself determinedly, military regulations notwithstanding, to the campaign of the "anti-candidate" who had not been foreseen by the authorities. The team around General Euler was, therefore, made up almost exclusively of dissident officers. Consequently, although he had the backing of some of the opposition and claimed to have "ordinary citizen" status, in seeking to stand for election the general was prolonging the series of conflicts between factions of officers, which constituted a large part of the political game under military rule.

THE RETURN OF THE FIRST HARD LINE

The dissident officers who rallied to Euler had different profiles but all, bar General Hugo Abreu, had been guilty of insubordination in the early years of the military regime. Most were linked more or less directly to that part of the "first hard line" of which Francisco Boaventura, removed from active service by AI-5 in May 1969, was the symbolic figure and leader. Euler's closest associates belonged to Boaventura's inner circle. This was true of his spokesman, Colonel Amerino Raposo Filho, and of campaign team members General Hélio Lemos and Colonel Sebastião Ferreira Chaves. Boaventura himself, while he did not appear in the press, attended the secret meetings that accompanied the establishment of Euler's candidacy. Colonel Dickson Grael and Colonel Tarcísio Nunes Ferreira also organized military support for the candidate, the former behind the scenes, the latter openly. Hugo Abreu recruited Colonel Kurt Pessek, linked since 1964 to the Boaventura group, to the team. Abreu was not himself a close associate of Boaventura, any more than Major Adalto Lupi Barreiros was, but Barreiros was connected to the network after taking part in the paratroopers' rebellion at the end of 1969 along with José Aurélio Valporto de Sá and Francimá de Luna Máximo. Their membership in the "Centelha Nativista" group linked them to Pessek who had also been a member for a while.

General Euler's military support was centered on two groups of officers with some links between them: Abreu's entourage and the group formerly linked to Boaventura. They were a handful of the most active men in the electoral campaign and the most likely to incur disciplinary sanctions. Other officers gravitated to this militant core, mostly from middle and junior ranks. The press hinted at their existence but the secret nature of their involvement prevented learning more about them. Nevertheless, Colonel Tarcísio recognized that the campaign had only limited success with the bulk of officers increasingly inclined to follow the decisions of their hierarchical leaders and the President's Office. The military elite threw their overwhelming support behind General Figueiredo.

What then explains these about-faces in officers so clearly entrenched on the far Right for so long? First, there was the hope of finally coming to power, even if the military could not admit such an ambition since their esprit de corps was built on hostility to private interest and the personal strategies of what they called politicagem. The spirit of vengeance against the group in power was more frequently acknowledged.[26] It was General Abreu's entourage that appeared to nurture the fiercest hatred for Golbery and the presidential group, as well as the greatest contempt for Figueiredo. This fierce animosity brought them closer to some on the radical Right and notably to the positions of General Frota. A letter Major Barreiros wrote to the former army minister in September 1978 when the presidential campaign was at its height is very revealing:

> Like you, [General Abreu] and I had the naivety to trust the President's moral code. Belatedly, we reached the conclusion that the government had no moral code and you know the reasons better than I do....
>
> I will go even further and say that I am in favor of any solution that would prevent this group having another government for the simple reason that I have seen the

key figures up close and I know who they are and where they will take the country. Consequently, I am in favor of the solution now offered as the only opportunity of opposing this tragedy of acts of cowardice, betrayal, servility, and aggression against the national will, against the Military Chiefs, and against the principles of the Military Institution.

I also know your attitude to this whole process, to the people who are its main protagonists.

But it is necessary to stop before it is too late. Either we protect the Army from popular disapproval or we spend thirty years staunching the institution's wounds. . . .

Perhaps, general, sir, we do not agree on everything but we do agree about the essentials. . . .

I am convinced that you have a contribution to make. Many people are expecting the authorities to say "no" to all this. The choice must be made from few options. It is necessary to forget about the differences and to opt, at least, for a lesser evil.[27]

Had General Hugo Abreu been obliged to explain his commitment to Euler's candidacy to Frota, he would probably have described it as "the lesser evil." Although it was compromised by Euler's links to the Left, he considered it more honest than the candidacy backed by the palace group.

Now, at the end of the 1970s, hostility to the incumbent authorities was increasingly expressed as opposition to a military "system" installed for the long term, even though, according to the dissidents, this had never been part of the revolutionaries' initial plan—which had been only for a short-term movement. It was a wry reworking of history, since it was precisely the "first hard line" that had encouraged long-term military rule in 1964 and 1965. At the end of September 1978, Hélio Lemos made public a document of support for General Euler. During the coup, he said: "We expected that military intervention would not last and the nation would soon be able to return to democratic normality but, as is often the way with exceptional regimes, the interests they generate and even encourage started to bring about the replenishment of the system, endorsing its continuity."

Criticism from former members of the "first hard line" borrowed from both the antidictatorial discourse of the camp to which they now belonged and from the old mindset of the military far right. In the same document, Lemos talks of the "permanent exercise of arbitrary rule," and the whole group forcefully condemned the overgrown security and intelligence community, even though some of them had played a part in its development. Amerino Raposo and Hélio Lemos, for example, belonged to the SNI in the years after the putsch. They all drew a distinction between themselves and the operatives of the machinery of repression who were responsible in 1976 and again from 1979 to 1981 for terrorist operations against organizations and individuals of the civilian Left, which culminated in one final act, an attack on the Riocentro Convention Center on April 30, 1981.

The undertaking was an utter disaster. The bomb went off as one of the perpetrators, who were members of the Rio DOI, was holding it, killing him and seriously injuring his accomplice. It is remembered as proof that the extremists in the machinery of repression were completely out of control. Several thousand people were there to attend a concert to celebrate May Day. Preparations for the attack had included sidelining a certain number of agents likely to have opposed it. Colonel Dickson Grael, for instance, a member of the "first hard-line" networks and responsible for security at the venue, was dismissed without explanation a month before the incident. After it, he became one of those fiercely opposed to the impunity of the DOI and SNI military servicemen responsible. In 1985 he published one of the first books reporting on and condemning far-right military terrorism.[28] Grael objected in particular to the outcome of the IPM military inquiry set up at the time, a charade designed to hush up the incident. Tarcísio Nunes Ferreira said he asked to be transferred to the reserve the day the results of the inquiry came out, after his truculent opposition to the perpetrators of the attacks had, he claimed, earned him several months of "terrible persecution" in the organization.[29] Hushing up the affair also led to a more significant resignation, that of the head of the Civil Cabinet, Golbery, who blamed the "radical Right" in the security agencies outright for the attack and a diminution of the regime.[30]

The first hard line's battle with the second was not solely down to an astonishing antidictatorial U-turn. It was also a reaction of the vanquished against the victors, as they seemed to be at the time at least, and a way of resisting ostracism within the institution by peers who saw their "democratic" attitudes and condemnations of crimes perpetrated by the military as just so many betrayals. They sought to win the sympathy of their comrades in arms by condemning the damage the regime had done to the military institution itself ("arbitrariness had begun to compromise not only the Armed Forces as a whole but also each of their members in person as a consequence of decisions to which they were not party but for which society held them automatically responsible," wrote Hélio Lemos in 1978[31]) and, especially, by once again taking up the topic of corruption, which was very popular with the military. Major Adalto Barreiros, for instance, made criticism of government corruption his trademark theme. Along with Dickson Grael and Colonel Raimundo Saraiva Martins, he was one of a group of officers involved in the systematic denunciation of presumed malpractice within the state apparatus, which had scandalized smaller groups of the military as of 1976.[32]

With the election of General Figueiredo as president of the Republic, the "first hard-line" officers who had backed his rival experienced their final political defeat. The military regime was coming to an end but the accelerated democratization the government set in motion and the return to civilian rule happened without them. Specifically, their involvement was now lost in that of civil organizations, political parties, the media, and the people who had taken to the streets to fight for the restoration or acquisition of political and social rights.

These officers were soon disenchanted by the New Republic born in 1985 and equipped with a new constitution as of 1988. Time and the transition to democracy, moreover, were conducive to attenuating the seriousness of the military's internal rifts. Faced with what they regarded as signs of "revanchism" from the Left and the vanquished, hard feelings between comrades in arms faded. In the 1990s and 2000, above all, when a "war of memory" set in between former opposition members, researchers, and victims' relatives on the one hand and putschists, mainly military, on the other, the majority of "first hard-line" officers softened their judgments of the military regime.[33] Some even joined organizations seeking to sweeten its memory and defend conservative and nationalist options. These brought together "hard-line" officers of different generations. Before it became dormant, for example, the 469 officers in the "Guararapes Group" in 2009 included Reserve General Antônio Bandeira, a second-generation radical who had supported Sylvio Frota and General Agnaldo del Nero, a former member of the machinery of repression, and a stalwart of the small far-right group Terrorism Never Again (Terrorismo Nunca Mais, which took its name in response to Torture Never Again, Tortura Nunca Mais, one of the most active movements of victims and their families since the 1980s), as well as Reserve General Hélio Lemos and Reserve Colonel Adalto Luiz Lupi Barreiros, labeled hard-liners in 1964–67 and 1969, respectively, but all members of General Euler Bentes Monteiro's team.[34]

The ambiguity of their role in history from radical putschists to militants favoring a return to barracks makes it easier for the latter to reconstruct their life stories according to the context or the expectations of their interlocutors. In talking to journalist Hélio Contreiras, therefore, who in a way can be taken as representing civil society critical of the dictatorship, Colonel Amerino Raposo of the "first hard line" depicted himself as dissenting from a regime that was not intended to become entrenched in authoritarianism, and regretted AI-5, "which imposed arbitrary rule, as well as its tools: censorship, and the excesses carried out by the DOI-CODIs, with the suspension of the civic safeguards."[35] When he spoke to peers during an exercise to collect testimonies organized by a general, however, what he said was very different: that he believed, for example, that the revolution had sacrificed security to development; and that it was President Costa e Silva's desire to liberalize too quickly that had led to AI-5.[36] After a fashion, in championing the democratic positions increasingly held by a civil society in the process of reorganization, these former "hard-line" officers offset their loss of status and prestige among their peers by presenting a positive identity to public opinion. This is one of the reasons that they easily agree to give interviews, unlike colleagues who feel they are systematically in an awkward position vis-à-vis civil society. The consistency given to lives lived in the orbit of a "surgical revolution" that never took place identifies them as long-standing dissidents and obscures the many ambiguities and contradictions in their political thinking.

CONCLUSION

The Brazilian military regime was built around the principle of hierarchy, like the conservative and police dictatorships of its Hispano-American neighbors. However, it differed from other military movements and governments—whether those with a similar ideology, such as Greece under the Colonels; or a dissimilar one, like the Cuba of the *barbudos* ("bearded men") or the Portugal of the Carnation Revolution. The men who gradually became its main actors and supporters, officers from the three armed forces, took with them into the state apparatus and into politics those forms of organization, and the precepts and criteria for authority, that were proper to their own institution: limited expression of internal differences of opinion, a declared distance from public debate, and above all, the supremacy of the high-ranking officers, particularly the four-star army generals. From 1964 to 1985, the highest office of the state was contested by some fifteen or so men of that rank while key ministries, the management of major public enterprises, and collegiate bodies advising and supervising the President's Office were staffed predominantly by officers, all of them generals.

Nevertheless, with the exception of the Years of Lead, politics continued to exist inside the Brazilian armed forces. Those involved were high- and middle-ranking officers in active service or the reserve, kept out of the main decision-making circles or frustrated in their greatest ambitions. The troops themselves, for their part, were kept in almost absolute political passivity.

With the exception of rare crisis moments, activism per se involved only a minority of officers who nevertheless often referred to an "opinion of the barracks" beyond the reach of the historian. Since the conspiracy during the Goulart government, middle-ranking officers had been far more than just an audience or a challenge for higher-ranking putschists. It was they who would go on to transmit anticommunist military doctrines such as the theory of revolutionary war, who would organize networks, and relay information and opinion inside an "archipelago" of the conspiracy's more high-profile generals.

After the coup, these junior officers claimed choice positions in the new regime. If some of them did secure what was regarded by the "revolutionaries" as the highly prestigious task of running political inquiries into allegedly "corrupt" and "subversive" persons (the IPMs), this role did not allow, much less guarantee, the radical purge they wanted—nor a decision-making say in the government's economic and institutional approaches. Exploiting the visibility and influence they acquired by running the inquiries, these colonels put crucial pressure on the first president, Castelo Branco. Linked to the regimental officers of their generation, they were part of the military consensus regarding the first authoritarian about-face at the end of 1965. They gave their decisive backing to the candidacy of War Minister General Costa e Silva, whose rise to the President's Office marked the regime's definitive militarization.

It was a Pyrrhic victory for the colonels of the "first hard line," however. The second military government did not in fact offer them the central role historiography has afforded them. Government was increasingly monopolized by generals, who denied the colonels the role of backstage critical advisers and shadow counselors that the latter felt they deserved. At this point, an initial group, made up of officers with highly distinguished professional careers, took their first steps on the road of dissent. The 1968 outburst and the emergence of armed struggle rudely interrupted their plans—although only for a time—while a second group opted for acts of far-right political violence. The first "hard-line" faction was linked to Colonel Francisco Boaventura Cavalcanti Júnior and typified by affiliation with the troops. We have called it "military," as distinct from the second faction, described here as "militant," which was more heterogeneous though still bound by shared experiences such as participation in the uprisings of the 1950s and in the far-right groups. These two strains of the "first hard line," with very few exceptions, backed the tougher authoritarianism that the Fifth Institutional Act made possible from December 1968. They were not its main architects, however. That responsibility fell to the generals at the heart of government, who at the same time imposed their dominance over a civilian political class, reduced to being merely the regime's democratic rubber stamp.

The foundations of the "generals' regime" were fragile, however. The institutions were still formally those of civil democracy so that regulating the political domain through military norms and values was merely a matter of custom. The army generals' political sovereignty was not based on any legislative or regulatory documents. Nor was it the subject of a specific propaganda strategy allowing it to be imposed on public opinion and military opinion in particular. Consequently, it was challenged by other legitimacies, those of liberal democracy, the "revolution," the fight against the communist enemy, and those of the armed forces as a corps—the incarnation of the people—for which a multitude of actors could claim to speak. Costa e Silva's sudden and total incapacitation in August 1969 exposed this symbolic ambiguity of the regime, which gave rise to demands for political participation within the officer corps. The Brazilian Army was thought of as highly professional, and the apoliticism of its mid-ranking officers was considered one of its hallmarks, and a key requirement. Despite this, its top brass were able to impose their candidate, General Medici, only at the cost of consulting the officers of all three forces—a consultation orchestrated by the highest-ranked among them. The result of the "election" was a foregone conclusion, but it showed that in the event of a presidential vacancy, there was no consensus about the foundations of "revolutionary" sovereignty.

This uncertainty was not apparent only at times of politico-military crisis. The bargaining and power struggles between officers at the center and on the periphery of power were standard for the regime. Moreover, the debate could not be summed up as a clash between the generals' hierarchical authority on the one hand and the claims of junior revolutionary officers on the other. Among the generals, the balances between the President's Office, the High Commands, and the military leaders who claimed to represent the officer corps in politics were also the subject of more or less muted conflicts. As the regime militarized and protesting officers were reduced to subjection, this jousting between the generals tended to take precedence over the demands of their subordinates.

This political dueling was largely stifled in the Years of Lead. Tensions resurfaced during the political abertura. Army Minister Sylvio Frota claimed to be the forerunner of the system that General Médici's "election" in 1969 appeared to have established: the supremacy of the Army High Command as a sort of supreme council of the revolution, of which the president was merely a delegate. Geisel confronted this military regime model with that of a virtually monarchical presidency on the grounds that it was essential that the armed forces as a whole, including those at the top of the hierarchy, were not involved in politics. Predictably enough, political disagreements, if not ideological divides, lay behind these conflicts of legitimacy. The president intended to "institutionalize the revolution," establishing an elitist and authoritarian regime for the long term. This was the plan of the castelista group that Geisel allowed back into government. Frota refused to abandon revolutionary exceptionality, citing the permanence of the "subversive threat" and the wild suspicion that a government plot had been hatched by the castelista Sorbonne with the ultimate aim of shifting Brazil's allegiances eastward.

A new generation of protesting officers supported this notion, most of them members of the machinery of repression, a new or "second hard line," arising partly, but not exclusively, from the most militant section of the first. The clandestine utterances of its members, which were confined to military circles, together with their acts of political violence, were now justified in terms of their identification as frontline fighters against the communist enemy. They no longer laid claim to greater involvement in political decision making. Now they were fighting to retain their place in a police state. Admittedly, there was a degree of continuity between the political activism of the agents of repression and that of the "first hard-line" colonels, a continuity of people, to some extent; of the ideal, which was authoritarian and repressive; and of the representation of the political arena, in which the enemy personified communism, imperialism, and anti-nation feeling beneath the reviled features of the civilian politician. The rationale for action was changing, however. In addition, a part of the first generation of activists opted at the end of the 1970s for protest of an unexpected kind, first hinted at some ten years before: a move into the democratic opposition, driven by political frustration, a spirit of vengeance, and disappointment with the regime's performance.

In this way, two successive generations of protesters appeared under the hard-line banner. The first was defeated by the "generals' regime" despite having helped define it and consolidate it in the years after the coup. With their ambitions thwarted, some of these officers embarked on a discreet process of dissent while others joined the arcane world of the machinery of repression. When this generation of protesters was neutralized, a particular sort of activism also vanished for a while. It had been a protest open to the public domain and based on questioning the military's apoliticism and the hierarchical order when "national destiny" was thought to be in jeopardy. By contrast, the second "hard line" was the product of the regime itself. Some of the agents of repression who made up its members were certainly long-term extremists and militants. Their political mobilization stemmed from their place in the state apparatus, however, and no longer challenged the generals' preeminence in politics: they were very keen to preserve the existing order, including the hierarchy.

At its peak, each of these hard lines left its mark on the choices made by the military governments. Nevertheless, once the fervor and chaos of the revolution had subsided, the young protesting officers were relegated to the periphery of power. The majority of them backed the regime's increasing move toward repressive authoritarianism and some allowed their anticommunist hatred to flourish in the police struggle against the movements of the armed Left. The main decision-making circles, however, were soon confined to the generals, who used the discontent of activist networks and the "opinion of the barracks" as a line of argument and a political resource. The military regime thus came to impose on its own supporters the hierarchical and disciplinary rule of abstention from any kind of political involvement, a demand the future putschists had made before 1964 of the sergeants calling for greater rights. In this way, the dictatorship paradoxically rendered the Brazilian forces politically powerless to a great extent. This in no way meant that this loss of political agency under the dictatorship would lead to the soldiers being less interventionist and activist once the yoke of the generals had been lifted. It did, however, correspond to a particular regime model that did not rely on a *politically* mobilized military base, but rather on the majority's tacit assent and a fanaticized and conservative police apparatus waging its own private war on "subversion."

The imposition of this type of regime did not proceed in consensual fashion. Several writers have stressed that the Brazilian military dictatorship did not devise a coherent, clearly defined system of legitimization, in which political sovereignty lay. The persistence of politics under the military regime was closely linked to this symbolic ambiguity: the conflicting parties had a wide range of justifications for their own political participation, which they could bring to bear depending on what was at stake. Furthermore, they rarely appealed to a single, unchanging discourse to legitimize the regime and their own action. On the whole, indeed, the officers shared a common mindset that valued the hierarchy alongside the "revolutionary," and contempt for politics alongside some recognition of the party-political system. In this sense, the junior military who rose up against the hegemony of the generals did not demonstrate a surviving ideal of the "citizen soldier" and individual political action within the army—an army schooled in what was regarded as "professional" apoliticism, and strict respect for hierarchy and discipline. Nor did the "castelista" group have a monopoly on the supremacy of a civilianized presidency facing the politicization of the armed forces. There were, of course, degrees of support for these suggestions, but the place of the actors in the political system and the issues they faced had a decisive influence on which aspect of political identity they chose to highlight. Changes in the discourse of certain "first hard-line" officers close to Colonel Boaventura provide a clear illustration of the point. In the aftermath of the coup, they emphasized their identity as "long-standing revolutionaries." When the legitimacy of the revolution gave way to that of "the opinion of the barracks," and the political ascent of General Costa e Silva militarized the regime, they became the spokesmen of the troops and junior officers. Last, at the end of the 1970s, when the political opening and the awakening of civil society made certain references to liberal democracy acceptable again, they joined forces with the opposition party and championed free elections in order to achieve power.

While the protesting officers used continuously renewed arguments to justify their utterances, their demands for participation, and resistance to the government's approaches, their discourse was constantly marked by a particular representation of politics. It was entirely organized around a stereotypical concept of the adversary as the mirror image of the patriotic, upstanding, selfless, and courageous soldier—the ideal they believed themselves to be. The enemy had all the features of the getulista politician, who was the pillar of the "overthrown system": a sell-out to foreigners and big capital, weak in the face of subversion's appeal, perhaps even in collusion with the "International Communist Movement," and, above all, morally lost, a traitor to his corps if he was a soldier, to the revolution if he was a putschist, and to the motherland every time. Whatever fights they had fought and despite some of their spectacular conversions, these "ultra" officers always interpreted public action in the light of this anticivilian moralism, fixated on an exclusive nationalism.

These power struggles, conflicts, negotiations, and battles for influence were *political where politics was not expected*, because they took place inside an institution that had become reluctant to engage in this type of debate and that was, moreover, living under a dictatorship. This was politics in which the categories of identification, the composition and the structure of groups and factions, and the discourses themselves had still to be invented even as power was being contested—and this within the context of a regime that was itself very vague about its principles and the sectors of society in which its sovereignty was invested. Despite the lengthy militant experience of most of the protagonists, and the apparent staunchness and radicalism of their convictions, this lack of definition and the need to be forever improvising courses of action created the conditions for a political interplay in constant flux, peppered with unnatural alliances and unlikely U-turns. It created a political world, moreover, in which personal relations, matters of honor, opportunism, and military organizational rationales often took priority over ideologies and long-standing convictions as drivers of behavior—a world difficult to understand in any case, given the binary templates for interpretation that held sway both before the coup and after the transition to democracy.

However, this way of doing politics was in no way devoid of any ethical standards or norms—first, because despite the regime's lack of definition, the men themselves were steeped in the highly prescriptive world of the institution to which they belonged. Regulations, customs, traditions, and the internal organization of the armed forces—even their contradictions—structured how politics was done; and second, because moments of greater clarity succeeded the phases of poor definition during which the political camps were very porous. When there was a head-on attack on the army or its "honor," the military closed ranks. When the "subversive threat" finally became a reality, anticommunism united the putschist camp and it fell silent. This reveals a political culture shared by these officers over and above their factions and differences, a culture made up of anticivilianism and a great sense of responsibility (as the military) for the nation; of ambitions of greatness and distrust of their own people; of the desire for order, hatred of the "reds," and the difficulty of abandoning all hope of some political pluralism. Of course, there were substantial variations, and different mindsets and plans applied depending on circumstance. What divided them above all, however, was their rank, from which stemmed their unequal legitimacy as political actors. From this point of view, the history in this book is a history of the vanquished, of the middle-ranking officers who were not able to prevent the consolidation of a hierarchical military regime despite their past, their involvement in the state apparatus, or even a "spirit of the times" that occasionally looked kindly on action by reform-minded junior officers. They wanted to be agents of history. Most often, they were simply a means to an end in the hands of their own commanders.

NOTES

INTRODUCTION: *The Unusual Face of the Brazilian Dictatorship*

1. Starling, *Os senhores das Gerais.*
2. Carvalho, *Forças armadas*, 7–8.
3. Ferreira, "O Nome e a coisa."
4. Pereira, *Ditadura e repressão.*
5. Castro, *Os militares e a república*, 18–81.
6. Carvalho, *Forças armadas*, 13–61.
7. Decree No. 2.429 of March 4, 1938.
8. Carvalho, *Forças Armadas*, 38–42.
9. Huntington, *Soldier and the State.*
10. Finer, *Man on Horseback*; Perlmutter, *Military and Politics*, 4–5. On the subject of Brazil, it was Alfred Stepan who insisted on a link between political intervention and military professionalism. He speaks of a "new professionalism" born in the 1960s in the context of a social, political, and moral crisis in *Os militares na política* and "New Professionalism."
11. Carvalho, *Forças armadas*, 42.
12. Proceedings of the Forty-Eighth meeting of the *Alto Comando do Exército*, cited by Elio Gaspari, *A ditadura escancarada*, 137. The date indicated by Gaspari (July 26, 1979) is wrong. The meeting quite likely took place in November 1969.
13. See, for example, Smallman, *Fear and Memory.*

CHAPTER 1: *Conspiracies*

Epigraph: De Souza, undated quotation, Archives of Colonel Manuel Soriano, File 6 (*Política Nacional* / Army Documentation Centre CDOC).

1. Humberto de Alencar Castelo Branco, "Os meios militares e a recuperação moral do País," Superior War School, in Castelo Branco Archives, File no.10, *Escola de Comando e Estado Maior do Exército* (ECEME).
2. Franco and Levín, *Historia reciente*, 15–16.
3. Carlos Lacerda, quotation from June 1950 found by Marina Gusmão de Mendonça, reproduced in *O Demolidor de Presidentes*, 115.
4. Labaki. *1961: A Crise de renúncia.* Appendix 1.
5. The abundance of officers' testimonies is peculiar to Brazil. It is not seen—or only much later—in neighboring countries. It is explained in particular by the amnesty law adopted in August 1979, relating both to opponents of the regime and to agents of the state implicated in political assassinations and serious human rights violations under the dictatorship. Protected from potential prosecution, many officers have been more inclined to talk. In 2018, despite numerous appeals, international injunctions, and the existence of a National Truth Commission, the amnesty law has never really been called into question.

6. Castro, "A origem social dos militares," 199.
7. The *A memória militar* trilogy, published by CPDOC researchers Maria Celina D'Araujo, Gláucio Ary Dillon Soares, and Celso Castro (*Visões do golpe*; *Os anos de chumbo*; *A volta aos quartéis*). The first volume deals with the conspiracy as well as the coup itself.
8. Fico, "Versões e controvérsias "
9. Martins Filho, "A guerra da memória."
10. Calculated based on figures provided by Cláudio Beserra Vasconcelos. For punishment of the military after the coup, see Vasconcelos, "A política repressiva."
11. In *Militares e militância*, Paulo Ribeiro da Cunha puts the military Left at around 10 percent of the total since the 1940s.
12. Zimmermann, "Sargentos de 1964."
13. Camargo and Góes, *Meio século de combate*, 566.
14. See the descriptions of Military Club meetings in 1963 in the Ulhoa Cintra archives (UCi g 1963.04.09/CPDOC).
15. Moreira Alves, *Estado e oposição no Brasil*, 33–52; Comblin, *A ideología da segurança nacional*.
16. Vanda Peres Costa Aderaldo, "A Escola Superior de Guerra"; Arruda, *A Escola Superior de Guerra*; and Ferraz, *A sombra dos carvalhos*.
17. Miguel, "Segurança e desenvolvimento."
18. On these connections, read the still relevant classic by René Armand Dreifuss, *1964: A conquista do estado*.
19. Ferraz, *A guerra que não acabou*.
20. Nabuco de Araujo, "Conquête des esprits et commerce," 12.
21. For U.S.-Brazilian relations during the Cold War, see Davis, *Brotherhood of Arms*.
22. Calandra and Franco, *La guerra fría cultural*, 3–10. Tota, *Seduction of Brazil*.
23. USIS Secret Report, "Internal Defense Plan for Brazil/Brazil—Country Internal Defense Plan," March 20, 1964, RG59, 1964–66, 24, box 42. Quoted in Fico, *O Grande Irmão*, 81. What follows is inspired by the latter study: 67–111. See also Parker, *1964*, and Leacock, *Requiem for Revolution*.
24. Motta, *Em guarda*, 231.
25. Cordeiro, *Direitas em movimento*.
26. "Internal Defense Plan for Brazil." Quoted in Fico, *O Grande Irmão*, 81.
27. Martins Filho, "A educação dos golpistas." Filho was the first to show that the Brazilian Army had appropriated the French theory of revolutionary war.
28. D'Araujo, Soares, and Castro, *Visões do golpe*, 77–78, as quoted in Martins Filho, "Os Estados Unidos," 77.
29. Nabuco de Araujo, "Conquête des esprits et commerce," 9.
30. Nabuco de Araujo, "Conquête des esprits et commerce," 22.
31. This statement, which runs counter to firmly established beliefs about the overwhelming ideological responsibility of the United States in triggering the 1964 putsch, may be seen in the developing interpretations of the Brazilian historian and political scientist João Roberto Martins Filho, who gradually came to specialize in foreign influences on the Brazilian Army in the 1950s–1970s. If, in 1999, he presupposed the importance of the Cuban Revolution and the U.S. ideological offensive in heightening Brazilian officers' anticommunist fixation, without being able to prove it ("Os Estados Unidos," 67–82), a few years later (2004) he commented on the prevalence of the imported French doctrine ("A educação dos golpistas").
32. An overview taken from the list of former Brazilian trainees at the U.S. Army School

of the Americas, accessible via the nongovernmental organization School of the Americas Watch at www.soaw.org (accessed December 2016).

33. Robin, *Les Escadrons de la mort*.

34. "A guerra revolucionária," *Mensário de Cultura Militar*, no. 110-11 (September-October 1957), 287-96. Translated from Ximenés (pseudonyms of generals Maurice Prestat and Pierre Saint-Macary), "La guerre révolutionnaire," *Revue Militaire d'Informations* 281 (February-March 1957).

35. These were General Moacyr Araújo Lopes, colonels Ferdinando de Carvalho, Amerino Raposo Filho, Raimundo Teles Pinheiro, and Ednardo d'Ávila Melo, Lieutenant Colonel Meira Mattos (subsequently regarded as one of the leading thinkers in adapting the revolutionary war theory and National Security Doctrine to Brazil) and Major Adyr Fiúza de Castro. The list is based on articles published in the *Mensário de Cultura Militar* from 1957 to 1961; from 1962 onward, the success of revolutionary war indoctrination widened the circle of officers involved.

36. Stepan, *Os militares na política*, 27-40.

37. "Inquérito sôbre a guerra moderna" (interview with General Zeno Estillac Leal), *Mensário de Cultura Militar*, no. 122-23, year XI (September-October 1958), 241-43.

38. Colonel Jacques Hogard, "A tática e a stratégia na Guerra Revolucionária," (original title and translator untraceable) *Mensário de Cultura Militar*, no. 132-33 (July 1959), 226-41.

39. Published under the pseudonym TAM in the *Revue Militaire Générale* in June 1960 and translated as "Da guerra subversiva à 'guerra'" in *Mensário de Cultura Militar*, no. 150 (April 1961), 210-17.

40. EME training directives of June 14, 1961, which gave rise to Instruction Note no. 1 of the *Diretoria Geral do Ensino* dated November 6, 1961, for application in 1962.

41. See several training documents in the Antônio Carlos Murici archives: ACM pm 1961.08.16.

42. Three of these lectures were reproduced in this issue of the *Mensário*: the one given by Castelo Branco at ECEME and a few days earlier at EsAO (December 15, 1961); those by General Augusto de Lira Tavares to AMAN (November 29, 1961) and by General Vasconcellos at the Sergeants' Improvement and Specialization Centre at Realengo (at the end of November), which he had also given to cadets at AMAN and the Army Sergeants' School (Escola de Sargentos das Armas) (November 27, 1961) and to students and trainers at EsAO (November 28, 1961).

43. João Roberto Martins Filho provides a detailed presentation and points out that this phase was predicted by the previous year's EME directive (in "A educação dos golpistas," 1-2). The EME published Castelo Branco's lecture ("Ação educativa contra Guerra Revolucionária") and the whole of the third stage course in 1965.

44. Introduction to the Military Duty special issue of the *Mensário de Cultura Militar*, Year XIV (February 1962), 3-5.

45. Colonel Otávio Costa, in discussion with the CPDOC researchers, published in *Visões do golpe*, 2nd ed., 93.

46. Cel. Francisco Ruas Santos, *A Guerra revolucionária comunista* (Academia Militar das Agulhas Negras / Ensino Fundamental / Seção de Ensino a Cadeira de História, n.d.), AMAN Archives.

47. See the testimony of General Geisel Ferrari, an AMAN trainer in 1964, in vol. 1 of *História oral do Exército*, 193, 203.

48. "Instrução Teórica de Oficiais sôbre Guerra Insurrecional," ACM pm 1961.08.16/ CPDOC.

49. ACM pm 1963.05.01/CPDOC.

50. Letter from Castelo Branco to Antônio Carlos Murici, June 3, 1963, ACM pm 1963.05.01/CPDOC.

51. General Agnaldo del Nero, in discussion with the author, Brasília, March 2008.

52. Ulhoa Cintra Archives, UCi g 1963.04.09/CPDOC.

53. Fico, *O Grande Irmão*, 101.

54. Dreifuss, *1964: A conquista do estado*.

55. *Jornal do Brasil*, Mar 15, 1978, 4. The romantic aspect of the "revolutionary fervor" this letter surely represents for the colonel is confirmed by the ease with which he put it on show: in 1978, when he was subject to disciplinary sanctions because of his political activism, he had it read out in the Chamber of Deputies to ensure it entered the Annals of Congress, as indeed it did.

56. Tarcísio Nunes Ferreira, interview given to the author, Rio de Janeiro, June 2006.

57. For Carlos Lacerda's career, see Dulles, *Carlos Lacerda*; and Mendonça, *O demolidor de presidentes*. We should point out that, paradoxically, Carlos Lacerda played little part in the secret negotiations and contacts that prepared the coup, primarily because of the suspicion aroused in many military leaders by his capacity to betray his allies and make peace with his former enemies for the sake of his political ambitions.

58. Daniel Krieger's address to the Senate on the subject of Colonel Francisco Boaventura Cavalcanti's letter to War Minister Jair Dantas Ribeiro, which earned him thirty days in prison. *Diário do Congresso Nacional*, section 2, November 23, 1963, 5.

59. Anonymous report [*Informe*] dated May 2, 1963. Cordeiro de Farias Archives, Cfa tv 1963.05.02/CPDOC.

60. See Rodrigo Patto Sá Motta, "A figura caricatural."

61. Antônio Carlos Murici Archives, ACM pm 1963.05.01/CPDOC. Hélio Silva and Maria Cecila Ribas Carneiro also talk of a five-hundred-name petition in support of the general (*1964—golpe ou contragolpe?* 270).

62. Bulletin distributed within the armed forces, June 1963. Odílio Denys Archives (OD vm 1961-12-13/CPDOC).

63. There are many studies of how the Intentona is remembered, particularly its commemoration, since 1936, on November 27. Ferreira, *Organização e poder*; Motta, *Em guarda*; Motta, "A 'Intentona Comunista'"; Castro, *A invenção do Exército*, 49–67.

64. Avelar Coutinho, interview given to the author, Rio de Janeiro, October 2006.

65. *Boletim do Exército* 51 (December 17, 1960), 16–18.

66. Smallman, *Fear and Memory*.

67. Capanema P. de Almeida, *Couleur et châtiment*; Love, *Revolt of the Whip*.

68. Carvalho, *Forças armadas*, 63; Parucker, *Praças em pé de guerra*.

69. A comparison can be made, for example, with the situation of Chile's soldiers and sailors thanks to a study by Magasich Airola, *Los que dijeron No*.

70. Aviso n.GR 32 D1, February 5, 1963. *Noticiário do Exército*, February 6, 1963, 1. We note that it appeared in this newspaper (produced by the ministry) even before it was published in the official newspaper (*Diário Oficial*), published on February 11, which clearly reveals the desire to distribute the recommendation at speed.

71. *Boletim do Exército*, no. 23, June 7, 1963, 31.

72. The adjective "tupiniquim," borrowed from the first indigenous people encountered by the Portuguese conquistadores in 1500, has become a synonym for "typically Brazilian." The rebels certainly had the Kronstadt Rebellion in mind and showed Sergei Eisenstein's *Battleship Potemkin* to an enthusiastic audience. Chagas, *A guerra das estrelas*, 23.

73. Lemos, *Justiça fardada*, 18.
74. Speech made at EsAO during the commemoration of the Brazilian Expeditionary Force victory at Monte Castelo and published in the *Mensário de Cultura Militar*, nos.183-84 (January-February 1964), 5-12.
75. Stepan, *Os militares na política* and "The New Professionalism." Finer, *Man on Horseback*; Perlmutter, *Military and Politics*.
76. Reserved circular from the army chief of staff, dated March 20, 1964.
77. Ulhoa Cintra Archives, UCi g 1963.04.09/CPDOC. Reproduced in a book of General Cordeiro de Farias's memoirs (Camargo and Góes, *Meio século de combate*, see the appendix). See the analysis by Daniel de Mendonça in "O discurso militar."
78. Article 177 of the 1946 Constitution says: "The Armed Forces are to defend the Motherland and to guarantee the constitutional powers, law and order."
79. UCi g 1963.04.09/CPDOC.
80. "Message to Young Soldiers. 3. Defend the Motherland, Despite Everything and Everyone," *O Globo*, April 10, 1964.
81. Stacchini Junior, *Março 64*, 37.
82. According to Cyro Etchegoyen, "1964 começou com coronéis," *A Folha de São Paulo*, March 20, 1994.
83. D'Araujo, Soares, and Castro, *Visões do golpe*, 127.
84. D'Araujo, Soares, and Castro, *Visões do golpe*, 175.
85. For more in-depth consideration of the use of the word, see Chirio "Le pouvoir en un mot."

CHAPTER 2: *Continuing the Revolution*

Epigraph: General Carlos de Meira Mattos, in discussion with D'Araujo, Soares, and Castro, in *Visões do golpe*, 114.

1. Colonel Gustavo Moares Rego Reis, in discussion with Maria Celina D'Araujo and Gláucio Ary Dillon Soares in Rio de Janeiro, July 1992 (Rio de Janeiro: CPDOC, 2005), 21, http://www.fgv.br/cpdoc/historal/arq/Entrevista631.pdf. For Boaventura, who publicly declared his opposition in May to press baron Roberto Marinho, thus providing the pretext to oust him from the cabinet on the grounds of an attack on the disciplinary rules, see *Jornal do Brasil*, May 19, 1964, 5.
2. One of the first appearances of this dichotomy in the press was the column written by journalist Castello Branco (no relation to the general of the same name) in the *Jornal do Brasil*, August 17, 1964, 4.
3. SNI, *Impresso Geral* no. 5 (September 7-14, 1964), Luis Viana Filho Archives, National Archives.
4. Anonymous manifesto distributed in the chamber by Deputy José Costa Cavalcanti, *Jornal do Brasil*, April 23, 1965, 4.
5. The first to raise this hard-line/moderate dichotomy was Alfred Stepan in *The Military in Politics*, translated into Portuguese by Italo Tronca as *Os militares na política*.
6. "Capitães do Exército Brasileiro!" speech made at the EsAO in July 1964 and published in *Noticiário do Exército*, July 8, 1964.
7. Testimony of Colonel Cyro Etchegoyen, in D'Araujo, Soares, and Castro, *Visões do golpe*, 182.
8. There are a numerous journalistic writings about this. See Chagas, *A guerra das estrelas*; Camargo and Góes, *O drama da sucessão*; and Bittencourt, *A quinta estrela*.
9. Linz, "Future of an Authoritarian Situation."
10. This image of moderation was subsequently qualified: João Roberto Martins Filho

showed in particular that the policies adopted by the Castelo Branco government were less enforced by right-wing pressure and more a response to it, as part of a power game where authoritarian measures strengthened the political influence of whoever adopted them. *O palácio e a caserna*, 66–68, 82–84.

11. Stepan, *The Military in Politics*, 239.

12. Stepan, *The Military in Politics*, 167.

13. Eduardo Svartman has suggested an interesting classification into three groups (insurrectional-rebel, technocrat, institutional-conspirator), which breaks away from earlier models and representations. *Guardiões da nação*.

14. The list taken as a working basis is the one Colonel Gustavo Moraes Rego gave the CPDOC researchers D'Araujo and Castro during their discussion in 2005, plus information from the memoirs of Jayme Portella de Mello, Ernesto Geisel, and Sylvio Frota; the published interviews of Antônio Carlos Murici and Osvaldo Cordeiro de Farias; and the author's own interviews with Amerino Raposo Filho, Kurt Pessek, Osnelli Martinelli, and Tarcísio Nunes Ferreira.

15. SNI, *Informe especial* no. 4 (July 5, 1965): file 1, 1.24–1.71, Luis Viana Filho Archives, National Archives.

16. *Jornal do Brasil*, July 21, 1964.

17. Three participants in the July 1922 rebellion entered the government in 1964: General Juarez Távora (1898–1975), transport minister; Brigadier Eduardo Gomes (1896–1981), air force minister for a short time; and General Cordeiro de Farias (1901–81), minister extraordinary for the coordination of regional agencies. Juracy Magalhães (1905–2001), a tenente from 1930 rather than 1922–24, was foreign minister at the end of General Castelo Branco's term of office.

18. Also on the cruiser was Deputy Carlos Lacerda, as were many other senior officers who would have leading roles under the dictatorship: Colonel Jurandir Bizarria Mamede, Major Jayme Portella (future éminence grise to General Costa e Silva), and lacerdista "hard-liner" Major Heitor Caracas Linhares. A fuller list is provided by Barbosa, *Confissões de generais*, 23. On this episode, see Carloni, *Forças armadas*.

19. Silva and Carneiro, *1964—golpe ou contragolpe?* 229.

20. SNI, *Informe especial* no. 4 (July 5, 1965), file 1, 1.24–1.71, Luis Viana Filho Archives, National Archives.

21. "The Brazilian Revolution (April 1964)," dispatch by the Military and Air Force Attaché to the French Embassy in Rio, July 1964. French Army Archives, 10T1109. Heck's growing opposition had him thrown off the admirals' council in April 1965.

22. Stacchini, *Março 64*, xvii, 2, 114.

23. *Jornal do Brasil*, August 5, 1964.

24. For the STM as a space for dissent and political expression by the military, see Lemos, *Justiça fardada*, and "Poder judiciário e poder militar."

25. The eleven generals mentioned by Moraes Rego are: Siseno Sarmento, Sylvio Frota, Ramiro Tavares Gonçalves, Arthur Duarte Candal, Afonso de Albuquerque Lima, Ednardo D'Ávila Melo, Oscar Luis da Silva, José Anchieta Paes, Henrique Assunção Cardoso, Clovis Brasil, and João Dutra de Castilho.

26. According to Colonel Moraes Rego, these were army officers: Osnelli Martinelli, Gérson de Pina, Ferdinando de Carvalho, Luis Alencar Araripe, Euclides de Oliveira Figueiredo Filho, Sebastião Ferreira Chaves, Amerino Raposo Filho, Hélio Ibiapina de Lima, Adyr Fiúza de Castro, Hélio Lemos, Hélio Mendes, Heitor Caracas Linhares, Rui Castro, Sebastião José Ramos de Castro, Florimar Campelo, César Montanha de Souza,

Antônio Erasmo Dias, Osvaldo Ferraro, Confúcio Danton de Paula Avelino, Joaquim Vitorino Portela Alves, Augusto Cid Camargo Ozório, Cabral Ribeiro. Plínio Pitaluga, Confúcio Pamplona, Antônio Carlos de Andrada Serpa, Luis Gonzaga Andrada Serpa, Valter Pires, and Antônio Bandeira. Moraes Rego, discussion, 24–25.

27. Colonel Tarcísio Nunes Ferreira, in discussion with the author, Rio de Janeiro, June 2006.

28. Colonel Osnelli Martinelli, in discussion with the author, Rio de Janeiro, April 2007.

29. Martinelli, discussion.

30. Ferdinando de Carvalho published all the results of his IPM (known as No. 709) in a series of books titled *O comunismo no Brasil*, and all the "orders of the day" for Intentona commemorations from 1936 to 1979, in *Lembrai-vos de 35!*

31. Ferreira, discussion.

32. Colonel José Eduardo de Castro Portela Soares, in discussion with the author, Rio de Janeiro, June 2006.

33. For the STM, see Moreira, "Ditadura e justiça."

34. Constitutional Amendment no. 9, July 22, 1964.

35. *Estimativa* no.3. Brasília, September 15, 1964, file 1, 1.24–1.71, Luis Viana Filho Archives, National Archives.

36. The "aircraft carrier crisis" was a dispute between high-ranking officers of the air force and navy over who has control of the aircraft loaded onto the Minas Gerais aircraft carrier purchased in 1956.

37. Portella de Mello, *A revolução e o governo*, 276.

38. Figures from a single press source and so subject to caution. *Jornal do Brasil*, April 25, 1965, 22.

39. The marshal stood down (without first abandoning his "hard-line" positions) when his son, an economist with progressive beliefs, Sérgio Rezende, was involved in an IPM within the Fourth Army. On the way, he tempered his repressive ambitions and joined the opposition MDB party in August 1966 (*Jornal do Brasil*, July 21, 1964, and August 18, 1966).

40. *Noticiário do Exército*, May 16, 17, 28; June 9, 1964.

41. A public interview given on October 30, and reproduced in part in *Jornal do Brasil*, November 13, 1964.

42. SNI, *Impresso Geral* no. 7, September 22–28, 1964. Luis Viana Filho Archives, National Archives.

43. Note from the French Military Attaché to the Prime Minister, October 14, 1964, "Radical Democratic League (October 1964)," Army Archives, 10T1111.

44. SNI information about the GAP is patchy. A November 1965 document mentions links to the Brazilian Anticommunist Legion (Legião Brasileira Anticomunista) but also notes that the informant knew nothing about its expansion into military circles. The report confirmed that the GAP was dependent on the LIDER (Grupo de Ação Popular e Grupo de Ação Patriótica—E0083264—1981. SNI Archives, Brasília Office of the National Archives).

45. Reproduced in Prospero Punaro Baratta Netto, who took part in the events. *Amazônia*.

46. Martinelli, discussion.

47. Colonel Amerino Raposo Filho, in discussion with the author, Rio de Janeiro, October 2006.

48. Martinelli, discussion.
49. Lemos, *Justiça fardada*, 23–25.
50. On CAMDE, see Cordeiro, *Direitas em movimento*.
51. Daniel Aarão Reis Filho initiated the process. See his *Ditadura e democracia*. One champion of retaining the term "military dictatorship" who has called for a genuine historiographical and memorial debate is João Roberto Martins Filho in "Adieu à la dictature?"
52. Luis Viana Filho Archives, National Archives. From the end of July 1965, only a few pages of documents have been preserved and provide no further useful information about the military.
53. *Impresso Geral* no.1, August 10–16, 1964, file 1, 1.24–1.71, Luis Viana Filho Archives, National Archives.
54. *Estimativa* no. 2, November 1964, file 1, 1.24–1.71, Luis Viana Filho Archives, National Archives.
55. *Apreciação das tendências contra-revolucionárias*, April 24, 1965, file 1, 1.24–1.71, Luis Viana Filho Archives, National Archives.
56. *Proposta de apreciação*, July 26–30, 1965, file 1, 1.24–1.71, Luis Viana Filho Archives, National Archives.
57. *Noticiário do Exército*, July 8, 1964.
58. *Noticiário do Exército*, June 22, 1965.
59. *Jornal do Brasil*, April 15, 1964.
60. *Jornal do Brasil*, April 2 and 3, 1965.
61. Transcription of the speech the general gave on October 6, 1965 at the Vila Militar. The recording is held in CPDOC's small Costa e Silva Archive. The applause punctuating the speech (highly inappropriate in a barracks setting) is one of the few signs of the Vila's great political mobilization at the time.
62. Letter dated July 19, 1965. Ulhoa Cintra Archives, UCi fm 1962.09.11/CPDOC.
63. Colonel Kurt Pessek, in discussion with the author, Brasília, March 2008.
64. D'Araujo and Castro, *Ernesto Geisel*, 180–92.
65. Marina Gusmão de Mendonça believes the key positions Lacerda adopted in the early years of the military regime should be interpreted in the light of his own presidential plans: *O demolidor de presidentes*, 326–28. Lacerda himself made no secret of this. During his first post-coup visit to the Presidential Palace on April 20, 1964, he delivered the impertinent "I would very much like to be living here in 1966." Neto, *Castello*, 277.
66. *Jornal do Brasil*, October 16, 1965.
67. Portella de Mello, *A revolução e o governo*, 300.
68. *Jornal do Brasil*, October 23, 1965. The background noise (Costa e Silva archives, CPDOC) once again reveals the excited atmosphere among the officers in attendance. Some of them are chanting, "Manda brasa, ministro!" (Stir things up, Minister!).
69. Term taken from Élio Gaspari (who used it with regard to the Vila Militar, in October 1965), *A ditadura envergonhada*, 123.
70. *Jornal do Brasil*, June 23, 1965.
71. *Noticiário do Exército*, July 8, 1964.
72. *Jornal do Brasil*, August 26, 1964.
73. Decree no. 54.062, July 28, 1964. Published in the *Boletim do Exército* no. 34, August 21, 1964.
74. Article 14 of the "Law on the Inactivity of Personnel from the Three Service Arms" (no. 4902, December 16, 1965) limited the length of time an officer could be kept away from active service, exercising elective or ministerial functions.
75. Denys, *O ciclo revolucionário brasileiro*, 9.

76. *Jornal do Brasil*, July 21, 1964.
77. *Jornal do Brasil*, January 7, 1965.
78. *Jornal do Brasil*, February 5, 1965.
79. Silvio Heck's second manifesto, *Jornal do Brasil*, October 31, 1964.
80. Mendonça, *O demolidor de presidentes*, 99, 280, 326.
81. Correspondência política—Governor Carlos Lacerda. Castelo Branco Archives / ECEME, letter of November 22, 1964.
82. *Jornal do Brasil*, February 5, 1965.
83. *Noticiário do Exército*, August 8, 1964.
84. The admiral's fourth manifesto at the end and at the height of the "IPM colonels" crisis, published in the *Jornal do Brasil*, June 30, 1965.
85. *Jornal do Brasil*, June 22, 1965. A few months before he died, Martinelli remained very proud of this letter and could quote passages by heart. Martinelli, discussion.
86. Manifesto of the Guanabara IPM colonels, *Jornal do Brasil*, May 13, 1965.
87. *Jornal do Brasil*, January 7, 1965.
88. *Jornal do Brasil*, April 23, 1965.
89. *Jornal do Brasil*, October 20, 1965.

CHAPTER 3: *Consolidation and Divergences*

Epigraph: Statement to ECEME students on December 16, 1968, three days after the enactment of AI-5. *Jornal do Brasil*, December 17, 1968.

1. Castelo Branco Archives, "Sucessão" File, ECEME. We note in passing that the president was sharing his thoughts and concerns with the generals, not the ARENA leaders or the government as a whole.
2. CS pi 1967.08.00/ CPDOC.
3. *Jornal do Brasil*, August 6, 1966.
4. Martins Filho, *O palácio e a caserna*, 82–95.
5. *Jornal do Brasil*, January 13, 1967.
6. *Jornal do Brasil*, February 14, 1967.
7. *Jornal do Brasil*, March 18, 1967.
8. Martinelli, discussion with the author, Rio de Janeiro, April 2007.
9. *Jornal do Brasil*, April 26, 1967.
10. *Jornal do Brasil*, June 1, 1967.
11. *Jornal do Brasil*, June 2, 1967.
12. *Jornal do Brasil*, June 17, 1967.
13. *Jornal do Brasil*, July 1, 1967.
14. *Jornal do Brasil*, February 18, 1968.
15. *Jornal do Brasil*, March 20, 1968.
16. *Jornal do Brasil*, April 28, 1968.
17. *Jornal do Brasil*, August 18, 1966.
18. *Tribuna da Imprensa*, July 22, 1967.
19. *Jornal do Brasil*, August 9, 1967.
20. The document was published in the *O Globo* issue of August 25, 1967, on Soldier's Day, one of the army's main celebrations.
21. *O Globo*, August 28, 1967.
22. *Jornal do Brasil*, September 28, 1967.
23. Lacerda, *Depoimento*, 463.
24. Lemos, "Por inspiração"; and the introduction to *Justiça fardada*.
25. Mourão Filho, *Memórias*, 419.

26. *Jornal do Brasil*, March 15, 1967. See also *Estado de São Paulo* of March 18, 1967, and its analysis by Eliézer Rizzo de Oliveira in *As forças armadas*, 84.

27. *Jornal do Brasil*, May 3, 1966.

28. *Jornal do Brasil*, August 11, 1966.

29. *Jornal do Brasil*, August 11, 1966. General Kruel was eventually elected as an MDB deputy in September 1968.

30. *Jornal do Brasil*, July 5, 1967.

31. O'Reilly, "A ideologia da Corrente Militar," 180–81.

32. Carlos Fico has shown the extent to which these images fed into the dictatorship's overall propaganda from 1969, when a propaganda machine was established, in *Reinventando o otimismo*.

33. *Registro Histórico*, AMAN Archives.

34. *Jornal do Brasil*, May 7, 1968.

35. *Jornal do Brasil*, August 10, 1968.

36. *Jornal do Brasil*, June 27, 1968.

37. *Jornal do Brasil*, July 5, 1968.

38. See Cowan, *Securing Sex*.

39. *Jornal do Brasil*, October 15, 1968.

40. Compagnon, "Le '68 des catholiques"; Jalles de Paula, *O bom combate*.

41. Deckes, *Radiografia*, 57–66; Argolo, *A direita explosiva*, 265; Gorender, *Combate nas trevas*, 149–52; Gaspari, *A ditadura envergonhada*.

42. Quoting Lieutenant Colonel Luiz Helvécio da Silveira Leite (himself an activist), in Argolo and Fortunato, *Dos quartéis à espionagem*, 215.

43. Testimony of colonels Alberto Fortunato and João Paulo Moreira Burnier, in Argolo, *A direita explosiva*.

44. This was the Vanguard's program, colored by revolutionary mystique and apolitism, and combined with support for the government. It was published in the *Jornal do Brasil*, November 3, 1968. The group came into being in August 1968.

45. Colonel Kurt Pessek, in discussion with the author, Brasília, March 2008.

46. Argolo, *A direita explosiva*, 314.

47. AI-5 subsequently forced Captain Sérgio Miranda out of the army. The CPDOC archives Cfa tv 1964.10.23 reveal the efforts made by Brigadier Eduardo Gomes and General Cordeiro de Farias (supported by Admiral Sílvio Heck and General Albuquerque Lima, according to *Folha de São Paulo*, February 18, 1978) between 1978 and 1980 to have him reinstated after being amnestied. This was only granted by the STF (together with a promotion) in 1992, but neither the air force minister of the day, Brigadier Sócrates da Costa Monteiro, nor the president of the Republic Fernando Collor de Mello, enforced the ruling. Captain Sérgio's reinstatement and promotion were achieved posthumously, in 1994.

48. This is a reference to recent manifestos from the "mothers of São Paulo" against the suppression of the secondary school and student movement.

49. The War of the Emboabas was a conflict over gold in Minas Gerais between 1707 and 1709 involving the established population of São Paulo versus new Portuguese colonists. After crushing and bloody defeats of their men, the *paulista* women of Piratininga were said to have denied their husbands their favors and their parents their affection until they achieved victory.

50. *Diário do Congresso Nacional*, Supplement, September 4, 1968, 9.

51. Moreira Alves, *68 mudou o mundo*.

52. Nunes Ferreira, discussion, Rio de Janeiro, June 2006. The testimony of Colonel

Amerino Raposo Filho (in a separate discussion with the author, Rio de Janeiro, November 2006) agrees with Ferreira's recollections.

53. Portella de Mello, *A revolução e o governo*, 625, 632, 568.

54. Telegram from the Embassy of Brazil to the State Department, Rio de Janeiro, December 20 1968. U.S. State Department Archives, National Archives and Records Administration, RG 59, Central Files 1967–69, POL 23-9 BRAZ. http://www.state.gov/r/pa/ho/frus/johnsonlb/xxxi/36293.htm.

55. *Jornal do Brasil*, November 23, 1968.

56. Ernani do Amaral Peixoto Archives—EAP df2 1968.11.18/CPDOC. The deputy's speech and his "affair" in general came to public awareness fairly belatedly through the press. It was first mentioned in the *Jornal do Brasil* on September 28, 1968.

57. *Jornal do Brasil*, September 8, 1968.

58. *Correio da Manhã*, November 1, 1968.

59. *Visão 33*, no. 11, November 22, 1968.

60. *Jornal do Brasil*, November 23, 1968.

61. *Jornal do Brasil*, December 7, 1968.

CHAPTER 4: *Shaking the Ground*

Epigraph: O'Reilly, "A ideologia da Corrente Militar," 250–53.

1. *Jornal do Brasil*, May 20, 1969.

2. Lacerda, *Depoimento*, 462.

3. Colonel Gustavo Moares Rego Reis, in discussion with Maria Celina D'Araujo and Gláucio Ary Dillon Soares in Rio de Janeiro, July 1992 (CPDOC: Rio de Janeiro, 2005), 66, accessed January 1, 2017, http://www.fgv.br/cpdoc/historal/arq/Entrevista631.pdf.

4. General Moniz de Aragão, letter to General Lira Tavares, reproduced in Chagas, *113 dias*, 199.

5. Letters from General Antônio Carlos Murici to General Aurélio de Lira Tavares, June 26, 1969. Antônio Carlos Murici Archives, ACM pm 1969.06.26/CPDOC; and letter from General Lira Tavares to General Aragão, June 30, 1969, reproduced in Chagas, *113 dias*, 203.

6. 42e ACE meeting. Rio de Janeiro, GB, July 21, 1969, in SNI Archives, Atitudes do Gen Ex Moniz de Aragão—A0063230—1980.

7. Ferreira, discussion.

8. O'Reilly, "A ideologia da Corrente Militar," 219.

9. O'Donnell, *Modernization*; Collier, *New Authoritarianism*; and Evans, *Dependent Development*.

10. See Prado and Earp, "O 'milagre' brasileiro."

11. Zirker, "Hugo Abreu."

12. Vizentini, "A ditadura foi Entreguista?"

13. Vanguarda Militar Nacionalista—A0213214—1969, SNI Archives.

14. Calculated on the basis of figures supplied to the author by Cláudio Beserra Vasconcelos.

15. d'Aguiar, *Ato 5*, 298. The Brazilian Senate published the text of this stillborn constitution (amounting to a single amendment to the 1967 document, which further strengthened the executive) in 2002 with the title: *A constituição que não foi história* [The constitution that never was] (Brasília: Senado Federal, 2002).

16. The term is taken from Chagas, *113 dias*, 12.

17. Ferreira, discussion.

18. Memorandum written on August 31, 1969, reproduced in O'Reilly, "A ideologia

da Corrente Militar," 222-24. According to this author, the memorandum was probably written together with generals Dutra de Castilho, Siseno Sarmento, and Moniz de Aragão.

19. Murici, *Depoimento*, 701.

20. While we do not have the original texts of these programs, we do have an unsigned and undated note describing them, in the archives of Air Force General Faria Lima (FL emfa 1969.08.00/CPDOC).

21. Order of the Day of the First Airborne Artillery Group, Airborne Brigade, First Army, November 7, 1969. Reproduced in Chagas, *113 dias*, 239-45.

22. GAAet Order of the Day, November 7, 1969.

23. *Veja*, March 15, 1978, transcribed in an SNI document sent to Third Army Headquarters in March 1981. Archives SNI—Grupo Centelha Nativista—G0023310—1981.

24. Ferreira, discussion. There was a newspaper of this name in the early 2000s, linked to the Movimento Nativista, which had become the more respectable Núcleo de Estudos Estratégicos Mathias de Albuquerque; in 2008 the "general coordinator" was reserve colonel Francimá de Luna Máximo and reserve colonel Adalto Barreiros was still a member in 2002.

25. Motta, *História oral*.

26. Anonymous note reporting the operation, Archives Cordeiro de Farias, Cfa tv 64.04.11/CPDOC.

27. Document reproduced in O'Reilly, "A ideologia da Corrente Militar," 238-40.

28. Letter from General Albuquerque Lima to General Murici, September 5, 1969. Reproduced in O'Reilly, "A ideologia da Corrente Militar," 242-44.

29. Letter in O'Reilly, "A ideologia da Corrente Militar," 245-47.

30. Taken from the personal archives of General Afonso de Albuquerque Lima and reproduced in O'Reilly, "A ideologia da Corrente Militar," 250-53. It was signed by 12 majors, 62 captains, 49 first lieutenants, 40 second lieutenants, and 26 officer cadets, a total of 189 serving officers, anonymized in the source.

31. Proceedings of the Forty-Fourth ACE meeting, September 15, 1969, in Élio Gaspari, "O Alto-Comando do Exército e a crise de 1969," *Arquivos da Ditadura* [The Dictatorship Archives] (blog), an online archive cum blog built by the Italian-born Brazilian journalist, http://arquivosdaditadura.com.br/documento/galeria/alto-comando-exercito-crise-1969.

32. Letter sent from Rio de Janeiro on October 5, 1969, to General Albuquerque Lima, reproduced in O'Reilly, "A ideologia da Corrente Militar," 302-4.

33. *Murici, Depoimento*, 724.

34. Unsigned and undated document held in the Air Force General Faria Lima Archive (FL emfa 1969.08.00—CPDOC). Furious handwritten annotations—"filthy lie," "probable lie"—crisscross the page.

35. Letter from Moniz de Aragão to the army minister, read out at the Forty-Fifth meeting on September 17. Proceedings of the Forty-Fifth ACE meeting, Antônio Carlos Murici Archive, ACM pm 1969.06.26—CPDOC.

36. Letter from General Afonso de Albuquerque Lima to General Aurélio de Lira Tavares, October 2, 1969, reproduced in Chagas, *113 dias*, 218-20.

37. Reply from Lira Tavares to Albuquerque Lima, October 3, 1969, reproduced in Chagas, *113 dias*, 222.

38. Martins Filho, *O palácio e a caserna*, 186.

39. Admiral Ernesto de Mello Batista, "Apelo ao governo e à opinião pública," Antônio Carlos Murici Archive, ACM pm 1969.06.26—CPDOC.

40. Couto, *Revolução de 1964*, 215.

41. Antônio Carlos Murici Archive, ACM pm 1969.06.26—CPDOC.
42. Latin, literally, "in the manner of a corpse." Though used earlier in medieval times, Loyola famously used the phrase in his constitution for the Jesuit order, when describing the total submission required of any follower, who could be moved about without any remonstration, just as though he were a corpse.
43. The descriptions are by Carlos Chagas (*113 dias*) and Élio Gaspari (*A ditadura Escancarada*), the interpretations by Eliézer Rizzo de Oliveira (*As forças armadas*) and João Roberto Martins Filho (*O palácio e a caserna*). For "models" of military regimes and the peculiar nature of the Brazilian hierarchy see Arceneaux, *Bounded Missions*.

CHAPTER 5: *At the Heart of the System*

Epigraph: D'Araujo, Castro, and Soares, *Os anos de chumbo*, 114.
1. The expression comes from Suzeley Kalil Mathias in his groundbreaking work on the "détente" period: *A distensão no Brasil*, 89.
2. In its June 9 and 18, 1978, editions when prepublication censorship was coming to an end in the press, the *Jornal do Brasil* drew up the full list of topics affected during the Years of Lead.
3. Castelo Branco gifted some of his personal archives to the ECEME library and Costa e Silva a few (a very few) documents to the CPDOC of the Fundação Getulio Vargas (Getulio Vargas Foundation). Geisel also gave a large proportion of his personal archive material to the CPDOC.
4. Quadrat, "A preparação dos agentes ."
5. This is the subject of current research by the author and Mariana Joffily. Chirio and Joffily, "A repressão condecorada," and "Moderniser la répression politique."
6. General Agnaldo del Nero, in discussion with the author, Brasília, March 2008.
7. Testimony of João Paulo Moreira Burnier on the creation of the NCISA and CISA in Argolo, *A direita explosiva*, 72.
8. João Paulo Moreira Burnier in discussion with Celso Castro and Maria Celina D'Araujo (212–13), Rio de Janeiro, December 1993 (CPDOC: Rio de Janeiro, 2005), 174, http://www.fgv.br/cpdoc/historal/arq/Entrevista633.pdf.
9. U.S. Defense Attaché Report (United States Defense Attaché Office, USDAO) to the State Department, "A Follow-up on the BURNIER Force-out," July 17, 1972. State Department Archives, João Paulo Moreira Burnier File.
10. SDECE note to the prime minister, dated February 17, 1970, "Hostilité du Haut Commandement de l'Armée à l'égard du président (février 1970)," Archive of the French Army, 10T1109.
11. D' Araujo, Castro and Soares, *A volta aos quartéis*, 191.
12. Osvaldo Cordeiro de Farias, *Sessão Especial Comemorativa do VI Aniversário da Revolução de Março de 1964,* Rio de Janeiro, ESG, March 31, 1970, 12–13. Quoted in Mathias, *A distensão no Brasil*, 59.
13. Ernesto Geisel, interviewed by Alfred Stepan, quoted in Stepan, *Os militares*, 46.
14. Testimony of Colonel Moraes Rego, in D' Araujo, Castro and Soares, *A volta aos quartéis,* 48.
15. The Communist Party of Brazil, founded in 1962, is a Maoist dissident faction of the Brazilian Communist Party, which has remained faithful to Moscow.
16. Carvalho, *O governo Médici*, 32; and Mathias, *A distensão no Brasil*, 39.
17. Ernesto Geisel Archive, EG pr 1974.07.10/CPDOC.
18. *Jornal do Brasil*, August 30, 1974.
19. Ernesto Geisel Archive EG pr 1978.00.00/CPDOC.

20. Oliveira, Velloso, and Gomes, *Estado Novo*, 84.

21. Mathias, *A distensão no Brasil*, 97.

22. The most recent study summarizing information on Brazil's participation in Operation Condor is the chapter titled "Conexões internacionais: A aliança repressiva no Cone Sul e a Operação Condor" in the National Truth Commission Report, vol, 2, 219–74. See also McSherry, *Los Estados depredadores*; and Palmar, *Onde foi*.

23. See the reflection of Celso Castro and Leslie Bethell in Bethell, *Cambridge History of Latin America*, 9:170.

24. The short list we have used is based on the testimonies published in D'Araujo, Castro, and Soares, *Os anos de chumbo*. It is not exhaustive.

25. Stepan, *Os militares*, 26.

26. The testimonies are those of colonels Alberto Fortunato, Luiz Helvécio da Silveira Leite, Pedro Maciel Braga, Freddie Perdigão, Octávio Moreira Borba, and Henrique Couto Ferreira Mello, published in Argolo, *A direita explosiva*; and Argolo and Fortunato, *Dos quartéis à espionagem*.

27. The statement is known by the name "Note on the Disappeared." *Jornal do Brasil*, February 7, 1975.

28. Memo titled "Anxiety in the Military Space" [*Inquietação na área militar*], dated March 17, 1975, and quoted in Gaspari, *A ditadura encurralada*, 70.

29. The number of "chapters" in the *Saga* and the period of time during which they were released are noted in Gaspari, *A ditadura encurralada*, 67. The journalist has read them all but only four are available to the academic community (Cordeiro de Farias Archive, Cfa tv 76.00.00/CPDOC). The information that the first chapter was released only to the intelligence community appears in the SNI Report of October 12, 1977, in the Ernesto Geisel Archive, EG pr 1974.03.00/CPDOC.

30. SNI Report of May 8m 1975, Ernesto Geisel Archive, EG pr 1974.03.00/CPDOC; and SNI Archives (National Archives), CIE Document dated March 1–31, 1975, Relatório periódico de informações—A0863154—1975.

31. Baffa, *Nos porões do SNI*, 51–54.

32. Document of the First Army, July 1975. SNI Archives (National Archives), Relatório periódico de informações—A0863154—1975..

33. SNI Report of September 15, 1975, Ernesto Geisel Archive, EG pr 1974.03.00/CPDOC.

34. *Jornal do Brasil*, August 2, 1975.

35. *Jornal do Brasil*, December 18, 1975.

36. This statement is based on Miranda and Tiburcio, *Os filhos deste solo*.

37. Social repression developed against the poorest sectors of the population at this time, carried out by the infamous Death Squads denounced in 1976 by lawyer and politician Bicudo, *Meu depoimento*; also Peralva, *Violência e democracia*.

38. SNI Report of February 2, 1976. Ernesto Geisel Archives, EG pr 1974.03.00/CPDOC.

39. Argolo, *A direita explosiva*, 308.

40. The Secret Army Organization (OAS) was a clandestine far-right militia, set up in France in 1961, which used terrorist action to fight Algerian independence.

41. Testimony given by Colonel Alberto Fortunato to José Amaral Argolo and Luiz Alberto Fortunato, *Dos quartéis à espionagem*, 222. Some of the pamphlets were accompanied by drawings of a hanged Golbery.

42. D' Araujo, Castro and Soares, *A volta aos quartéis*, 253.

43. In French in the original.
44. Cordeiro de Farias, Cfa tv 76.00.00/CPDOC.
45. *Veja*, September 23, 1987. The review was given the document by Élio Gaspari.
46. *Jornal do Brasil*, August 20, 1976.
47. "Objetivo Nacional Permanente: O Brasil na posição socialista," SNI Archives (National Archives), Candidatura do General Euler Bentes, Frente Nacional de Redemocratização—E0072114—1981.
48. "Objetivo Nacional Permanente."
49. Chirio and Joffily, "La repression en chair et en os".
50. *Ernesto Geisel*, 362.
51. *Jornal do Brasil*, September 3, 1976. The minister entered parliament escorted by forty general officers.
52. Testimony given to Maria Celina D'Araujo and Celso Castro, published in *Ernesto Geisel*, 361-62.
53. January 21, 1976. Chronology of Frota's actions, Ernesto Geisel Archive, EG pr 1974.03.25/3/CPDOC.
54. Frota, *Ideais traidos*, 436.
55. *Jornal do Brasil*, December 23, 1976.
56. *Jornal do Brasil*, October 13, 1977.
57. SNI Report of October 26, 1977, Ernesto Geisel Archives, EG pr 1974.03.00/CPDOC.
58. Stepan, *Os militares*, 55.

CHAPTER 6: *The Final Campaign*

Epigraph: Undated campaign speech. ARENA archives (although General Euler was standing for the MDB), ARENA d 1973.05.10/CPDOC.

1. The document is republished in Abreu, *O outro lado do poder*, 134.
2. Bittencourt, *A quinta estrela*; Stumpf and Filho, *A segunda guerra*; the chapter dealing with this election in Chagas: *A guerra das estrelas*; as well as Góes, *O Brasil do General Geisel*.
3. Abreu, *O outro lado do poder*, 174.
4. Elio Gaspari, despite his latest work being so rich and detailed regarding the power games of the Figueiredo government, bats aside the question of the "first hard-line" officers' political trajectories with a sweep of the hand: in a minority and atypical, they are given only a few lines in the book. *A ditadura acabada*, 101.
5. These are the expressions used by Colonel Ênio dos Santos Pinheiro in D'Araujo, Castro, and Soares, *A volta aos quartéis*, 225. Colonels José Eduardo de Castro Portela Soares and Fernando da Graça Lemos were just as highly critical of the political opening and used similar terms in the interviews they gave the author.
6. D'Araujo, Castro, and Soares, *A volta aos quartéis*, 55.
7. SNI Report of June 15, 1974. See also those dated September 5, 1974, June 12, 1975, and November 26, 1975. Ernesto Geisel Archive, EG pr 1974.03.00/CPDOC.
8. Movimento Nacionalista Popular pro Governo Geisel—A0950713—1976, SNI Archives (National Archives-Brasília Branch).
9. Testimony given to Camargo and Góes, *Meio século de combate*, 519-20.
10. The letters are held in the General Cordeiro de Farias Archive, Cfa tv 1964.10.23/CPDOC. Zuzu Angel would herself die in suspicious circumstances in April 1976.
11. Grupo Centelha Nativista—G0023310—1981, SNI Archives (National Archives-Brasília Branch).

12. MMDC Manifesto, April 21, 1977. Cordeiro de Farias Archive, Cfa tv 64.04.11/CPDOC.

13. *O Estado de São Paulo*, August 19, 1977.

14. Colonel Tarcísio Nunes Ferreira, "Participation and Responsibility" (speech, Ponta Grossa Lions Club, Paraná, Brazil, March 4, 1978), personal archive of Col. Ferreira, shown to the author.

15. *Jornal do Brasil*, March 11, 1978.

16. *Jornal do Brasil*, April 13, 1978.

17. Ferreira, discussion. "Pombo correio" is a musical variety song composed and sung by Moraes Moreira in 1975.

18. *Jornal do Brasil*, April 1, 1978.

19. SNI Report of January 18, 1978, Ernesto Geisel Archive, EG pr 1974.03.00/CPDOC.

20. Abreu, *O outro lado do poder*, 78.

21. Abreu, *O outro lado do poder*, 21.

22. Abreu, *Tempo de crise*, 98.

23. See, for example, the joint meeting held by Magalhães Pinto and Euler Bentes Monteiro in São Paulo, June 31, 1978. *Jornal do Brasil*, July 1, 1978. His full program once he was officially endorsed by the MDB was published in the *Jornal do Brasil*, August 24, 1978.

24. *Jornal do Brasil*, August 24, 1978.

25. Frota, *Ideais traídos*, 593–94.

26. A recent article by Daniel Zirker defends the theory that nationalist convictions were stronger in this group of officers, seeing them as a determining factor in their U-turn at the end of Geisel's government. Zirker, "Hugo Abreu."

27. Letter quoted in Frota, *Ideais traídos*, 570–71.

28. Grael, *Aventura corrupção terrorismo*.

29. Ferreira, discussion.

30. See his resignation note, published in *Jornal do Brasil*, August 6, 1981.

31. *Jornal do Brasil*, September 21, 1978.

32. Grael, *Aventura corrupção terrorismo*, 24.

33. Martins Filho, "A guerra da memória."

34. Figures taken from the Guararapes Group Web site, since disabled. On this subject, see Santos, "Extrema direita, volver!"

35. Testimony given to Contreras, *Militares*, 91–92.

36. The collection was organized by Motta, *História oral do Exército*.

BIBLIOGRAPHY

BRAZILIAN NATIONAL ARCHIVES (BRASÍLIA/RIO DE JANEIRO)

Security and Information Division (DSI). Department of Justice. Rio de Janeiro
Case 62135/75. Serie MC. 1965-85 (Tradition, Family, Property).
Case 65774. Serie MC. 1976 (Nationalist Party).
Case 30070/66. Serie MC. 1976.
Case 100055. Serie MC. 1981.

Luis Viana Filho Personal Archives. Rio de Janeiro
1st File. 1.24 à 1.71 (National Information Service Impresso Geral).
3rd File. 3.88, 3.111 to 3.115 (National Information Service Bulletins).

National Information Service (SNI) Archives. Brasília
ADNAM, Associação Democrática e Nacionalista de Militares—A0369937—1983.
AMAN—C0112173—1968.
Atentado à bomba no Riocentro Rio de Janeiro—A0159190—1981.
Atitudes do Gen Ex Moniz de Aragão—A0063230—1980.
Atividades diversas—A0820271—1975.
Atividades do Grupo Centelha em Salvador BA—A0126603—1981.
Campanha subversiva contra o governo revolucionário—A0206477—1969.
Candidatura do General Euler Bentes. Frente Nacional de Redemocratização—E0072114—1981.
Centelha Nativista—C0032335—1980.
Chapas concorrentes à eleição no Clube Militar—A0393186—1984.
Difusão de manifesto a oficiais do Exército Brasileiro de autoria do autodenominado Comando Delta—E0086411—1981.
Grupo Centelha atividades de Kurt Pessek—A0114443—1980.
Grupo Centelha Nativista—A0091972—1980.
Grupo Centelha Nativista—G0023310—1981.
Grupo de Ação Patriótica—G0121770—1981.
Grupo de Ação Popular e Grupo de Ação Patriótica—E0083264—1981.
Grupo Serpa, reunião de militares e políticos—A0461258—1984.
Manifestações de organizações de extrema direita—R0055967—1983.
Manifesto do comando Delta—A0202710—1981.
Movimento Nacionalista Popular pro Governo Geisel—A0950713—1976.
Palestra do CIE para cadetes da AMAN—A0467108—1984.
Panfleto endereçado a oficiais alunos da EsAO—A0114686—1980.

Panfleto Proclamação ao povo brasileiro—A0200062—1969.
Propaganda adversa campo militar São Paulo—A0089485—1980.
Relatório de informações do II Exército—A0339167—1971.
Relatório periódico de informações—A0863154—1975.
Relatório periódico de informações—A0909014—1976.
Relatório periódico de informações do II Exército—A0495700—1972.
Reunião de militares no Rio de Janeiro—A0123857—1981.
Sergio Mauricio Lipkin, DCE Mario Prata UFRJ—A0035403—1979.
Vanguarda Militar Nacionalista—A0206507—1969.
Vanguarda Militar Nacionalista—A0213214—1969.

CENTER FOR THE RESEARCH AND DOCUMENTATION OF CONTEMPORARY BRAZILIAN HISTORY (CPDOC) ARCHIVES. GETULIO VARGAS FOUNDATION (FGV). RIO DE JANEIRO

Augusto do Amaral Peixoto Archives
AAP rev64 1964.00.00/1.
AAP rev64 1964.00.00/2.
AAP c 1969.01.031.

Antônio Carlos Murici Archives
ACM pm 1961.08.16.
ACM pm 1963.05.01.
ACM pm 1963.05.30.
ACM pm1964.10.00.
ACM pm 1969.06.26.

ARENA Archives
ARENA d 1973.05.10.

Bertoldo Klinger Archives
BK ger 1963.09.00.
BK ger 1964.03.26/1.

Clemente Mariani Archives
CMa cg 1959.05.23.

Cordeiro de Farias Archives
CFa foto 274.
Cfa tv 1963.05.02.
Cfa tv 1964.10.23.
Cfa tv 64.04.11.
Cfa tv 76.00.00.

Costa e Silva Archives
CS pi 1967.08.00.

Ernâni do Amaral Peixoto Archives
EAP df2 1968.11.18.

Ernesto Geisel Archives
EG pr 1974.03.00.
EG pr 1974.03.23/3.
EG pr 1974.03.25/1.
EG pr 1974.03.25/3.
EG pr 1974.07.10.
EG pr 1974.09.21.
EG pr 1975.00.00.
EG pr 1975.05.02.

Faria Lima Archives
FL emfa 1969.08.00.

João Goulart Archives
JG vpr 1959.00.00/2.
JG pr 1963.11.05.
JG pr 1964.02.19.

João Punaro Bley Archives
JPB d 1961.00.00.

Juarez Távora Archives
JT dpf 1969.01.21.
JT dpf 1969.05.22.

Juracy Magalhães Archives
JM pi Ministério da Guerra 1965.11.00.

Lourenço Filho Archives
LF t DEEX.

Moreira Lima Archives
ML rj 1956.02/03.00/ [1-10].

Ulhoa Cintra Archives
UCi fm 1962.09.11.
UCi g 1959.01.03.
UCi g 1959.01.08.
UCi g 1963.04.09.

AGULHAS NEGRAS MILIARY ACADEMY (AMAN) ARCHIVES. RESENDE (RJ)

Curricula
Planos Gerais de Ensino (PGE), 1964–70.
Programa de Instrução. Corpos dos Cadetes. Curso de Comunicações. 2°-3° ano. 1961.
Programa de Instrução. Corpo dos Cadetes. Curso de Intendência.1964.
Programa de Instrução. Corpo dos Cadetes. Curso de Material Bélico. 1964.

Historical Register (Registro do Histórico), 1958–76

Textbooks
AMAN, *Histórico da AMAN*, 1980,
AMAN/Divisão de ensino/Cadeira de História Militar, *Revoluções no Brasil após a República*,1980.
Estado Maior das Forças Armadas, *Manual de vocábulos das Forças Armadas*, Presidência da República/EMFA, Rio de Janeiro, 1967.
Ministério do Exército, *Instruções provisórias de defesa interna*, Ministério do Exército/ EME, 1969.
Ministério do Exército/Estado-Maior do Exército, *Instruções Provisórias: o pequeno escalão das operações contraguerrilhas*, 1973.
Ministério do Exército/Estado-Maior do Exército, *Instruções Provisórias: Operações*, 1975.
Ministério do Exército/Estado-Maior do Exército, *Relação das Publicações do Exército*, 1982
Santos, Francisco Ruas, *A Guerra Revolucionário Comunista*, Academia Militar das Agulhas Negras/Ensino Fundamental/Seção de Ensino, n.d.

Cadets' Individual Files: 1961, 1965, 1973 (all of it); 1954, 1968, 1969, 1971 (partially)

ARMY COMMAND AND GENERAL STAFF SCHOOL (*ESCOLA DE COMANDO E ESTADO MAIOR*, ECEME) ARCHIVES. RIO DE JANEIRO

Marshal Humberto de Alencar Castelo Branco Archives
Files: *Sucessão, Correspondência Política—Gov. Carlos Lacerda, Carlos Lacerda* and *Assuntos gerais* nos. 3, 10, 21, 22, 30–32, 41–44.

ARMY STAFF STUDIES CENTER (*CENTRO DE ESTUDOS DO PESSOAL*, CEP) ARCHIVES. RIO DE JANEIRO

Operações psicológicas—355.3434-94 OPS/01 01–10.
ECEME, *Operações psicológicas*, 1971.
EsNI, *Controle da propaganda adversa—A arma psicológica*, 1976.
Aula inaugural Palestras Conferências—355.04 PC/1 1–14.

ARMY DOCUMENTATION CENTER (CENTRO DE DOCUMENTAÇÃO DO EXÉRCITO, CDOC) ARCHIVES. BRASÍLIA

Colonel Manuel Soriano Personal Archives
Boxes: *Política Nacional* (1 to 7); *Revolução 31 de março de 1964* (1 to 5); *Guerra Revolucionária*; *Nacionalismo*; *Ideologia*.

PRESS

General-Interest Press
Jornal do Brasil (1964–78).
Visão (1964–65 and 1968).
O Estado de São Paulo (1977).
Manchete (1968–69).
O Globo (1961, 1964, 1967).

Correio da Manhã, Tribuna da Imprensa, Diário de Notícias, Última Hora, Folha de São Paulo, Jornal da Tarde, Jornal do Comércio, Veja (punctually)

Military Press
Boletim de Informações do Estado Maior do Exército (1960–67),
Boletim do Exército (1960–78).
Mensário de Cultura Militar (1957–70).
Noticiário do Exército (1962–69).

FRENCH MINISTER OF FOREIGN AFFAIRS (QUAI D'ORSAY) ARCHIVES. LA COURNEUVE

FR MAE Amérique Brésil 1964–70 ; 1971–75.

FRENCH ARMY ARCHIVES. VINCENNES
10T1109, 10T1111, and 10T1112.

U.S. DEPARTMENT OF STATE ARCHIVE (ONLINE)

Kennedy Administration. Vol. 12. American Republics

Johnson administration. Vol. 33. South and Central America; Mexico

DISCUSSIONS WITH THE AUTHOR

Aguiar Borges, Zenóbio Cid de (Reserve Colonel). Rio de Janeiro, October 2006.
Albuquerque Lima, Fernando de (Reserve Colonel). Rio de Janeiro, April 2007.
Avelar Coutinho, Sérgio Augusto de (Reserve General). Rio de Janeiro, October 2006.
Carneiro, Luis Carlos (Reserve Colonel). Rio de Janeiro, June 2006 and September 2006.
Carvalho Nunes Ferreira, Tarcísio Célio (Reserve Colonel). Rio de Janeiro, June 2006.
Del Nero Augusto, Agnaldo (Reserve General). Brasília, March 2008,
Lemos, Fernando da Graça (Reserve Colonel). Rio de Janeiro, October 2006.
Martinelli, Osnelli (Reserve Colonel). Rio de Janeiro, April 2007.
Meira Mattos, Carlos de (Reserve General). Rio de Janeiro, October 2007.
Passarinho, Jarbas (Reserve Colonel). Brasília, March 2008.
Pessek, Kurt (Reserve Colonel). Brasília, March 2008.
Portela Soares, José Eduardo de Castro (Reserve Colonel). Rio de Janeiro, June 2006.
Raposo Filho, Amerino (Reserve Colonel). Rio de Janeiro, October–November 2006.

PUBLICATIONS

Aarão Reis Filho, Daniel. *Ditadura e democracia no Brasil*. Rio de Janeiro: Zahar, 2014.
Aarão Reis Filho, Daniel, Marcelo Ridenti, and Rodrigo Patto Sá Motta. *O golpe e a ditadura militar: quarenta anos depois (1964–2004)*. Bauru, São Paulo: EDUSC, 2004.
Abreu, Hugo. *O outro lado do poder*. Rio de Janeiro: Nova Fronteira, 1979.
Abreu, Hugo. *Tempo de crise*. Rio de Janeiro: Nova Fronteira, 1980,
Aderaldo, Vanda Peres Costa. "A Escola Superior de guerra: um estudo de currículos." Master's thesis, Instituto Universitário de Pesquisas do Rio de Janeiro (IUPERJ), 1978.
Arceneaux, Craig L. *Bounded Missions: Military Regimes and Democratization in the Southern Cone and Brazil*. University Park: Pennsylvania State University Press, 2001.

Argolo, José Amaral, ed. *A direita explosiva no Brasil.* Rio de Janeiro: Mauad, 1996.

Argolo, José Amaral, and Luiz Alberto Fortunato. *Dos quartéis à espionagem: caminhos e desvios do poder military.* Rio de Janeiro: Mauad, 2004.

Arruda, Antônio de. *A Escola Superior de Guerra: história de sua doutrina,* São Paulo: GRD/Brasília: INL, 1983.

Arturi, Carlos Schmidt. *Le Brésil: une tentative de démocratisation octroyée (1974–1985).* Villeneuve d'Ascq: Presses Universitaires du Septentrion, 1999.

Baffa, Ayrton. *Nos porões do SNI: o retrato do monstro de cabeça oca.* Rio de Janeiro: Objectiva, 1989.

Baratta Netto, Prospero Punaro. *Amazônia: tua vida é minha história.* N.p., n.d.

Barbosa, Eurico. *Confissões de generais.* Brasília: Thesaurus Editora, 1988.

Barros, Alexandre de Sousa Costa. "The Brazilian Military: Professional Socialization, Performance and State Building." PhD diss., University of Chicago, 1978.

Beattie, Peter. *The Tribute of Blood: Army, Honor, Race, and Nation in Brazil, 1864–1945.* Durham, NC: Duke University Press, 2001.

Benevides, Maria Victória de Mesquita. *A UDN e o udenismo: ambigüidades do liberalismo brasileiro (1945–1965).* Rio de Janeiro: Paz e Terra, 1981.

Bethell, Leslie, ed. *The Cambridge History of Latin America. Volume 9: Brazil since 1930.* Cambridge: Cambridge University Press, 2008.

Bicudo, Hélio. *Meu depoimento sobre o esquadrão da morte.* São Paulo: PUC-SP/Comissão de Justiça e Paz de São Paulo, 1976.

Bittencourt, Getúlio. *A Quinta Estrela: como se tenta fazer um presidente no Brasil.* São Paulo: Editora Ciências Humanas, 1978.

Borges, Vavy Pacheco. *Tenentismo e revolução brasileira.* São Paulo: Brasiliense, 1992.

Branche, Raphaëlle. *La guerre d'Algérie: une histoire apaisée?* Paris: Editions du Seuil, 2005.

Calandra, Benedetta, and Marina Franco, eds. *La guerra fría cultural en América Latina.* Buenos Aires: Biblos, 2013.

Calil, Gilberto Grassi. *O integralismo no pós-guerra: a formação do PRP (1945–1960).* Porto de Alegre: EDIPUCRS, 2001.

Camargo, Aspásia, and Walder de Góes. *Meio século de combate: Diálogo com Cordeiro de Farias.* Rio de Janeiro: Nova Fronteira, 1981.

Camargo, Aspásia, and Walder de Góes. *O drama da sucessão e a crise do regime.* Rio de Janeiro: Nova Fronteira, 1984.

Capanema P. de Almeida, Silvia. *Couleur et châtiment: la modernisation de la Marine brésilienne et la revolte des matelots de 1910 contre l'usage du fouet.* Paris: Armand Colin, 2014.

Carloni, Karla. *Forças armadas e democracia no Brasil: o 11 de novembro de 1955.* Rio de Janeiro: Editora Garamond, 2012.

Carvalho, Aloysio de. "Geisel, Figueiredo e a liberalização de regime autoritário (1974–1985)." *Dados* 48, no.1 (January–March 2005), 115–46.

Carvalho, Aloysio de. *O governo Médici e o Projeto de Distensão Política (1969–1973).* Rio de Janeiro: IUPERJ, 1989.

Carvalho, Ferdinando de. *Lembrai-vos de 35!* Rio de Janeiro: Biblioteca do Exército Editora, 1981.

Carvalho, Ferdinando de. *O comunismo no Brasil.* 4 vols. Rio de Janeiro: Bibliotéca do Exército Editora, 1966–67.

Carvalho, José Murilo de. *Forças armadas e política no Brasil.* Rio de Janeiro: Zahar, 2005.

Castello Branco, Carlos. *Os militares no poder: o Ato 5.* Rio de Janeiro: Nova Fronteira, 1978.

Castello Branco, Carlos. *Os militares no poder: o baile das solteironas*. Rio de Janeiro: Nova Fronteira, 1979.

Castro, Celso. *A invenção do Exército brasileiro*. Rio de Janeiro: Zahar, 2002.

Castro, Celso. "A origem social dos militares." In Raposo, *1964*, 199–203.

Castro, Celso. "Interviewing the Brazilian Military: Reflections on a Research Experience." In *International Oral History Conference, XI International Oral History Conference*, vol. 1, 110–15. Istanbul: International Oral History Association University, 2000.

Castro, Celso. *Os militares e a república: um estudo sobre cultura e ação política*. Rio de Janeiro: Zahar, 1995.

Castro, Celso, Vitor Izecksohn, and Hendrick Kraay. "Da história militar a 'nova' história military." In *Nova história militar brasileira*, edited by Celso Castro, Vitor Izecksohn, and Hendrick Kraay, 11–42. Rio de Janeiro: FGV Editora, 2004.

Chagas, Carlos. *A guerra das estrelas (1964/1984): os bastidores das successões presidenciais*. Porto Alegre: L&PM, 1985.

Chagas, Carlos. *113 dias de angústia: impedimento e morte de um presidente*. Porto Alegre: L&PM Editores, 1979.

Chirio, Maud. "Le pouvoir en un mot: les militaires brésiliens et la 'révolution' du 31 mars 1964." Proceedings of the colloquium: La notion de révolution en Amérique Latine. 19e–20e siècle. Université Paris I, January 26–37, 2007, edited by Marianne González-Alemán and Eugénia Paliéraki. *Nuevo mundo–mundos nuevos* 8 (2007). https://nuevomundo.revues.org/3887.

Chirio, Maud, and Mariana Joffily. "A repressão condecorada: a atribuição da Medalha do Pacificador a agentes do aparato de segurança (1964–1985)." *História Unisinos* 18, no. 2 (May–August 2015), 140–51.

Chirio, Maud, and Mariana Joffily. "La répression en chair et en os: les listes d'agents de l'État accusés d'actes de torture sous la dictature militaire brésilienne." *Brésil(s). Sciences humaines et sociales*, no. 5 (June 2014), 77–103.

Chirio, Maud, and Mariana Joffily. "Moderniser la répression politique: la stratégie de formation de 'l'homme de renseignement' sous la dictature brésilienne." *Histoire@Politique*, no. 34 (January–April 2018). www.histoire-politique.fr.

Codato, Adriano Nervo. "O golpe de 64 e o regime de 68." *História: Questões e debates* 40 (2004), 11–36.

Coelho, Edmundo Campos. *Em busca de identidade: o Exército e a política na sociedade brasileira*. Rio de Janeiro: Record, 2000.

Collier, David. *The New Authoritarianism in Latin America*. Princeton, NJ: Princeton University Press, 1979.

Comblin, Joseph. *A ideología da segurança nacional: o poder militar na América Latina*. Rio de Janeiro: Civilização Brasileira, 1978.

Compagnon, Olivier. "Le 68 des catholiques latino-américains dans une perspective transatlantique." *Nuevo Mundo–Mundos Nuevos* (2008). https://nuevomundo.revues.org/47243.

Contreiras, Hélio. *Militares: Confissões—Histórias secretas do Brasil*. Rio de Janeiro: Mauad, 1998.

Cordeiro, Janaina Martins. *Direitas em movimento: a Campanha da Mulher pela democracia e a ditadura no Brasil*. Rio de Janeiro: FGV Editora, 2009.

Couto, Adolfo João de Paula. *Revolução de 1964: a versão e o fato*. Porto Alegre: Gente do Livro, 1999.

Couto, Ronaldo Costa. *História indiscreta da ditadura e da abertura: Brasil: 1964–1985*. Rio de Janeiro: Record, 1998.

Cowan, Benjamin A. *Securing Sex: Morality and Repression in the Making of Cold War Brazil*. Chapell Hill: University of North Carolina Press, 2016.
Cunha, Paulo Ribeiro da. *Militares e militância*. São Paulo: UNESP, 2014.
D'Aguiar, Hernani. *Ato 5: a verdade tem duas faces*. Rio de Janeiro: Razão Cultural, 1999.
D'Araújo, Maria Celina. *Ainda em busca de identidade: desafios das Forças Armadas na Nova República*. Rio de Janeiro: Centro de Pesquisa e Documentação de História Contemporânea do Brasil (CPDOC), 2000.
D'Araújo, Maria Celina. "Ouvindo os militares: imagens de um poder que se foi." In *Entrevistas: abordagens e usos da história oral*, edited by Marieta de Moraes, 147–72. Rio de Janeiro: FGV Editora, 1994.
D'Araújo, Maria Celina, and Celso Castro, eds. *Democracia e forças armadas no Cone Sul*. Rio de Janeiro: Editora FGV, 2000.
D'Araújo, Maria Celina, and Celso Castro. *Dossiê Geisel*. Rio de Janeiro: FGV Editora. 2002.
D'Araujo, Maria Celina, and Celso Castro. *Ernesto Geisel*. Rio de Janeiro: FGV Editora, 1997.
D'Araujo, Maria Celina, Celso Castro, and Gláucio Ary Dillon Soares. *A volta aos quartéis: a memória militar sobre a abertura*. Rio de Janeiro: Relume-Dumará, 1995.
D'Araujo, Maria Celina, Celso Castro, and Gláucio Ary Dillon Soares. *Os anos de chumbo: a memória militar sobre a repressão*. Rio de Janeiro: Relume-Dumará, 1994.
D'Araujo, Maria Celina, Celso Castro, and Gláucio Ary Dillon Soares. *Visões do golpe: a memória militar sobre 1964*. Rio de Janeiro: Relume-Dumará, 1994.
Davies, Thomas M., and Brian Loveman, eds. *The Politics of Antipolitics: The Military in Latin America*. Lincoln: University of Nebraska press, 1978.
Davis, Sonny. *A Brotherhood of Arms: Brazil–United States Military Relations, 1945–1977*. Niwot: University Press of Colorado, 1996
Deckes, Flávio. *Radiografia do terrorismo no Brasil–1966/1980*. São Paulo: Ícone, 1985.
Denys, Odílio. *O ciclo revolucionário brasileiro*. Rio de Janeiro: Biblioteca do Exército Ed., 1993.
Dreifuss, René Armand. *1964: a conquista do Estado. Ação política, poder e golpe de classe*. Petrópolis: Vozes, 1981.
Dulles, John W. Foster. *Carlos Lacerda: Brazilian Cruzader, volume 1: 1914–1960, volume 2: 1960–1977*. Austin: University of Texas Press, 1991.
Etchegoyen, Cyro. "1964 começou com coronéis." *Folha de São Paulo*, March 20, 1994.
Evans, Peter. *Dependent Development: The Alliance of Multinational State and Local Capital in Brazil*. Princeton, NJ: Princeton University Press, 1979.
Ferraz, Francisco César Alves. *A guerra que não acabou: a reintegração social dos veteranos da Força Expedicionária Brasileira (1945–2000)*. Londrina: Editora da Universidade Estadual de Londrina, 2012.
Ferraz, Francisco César Alves. *A sombra dos carvalhos: Escola Superior de Guerra e Política no Brasil: 1948–1955*. Londrina: UEL, 1997.
Ferreira, Jorge. "O Nome e a coisa: o populismo na política brasileira." In Ferreira, *O Populismo e sua história*, 59–124.
Ferreira, Jorge, ed. *O Populismo e sua história: debate e crítica*. Rio de Janeiro: Civilização Brasileira, 2001.
Ferreira, Marieta de Moares, ed. *João Goulart: entre a memória e a história*. Rio de Janeiro: Editora FGV, 2006.
Ferreira, Roberto Martins. *Organização e poder: análise do discurso anticomunista do Exército Brasileiro*. São Paulo: Editora Annablume, 2004.

Fico, Carlos. *Além do golpe: versões e controvérsias sobre 1964 e a ditadura military*. Rio de Janeiro: Record, 2004.

Fico, Carlos. *Como eles agiam: os subterrâneos da ditadura militar: espionagem e polícia política*. Rio de Janeiro: Record, 2001.

Fico, Carlos. *O Grande Irmão: Da Operação Brother Sam aos Anos de Chumbo*. Rio de Janeiro: Record, 2008.

Fico, Carlos. *Reinventando o otimismo: ditadura, propaganda e imaginário social no Brasil*. Rio de Janeiro: FGV, 1997.

Fico, Carlos. "Versões e controvérsias sobre 1964 e a ditadura militar." *Revista Brasileira de História* 24, no. 47 (2004), 29-60.

Fico, Carlos, Maria Paula Araujo, Marieta de Moraes Ferreira, and Samantha Viz Quadrat, eds. *Ditadura e Democracia na América Latina: balanço histórico e perspectiva*. Río de Janeiro: FGV, 2008.

Figueiredo, Eurico de Lima. *Os militares e a democracia: análise estrutural da ideologia do Presidente Castelo Branco*. Rio de Janeiro: Graal, 1980.

Finer, Samuel. *The Man on Horseback: The Role of the Military in Politics*. Londres: Penguin Books, 1976 (1st ed. 1962).

Fitch, John Samuel, and Abraham F. Lowenthal. *The Armed Forces and Democracy in Latin America*. Baltimore: Johns Hopkins University Press, 1998.

Franco Marina, and Florencia Levín. *Historia reciente: perspectivas y desafíos para un campo en construcción*. Buenos Aires: Paídos, 2008.

Frota, Sylvio. *Ideais traídos: a mais grave crise dos governos militares narrada por um de seus protagonistas*. Rio de Janeiro: Jorge Zahar, 2006.

Gaio, André Moysés. "Afinidades eletivas entre a União Democrática Nacional (UDN) e as forças armadas brasileiras." *Diálogos* 6 (2002), 31-40.

Gaio, André Moysés. *Em busca da remissão: os militares contra o regime: uma análise das eleições do Clube Militar em 1984*. Master's thesis, *Universidade Federal de Minas Gerais* (UFMG), 1992.

Gaspari, Elio. *A ditadura acabada*. Rio de Janeiro: Intrínseca, 2016.

Gaspari, Elio. *A ditadura encurralada*. São Paulo: Companhia das Letras, 2003.

Gaspari, Elio. *A ditadura envergonhada*. São Paulo: Companhia das Letras, 2002.

Gaspari, Elio. *A ditadura escancarada*. São Paulo: Companhia das Letras, 2002.

Góes, Walder de. *O Brasil do general Geisel: estudo do processo de tomada de decisão no regime militar-burocrático*. Rio de Janeiro: Nova Fronteira, 1978.

Gorender, Jacob. *Combate nas trevas: a esquerda brasileira: das ilusões perdidas à luta armada*. 3rd ed. São Paulo: Ática, 1987.

Grael, Dickson M. *Aventura corrupção terrorismo: à sombra da impunidade*. Petrópolis: Vozes, 1985.

Guimarães, Carlos Eduardo. "A crise da ditadura: a reação militar à abertura e o terrorismo de direita: o caso Riocentro como paradigma." Master's thesis, Universidade Federal de São Carlos (UFSCar), 2000.

Hunter, Wendy. *Eroding Military Influence in Brazil: Politicians against Soldiers*. Chapel Hill: University of North Carolina Press, 1997.

Huntington, Samuel. *The Soldier and the State: The Theory and Politics of Civil–Military Relations*. Cambridge, MA: Belknap Press of Harvard University Press, 1995 (1st ed. 1957).

Jalles de Paula, Christiane. *O bom combate: Gustavo Corção na imprensa brasileira (1953–1976)*. Rio de Janeiro: FGV Editora, 2015.

Joffily, Mariana. "No centro da engrenagem: os interrogatórios na Operação Bandeirante e no DOI de São Paulo (1969-1975)." PhD diss., Universidade de São Paulo, 2008.

Kinzo, Maria D'Alva Gil. *Oposição e autoritarismo: genêse e trajetória do MDB, 1966/1979*. São Paulo: Sumaré, 1990.

Klein, Lúcia, and Marcus F. Figueiredo. *Legitimidade e coação no Brasil pós-64*. Rio de Janeiro: Forense Universitária, 1978.

Labaki, Amir. *1961: A Crise da renúcia e a solução parlamentarista*. São Paulo: Brasiliense, 1986.

Lacerda, Carlos. *Depoimento*. Rio de Janeiro: Nova Fronteira, 1978.

Leacock, Ruth. *Requiem for Revolution: The United States and Brazil, 1961-1969*. Kent, OH: Kent State University Press, 1990.

Lemos, Renato. *Justiça fardada: o General Peri Bevilacqua no Superior Tribunal Militar (1965-1969)*. Rio de Janeiro: Bom Texto, 2004.

Lemos, Renato. "Poder judiciário e poder militar (1964-1969)." In *Nova história militar brasileira*, edited by Celso Castro, Vitor Izecksohn, and Hendrik Kraay, 409-38. Rio de Janeiro: Editora FGV/Bom Texto, 2004.

Lemos, Renato. "Por inspiração de Dona Tiburtina: o general Peri Bevilacqua no Superior Tribunal Militar." In *Locus: Revista de História* 9, no. 1 (January-June 2003), 113-24.

Linz, Juan. "The Future of an Authoritarian Situation or the Institutionalization of an Authoritarian Regime: The Case of Brazil." In Stepan, *Authoritarian Brazil*, 233-54.

Lopez, Ernesto. *Seguridad nacional y sedición military*. Buenos Aires: Legaz, 1988.

Love, Joseph L. *The Revolt of the Whip*. Stanford, CA: Stanford University Press, 2012.

Loveman, Brian. *For la Patria: Politics and the Armed Forces in Latin America*. Wilmington, DE: SR Books, 1999.

Magasich Airola, Jorge. *Los que dijeron No: historia del movimiento de los marinos antigolpistas de 1973*. Santiago: Lom Ediciones, 2008.

Manor, Paul. "Factions et Idéologie dans l'Armée Brésilienne: 'Nationalistes' et 'libéraux,' 1946-1951." *Revue d'Histoire Moderne et Contemporaine* (October-December1978), 556-86.

Markoff, John, and Silvio R. Duncan Baretta. "Professional Ideology and Military Activism in Brazil: Critique of a Thesis of Alfred Stepan." *Comparative Politics* 2 (1985), 175-91.

Martins Filho, João Roberto. "A educação dos golpistas: cultura militar, influência francesa e golpe de 1964." Paper presented at the Cultures of Dictatorship Symposium, University of Maryland, 2004. www2.ufscar.br/uploads/forumgolpistas.doc.

Martins Filho, João Roberto. "A guerra da memória: a ditadura militar nos depoimentos de militantes e militares." *Varia História* 28 (2002), 178-201.

Martins Filho, João Roberto. "Adieu à la dictature militaire ?" *Brésil(s): sciences humaines et sociales* 5 (May 2014), 17-32.

Martins Filho, João Roberto, ed. *O golpe e o regime militar: novas perspectivas*. São Carlos, São Paulo: EUFSCAR/FAPESP, 2006.

Martins Filho, João Roberto. *O palácio e a caserna: a dinâmica militar das crises políticas na ditadura, 1964-1969*. São Carlos, São Paulo: Universidade Federal de São Carlos (UFSCar), 1995.

Martins Filho, João Roberto. "Os Estados Unidos, a revolução cubana e a contra-insurreção." *Revista de Sociologia e Política* 12 (June 1999), 67-82.

Mathias, Suzeley Kalil. *A distensão no Brasil: o projeto militar (1973-1979)*. Campinas: Papirus, 1995.

McCann, Franck. *Soldiers of the Pátria: A History of the Brazilian Army, 1889-1937*. Stanford, CA: Stanford University Press, 2004.

McSherry, J. Patrice. *Los Estados depredadores: la Operación Condor y la guerra encubierta en América Latina*. Montevideo: Ediciones de la Banda Oriental, 2009.

Mendonça, Daniel de. "O discurso militar da ordem: uma análise dos pronunciamentos militares durante o governo Goulart (1961-1964)." *Teoria e pesquisa* 14, no.1 (January-June 2007), 167-98.

Mendonça, Marina Gusmão de. *O demolidor de presidentes: a trajetória política de Carlos Lacerda: 1930-1968*. São Paulo: Codex, 2002.

Mendonça, Marina Gusmão de. "Rebelião de Aragarças: um tema a investigar." *Revista de Economia Política e História Econômica* 9 (December 2007), 5-25.

Miguel, Luis Felipe. "Segurança e desenvolvimento: Peculiaridades da ideologia de Segurança Nacional no Brasil." *Diálogos latinoamericanos* 5 (2002), 40-56.

Miranda, Nilmário, and Carlos Tibúrcio. *Os filhos deste solo. Mortos e desaparecidos políticos durante a ditadura militar: a responsabilidade do Estado*. São Paulo: Boitempo, Fundação Perseu Abramo, 1999.

Moraes, João Quartim de. "Les militaires et les régimes politiques au Brésil de Deodoro à Figueiredo, 1889-1979." PhD diss., Paris, Institut d'études politiques, 1982.

Moreira Alves, Márcio. *68 mudou o mundo*. Rio de Janeiro: Nova Fronteira, 1993.

Moreira Alves, Márcio. *Tortura e torturados*. Rio de Janeiro: Idade Nova. 1966.

Moreira Alves, Maria. *Estado e oposição no Brasil, 1964-1984*. Petrópolis: Vozes, 1987.

Moreira D. da Silva, Angela. "Ditadura e justiça militar no Brasil: a atuação do Superior Tribunal Militar (1964-1980)." PhD diss., Centro de Pesquisa e Documentação de História Contemporânea do Brasil (CPDOC), 2011.

Motta, Aricildes de Moraes, ed. *História oral do Exército: 1964, 31 de março*. 14 vols. Rio de Janeiro: Bibliotéca do Exército Editora, 2003.

Motta, Rodrigo Patto Sá. "A figura caricatural do gorila nos discursos da esquerda." *Art-Cultura* 9, no. 15 (July-December 2007), 195-212.

Motta, Rodrigo Patto Sá. "A 'Intentona Comunista' ou a construção de uma legenda negra." *Tempo* 7, no. 13 (July 2002), 189-209.

Motta, Rodrigo Patto Sá. *Em guarda contra o "perigo vermelho": o anticomunismo no Brasil (1917-1964)*. São Paulo: Perspectiva, 2002.

Mourão Filho, Olímpio. *Memórias: A verdade de um revolucionário*. Porto Alegre: L&PM Editores, 1978.

Murici, Antônio Carlos. *Depoimento, 1981*. Rio de Janeiro: Centro de Pesquisa e Documentação de História Contemporânea do Brasil (CPDOC), 1993.

Nabuco de Araujo, Rodrigo. "Conquête des esprits et commerce des armes: la diplomatie française au Brésil (1947-1974)." PhD diss., Université Toulouse II-Le Mirail, 2011.

National Truth Commission. *National Truth Commission Report*, December 2014.

Neto, Lira. *Castello: a marcha para a ditadura*. São Paulo: Contexto, 2004.

Nunn, Frederick M. "Military Professionalism and Professional Militarism in Brazil, 1870-1970: Historial Perspectives and Political Implications." *Journal of Latin American Studies* 4, no. 1 (1972), 29-54.

Nunn, Frederick M. *The Time of the Generals: Latin American Professional Militarism in World Perspective*. Lincoln: University of Nebraska Press, 1992.

O'Donnell, Guillermo. *Modernization and Bureaucratic Authoritarianism*. Berkeley: Institute of International Studies, University of California Press, 1973.

O'Donnell, Guillermo, and Philippe C. Schmitter. *Transições do regime autoritário: America Latina*. São Paulo: Vertice, 1988.

O'Reilly, Marcos de Mendonça. "A ideologia da Corrente Militar 'Revolucionário Nacionalist' (1967-1969)." Master's thesis, Universidade Federal Fluminense, 1985.

Oliveira, Eliézer Rizzo de, ed. *As forças armadas no Brasil*. Rio de Janeiro: Espaço e Tempo, 1987.

Oliveira, Eliézer Rizzo de. *As forças armadas: política e ideologia no Brasil (1964–1969)*. Petrópolis: Vozes, 1976.

Oliveira, Eliézer Rizzo de. *De Geisel a Collor: forças armadas, transição e democracia*. Campinas, São Paulo: Papirus, 1994.

Oliveira, Lúcia Lippi, Mônica Pimenta Velloso and Ângela de Castro Gomes. *Estado Novo: ideologia e poder*. Rio de Janeiro: Zahar, 1982.

Palmar, Aluízio. *Onde foi que vocês enterraram nossos mortos?* Curitiba: Travessa dos Editores, 2006.

Parker, Phyllis R. *1964: o papel dos Estados Unidos no golpe de Estado de 31 de março*. Rio de Janeiro: Civilização Brasileira, 1977.

Parucker, Paulo Eduardo. *Praças em pé de guerra: o movimento político dos subalternos militares no Brasil, 1961–1964*. São Paulo: Expressão Popular, 2009.

Peixoto, Antônio Carlos, Eliézer Rizzo de Oliveira, Manuel Domingos Neto, and Alain Rouquié. *Les Partis militaires au Brésil*. Paris: Presses de la Fondation nationale des sciences politiques, 1980.

Peralva, Angelina. *Violência e democracia: o paradoxo brasileiro*. São Paulo: Paz e Terra, 2000.

Pereira, Anthony W. *Ditadura e repressão: o autoritarismo e o Estado de direito no Brasil*. São Paulo: Paz e Terra, 2010.

Périès, Gabriel. "Du corps au cancer: la construction métaphorique de l'ennemi intérieur dans le discours militaire pendant la Guerre Froide." *Cultures et Conflits* 43 (Autumn 2001).

Perlmutter, Amos. *The Military and Politics in Modern Times*. New Haven, CT: Yale University Press, 1977.

Portella de Mello, Jayme. *A revolução e o governo Costa e Silva*. Rio de Janeiro: Guavira, 1979.

Prado, Luiz Carlos Delorme, and Fábio Sá Earp. "O 'milagre' brasileiro: crescimento acelerado, integração internacional e concentração de renda (1967–1973)." In *O Brasil Republicano, 4: O tempo da ditadura—regime militar e movimentos sociais em fins do século XX*, edited by Jorge Ferreira and Lucilia de Almeira Neves Delgado, 207–41. Rio de Janeiro: Civilização Brasileira, 2007.

Prost, Catherine, and Yves Lacoste. *L'armée brésilienne: organisation et rôle géopolitique de 1500 à nos jours*. Paris: L'Harmattan, 2003.

Quadrat, Samantha. "A preparação dos agentes de informação e a ditadura civil-militar no Brasil (1964–1985)." *Varia Historia* 28, no. 47 (January–June 2012), 19–41.

Raposo, Eduardo, ed. *1964: 30 anos depois*. Rio de Janeiro: Agir, 1994.

Rezende, Maria José de. *A ditadura militar no Brasil: repressão e pretensão de legitimidade, 1964–1984*. Londrina: UEL, 2001.

Ridenti, Marcelo, and Rodrigo Patto Sá Motta, eds. *O golpe e a ditadura militar: 40 anos depois (1964–2004)*. Bauru: EDUSC, 2004.

Robin, Marie-Monique. *Les Escadrons de la mort: l'école française*. Paris: La Découverte, 2004.

Rouquié, Alain. *L'État militaire en Amérique latine*. Paris: Éditions du Seuil, 1982.

Santos, Cecilia MacDowell, Edson Luís de Almeida Teles, and Janaína de Almeida Teles, eds. *Desarquivando a ditadura: memória e justiça no Brasil*. São Paulo: Editora Hucitec, 2009.

Santos, Eduardo Heleno de Jesus. "Extrema direita, volver! Memória, ideologia e política dos grupos formados por civis e a reserva milita." Master's thesis, Niterói, Universidade Federal Fluminense (UFF), 2009.
Santos, Wanderley Guilherme dos. *Sessenta e quatro: anatómia da crise*. São Paulo: Vertice, 1986.
Silva, Hélio, and Maria Cecila Ribas Carneiro. *1964: golpe ou contragolpe?* Rio de Janeiro: Civilização Brasileira, 1975.
Skidmore, Thomas. *Brasil: de Castelo a Tancredo*. Rio de Janeiro: Paz e Terra, 1988.
Smallman, Shawn. *Fear and Memory in the Brazilian Army and Society, 1889–1954*. Chapel Hill: University of North Carolina Press, 2002.
Soares, Gláucio Ary Dillon, and Maria Celina D'Araujo. *21 anos de regime militar: balanços e perspectivas*. Rio de Janeiro: FGV Editora, 1994.
Soares, Samuel Alves. *Controles e autonomia: as Forças Armadas e o sistema político brasileiro, 1974–1999*. São Paulo: Universidade Estadual Paulista (UNESP), 2006.
Sodré, Nelson Werneck. *História militar do Brasil*. Rio de Janeiro: Civilização Brasileira, 1979.
Stacchini Junior, José. *Março 64: Mobilização da Audácia*. São Paulo: Companhia Editora Nacional, 1965.
Starling, Heloisa. *Os senhores das Gerais: os novos inconfidentes e o golpe de 1964*. Rio de Janeiro: Vozes, 1985.
Stepan, Alfred, ed. *Authoritarian Brazil: Origins, Policies, and Future*. New Haven, CT: Yale University Press, 1973.
Stepan, Alfred, ed. *Democratizing Brazil: Problems of Transitions and Consolidation*. New York: Oxford University Press, 1989.
Stepan, Alfred. "The New Professionalism of Internal Warfare and Military Role Expansion." In Stepan, *Authoritarian Brazil*, 47–65.
Stepan, Alfred. *Os militares na política: as mudanças de padrões na vida brasileira*. Translated by Italo Tronca. Rio de Janeiro: Artenova, 1975.
Stepan, Alfred. *Os militares: da abertura a Nova República*. Rio de Janeiro: Paz e Terra, 1986.
Stepan, Alfred. *The Military in Politics: Changing Patterns in Brazil*. Princeton, NJ: Princeton University Press, 1971.
Stepan, Alfred. *Rethinking Military Politics: Brazil in the Southern Cone*. Princeton, NJ: Princeton University Press, 1988.
Stumpf, André Gustavo, and Merval Pereira Filho. *A segunda guerra: a successão de Geisel*. São Paulo: Brasiliense, 1979.
Svartman, Eduardo. *Guardiões da nação: formação profissional, experiências compartilhadas e engajamento político dos generais de 1964*. Passo Fundo: Méritos, 2006.
Toledo, Caio Navarro de, ed. *1964: visões críticas do golpe: democracia e reformas no populismo*. Campinas, São Paulo: Editora da Unicamp, 1997.
Tota, Antonio Pedro. *The Seduction of Brazil: The Americanization of Brazil during Word War II*. Austin: University of Texas Press, 2009.
Valdivia Ortiz de Zárate, Verónica. *El golpe después del golpe: Leigh vs. Pinochet: Chile 1960–1980*. Santiago de Chile: LOM Ediciones, 2003.
Vasconcelos, Cláudio Beserra. "A política repressiva contra militares no Brasil após o golpe de 1964." PhD diss., Rio de Janeiro Universidade Federal do Rio de Janeiro (UFRJ), 2010.
Villatoux, Marie-Catherine. "Hogard et Némo: deux théoriciens de la 'guerre révolutionnaire.'" *Revue historique des armées* 232 (2003).

Vizentini, Paulo Gilberto Fagundes. "A ditadura foi entreguista? política externa e desenvolvimento no regime militar brasileiro." *Estudos em História* 8, no. 1 (2001), 301-20.

Zimmermann, Lausimar José. "Sargentos de 1964: como a disciplina superou a política." Master's thesis, Rio de Janeiro, Centro de Pesquisa e Documentação de História Contemporânea do Brasil (CPDOC), 2013.

Zirker, Daniel. "'Hugo Abreu e Afonso de Albuquerque Lima': mudança quixotesca da linha dura para o centro." *Historiæ* 5, no. 2 (2014), 325-60.

INDEX OF NAMES

Abreu, Hugo de Andrade, 190, 204, 207, 210, 212, 222, 223, 224, 225, 227, 228, 229
Albuquerque, Mario Cavalcanti de, 63
Aleixo, Pedro, 137, 151, 152, 157
Almeida, Reinaldo de, 202
Alves, Márcio Moreira, 130, 131, 133
Alves, Osvino Ferreira, 42, 43
Andrade, Auro de Moura, 2
Angel, Stuart, 175
Angel, Zuzu, 215
Aragão, Augusto César Moniz, 48, 49, 66, 105, 113, 142, 143, 144, 145, 146, 153, 158, 162, 218, 223
Araripe, Luis Alencar, 109
Araujo, Adauto Bezerra de, 155
Archer, Renato, 132
Arns, Dom Paulo Evaristo, 192
Arraes, Miguel, 72, 74, 78, 80
Arzua, Ivo, 220
Augusto, Agnaldo del Nero, 33, 173, 231
Avelino, Confúcio Danton de Paula, 184, 192, 202, 247

Bandeira, Antônio, 186, 231, 247
Barreiros, Adalto Luiz Lupi, 155, 156, 224, 225, 228, 231
Bastos, Justino Alves, 103, 119, 120
Batista, Ernesto de Melo, 63, 164
Beck, Marino, 120
Beloch, Israel, 150
Beltrão, Hélio, 147, 149
Bethlem, Fernando Belfort, 208
Bevilacqua, Peri Constant, 44, 63, 77, 117, 120, 140, 215
Bittencourt, José Alberto, 62, 63, 75
Boaventura, Sinval, 203
Bonecker, Cléber, 75, 78

Borba, Octávio Moreira, 129, 190, 193
Borges, Gustavo, 68, 69, 141
Borges, Mauro, 71, 74
Branco, Humberto de Alencar Castelo, 2, 11, 15, 16, 22, 24, 30, 32, 44, 45, 47, 48, 49, 50, 51, 54, 55, 56, 57, 58, 60, 63, 65, 66, 68, 71, 72, 74, 75, 78, 79, 81, 82, 83, 84, 85, 86, 87, 88, 89, 90, 91, 96, 97, 99, 100, 101, 102, 103, 104, 108, 109, 110, 111, 112, 113, 118, 119, 120, 121, 142, 148, 154, 171, 176, 177, 179, 180, 185, 186, 195, 198, 205, 215, 223, 234
Brandini, Roberto, 68
Brizola, Leonel, 18, 32, 33, 35, 38, 43, 74, 120, 197
Brumini, Raul, 120
Bulhões, Octávio Gouvêa de, 57, 148, 149
Burnier, João Paulo Moreira, 50, 68, 76, 126, 129, 173, 174, 175

Caetano, Marcelo, 213
Câmara, Dom Helder, 129
Campelo, Florimar, 104, 247
Campos, Roberto, 57, 90, 113, 148
Candal, Arthur Duarte, 153, 221, 246
Cardoso, Adauto Lúcio, 101
Carvalho, Ferdinando de, 28, 68, 72, 74, 78, 84, 109, 146, 243
Carvalho, Sérgio Miranda de, 129
Castilho, João Dutra de, 64, 141, 155, 156, 157
Castro, Adyr Fiúza de, 28, 52, 176, 186
Castro, Fidel, 4
Castro, Rui, 106, 108, 110, 120, 214, 218, 219, 220
Cavalcanti Júnior, Francisco Boaventura, 37, 55, 64, 65, 66, 67, 68, 69, 76, 77, 78, 83, 84, 85, 103, 104, 106, 107, 108,

Cavalcanti Júnior, Francisco Boaventura (*cont.*), 109, 115, 126, 132, 136, 140, 141, 142, 143, 144, 146, 147, 154, 156, 157, 158, 159, 164, 203, 214, 218, 219, 222, 227, 228, 234, 238
Chaves, Francisco Leite, 202
Chaves, Sebastião Ferreira, 214, 227, 246
Cintra, José Pinheiro Ulhôa, 34, 35, 48, 83
Coelho Netto, José Luiz, 186
Contreras, Manuel, 184
Coqueiro, Márcio César Leal, 68
Corção, Gustavo, 124
Costa, Otávio, 26, 31
Costa, Roberto Hipólito da, 68, 174
Coutinho, Sérgio de Avelar, 40
Couto, Adolfo João de Paula, 164
Covas, Mário, 132

Delfim Netto, Antônio, 108, 146, 149, 222
Dellamora, Carlos Afonso, 68, 174
Denys, Odílio, 18, 40, 61, 62, 88, 204
Dorias, João de Seixas, 74
Dutra, Eurico Gaspar, 12

Elbrick, Charles Burke, 154
Etchegoyen, Cyro Guedes, 52, 57, 168, 195, 196, 197

Falcão, Armando, 179, 181, 189, 202
Farias, Osvaldo Cordeiro de, 20, 22, 177, 214, 215
Fernandes, Alexander Murillo, 187, 192
Fernandes, Hélio, 112, 113, 142
Ferreira, Tarcísio Nunes, 36, 65, 66, 69, 76, 132, 146, 152, 156, 219, 220, 227, 228, 230
Figueiredo, João Batista, 11, 176, 184, 187, 195, 203, 208, 209, 210, 211, 216, 217, 218, 219, 220, 222, 224, 225, 226, 227, 228, 231
Fleury, Sérgio de Paranhos, 193
Fortunato, Alberto, 76, 126, 190
Fortunato, Gregório, 196
Friedman, Milton, 6
Frota, Sylvio, 184, 186, 187, 192, 200, 201, 202, 203, 204, 205, 206, 208, 213, 218, 222, 223, 224, 227, 228, 229, 235, 236
Furtado, Celso, 104, 148

Gama, Saldanha da, 63
Geisel, Ernesto, 8, 11, 83, 128, 149, 169, 170, 171, 176, 177, 178, 179, 180, 181, 182, 193, 185, 186, 187, 188, 190, 191, 192, 193, 195, 196, 197, 198, 200, 201, 202, 203, 204, 208, 209, 210, 211, 212, 213, 214, 215, 217, 218, 220, 221, 222, 223, 224, 226, 227, 236
Geisel, Orlando, 11, 176, 177, 201, 210
Gomes, Eduardo, 12, 129
Gomes, Severo, 183, 221
Gonçalves, Leonidas Pires, 51
Gordon, Lincoln, 25
Goulart, João, 1, 2, 3, 4, 5, 8, 13, 16, 17, 18, 21, 24, 25, 28, 30, 31, 32, 33, 34, 37, 38, 39, 41, 42, 44, , 47, 50, 52, 61, 63, 64, 65, 67, 81, 86, 106, 110, 113, 114, 117, 120, 134, 148, 150, 162, 216, 234
Gudin, Eugênio, 148
Guevara, Ernesto, 4, 154, 178
Guimarães, Ulysses, 215

Hauser, Ivan Zanoni, 127
Heck, Sílvio de Azevedo, 18, 60, 61, 62, 63, 75, 77, 83, 88, 89, 90, 92, 103, 113, 122, 124, 130, 136, 166
Henkin, Henrique, 120
Herba, Charles, 76
Herzog, Vladimir, 191, 192, 202
Hipólito, Dom Adriano, 194
Hogard, Jacques, 28, 29, 32
Honaiser, Dalmo, 150

Ibiapina, Hélio, 175

Jahn, Mário, 184

Kennedy, John Fitzgerald, 24
Kozel Filho, Mário, 123
Krieger, Daniel, 37
Kruel, Amaury, 42, 44, 111, 119, 120
Kubitschek, Juscelino, 4, 12, 13, 16, 28, 36, 61, 66, 71, 104, 106, 111, 129

Lacerda, Carlos, 13, 17, 36, 37, 51, 55, 63, 67, 68, 76, 82, 83, 84, 85, 87, 90, 91, 96, 107, 109, 110, 111, 112, 113, 114, 115, 116, 117, 120, 122, 126, 129, , 130, 137, 138, 141, 146, 147, 157, 196, 213

Index

Lamarca, Carlos, 140
Leal, Newton Estillac, 28, 221
Leite, Luiz Helvécio da Silveira, 126, 173, 187
Lemos, Hélio, 65, 66, 85, 108, 146, 214, 218, 219, 227, 229, 230, 231
Lima, Afonso de Albuquerque, 64, 83, 103, 104, 105, 120, 121, 122, 124, 134, 135, 137, 138, 143, 146, 147, 149, 150, 152, 153, 156, 157, 158, 159, 161, 162, 163, 166, 172, 176, 201, 221, 222, 246
Linhares, Heitor Caracas, 83, 203
Linhares, Marcelo, 203
Lisbôa, Manuel Carvalho, 105, 123
Lopes, Joaquim Pessoa Igrejas, 75, 77
Lopes, Moacir Araújo, 124, 243
Lott, Henrique Teixeira, 12

Magalhães, Juracy, 77
Magalhães, Rafael de Almeida, 103
Maggessi, Augusto da Cunha, 117
Mamede, Jurandir Bizarria, 109, 160
Marinho, Roberto, 194
Mariz, Dinarte, 203
Martinelli, Osnelli, 67, 68, 74, 75, 76, 77, 78, 84, 85, 90, 92, 94, 103, 104, 122, 126
Martins, Egydio, 192
Martins, Raimundo Saraiva, 231
Mattos, Carlos de Meira, 54, 72, 102, 243
Máximo, Francima de Luna, 155, 224, 228
Mazzili, Pascoal Ranieri, 2
Médici, Emílio Garrastazu, 11, 31, 103, 128, 151, 152, 155, 160, 163, 164, 166, 168, 169, 170, 171, 172, 175, 176, 177, 178, 179, 183, 190, 195, 201, 203, 217, 224, 235
Mello, Jayme Portella de, 72, 85, 103, 108, 132, 142, 143, 160, 204
Mello, Márcio de Souza e, 103, 152, 174
Mello, Vieira de, 120
Melo, Ednardo D'Ávila, 189, 192, 202, 243
Mesquita Filho, Júlio de, 35
Monteiro, Euler Bentes, 147, 208, 209, 210, 211, 220, 221, 222, 224, 225, 226, 227, 228, 229, 231
Monteiro, Pedro Aurélio de Góis, 10
Moraes Neto, Luis Mendes de, 75, 76

Moss, Gabriel Grün, 18, 61
Mourão Filho, Olímpio, 1, 2, 62, 63, 77, 104, 105, 112, 118, 119, 120, 129
Murici, Antônio Carlos, 32, 38, 43, 144, 153, 156, 160, 162

Neves, Iese Rego Alves, 210

Oliveira, Plínio Corrêa de, 125

Perón, Isabel Martínez de, 8
Pessek, Kurt, 66, 83, 127, 128, 156, 224, 225, 228, 78, 108
Pina, Gérson de, 74, 76, 246
Pinheiro, Israel, 82, 85
Pinto, Magalhães, 87, 90, 217, 220, 221, 224, 225
Pinto, Olavo Bilac, 33
Pitaluga, Plínio, 83
Portela, Petrônio, 198
Potyguara, Moacyr Barcellos, 27, 28, 31

Quadros, Jânio da Silva, 4, 12, 13, 18, 30, 36

Rademaker, Augusto, 63, 78, 103, 122, 152, 204
Ramalho, Thales, 215
Ramos, Rodrigo Otávio Jordão, 142, 153, 215, 221
Raposo Filho, Amerino, 28, 65, 76, 77, 108, 214, 227, 230, 232, 243
Rego, Gustavo Moraes, 141
Reis, Levi Pena Aarão, 63
Rezende, Estevão Taurino de, 73, 111
Ribeiro, Jair Dantas, 37
Ribeiro, Nina, 78
Rocha, Itamar, 129

Sá, José Valporto de, 127, 224, 228
Santos, Francisco Ruas, 31
Sarmento, Siseno, 105, 155, 156
Shibata, Harry, 192
Sigaud, Dom Geraldo, 122
Silva, Artur da Costa e, 11, 49, 50, 54, 55, 72, 76, 81, 82, 83, 84, 85, 96, 97, 98, 99, 100, 101, 102, 105, 110, 111, 112, 113, 114, 116, 118, 119, 120, 121, 127, 135, 136, 141, 146, 147, 149, 150, 151, 152,

Silva, Artur da Costa e (*cont.*), 153, 157, 159, 160, 171, 175, 177, 186, 195, 201, 217, 219, 220, 232, 234, 235, 238
Silva, Golbery do Couto e, 22, 65, 91, 176, 177, 179, 190, 193, 195, 196, 197, 198, 215, 216, 217, 223, 228, 230
Simonsen, Mário Henrique, 183
Soares, José Eduardo de Castro Portela, 70
Souto, Edson Luís de Lima, 115
Souza, Milton Tavares de, 15, 186

Tavares, Aurélio de Lira, 105, 106, 122, 133, 134, 135, 143, 144, 145, 146, 152, 158, 163, 200

Tavares, Maria de Conceição, 148
Távora, Juarez, 12, 103
Torres, Alberto, 23

Ururahy, Otacílio, 72, 83, 92
Ustra, Carlos Brilhante, 193

Valente, Júlio, 68, 78
Vargas, Getúlio Dornelles, 3, 4, 10, 12, 13, 16, 17, 18, 37, 38, 53, 54, 69, 70, 88, 91, 103, 104, 126, 147, 177, 196
Vaz, Rubens, 37, 126
Veid, Jean-Marc von der, 150
Viana, Francisco José de Oliveira, 23